UNDERSTAND, ADD & SUBTRACT FRACTIONS VISUALLY

Ages 5 – 11

Ali Alex Ella Asha

1st Edition

The only visual fractions book you need to **understand**, **add** & **subtract** fractions. It is comprehensive, convenient and completely visual.

3-in-1 *Visual Maths Fractions:*

Understanding Fractions Visually

Visual Fractions Charts, Introductions to Fractions, Visual Fractions, Equivalent Fractions, Decimal Fractions and Percentages. Quick Quizzes.

Adding Fractions Visually

How To Add Fractions with **Same** & **Different Denominators**, Simplifying Fractions, Finding LCM. Many Different Ways of Adding Halves, Quarters, Eighths, Fifths, Tenths, Thirds, Sixths, Ninths and Twelfths. Quick Quizzes.

Subtracting Fractions Visually

How To Subtract Fractions with **Same** & **Different Denominators**. Finding LCM. Simplifying Fractions. Subtracting Halves, Quarters, Eighths, Fifths, Tenths, Thirds, Sixths, Ninths & Twelfths in Combinations. Quick Quizzes.

Copyright © Eng S Jama

All rights reserved.

author.to/FractionsVisually

Understanding Fractions Visually

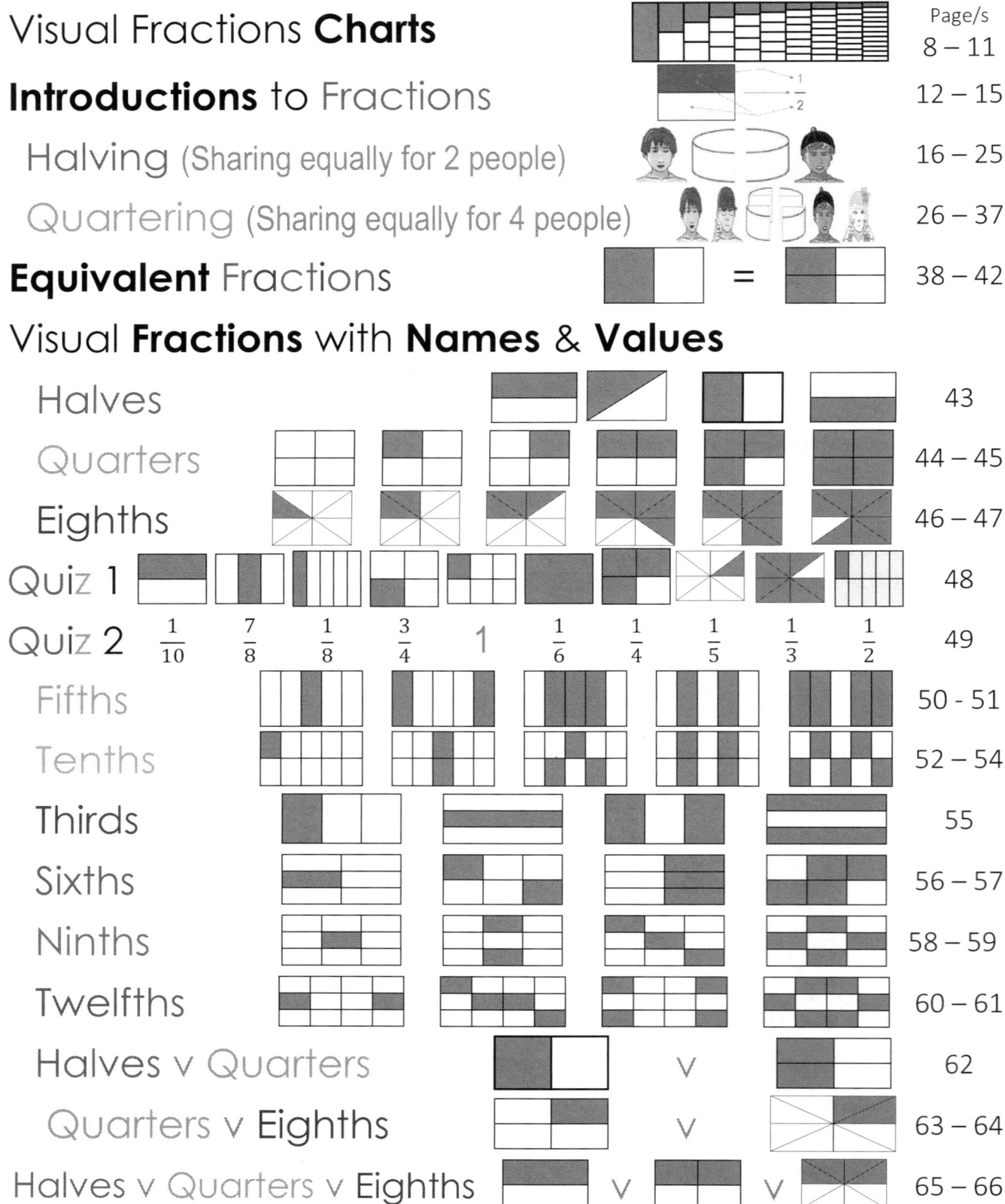

	Page/s
Visual Fractions **Charts**	8 – 11
Introductions to Fractions	12 – 15
Halving (Sharing equally for 2 people)	16 – 25
Quartering (Sharing equally for 4 people)	26 – 37
Equivalent Fractions	38 – 42
Visual **Fractions** with **Names** & **Values**	
Halves	43
Quarters	44 – 45
Eighths	46 – 47
Quiz 1	48
Quiz 2	49
Fifths	50 - 51
Tenths	52 – 54
Thirds	55
Sixths	56 – 57
Ninths	58 – 59
Twelfths	60 – 61
Halves v Quarters	62
Quarters v Eighths	63 – 64
Halves v Quarters v Eighths	65 – 66

Understanding Fractions Visually

			Page/s
Fifths v Tenths	v		67 – 69
Thirds v Sixths	v		70 – 71
Sixths v Ninths	v		72 – 73
Thirds v Sixths v Ninths	v ... v		74 – 75
Thirds v Twelfths	v		76
Quarters v Twelfths	v		77
Sixths v Twelfths	v		78

Equivalent **Fractions** and **Decimals**

		Page
Halves, Quarters and Eighths	$\frac{1}{2} = \frac{2}{4} = \frac{4}{8} = 0.50$	79
Fifths and Tenths	$\frac{1}{5} = \frac{2}{10} = 0.20$	80
Thirds, Sixths and Ninths	$\frac{1}{3} = \frac{2}{6} = \frac{3}{9} = 0.333$	81
Halves, Quarters and Twelfths	$\frac{1}{2} = \frac{2}{4} = \frac{6}{12} = 0.50$	82
Thirds, Sixths and Twelfths	$\frac{1}{3} = \frac{2}{6} = \frac{4}{12} = 0.333$	83

Fractions, **Decimals** and **Percentages**

		Page
Halves, Quarters and Eighths	$\frac{1}{2} = 0.50 = 50\%$	84 – 85
Fifths and Tenths	$\frac{1}{5} = 0.20 = 20\%$	86 – 87
Thirds, Sixths and Ninths	$\frac{1}{3} = 0.333 = 33.3\%$	88 – 89
Halves, Quarters and Twelfths	$\frac{1}{4} = 0.25 = 25\%$	90
Thirds, Sixths and Twelfths	$\frac{1}{6} = 0.166 = 16.6\%$	91 – 92
Answers and explanation to fractions story questions		93

Adding Fractions Visually

Adding Like Fractions
Page/s

How to add fractions with **same** denominators — 94

Simplifying Fractions — 95

Adding Halves  +  96 – 97

Adding Quarters 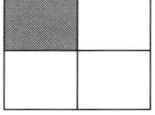 + 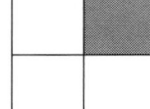 98 – 100

Adding Eighths 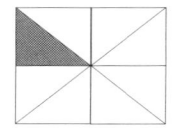 +  101 – 105

Quiz 1 $\frac{1}{8}+\frac{1}{8}$ $\frac{1}{2}+\frac{1}{2}$ $\frac{1}{3}+\frac{1}{3}$ $\frac{1}{4}+\frac{1}{4}$ $\frac{1}{5}+\frac{1}{5}$ $\frac{1}{6}+\frac{1}{6}$ $\frac{2}{10}+\frac{2}{10}$ 106

Adding Fifths 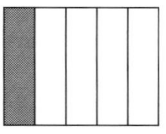 +  107 – 109

Adding Tenths 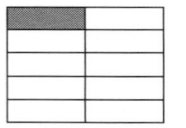 + 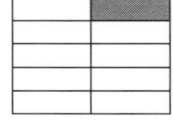 110 – 115

Adding Thirds  +  116 – 117

Adding Sixths 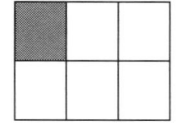 + 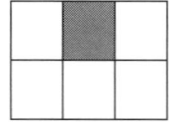 118 – 121

Adding Ninths 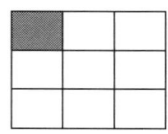 + 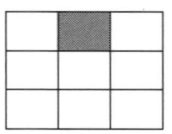 122 – 126

Adding Twelfths 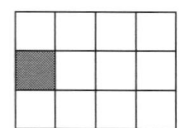 + 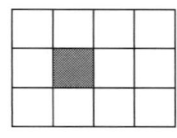 127 – 131

Quiz 2 $\frac{2}{10}+\frac{2}{10}$ $\frac{1}{6}+\frac{1}{6}$ $\frac{1}{5}+\frac{1}{5}$ $\frac{1}{4}+\frac{1}{4}$ $\frac{1}{3}+\frac{1}{3}$ $\frac{1}{2}+\frac{1}{2}$ $\frac{1}{8}+\frac{1}{8}$ 132

Adding Fractions Visually

Adding Unlike Fractions Page/s 133 – 138

How to add fractions with **different** denominators

Finding the Lowest Common Multiples

Examples of fractions with different denominators

Simplifying Fractions

Halves + Quarters	▨ + ▨	139
Halves + Eighths	▨ + ▨	140 – 141
Quarters + Eighths	▨ + ▨	142 – 145
Halves+Quarters+Eighths	▨ + ▨ + ▨	146
Fifths + Tenths	▨ + ▨	147 – 153
Thirds + Sixths	▨ + ▨	154 – 156
Thirds + Ninths	▨ + ▨	157 – 161
Sixths + Ninths	▨ + ▨	162 – 172
Thirds + Sixths + Ninths	▨ + ▨ + ▨	173 – 177
Halves + Thirds + Sixths	▨ + ▨ + ▨	178
Halves+Quarters+Twelfths	▨ + ▨ + ▨	179
Thirds +Sixths +Twelfths	▨ + ▨ + ▨	180 – 183

Subtracting Fractions Visually

Page/s

Subtracting Like Fractions 184

How to subtract fractions with **same** denominators and simplify results

Subtracting Halves — 185

Subtracting Quarters — 186 – 187

Subtracting Eighths — 188 – 191

Subtracting Fifths — 192 – 193

Subtracting Tenths — 194 – 197

Subtracting Thirds — 198 – 199

Subtracting Sixths — 200 – 202

Quiz 1 $\frac{3}{8}-\frac{1}{8}$ $\frac{2}{2}-\frac{1}{2}$ $\frac{3}{3}-\frac{1}{3}$ $\frac{3}{4}-\frac{1}{4}$ $\frac{3}{5}-\frac{1}{5}$ $\frac{3}{6}-\frac{1}{6}$ $\frac{6}{10}-\frac{2}{10}$ 203

Subtracting Ninths — 204 – 207

Subtracting Twelfths — 208 – 212

Subtracting Unlike Fractions 213 – 216

How to subtract fractions with **different** denominators, how to find their **Lowest Common Multiple (LCM)** plus how to **simplify** the **results**

Examples of fractions with **different** denominators 216 – 217

Halves - Quarters — 218 – 219

Halves - Eighths — 220 – 222

Subtracting Fractions Visually

		Page/s
Quarters - Halves		223
Quarters - Eighths		224 – 226
Eighths - Halves		227
Eighths - Quarters		228 – 229
Halves-Quarters-Eighths		230 – 233
Fifths - Tenths		234 – 237
Tenths - Fifths		238 – 239
Thirds - Sixths		240 – 241
Thirds - Ninths		242 – 244
Sixths - Thirds		245
Sixths - Ninths		246 – 251
Ninths - Thirds		252
Ninths - Sixths		253 – 256
Thirds - Sixths - Ninths		257 – 263
Sixths - Halves		264
Halves - Thirds - Sixths		265
Quarters - Twelfths		266 – 270
Halves-Quarters-Twelfths		271 – 276
Thirds - Twelfths		277 – 281
Sixths - Twelfths		282 – 285
Thirds - Sixths - Twelfths		286 – 293
Quiz 2 $\frac{7}{10}-\frac{3}{10}$ $\frac{5}{6}-\frac{3}{6}$ $\frac{4}{5}-\frac{2}{5}$ $\frac{3}{4}-\frac{1}{4}$ $\frac{3}{3}-\frac{1}{3}$ $\frac{2}{2}-\frac{1}{2}$ $\frac{3}{8}-\frac{1}{8}$		294

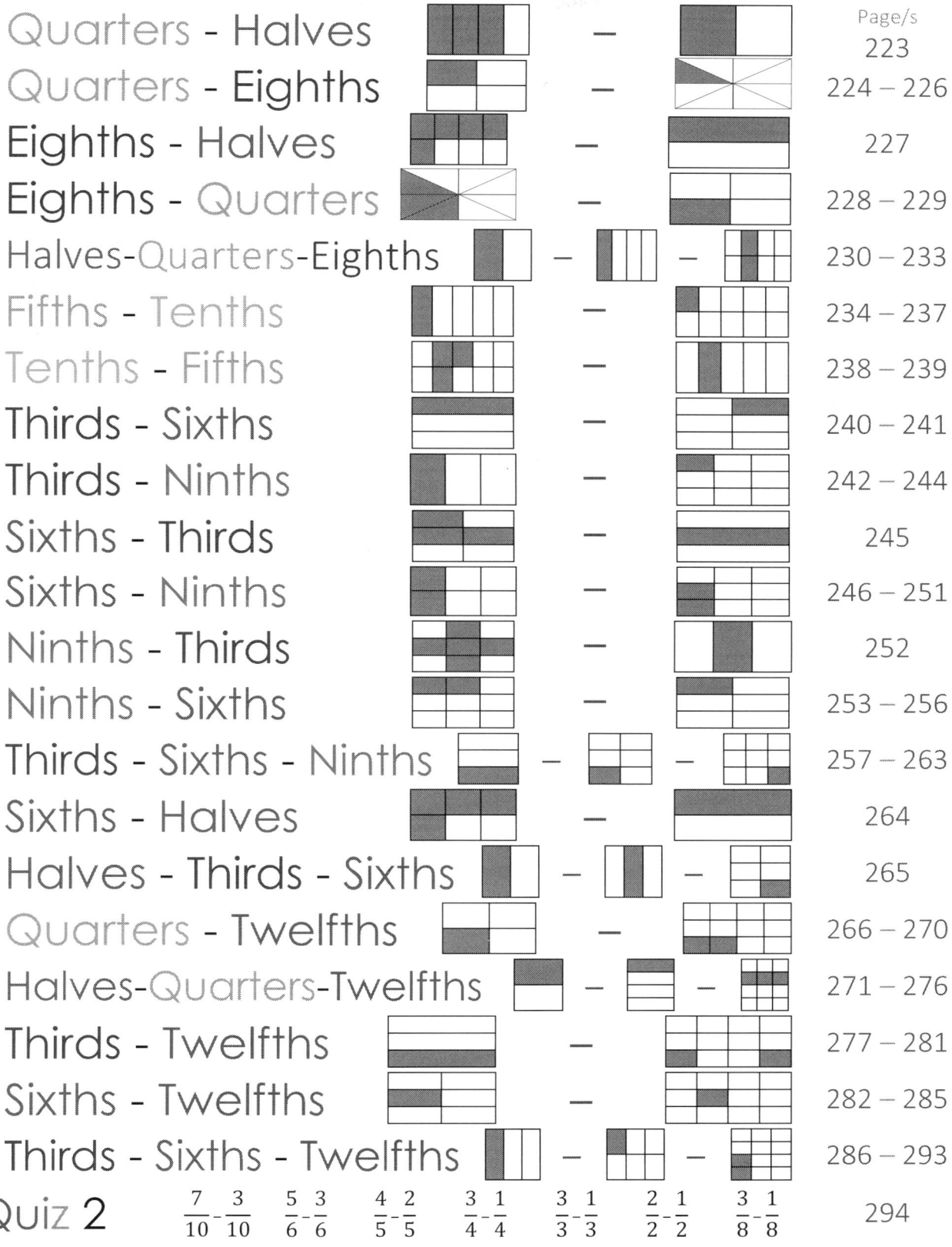

7

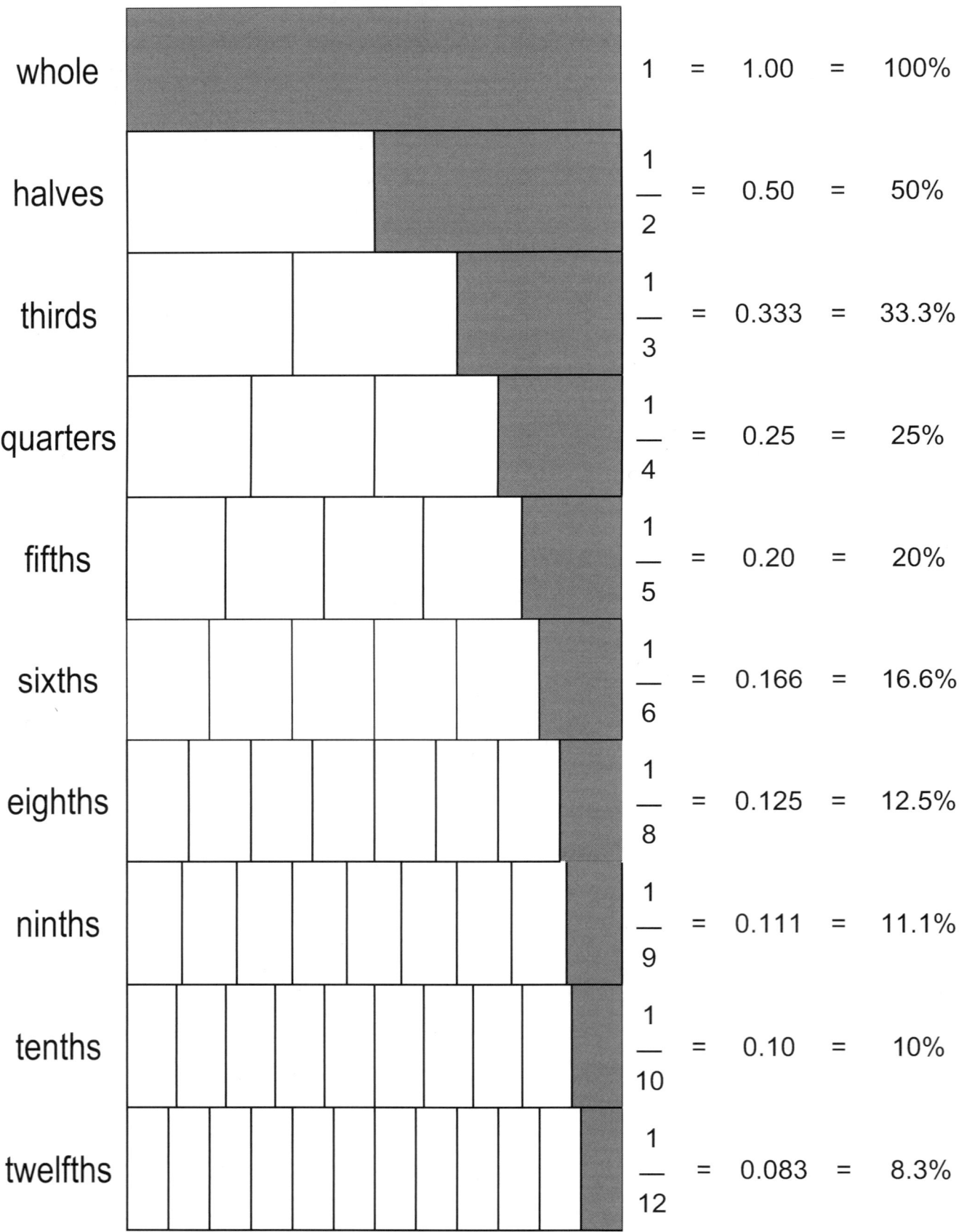

Fractions Chart 2

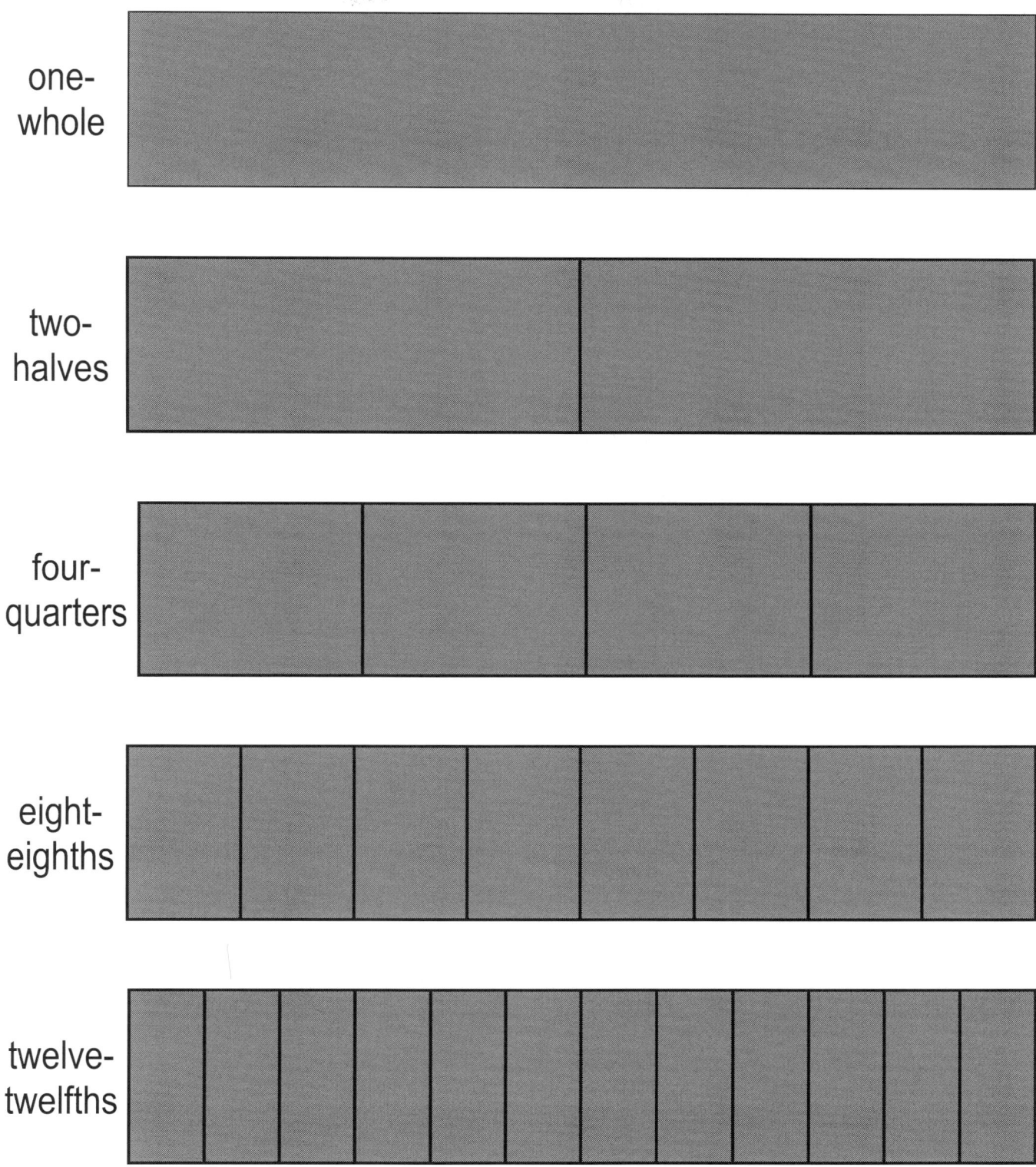

Fractions Chart 3

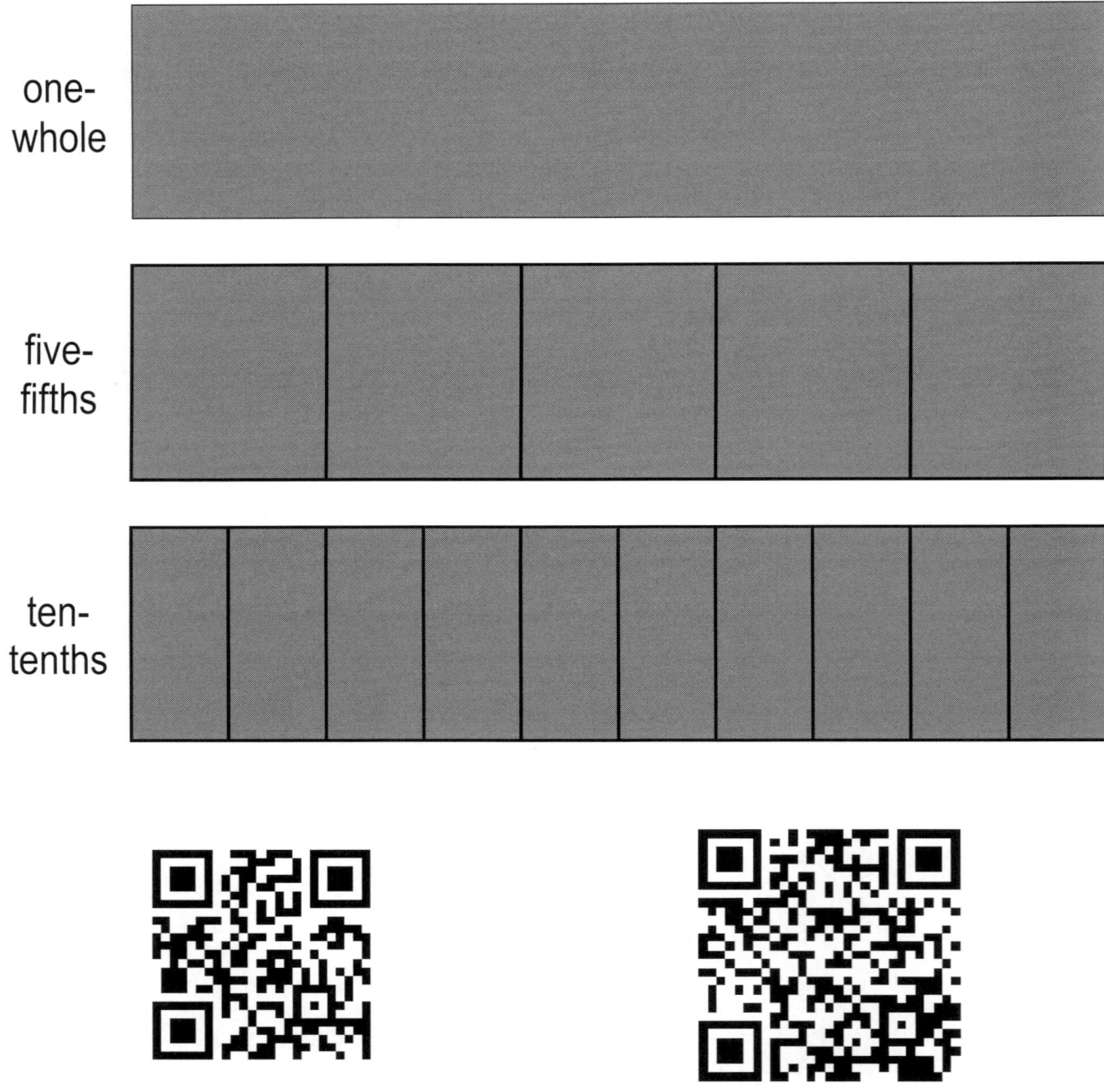

one-whole

five-fifths

ten-tenths

mybook.to/B-4

author.to/FractionsVisually

Fractions Chart 4

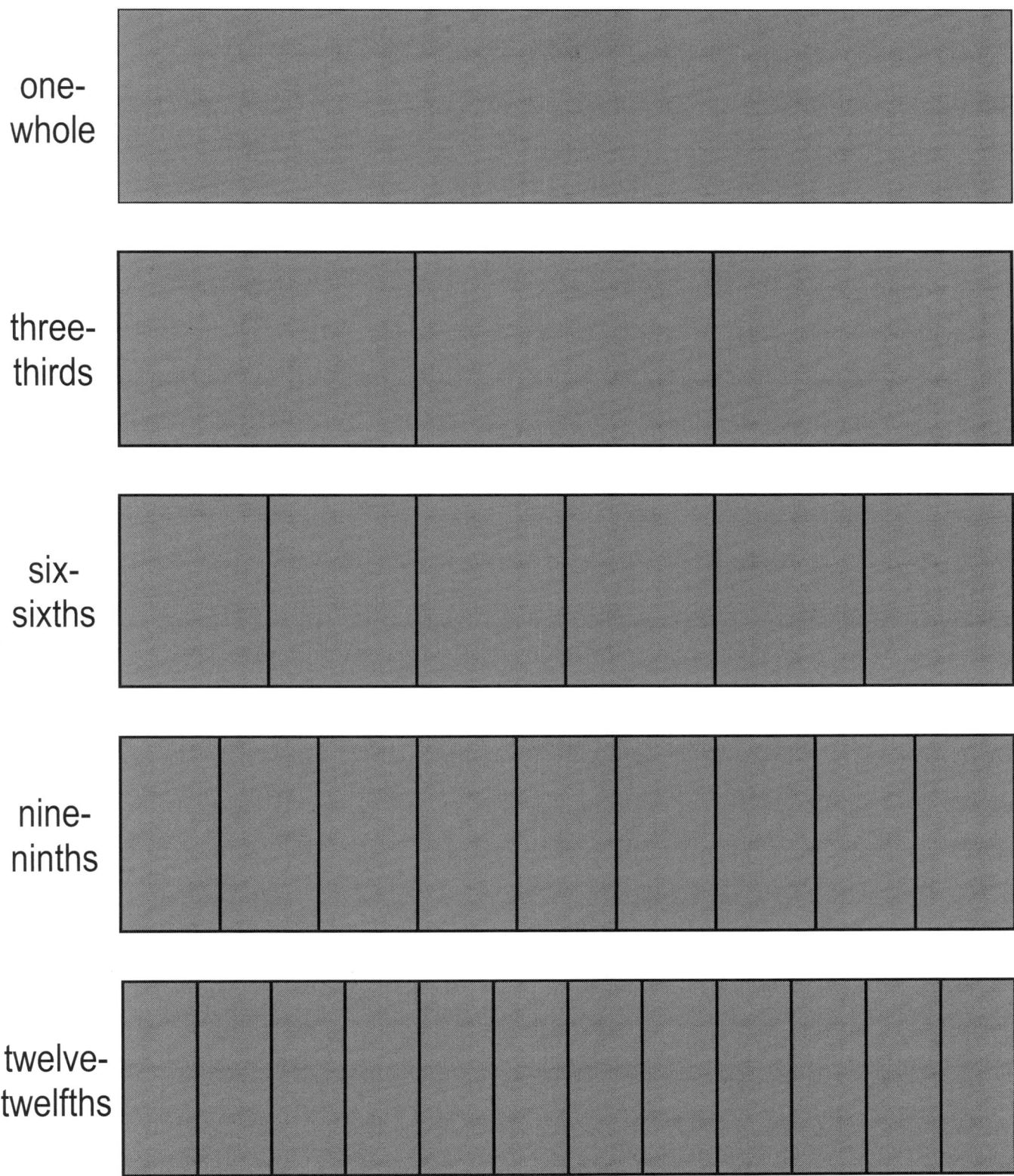

Introduction

Once upon a time, a mother went to a take-away.

She bought a pizza for her 3 children.

Mum divided the pizza like this.

But the younger boy was not happy!

Why was he not happy?

What could be the problem?

Any idea?

Next, their shares of the pizza were swapped for the younger boy and the older boy.

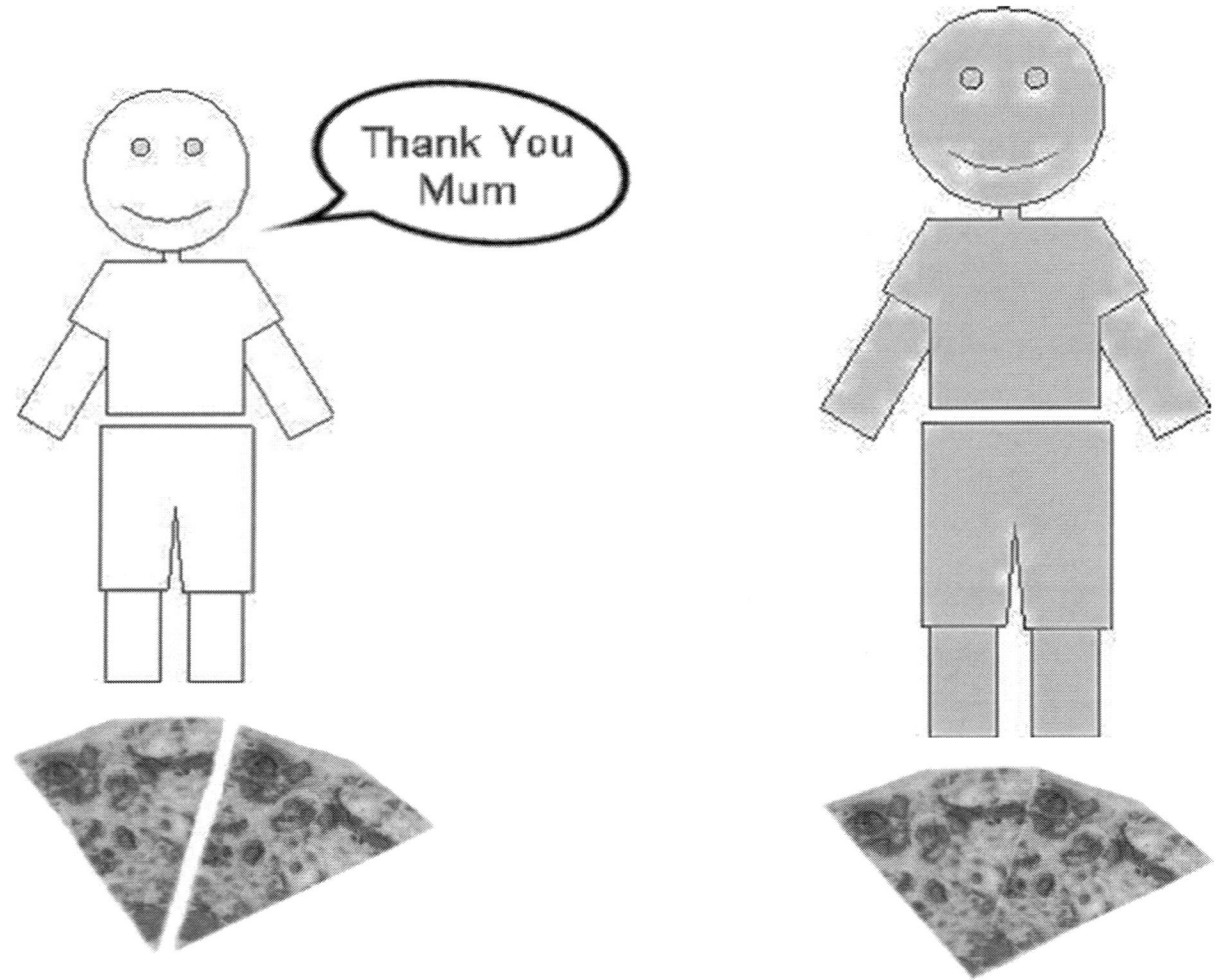

Then, the younger boy was happy!

What was the problem?

What do you think?

Check your answers (and explanation) on page 93.

What is a fraction?

Fraction is a **part** or **parts** of a **whole**.

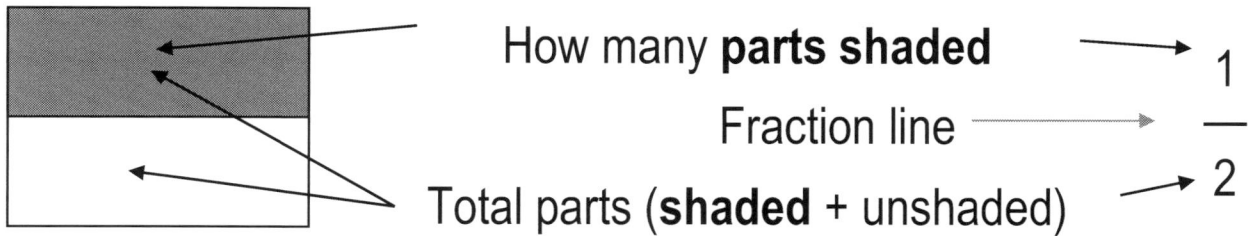

- Top number (*numerator*) shows how many parts (out of a whole)
- Bottom number (*denominator*) means total parts (to make a whole)

One part is shaded out of two parts.
That is a **half** or **one-half**. $\dfrac{1}{2}$

Also, one part is *unshaded* out of two parts.
That is another half or one-half. $\dfrac{1}{2}$

And $\dfrac{1}{2}$ + $\dfrac{1}{2}$ = $\dfrac{2}{2}$ 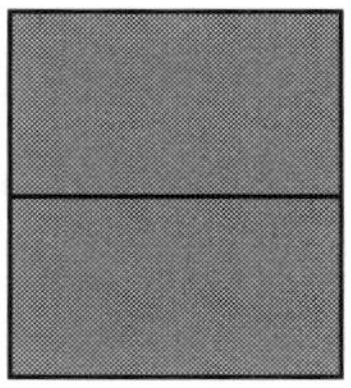 = 1

A fraction can be   small,   medium   or   big:

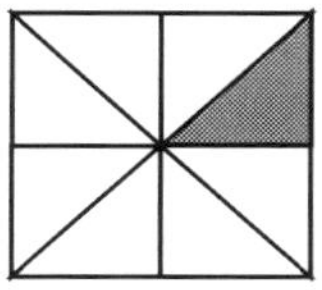

$\dfrac{1}{8}$, $\dfrac{1}{2}$, $\dfrac{7}{8}$

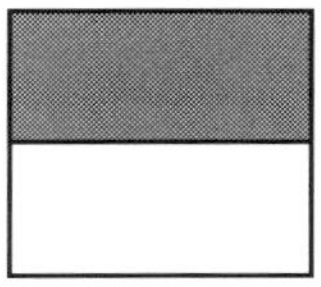

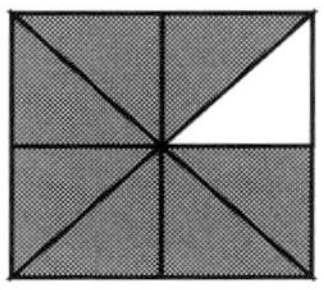

But not as big as a whole like 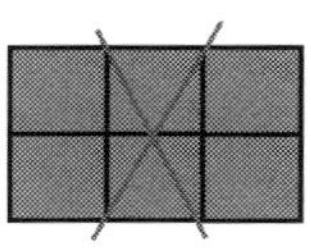   or

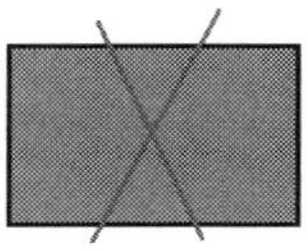

- A proper **fraction** is always *smaller* or *less* than a **whole**!

Halving 2, 4

Ali and Asha are friends and often share things. For the following shapes, one of them gets the **shaded** part and the other will get the *unshaded* part.

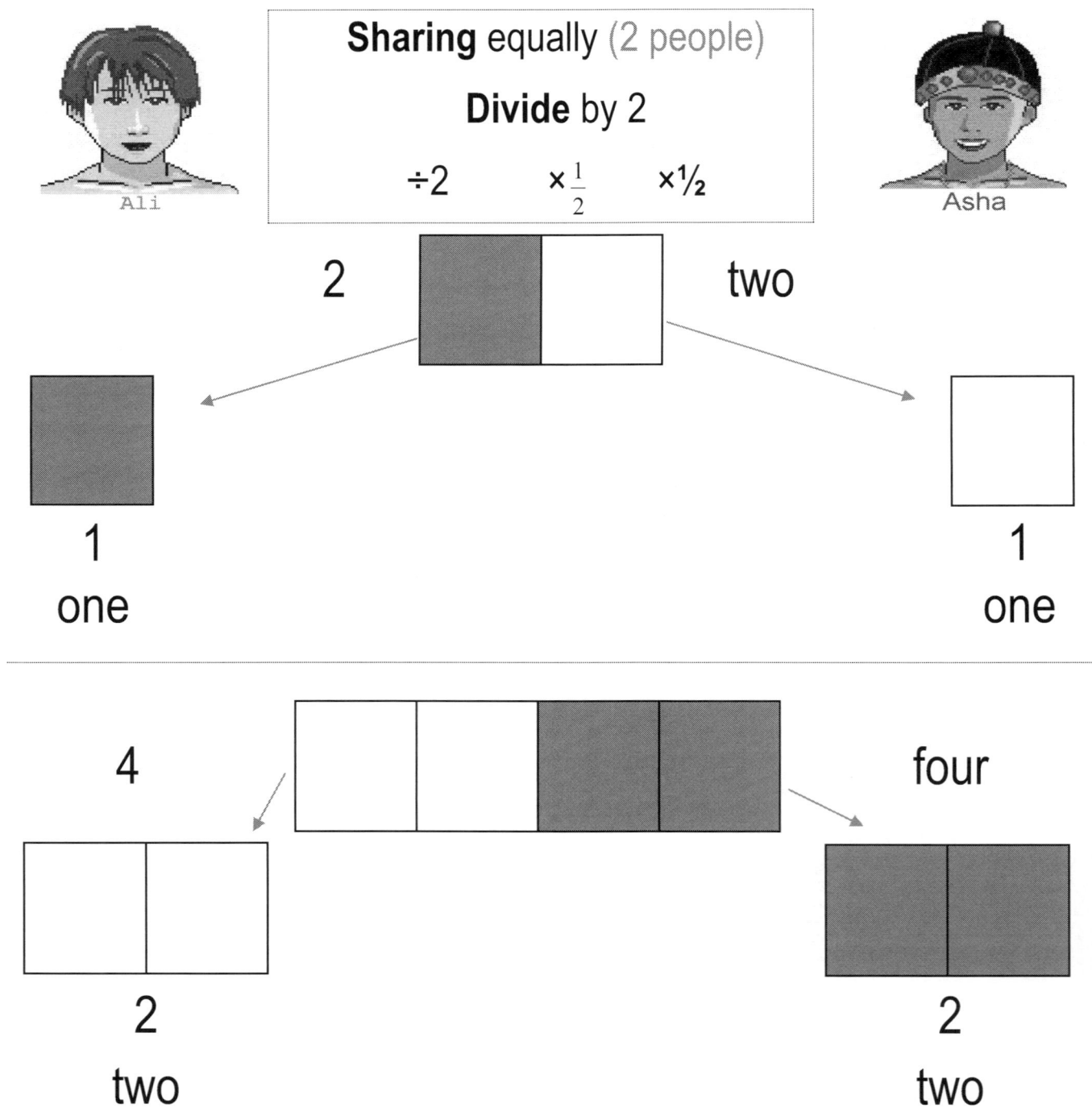

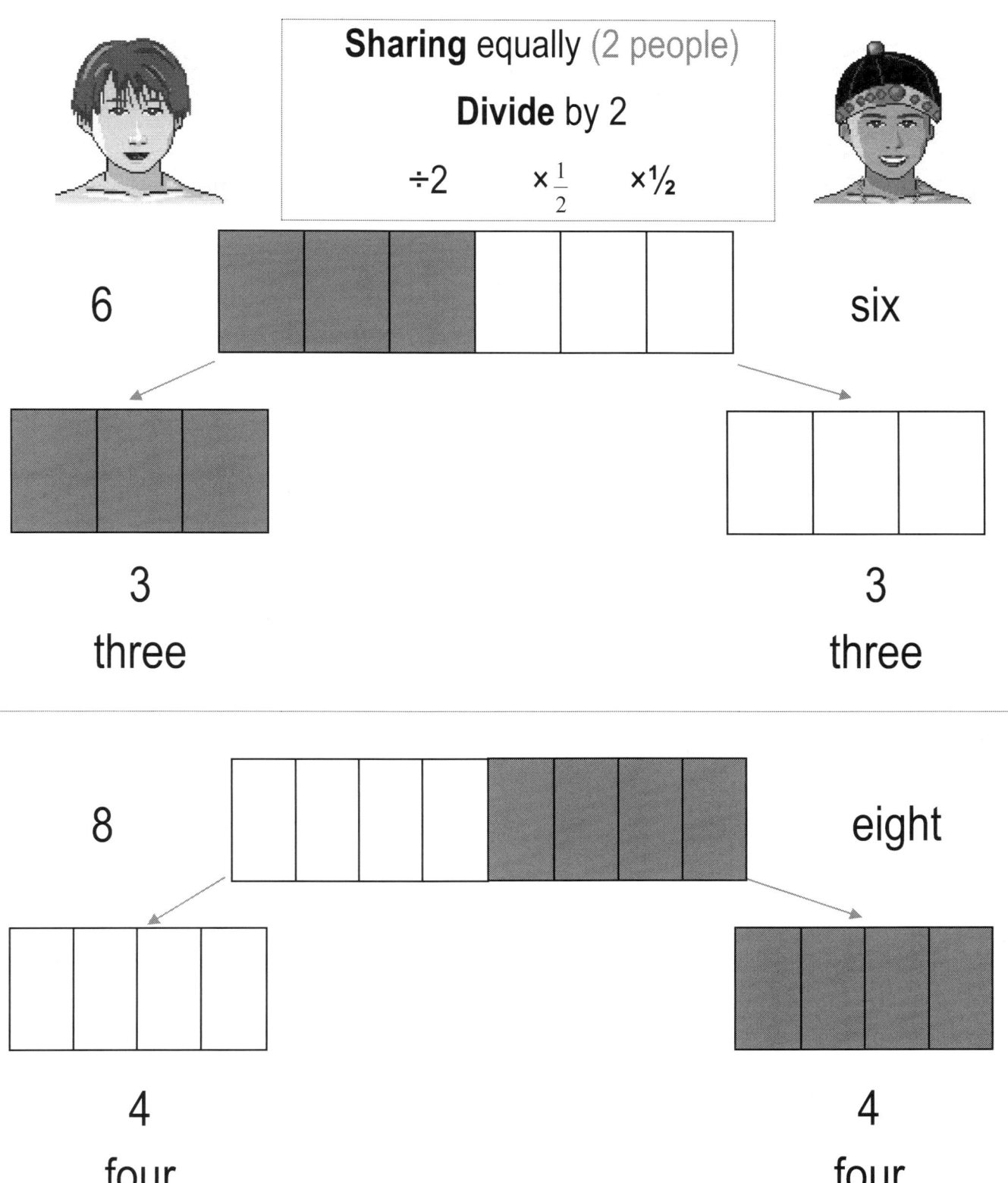

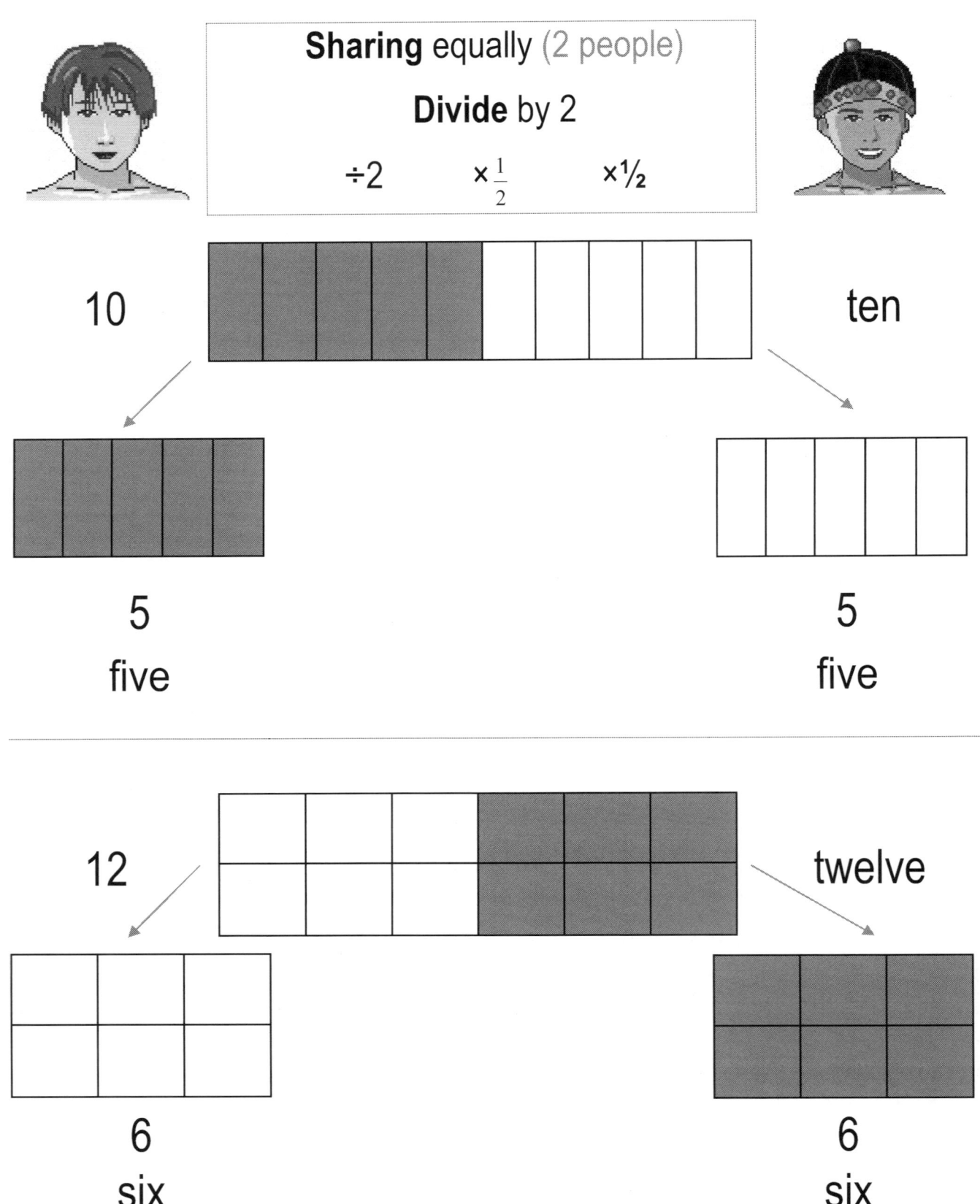

Halving 14, 16

Sharing equally (2 people)
Divide by 2
÷2   ×$\frac{1}{2}$ ×½

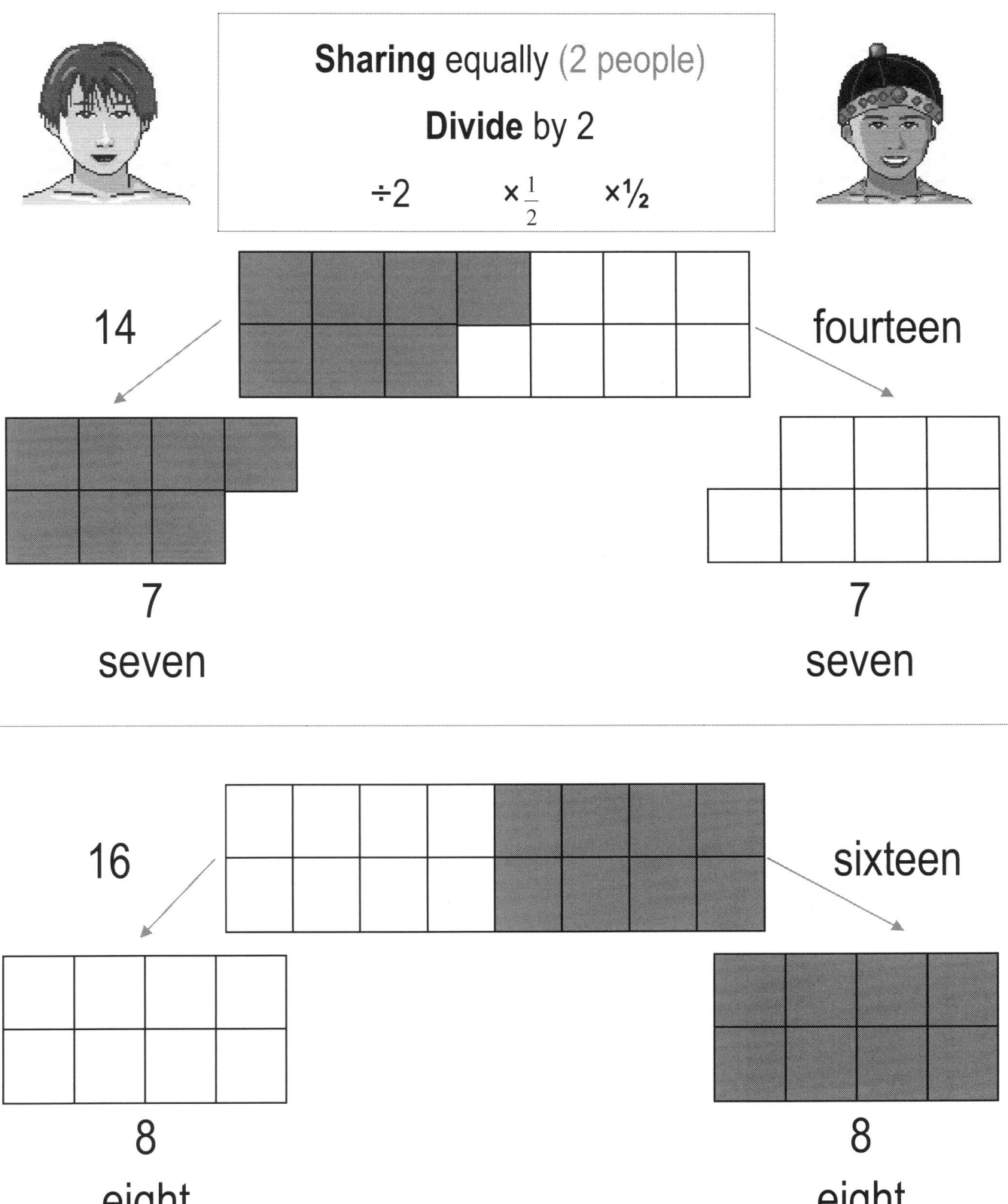

19

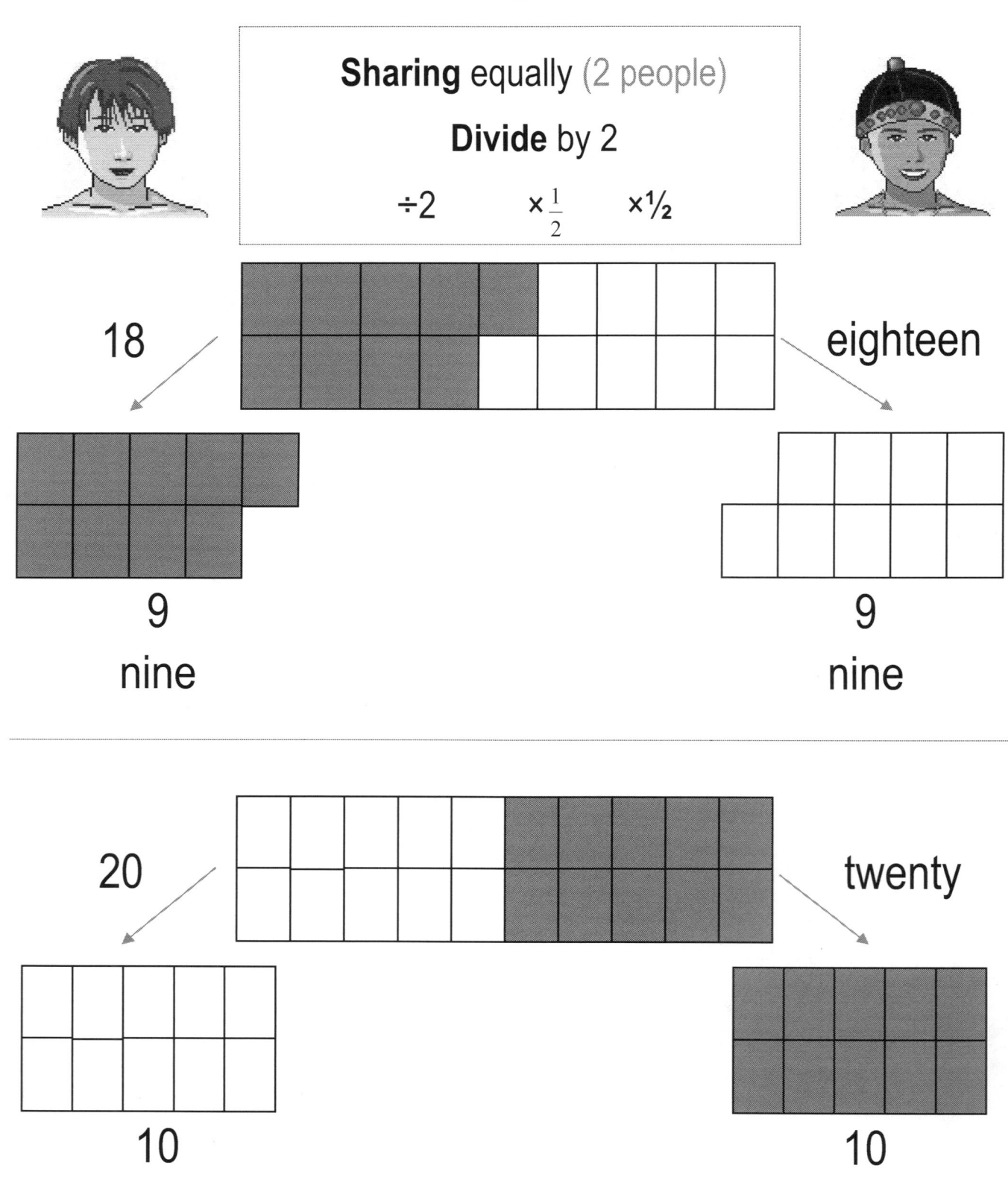

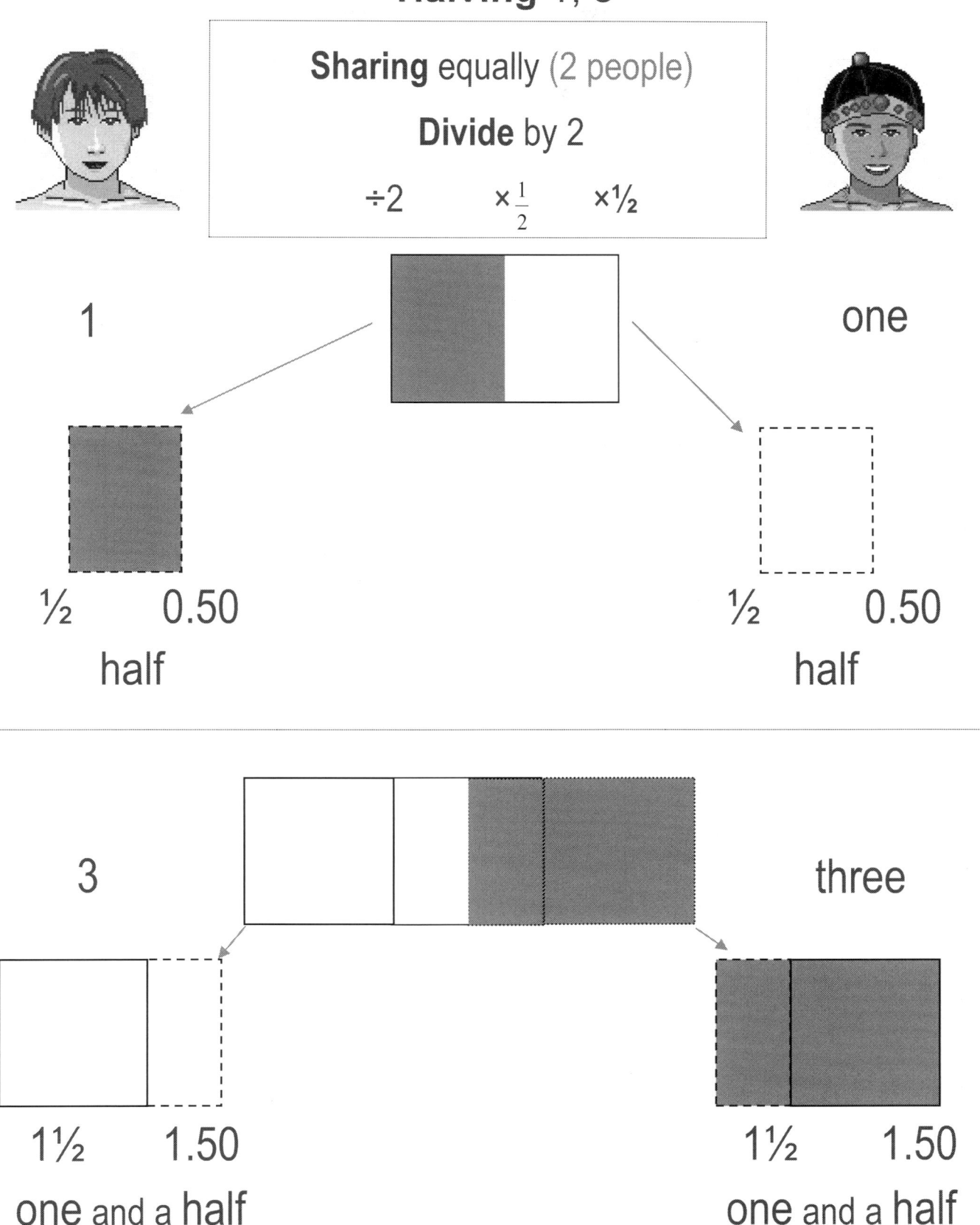

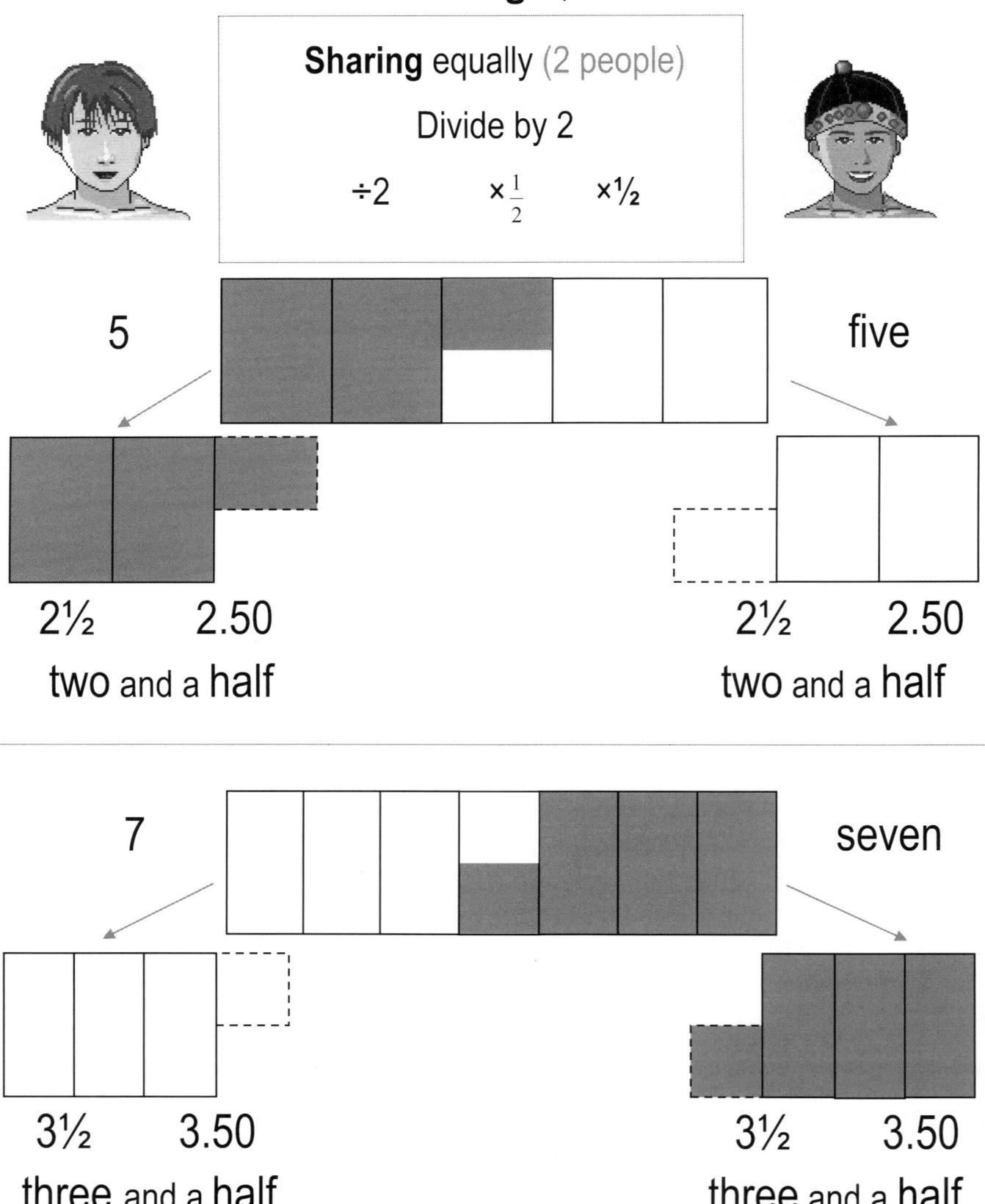

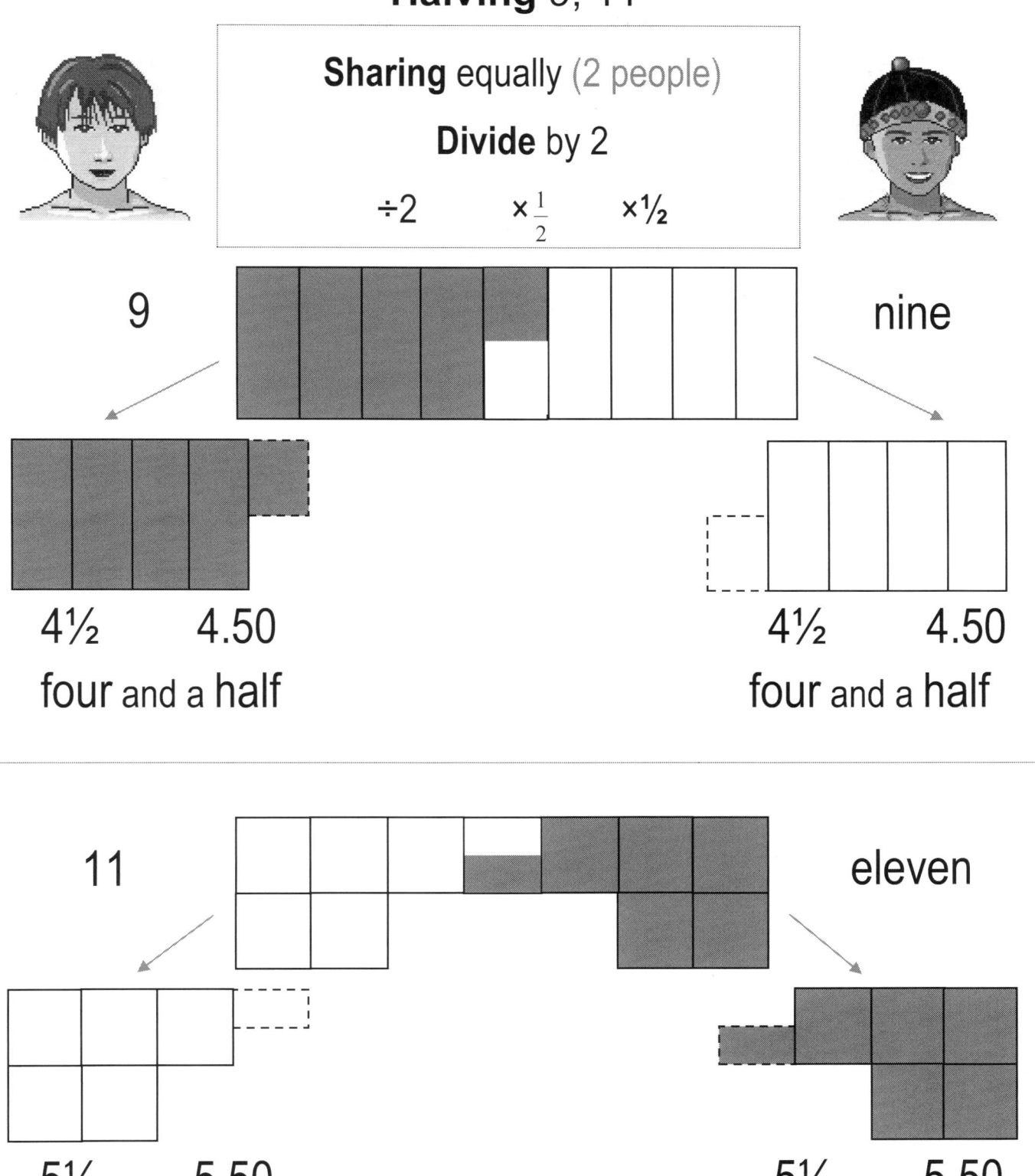

Halving 13, 15

Sharing equally (2 people)

Divide by 2

÷2   ×$\frac{1}{2}$ ×½

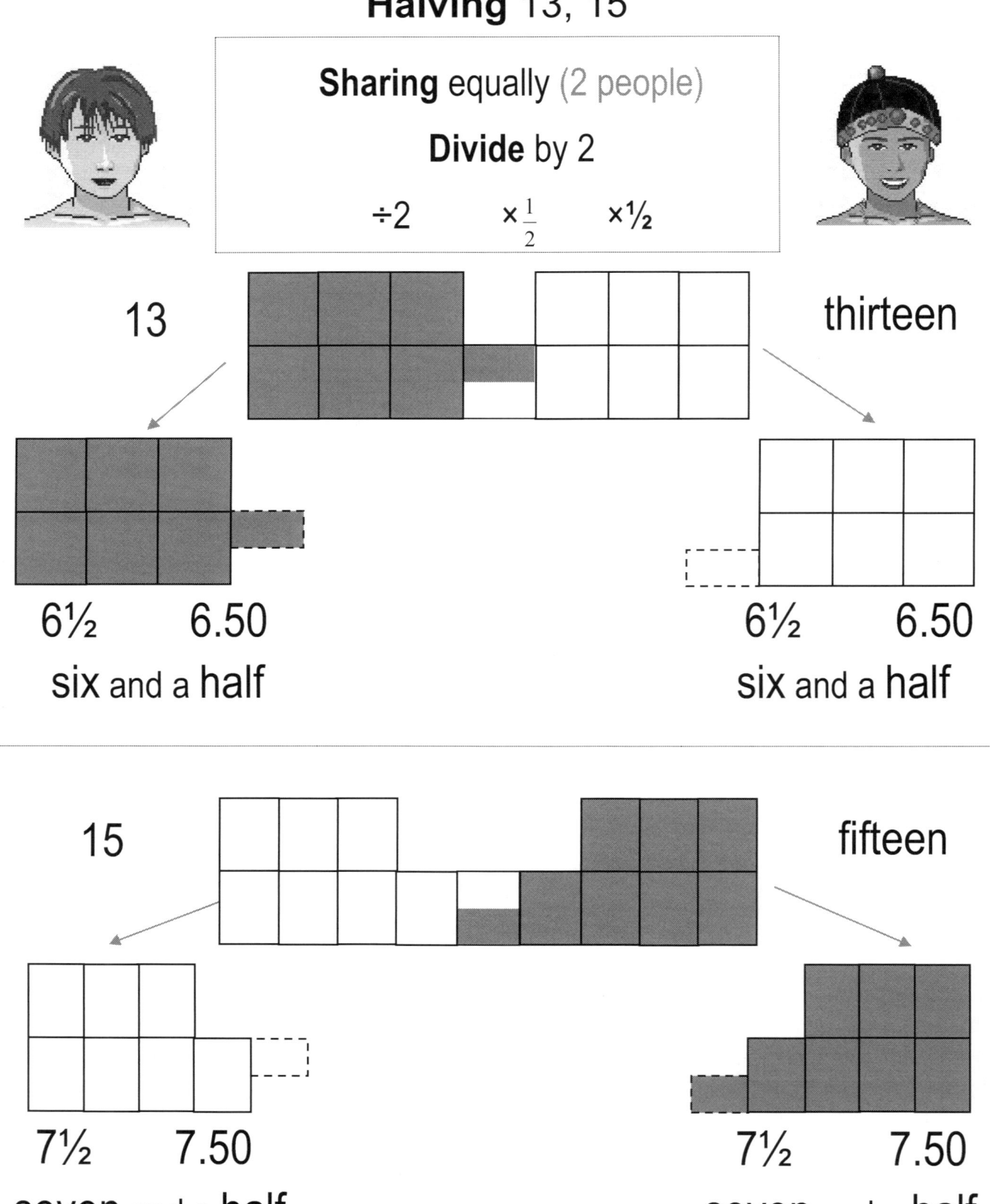

13 — thirteen

6½   6.50
six and a half

6½   6.50
six and a half

15 — fifteen

7½   7.50
seven and a half

7½   7.50
seven and a half

Halving 17, 19

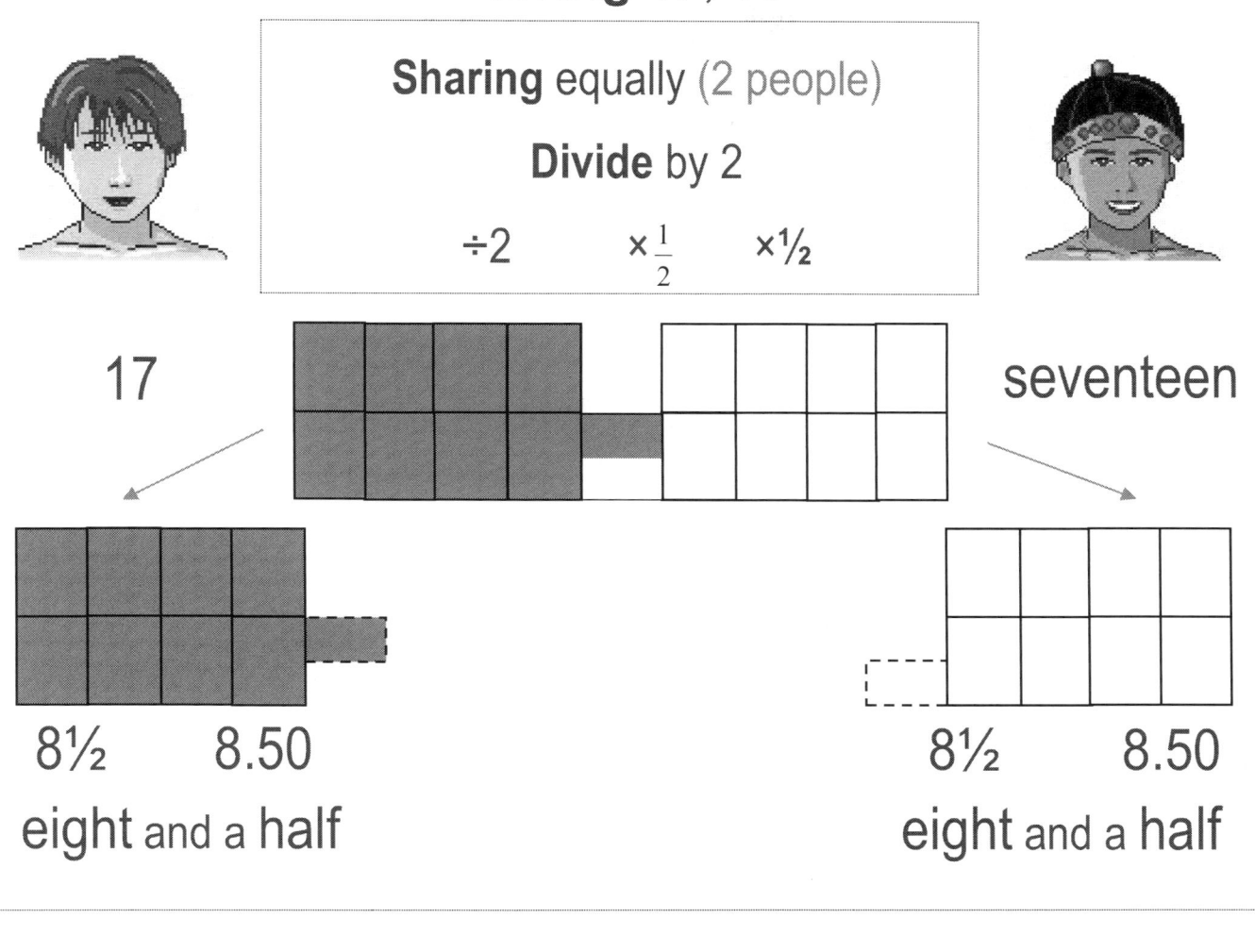

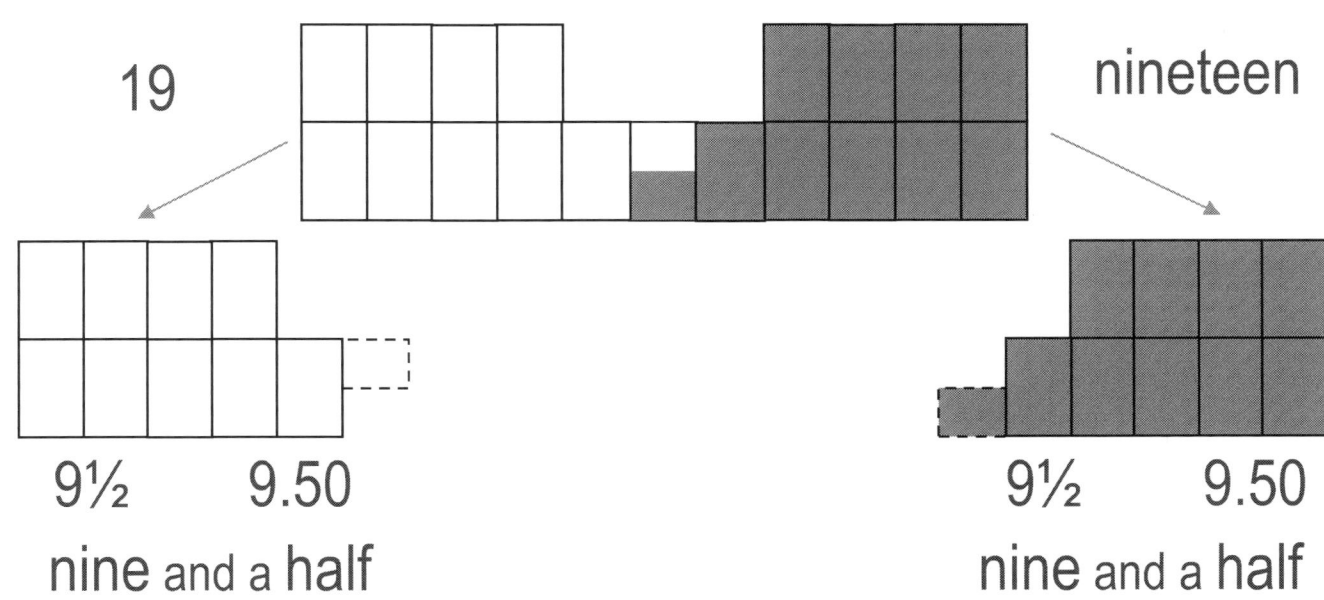

Sharing equally (2 people)
Divide by 2

$÷2 \quad ×\frac{1}{2} \quad ×½$

17 seventeen

8½   8.50
eight and a half

8½   8.50
eight and a half

19 nineteen

9½   9.50
nine and a half

9½   9.50
nine and a half

Quartering 4

Ali and Asha also share things with their friends Alex and Ella. For the following shapes, everyone gets a **quarter** (one-fourth) or **half** of **half**! That's halving for two groups, then halving *again* for each child.

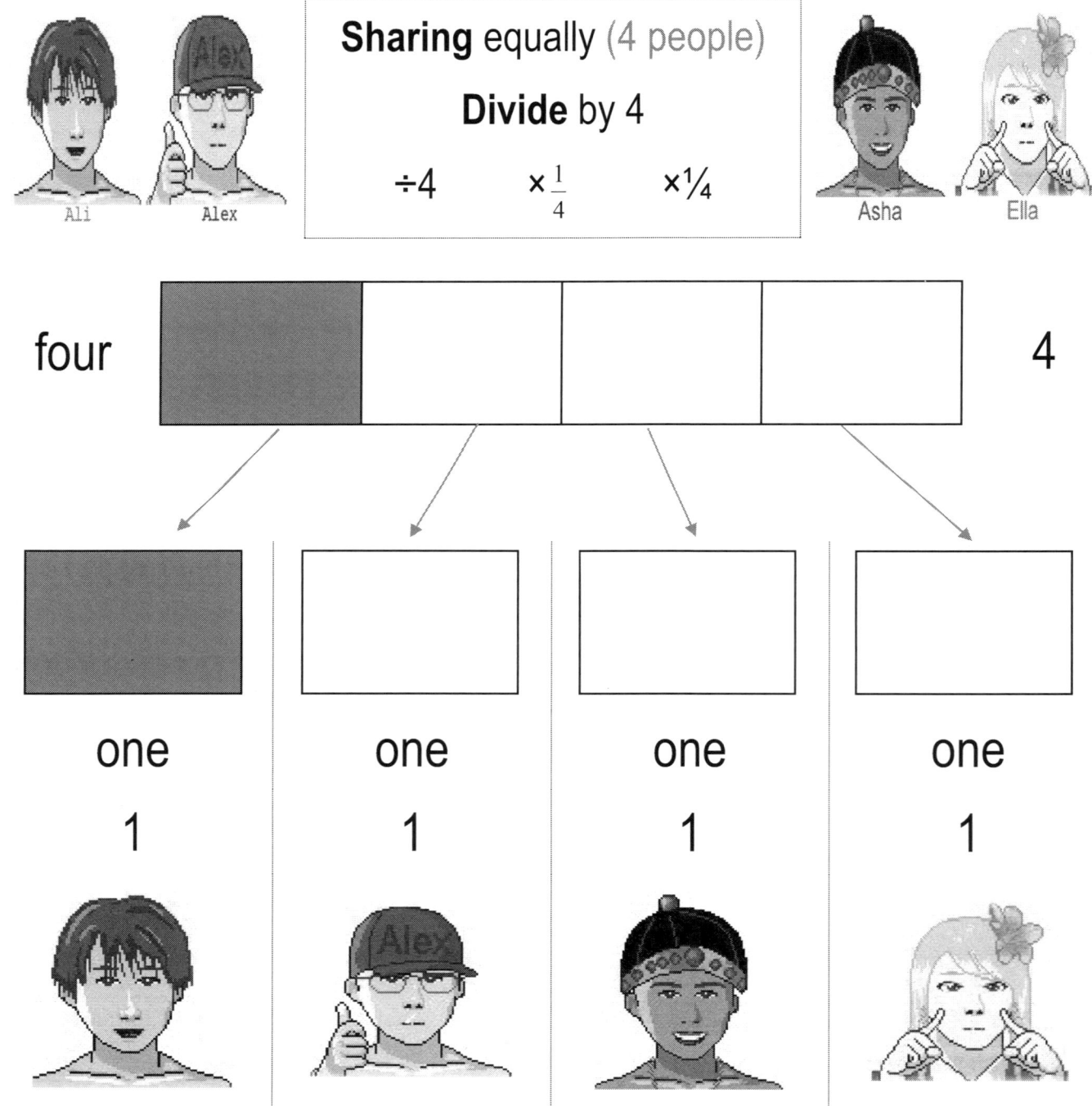

Quartering 8, 12

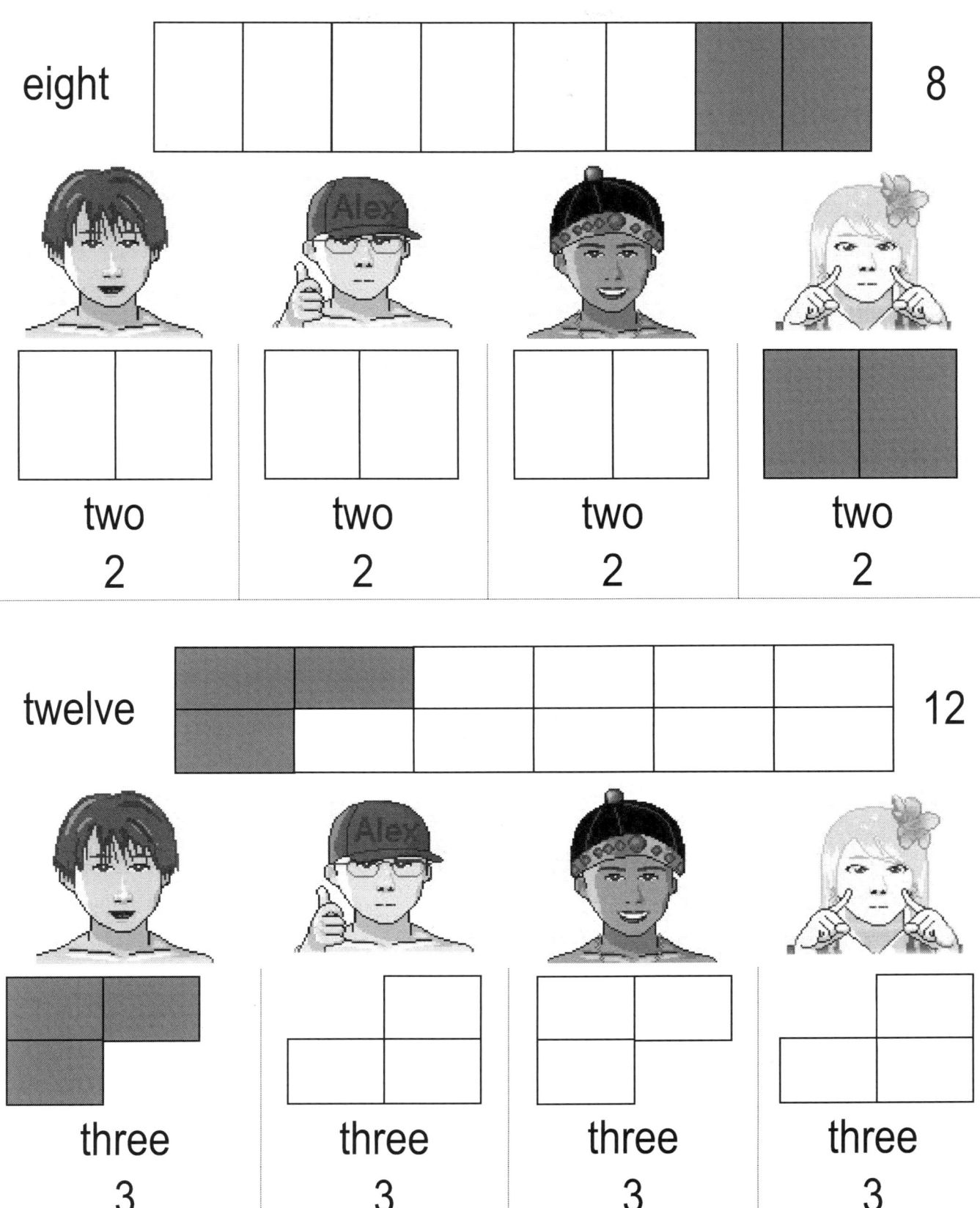

Quartering 16, 20

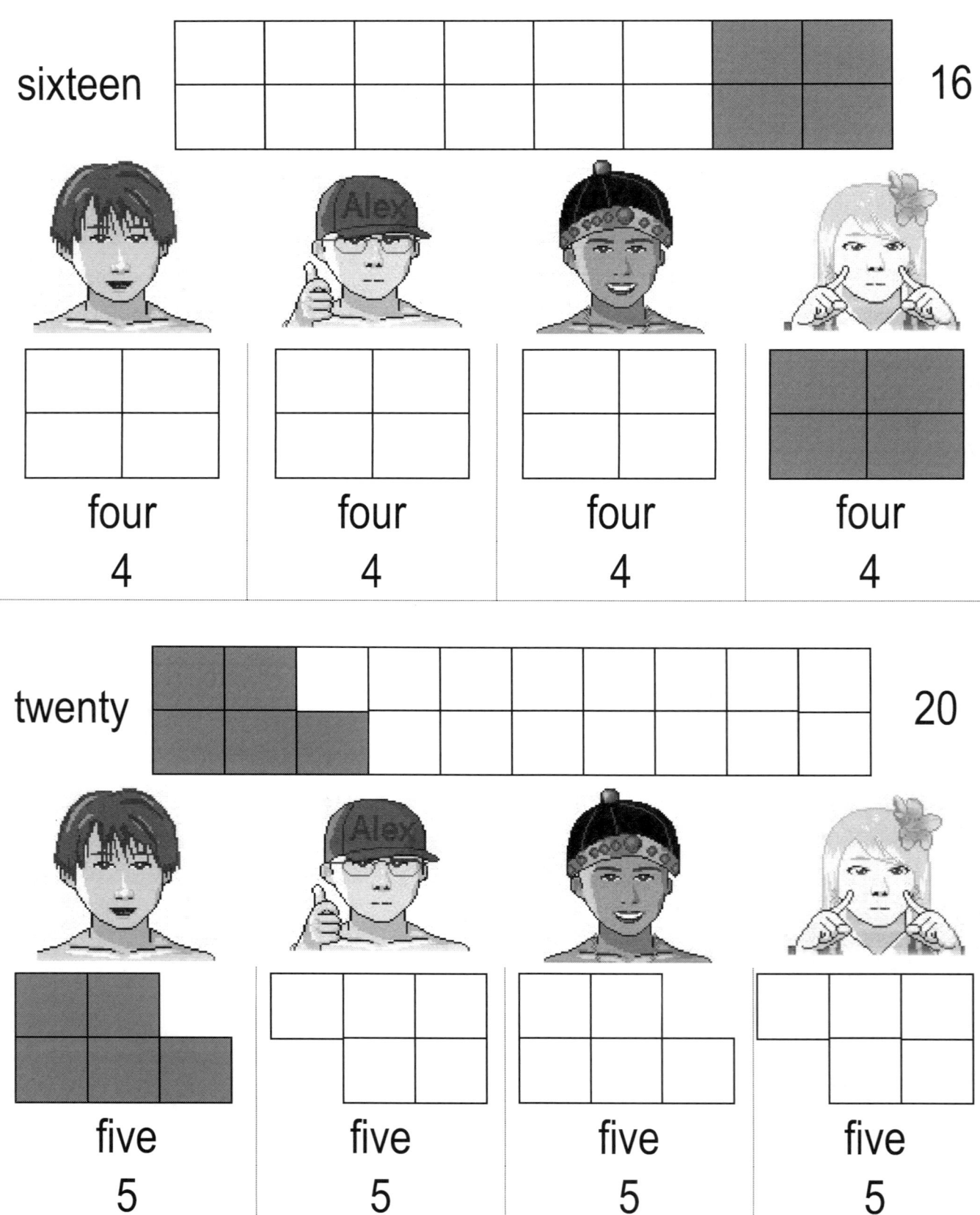

Quartering 2

Sharing equally (4 people)
Divide by 4

÷4   × $\frac{1}{4}$ ×¼

two 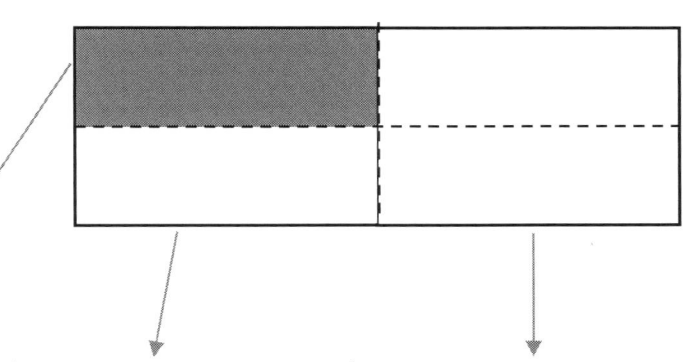 2

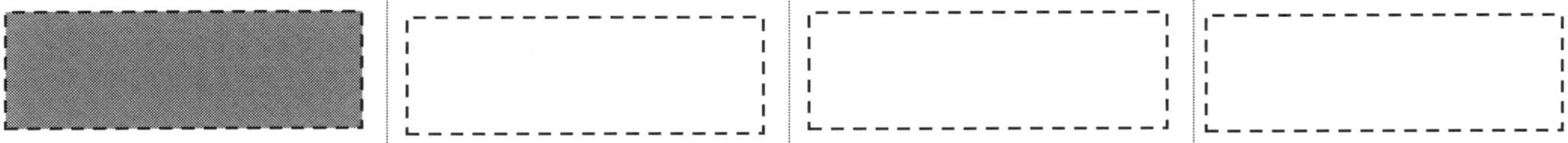

half   half   half   half

$\frac{1}{2}$ $\frac{1}{2}$ $\frac{1}{2}$ $\frac{1}{2}$

0.50   0.50   0.50   0.50

  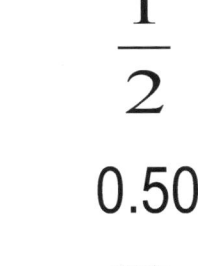 

Quartering 6, 10

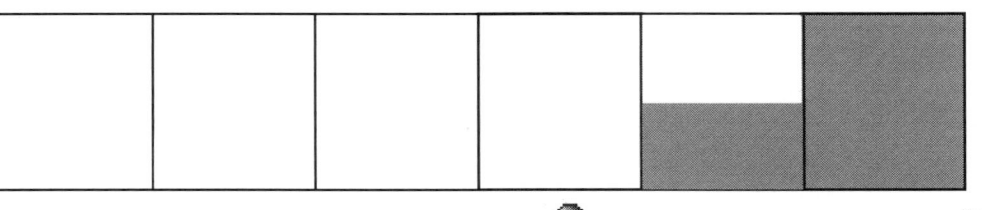

six 6

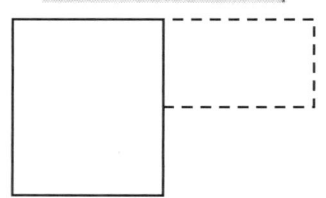 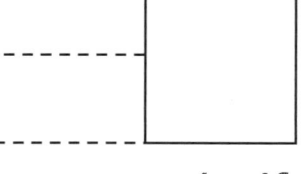 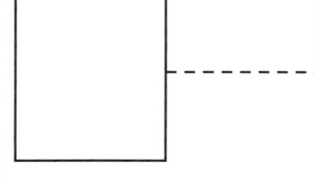 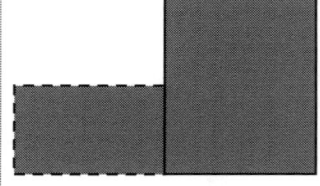

one and half	one and half	one and half	one and half
$1\frac{1}{2}$ 1.50	$1\frac{1}{2}$ 1.50	$1\frac{1}{2}$ 1.50	$1\frac{1}{2}$ 1.50

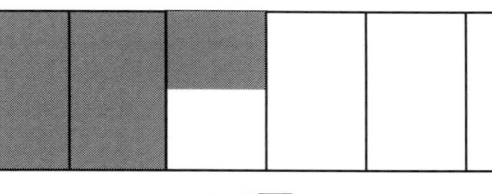

ten 10

 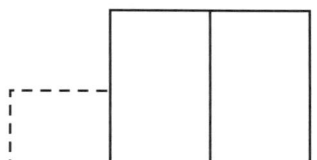 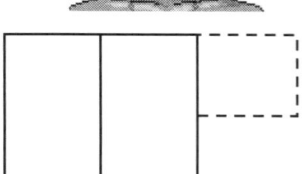 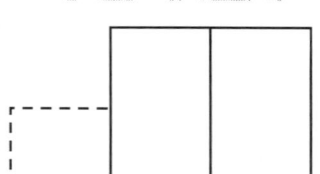

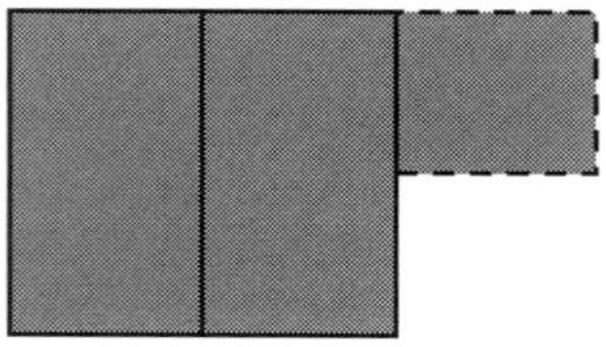

two and half	two and half	two and half	two and half
$2\frac{1}{2}$ 2.50	$2\frac{1}{2}$ 2.50	$2\frac{1}{2}$ 2.50	$2\frac{1}{2}$ 2.50

Quartering 14, 18

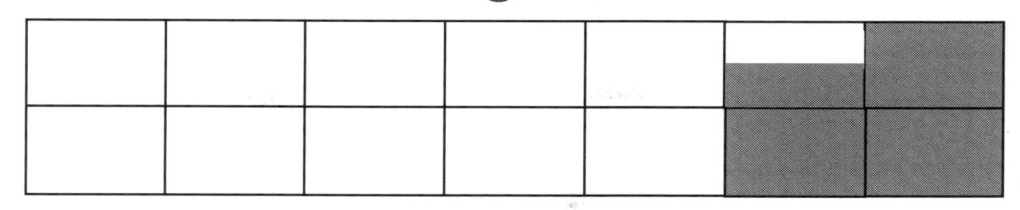

fourteen ... 14

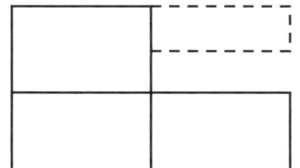 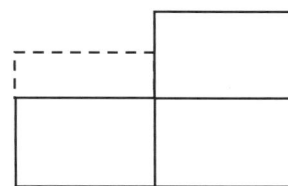  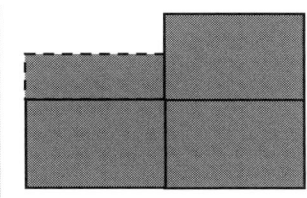

three and half	three and half	three and half	three and half
$3\frac{1}{2}$ 3.50	$3\frac{1}{2}$ 3.50	$3\frac{1}{2}$ 3.50	$3\frac{1}{2}$ 3.50

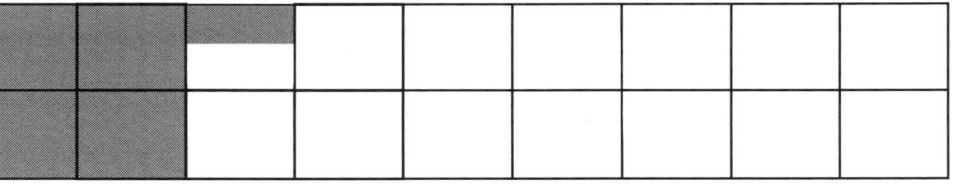

eighteen ... 18

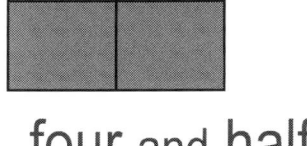 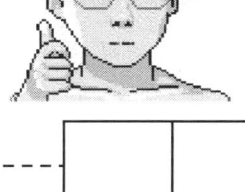 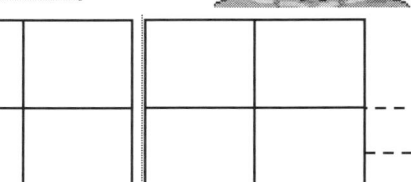 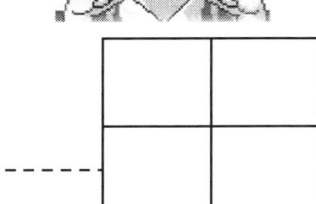

four and half	four and half	four and half	four and half
$4\frac{1}{2}$ 4.50	$4\frac{1}{2}$ 4.50	$4\frac{1}{2}$ 4.50	$4\frac{1}{2}$ 4.50

Quartering 1

Sharing equally (4 people)
Divide by 4
÷4   ×$\frac{1}{4}$ ×¼

one 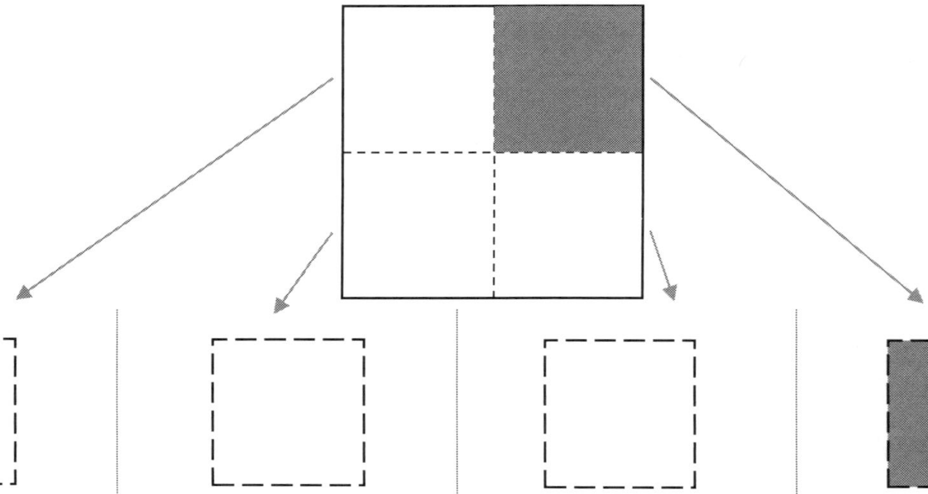 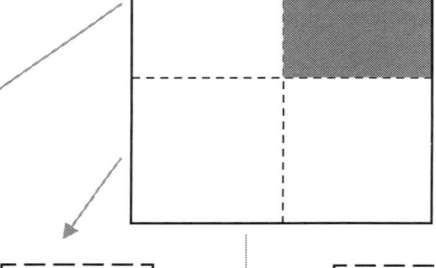 1

quarter	quarter	quarter	quarter
$\frac{1}{4}$	$\frac{1}{4}$	$\frac{1}{4}$	$\frac{1}{4}$
0.25	0.25	0.25	0.25

32

Quartering 5, 9

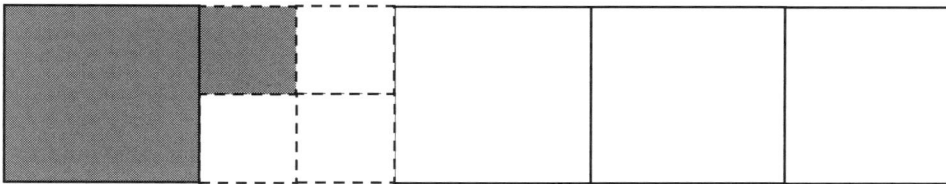

five   5

one and quarter	one and quarter	one and quarter	one and quarter
$1\frac{1}{4}$ 1.25	$1\frac{1}{4}$ 1.25	$1\frac{1}{4}$ 1.25	$1\frac{1}{4}$ 1.25

nine   9

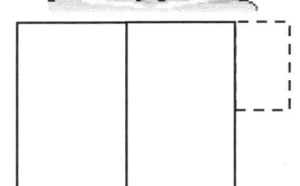 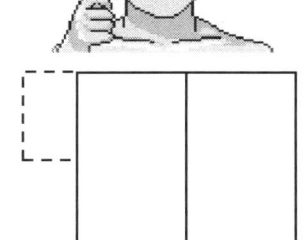 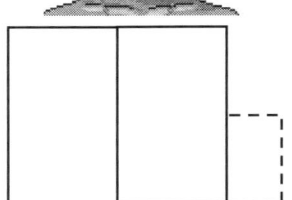 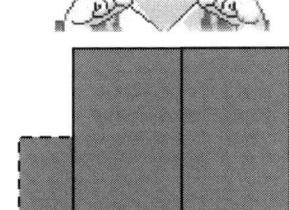

two and quarter	two and quarter	two and quarter	two and quarter
$2\frac{1}{4}$ 2.25	$2\frac{1}{4}$ 2.25	$2\frac{1}{4}$ 2.25	$2\frac{1}{4}$ 2.25

Quartering 13, 17

thirteen   13

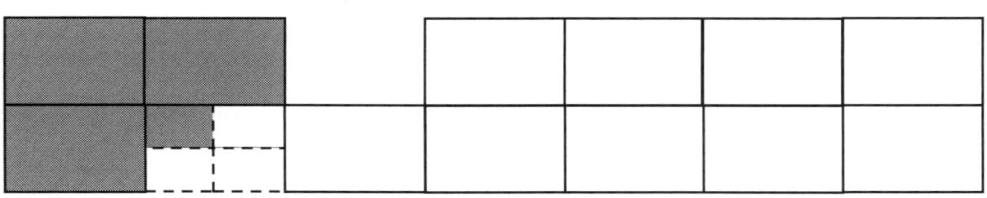

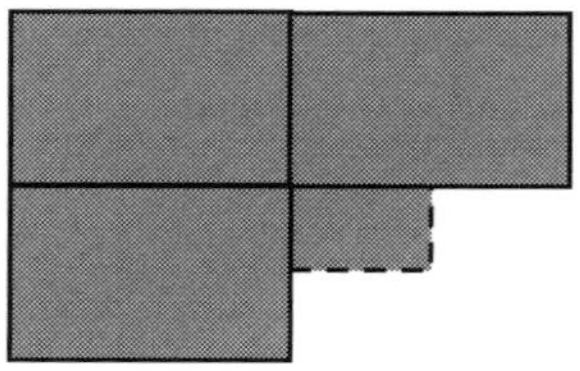

three and quarter	three and quarter	three and quarter	three and quarter
$3\frac{1}{4}$ 3.25	$3\frac{1}{4}$ 3.25	$3\frac{1}{4}$ 3.25	$3\frac{1}{4}$ 3.25

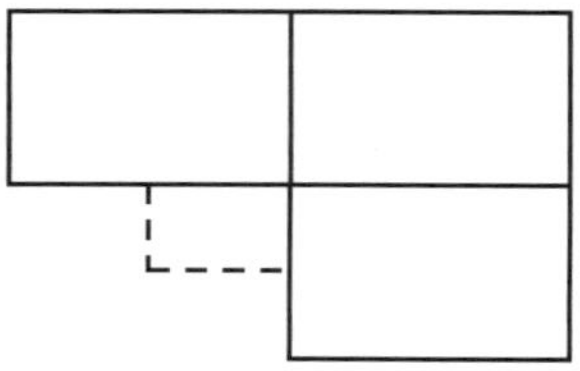

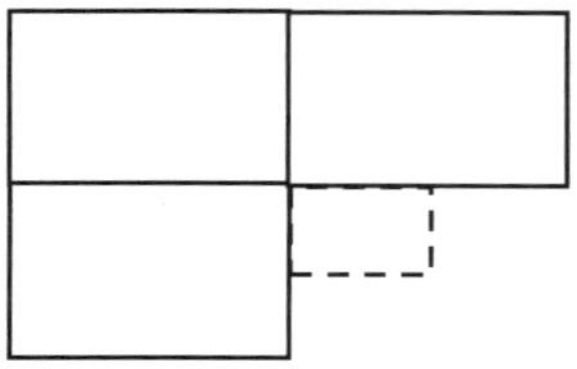

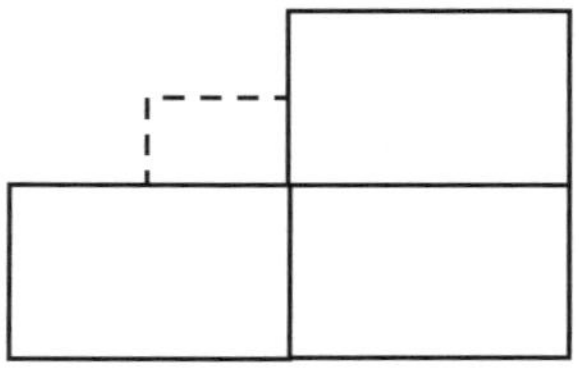

seventeen 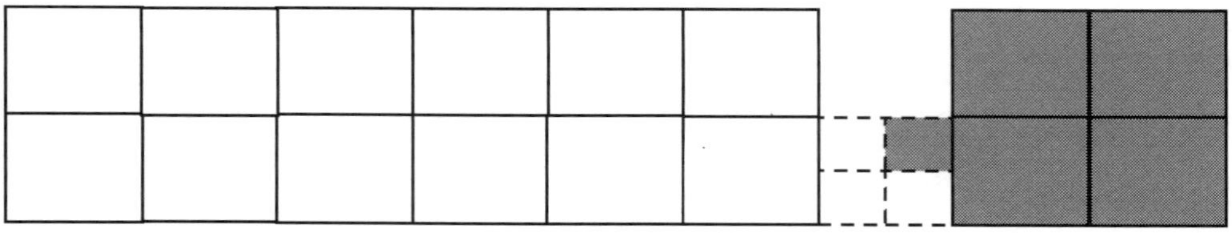   17

four and quarter	four and quarter	four and quarter	four and quarter
$4\frac{1}{4}$ 4.25	$4\frac{1}{4}$ 4.25	$4\frac{1}{4}$ 4.25	$4\frac{1}{4}$ 4.25

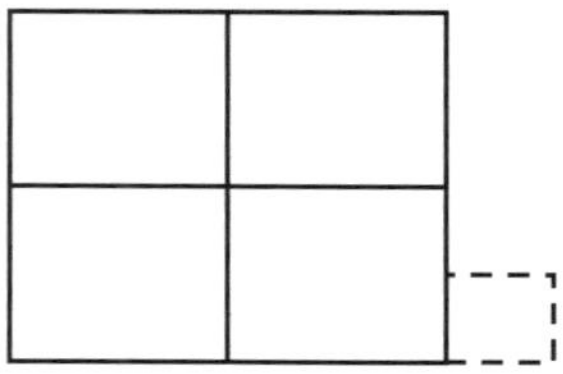

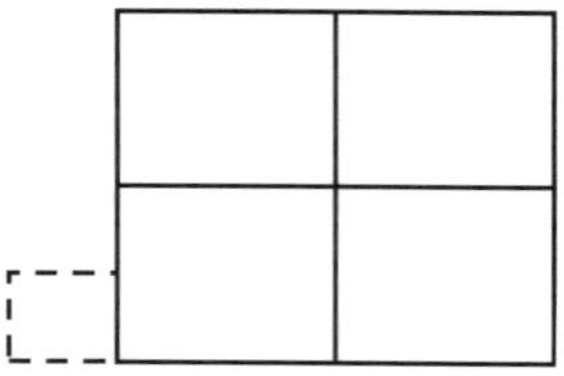

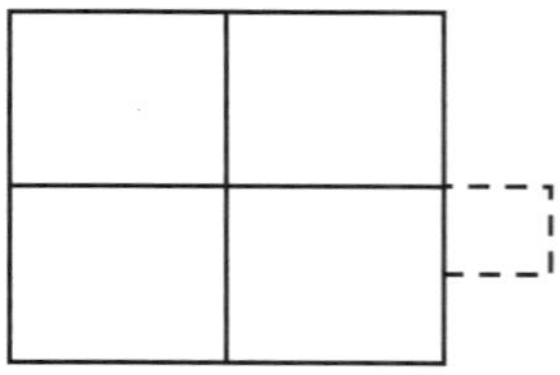

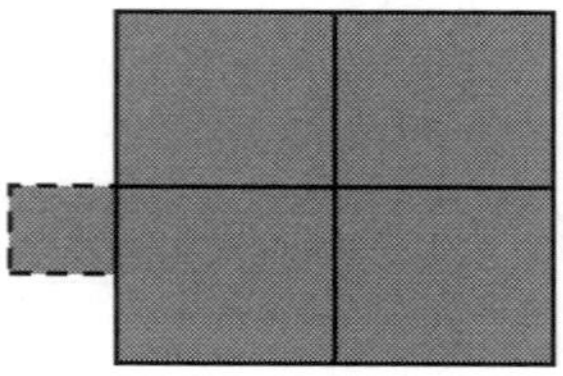

Quartering 3

Sharing equally (4 people)
Divide by 4

÷4   × $\frac{1}{4}$ ×¼

three 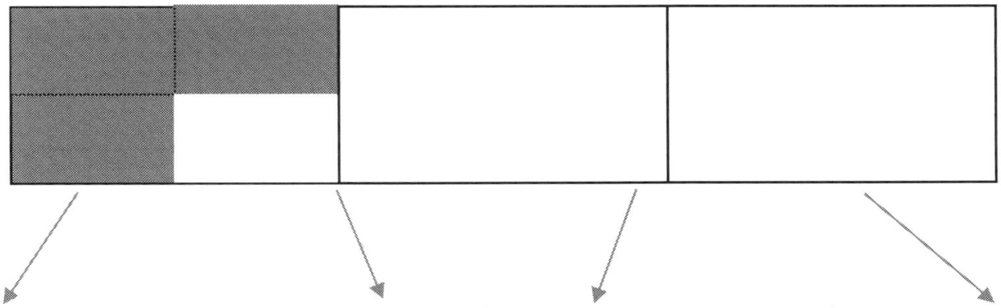   3

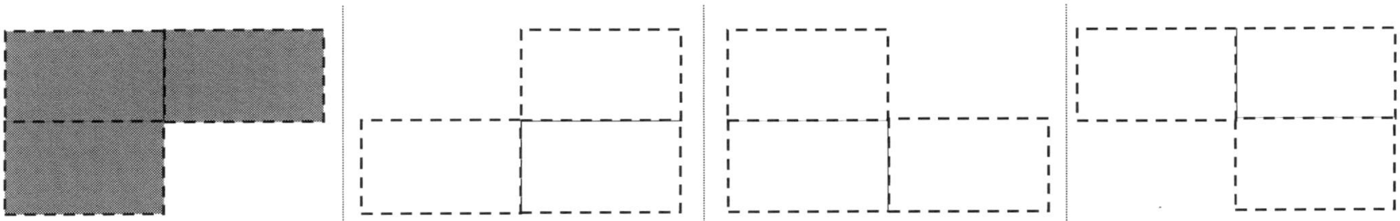

three-quarters	three-quarters	three-quarters	three-quarters
$\frac{3}{4}$	$\frac{3}{4}$	$\frac{3}{4}$	$\frac{3}{4}$
0.75	0.75	0.75	0.75

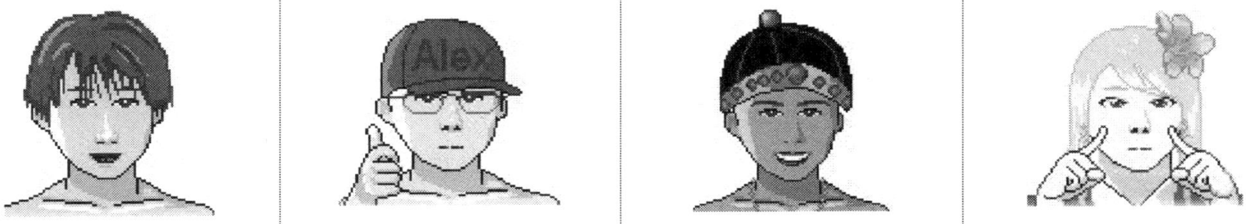

35

Quartering 7, 11

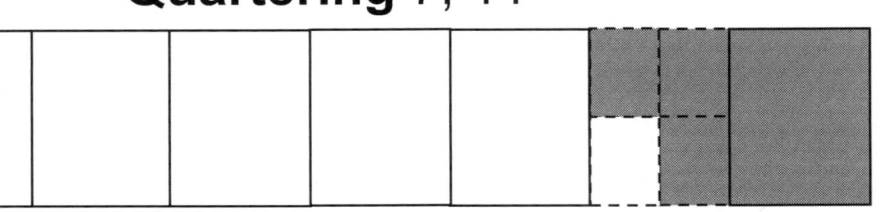

seven   7

  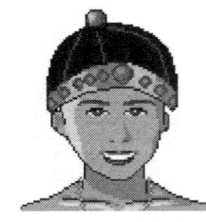 

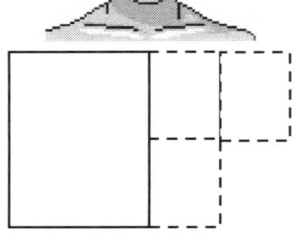 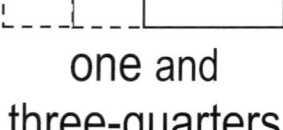 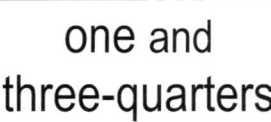 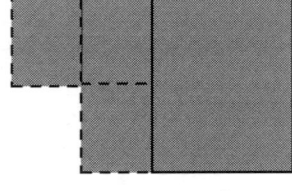

one and three-quarters	one and three-quarters	one and three-quarters	one and three-quarters
$1\frac{3}{4}$ 1.75	$1\frac{3}{4}$ 1.75	$1\frac{3}{4}$ 1.75	$1\frac{3}{4}$ 1.75

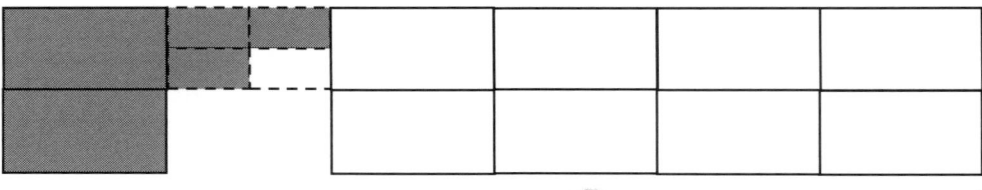

eleven   11

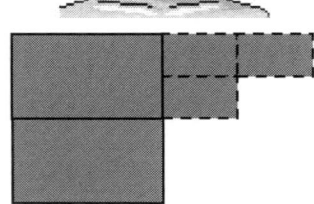 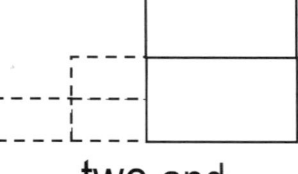 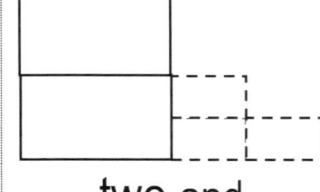

two and three-quarters	two and three-quarters	two and three-quarters	two and three-quarters
$2\frac{3}{4}$ 2.75	$2\frac{3}{4}$ 2.75	$2\frac{3}{4}$ 2.75	$2\frac{3}{4}$ 2.75

Quartering 15, 19

fifteen 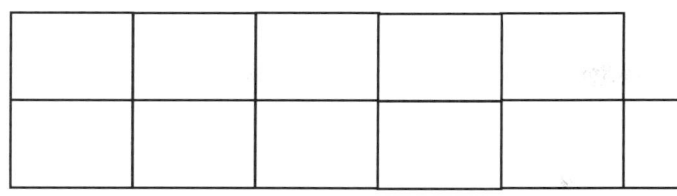 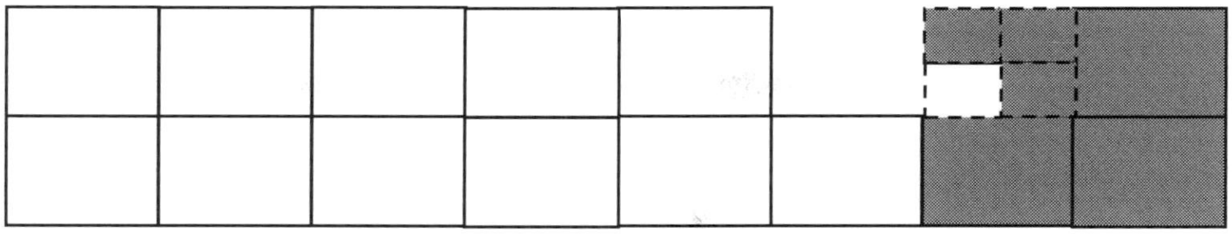   15

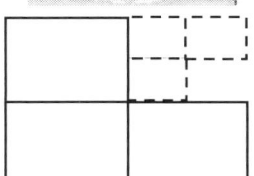

three and three-quarters	three and three-quarters	three and three-quarters	three and three-quarters
$3\frac{3}{4}$ 3.75	$3\frac{3}{4}$ 3.75	$3\frac{3}{4}$ 3.75	$3\frac{3}{4}$ 3.75

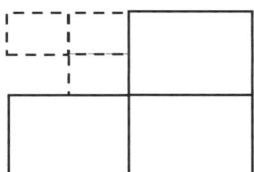

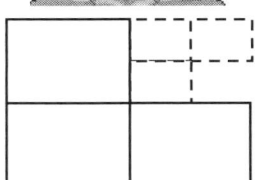

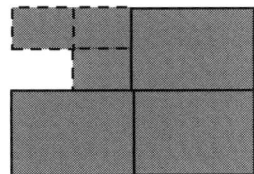

nineteen 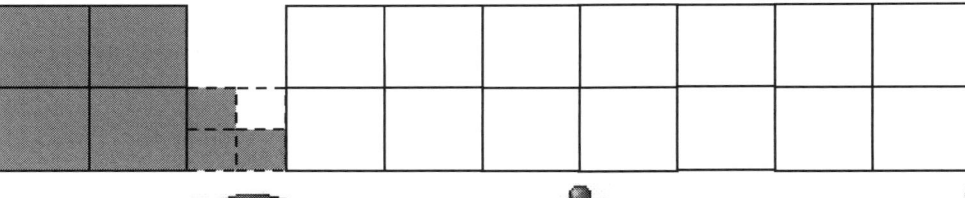   19

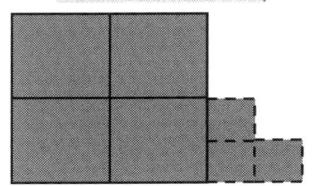

four and three-quarters	four and three-quarters	four and three-quarters	four and three-quarters
$4\frac{3}{4}$ 4.75	$4\frac{3}{4}$ 4.75	$4\frac{3}{4}$ 4.75	$4\frac{3}{4}$ 4.75

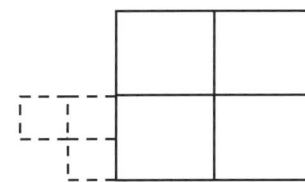

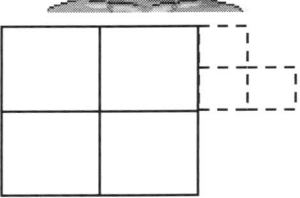

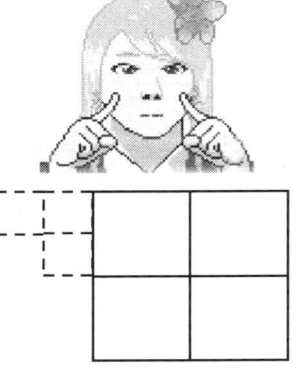

Equivalent Fractions

Equivalent means *equal in value*.

For example, if 2 children share 1 whole cake, they each get a **half**.

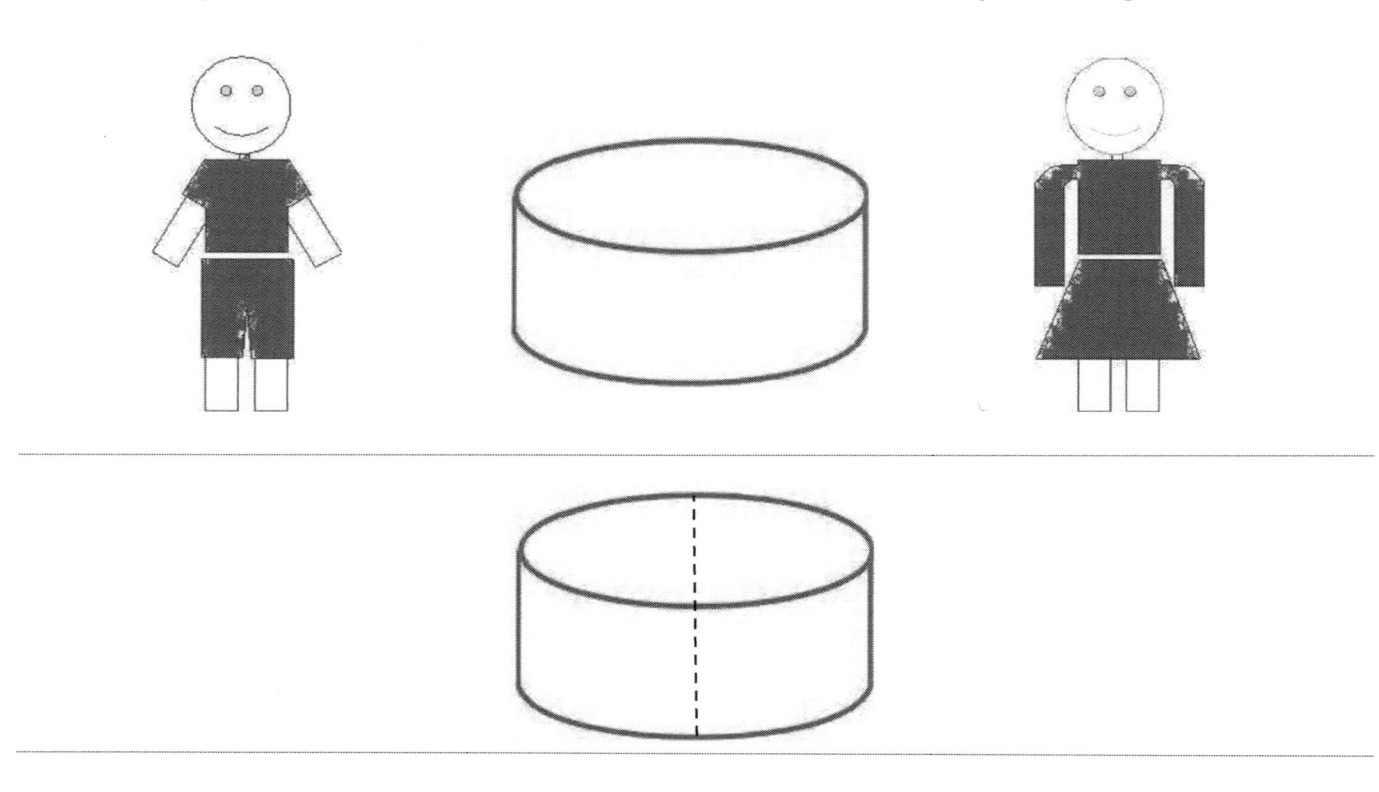

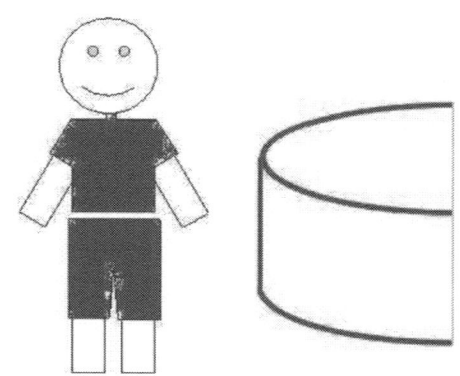

half

$\frac{1}{2}$

0.50

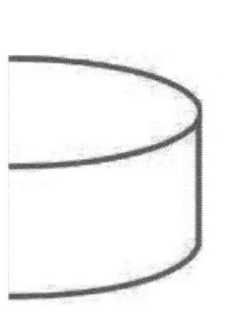

half

$\frac{1}{2}$

0.50

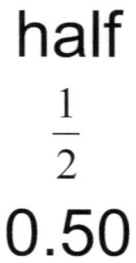

Also, if the same two children share the same whole cake, they can have **two-quarters** each. Quarter means **half** of a **half**.

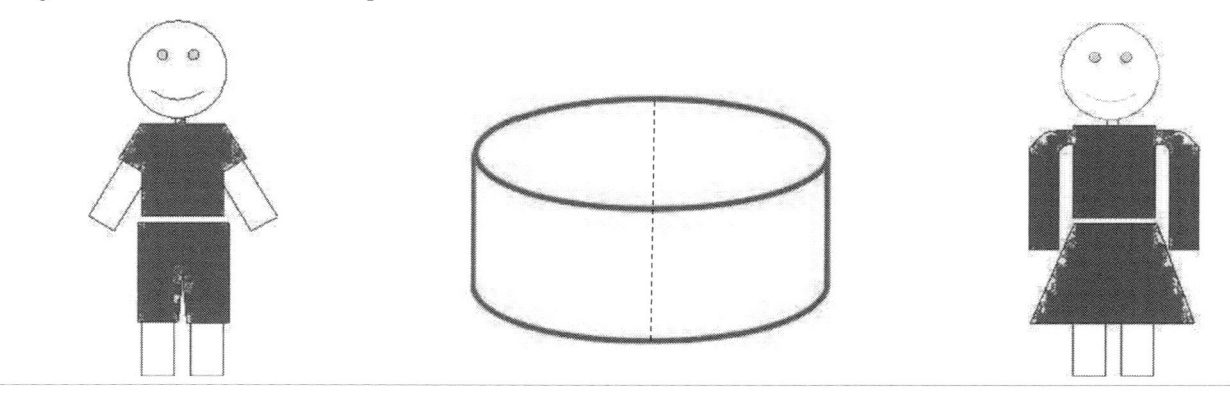

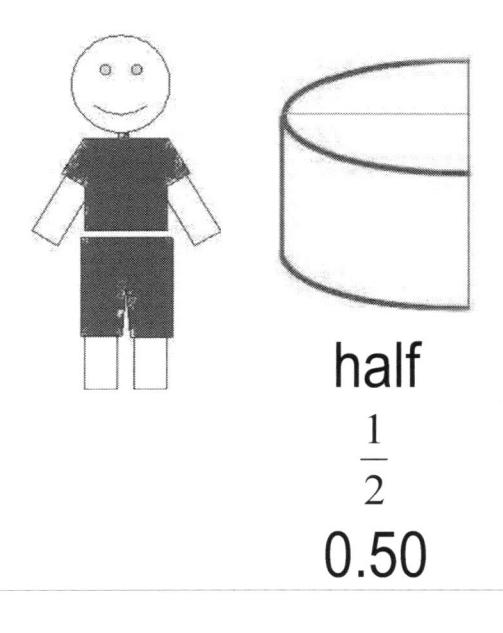

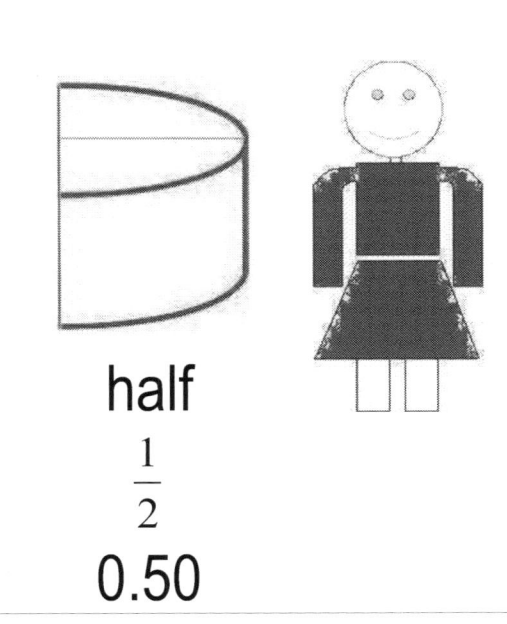

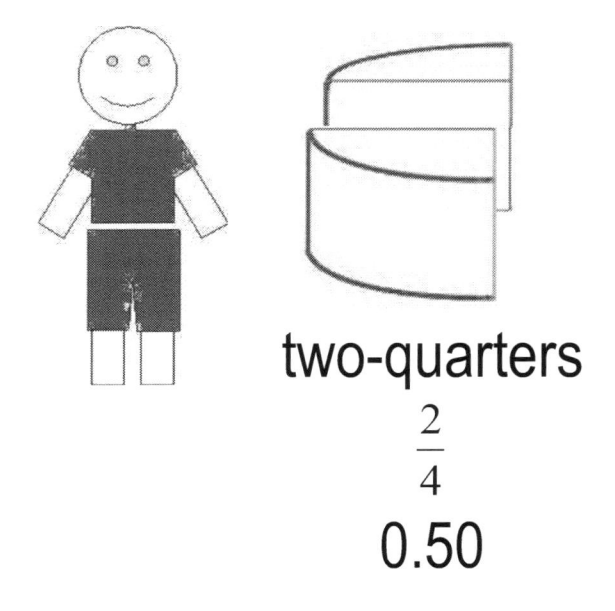

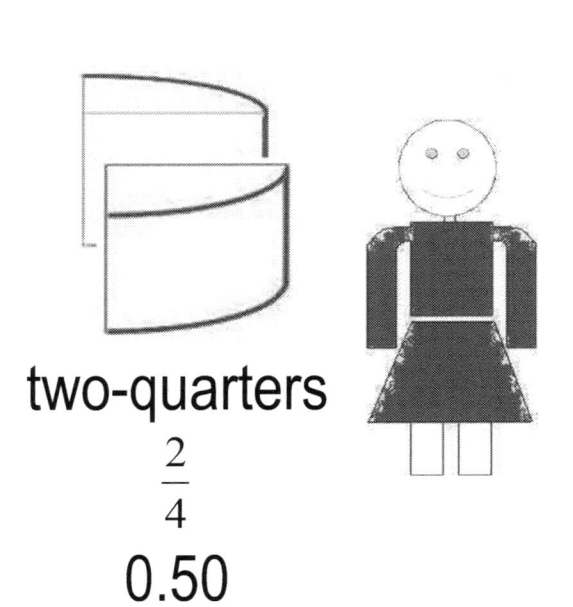

half
$\frac{1}{2}$
0.50

half
$\frac{1}{2}$
0.50

two-quarters
$\frac{2}{4}$
0.50

two-quarters
$\frac{2}{4}$
0.50

So, you can divide one whole cake into two halves (*each child gets a half*) or into four quarters (*each child can have two-quarters*).

Therefore, **half** is the same as **two-quarters**; both equal to 0.50!

$$\frac{1}{2} = \frac{2}{4} = 0.50.$$

Equivalent fractions are fractions with the **same value** even though their **numerators** and **denominators** may be **different**.

For example,

$$\frac{1}{2} \xrightarrow{\times 2} = \frac{2}{4}$$
$$\times 2$$

$$\times \frac{2}{2} (=1) =$$

That is, if you **multiply** (or **divide**) both the numerator and the denominator of a fraction by the same non-zero number, **the value** of that fraction **always stays the same**!
The fraction only changes into a different equivalent fraction.

This is because multiplying the top and the bottom of a fraction by the same non-zero number is the same as multiplying that fraction by one!

This is the principle of **equivalent fractions**.

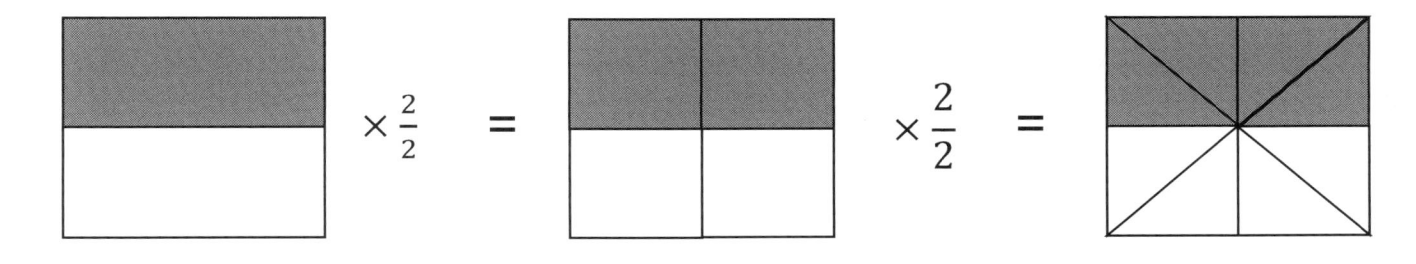

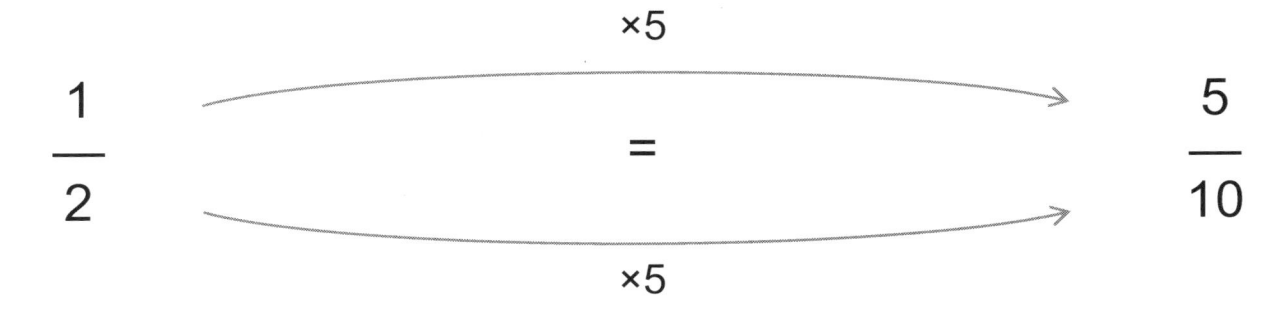

$$\frac{1}{2} \xrightarrow{\times 2} = \frac{2}{4} \xrightarrow{\times 2} = \frac{4}{8}$$

$$\square \times \frac{2}{2} = \square \times \frac{2}{2} = \square$$

$$\frac{1}{2} \xrightarrow{\times 5} = \frac{5}{10}$$

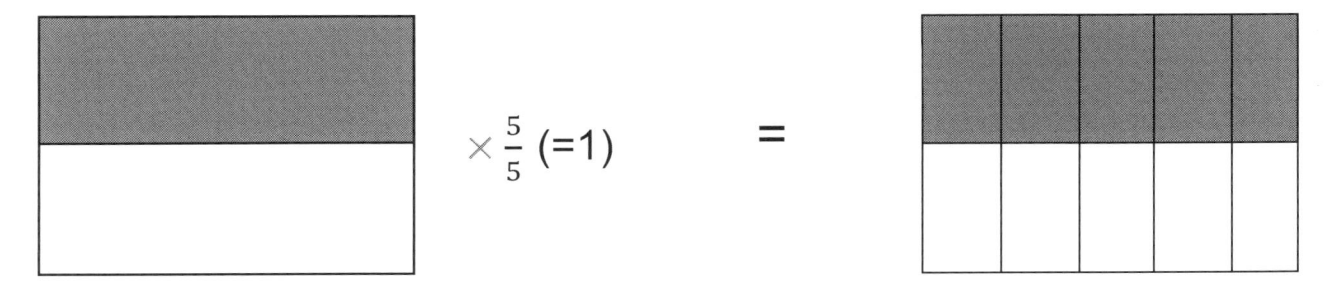

$$\square \times \frac{5}{5} (=1) = \square$$

Likewise,

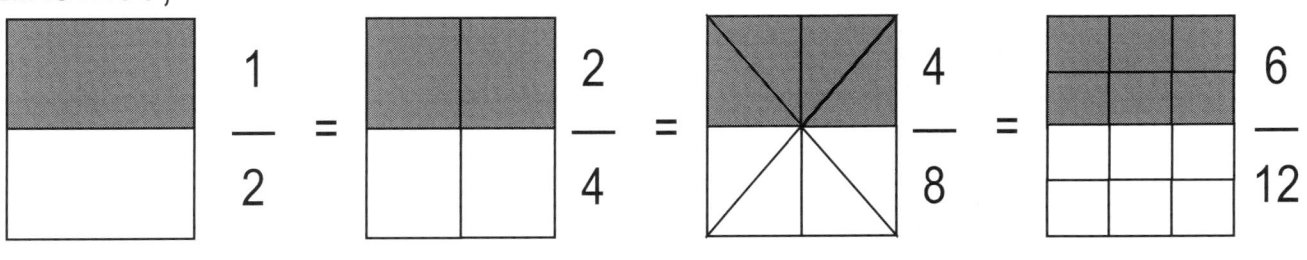

$$\frac{1}{2} = \frac{2}{4} = \frac{4}{8} = \frac{6}{12}$$

The principle of equivalent fractions (continued).

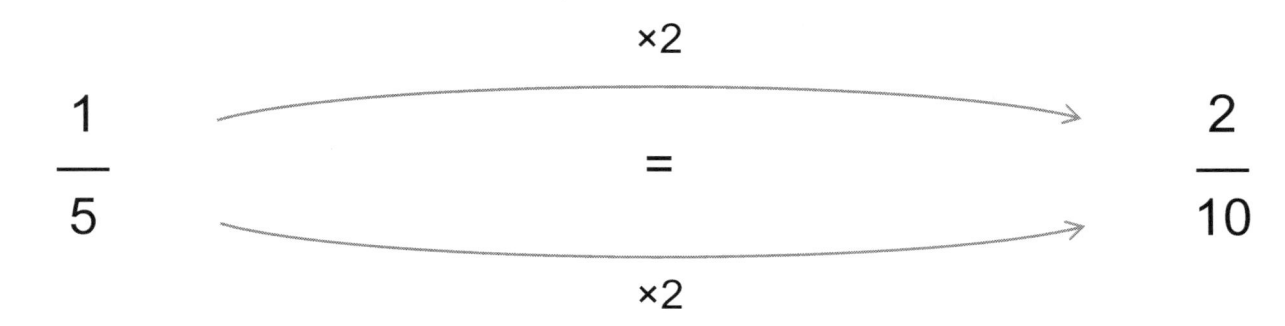

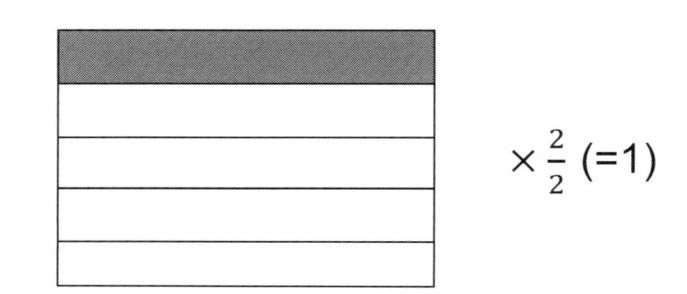

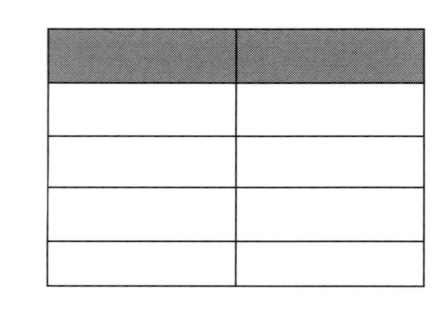

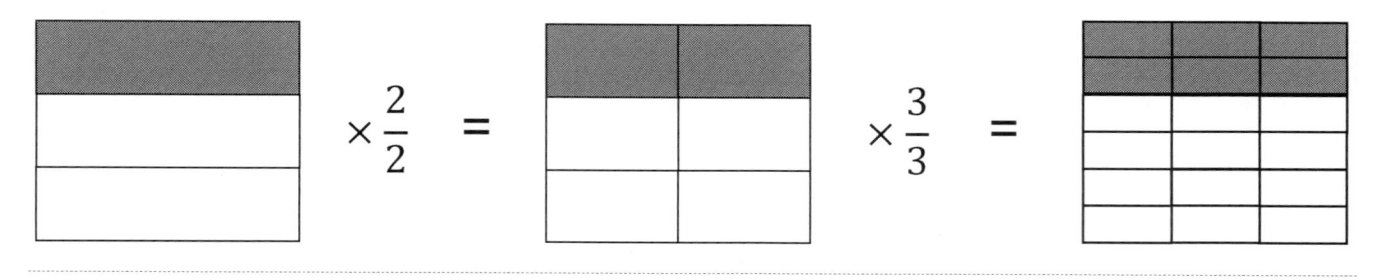

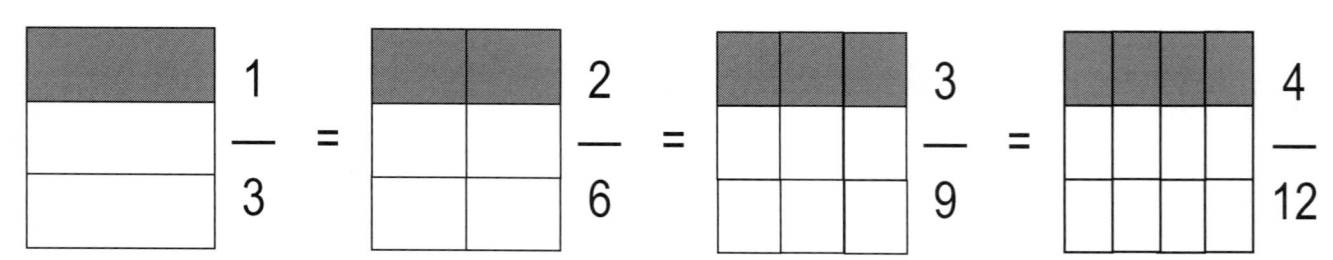

$$\frac{1}{5} \xrightarrow{\times 2} = \xrightarrow{\times 2} \frac{2}{10}$$

$$\times \frac{2}{2} (=1) \quad =$$

$$\frac{1}{3} \xrightarrow{\times 2} = \xrightarrow{\times 2} \frac{2}{6} \xrightarrow{\times 3} = \xrightarrow{\times 3} \frac{6}{18}$$

$$\times \frac{2}{2} = \quad\quad \times \frac{3}{3} =$$

$$\frac{1}{3} = \frac{2}{6} = \frac{3}{9} = \frac{4}{12}$$

And so on.

Halves

| Fraction | → | Equivalent Fraction | → | Decimal |

$\dfrac{0}{2}$ = $\dfrac{0}{1}$ = 0 = 0.00

nothing   nothing

$\dfrac{1}{2}$ = 0.50

one-half

$\dfrac{2}{2}$ = $\dfrac{1}{1}$ = 1 = 1.00

two-halves   one-whole

Quarters

| Fraction | → | Equivalent Fraction(s) | → | Decimal |

$\dfrac{0}{4}$ = $\dfrac{0}{2}$ = $\dfrac{0}{1}$ 0

nothing   nothing   nothing

$\dfrac{1}{4}$ = 0.25

one-quarter

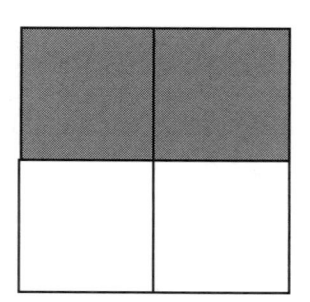

$\dfrac{2}{4}$ = $\dfrac{1}{2}$ = 0.50

two-quarters   half

Quarters

Fraction	→	Equivalent Fraction(s)	→	Decimal

$$\frac{2}{4} = \frac{1}{2} = 0.50$$

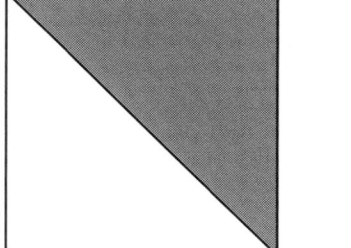

two-quarters   one-half

$$\frac{3}{4} = 0.75$$

three-quarters

$$\frac{4}{4} = \frac{2}{2} = \frac{1}{1} 1.00$$

four-quarters   two-halves   one-whole

45

Eighths

Shape Fraction	→	Shape Fraction	→	Shape Fraction	→	Shape Fraction	Decimal

$\dfrac{0}{8}$ = $\dfrac{0}{4}$ = $\dfrac{0}{2}$ = $\dfrac{0}{1}$ = 0

$\dfrac{1}{8}$ = 0.125

$\dfrac{2}{8}$ = $\dfrac{1}{4}$ = 0.25

$\dfrac{3}{8}$ = 0.375

$\dfrac{4}{8}$ = $\dfrac{2}{4}$ = $\dfrac{1}{2}$ = 0.50

46

Eighths

Shape Fraction	→	Shape Fraction	→	Shape Fraction	Decimal

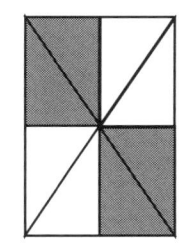

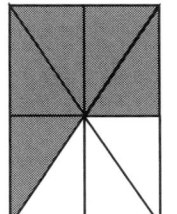

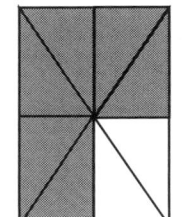

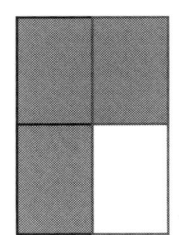

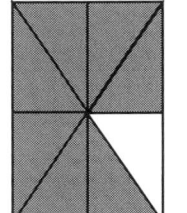

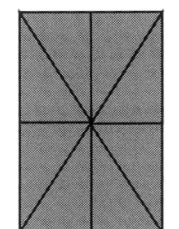

$\dfrac{4}{8}$ = $\dfrac{2}{4}$ = $\dfrac{1}{2}$ = 0.50

$\dfrac{5}{8}$ = 0.625

$\dfrac{6}{8}$ = $\dfrac{3}{4}$ = 0.75

$\dfrac{7}{8}$ = 0.875

$\dfrac{8}{8}$ = $\dfrac{4}{4}$ = $\dfrac{2}{2}$ = $\dfrac{1}{1}$ = 1.00

Quiz 1

Find the **odd one** out?
Which of the following shapes is **not** a proper **fraction** (*tick*)?

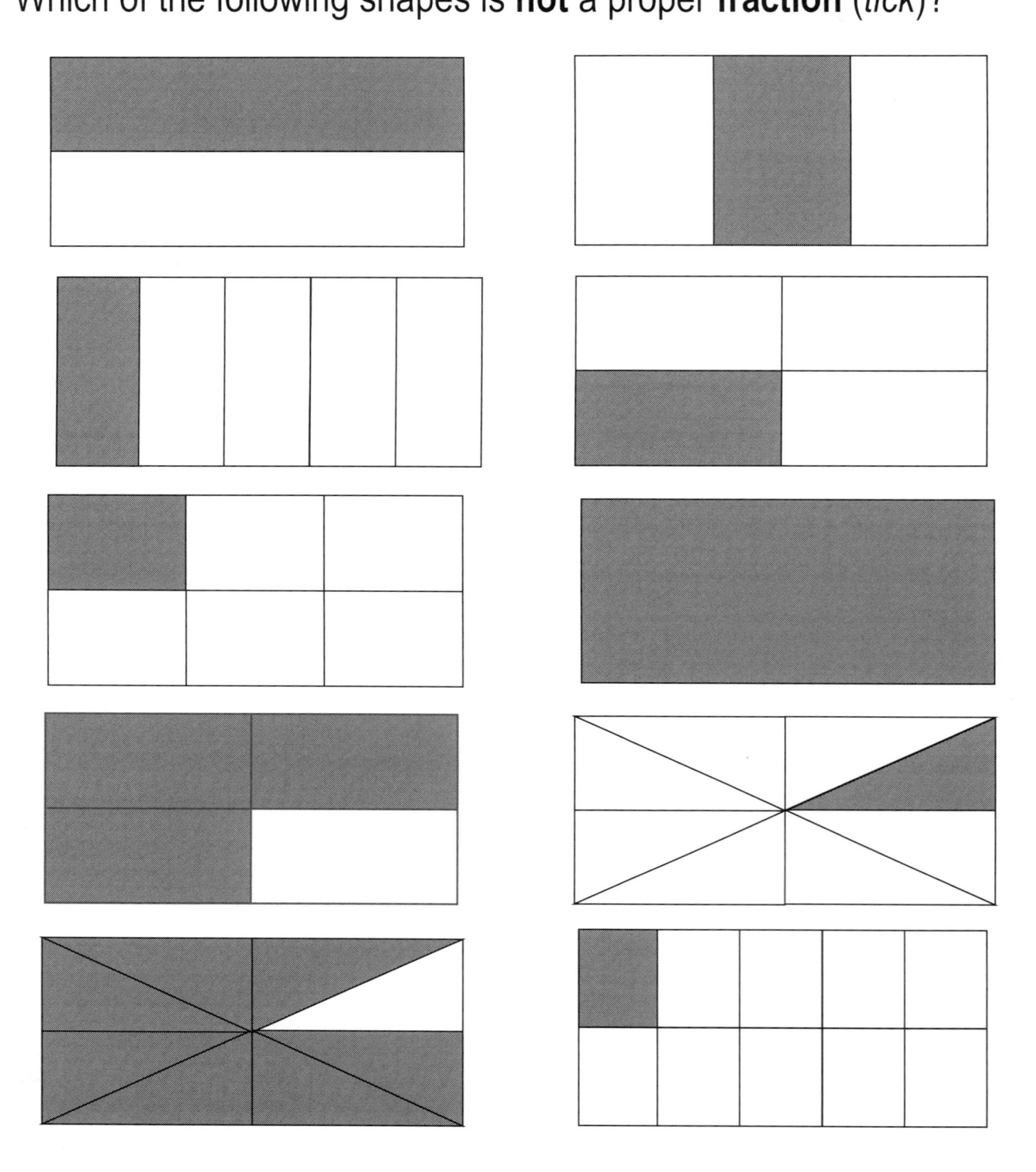

Quiz 2

Find the **odd one** out!

Which of the following numbers is **not** a proper **fraction** (*circle*)?

$$\frac{1}{2} \qquad \frac{1}{3}$$

$$\frac{1}{5} \qquad \frac{1}{4}$$

$$\frac{1}{6} \qquad \frac{1}{9}$$

$$\frac{1}{7} \qquad \frac{3}{4} \qquad \frac{1}{8}$$

$$\frac{1}{10} \qquad \frac{1}{1} \qquad 1$$

Fifths

Shape	Fraction	→	Shape	Fraction	→	Decimal

$\dfrac{0}{5}$ = $\dfrac{0}{1}$ = 0 = 0.00

$\dfrac{1}{5}$ = 0.20

$\dfrac{2}{5}$ = 0.40

$\dfrac{2}{5}$ = 0.40

Fifths

Shape	Fraction	→	Shape	Fraction	→	Decimal
	$\dfrac{3}{5}$				=	0.60
	$\dfrac{3}{5}$				=	0.60
	$\dfrac{4}{5}$				=	0.80
	$\dfrac{5}{5}$	=		$\dfrac{1}{1}$	= 1 =	1.00

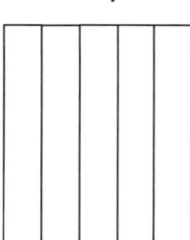

Tenths

| Fraction → | Equivalent Fraction(s) | → Decimal |

Shape $\dfrac{0}{10}$ = Shape $\dfrac{0}{5}$ = Shape $\dfrac{0}{1}$ = 0 = 0.00

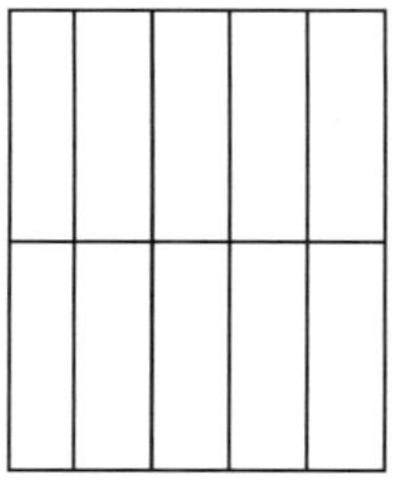

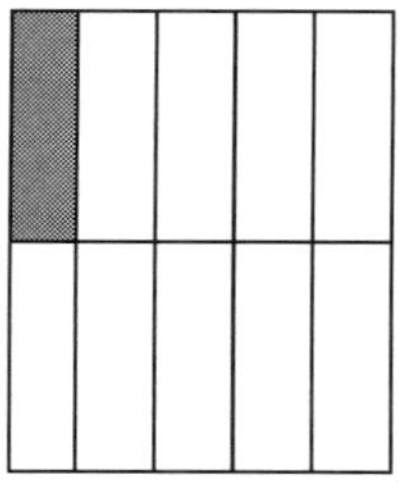

$\dfrac{1}{10}$ = 0.10

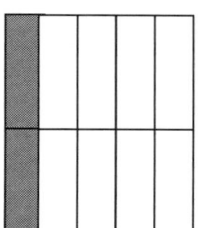

$\dfrac{2}{10}$ = $\dfrac{1}{5}$ = 0.20

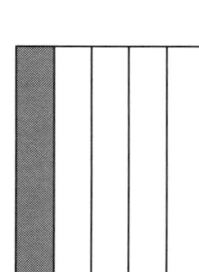

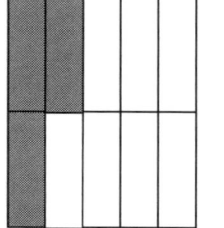

$\dfrac{3}{10}$ = 0.30

Tenths

| Fraction Shape | → | Equivalent Fraction Equivalent Shape | → | Decimal |

$\dfrac{4}{10}$ = $\dfrac{2}{5}$ = 0.40

$\dfrac{5}{10}$ = 0.50

$\dfrac{6}{10}$ = $\dfrac{3}{5}$ = 0.60

Tenths

Fraction	→	Equivalent Fraction	→	Decimal

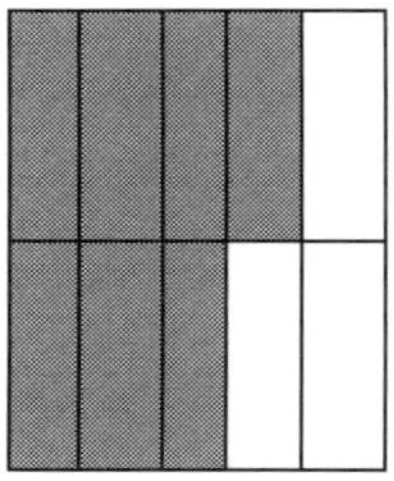

$\dfrac{7}{10}$ =   0.70

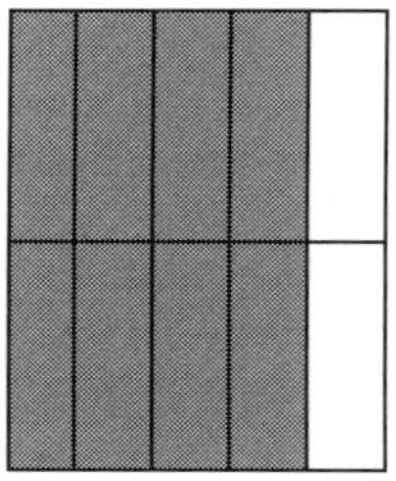

$\dfrac{8}{10}$ 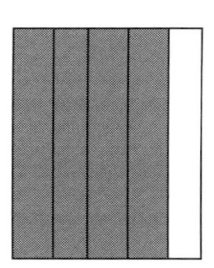 = $\dfrac{4}{5}$ = 0.80

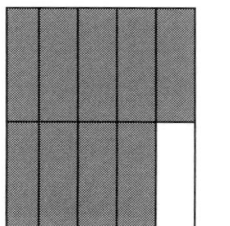

$\dfrac{9}{10}$ =   0.90

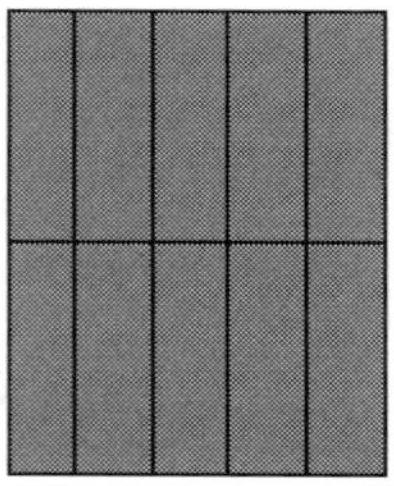

$\dfrac{10}{10}$ 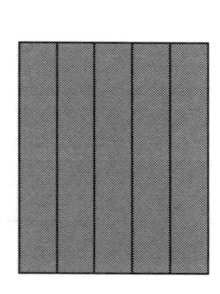 = $\dfrac{5}{5}$ = $\dfrac{1}{1}$ = 1.00

54

Thirds

| Shape | Fraction | → | Equivalent Shape / Equivalent Fraction | → | Decimal |

$\dfrac{0}{3} = \dfrac{0}{1} = 0 = 0.00$

$\dfrac{1}{3} = = 0.333$

$\dfrac{2}{3} = = 0.666$

$\dfrac{3}{3} = \dfrac{1}{1} = 1 = 1.00$

55

Sixths

| Shape Fraction → | Equivalent Shape(s)
 Equivalent Fraction(s) | → Decimal |

$$\frac{0}{6} = \frac{0}{3} = \frac{0}{1} = 0$$

$$\frac{1}{6} = 0.166$$

$$\frac{2}{6} = \frac{1}{3} = 0.333$$

56

Sixths

| Shape Fraction → | Equivalent Shape
Equivalent Fraction | → Decimal |

$\dfrac{3}{6}$ = $\dfrac{1}{2}$ = 0.50

$\dfrac{4}{6}$ = $\dfrac{2}{3}$ = 0.666

$\dfrac{5}{6}$ = 0.833

$\dfrac{6}{6}$ = $\dfrac{3}{3}$ = $\dfrac{1}{1}$ = 1.00

Ninths

Shape Fraction →	Shape Fraction →	Shape Fraction	Decimal

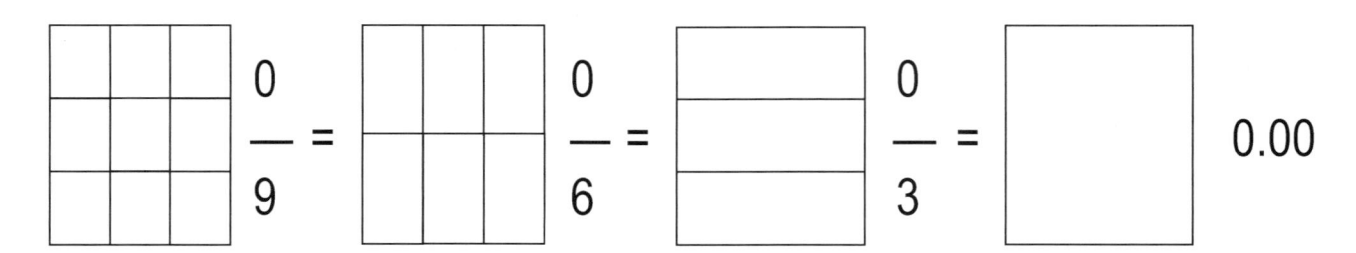

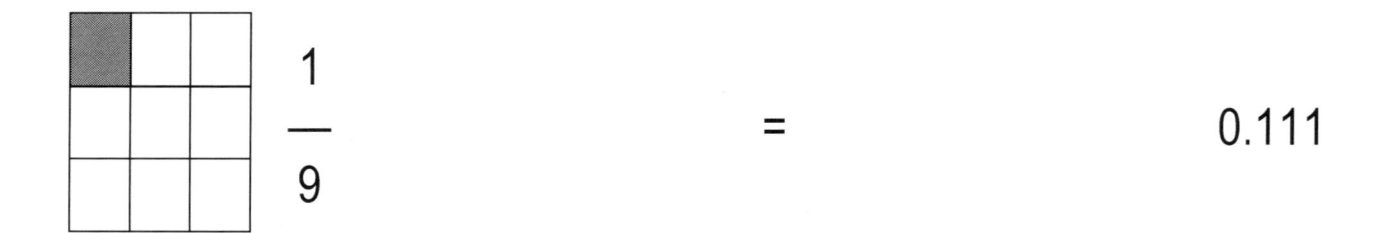

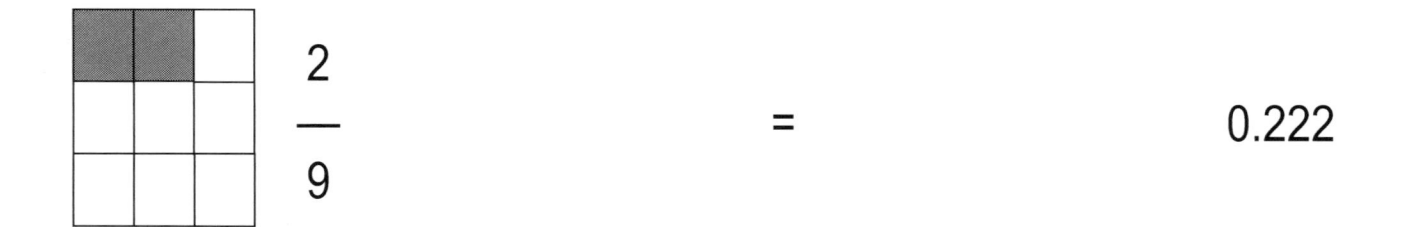

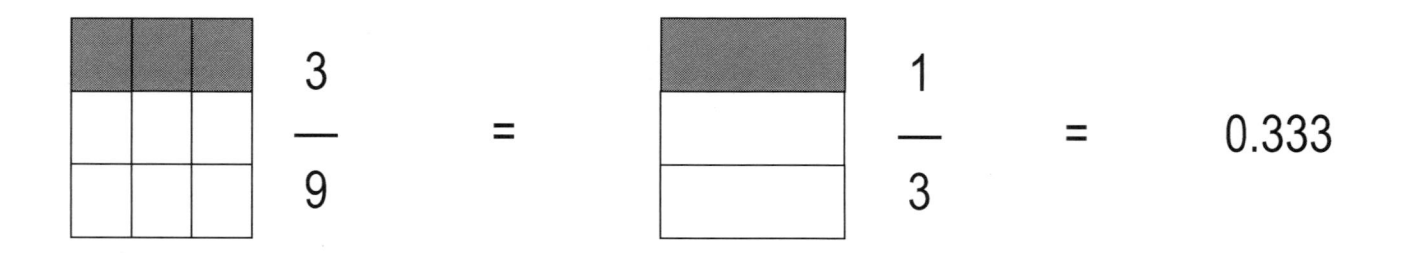

$\dfrac{0}{9}$ = $\dfrac{0}{6}$ = $\dfrac{0}{3}$ = 0.00

$\dfrac{1}{9}$ = 0.111

$\dfrac{2}{9}$ = 0.222

$\dfrac{3}{9}$ = $\dfrac{1}{3}$ = 0.333

$\dfrac{4}{9}$ = 0.444

Ninths

Shape Fraction →	Shape Fraction →	Shape Fraction	Decimal

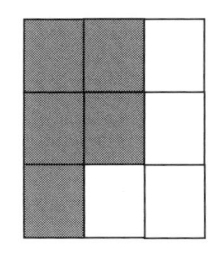

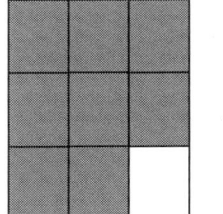

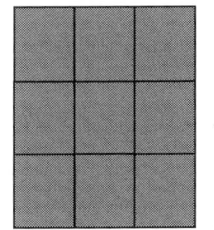

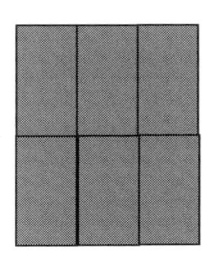

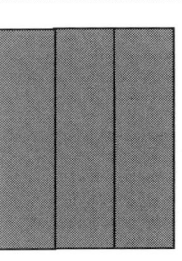

$\dfrac{5}{9}$ = 0.555

$\dfrac{6}{9}$ = $\dfrac{4}{6}$ = $\dfrac{2}{3}$ = 0.666

$\dfrac{7}{9}$ = 0.777

$\dfrac{8}{9}$ = 0.888

$\dfrac{9}{9}$ = $\dfrac{6}{6}$ = $\dfrac{3}{3}$ = 1.00

Twelfths

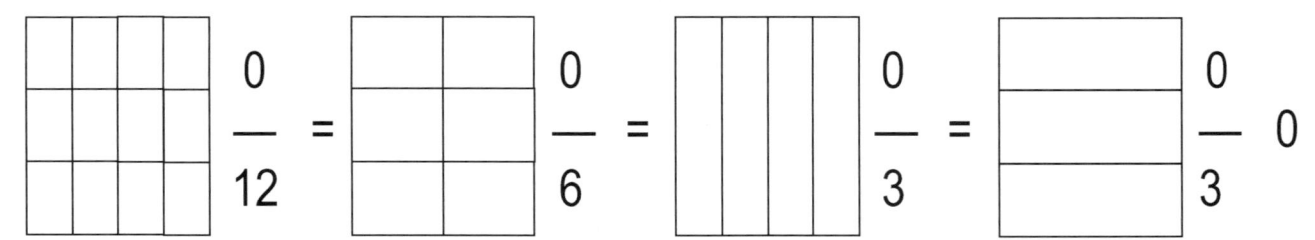

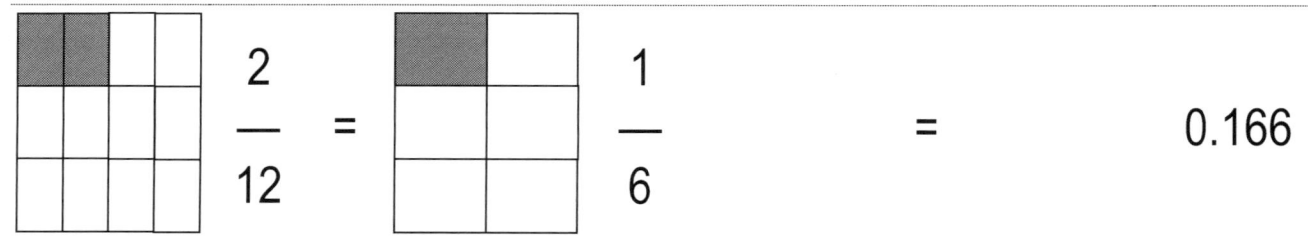

$\dfrac{0}{12}$ = $\dfrac{0}{6}$ = $\dfrac{0}{3}$ = $\dfrac{0}{3}$ 0

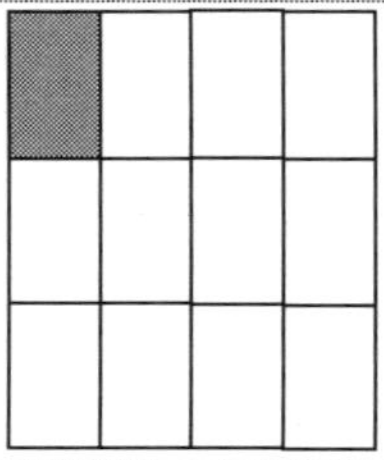

$\dfrac{1}{12}$ = 0.083

$\dfrac{2}{12}$ = $\dfrac{1}{6}$ = 0.166

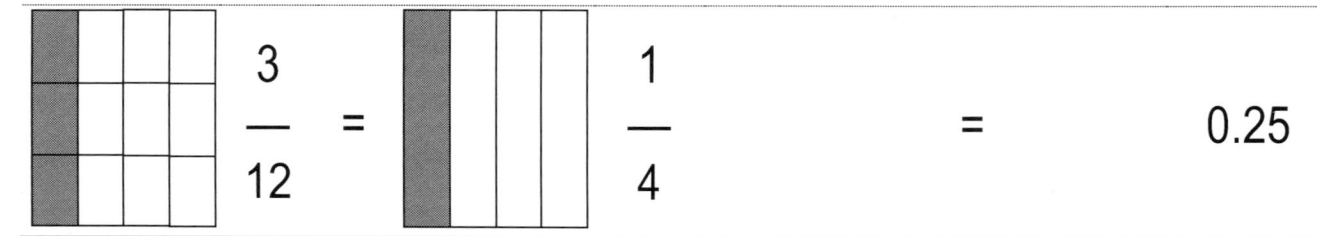

$\dfrac{3}{12}$ = $\dfrac{1}{4}$ = 0.25

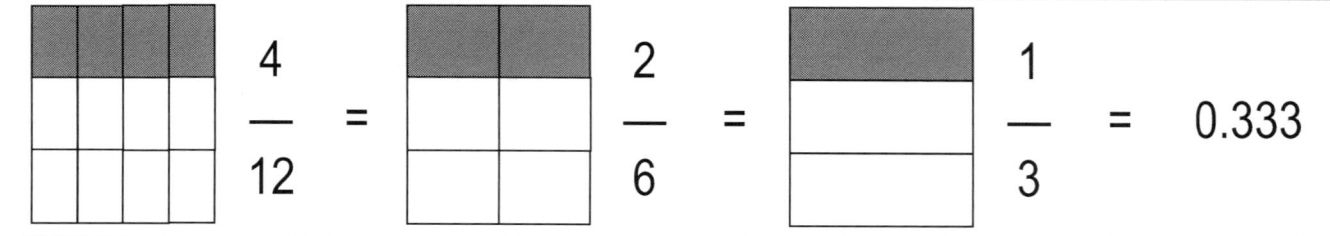

$\dfrac{4}{12}$ = $\dfrac{2}{6}$ = $\dfrac{1}{3}$ = 0.333

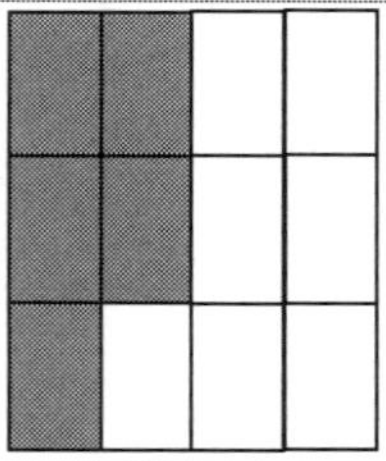

$\dfrac{5}{12}$ = 0.416

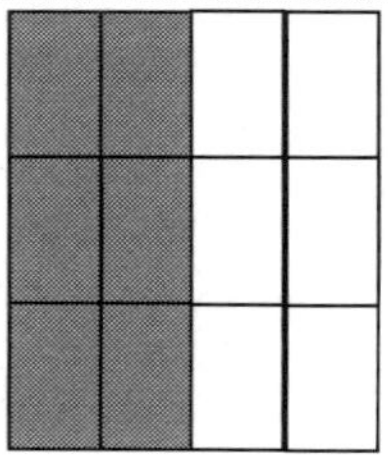

$\dfrac{6}{12}$ = $\dfrac{3}{6}$ = $\dfrac{1}{2}$ = 0.50

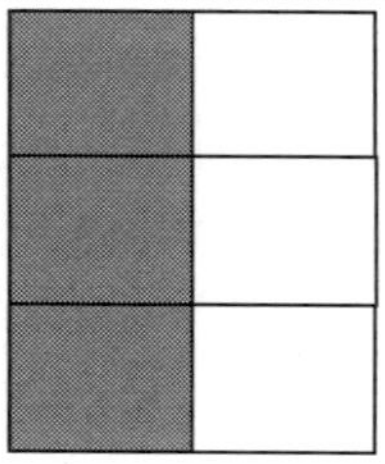

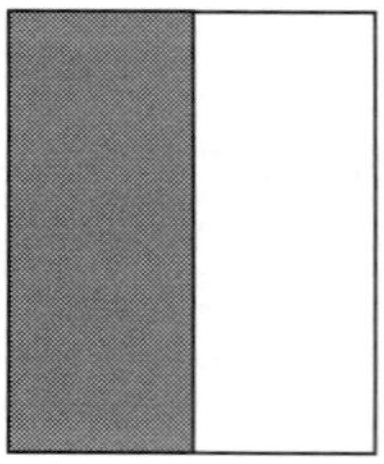

Twelfths

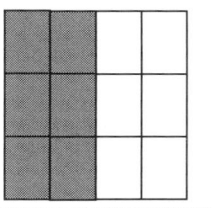

$$\frac{6}{12} = \frac{2}{4} = \frac{1}{2} = 0.50$$

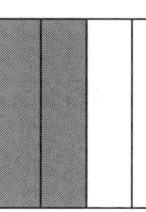

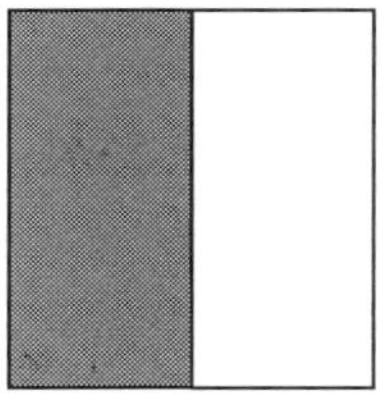

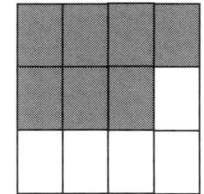

$$\frac{7}{12} = \quad = 0.583$$

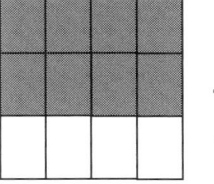

$$\frac{8}{12} = \frac{4}{6} = \frac{2}{3} = 0.666$$

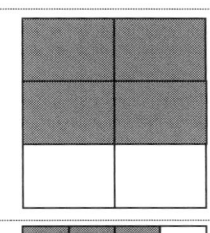

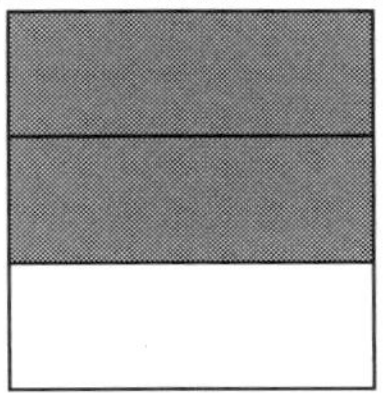

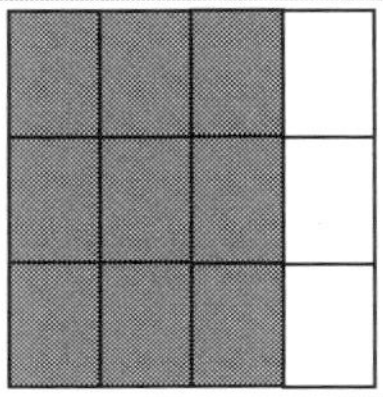

$$\frac{9}{12} = \frac{3}{4} = 0.75$$

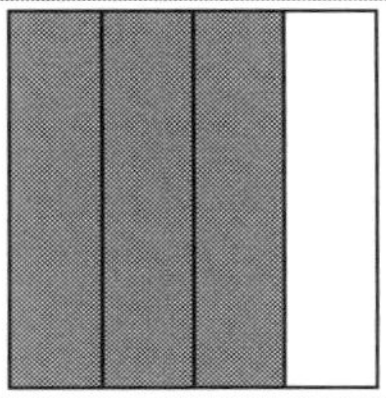

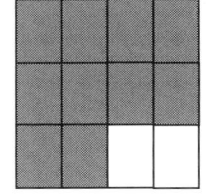

$$\frac{10}{12} = \frac{5}{6} = 0.833$$

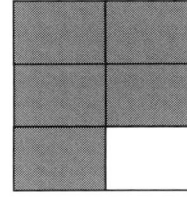

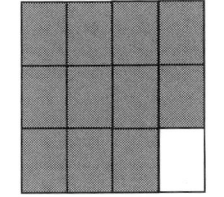

$$\frac{11}{12} = 0.916$$

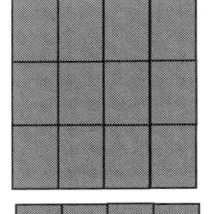

$$\frac{12}{12} = \frac{6}{6} = \frac{3}{3} = 1.00$$

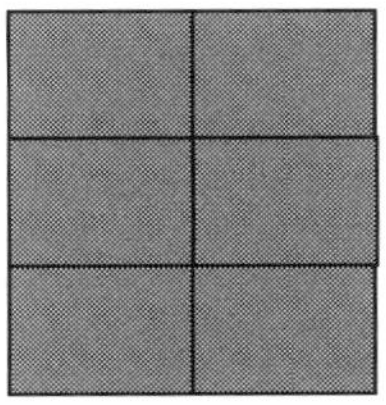

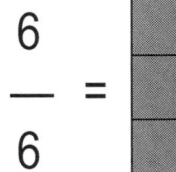

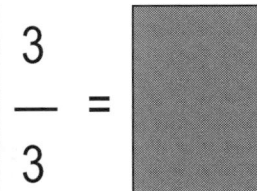

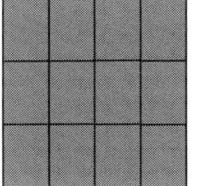

$$\frac{12}{12} = \frac{4}{4} = \frac{2}{2} = 1.00$$

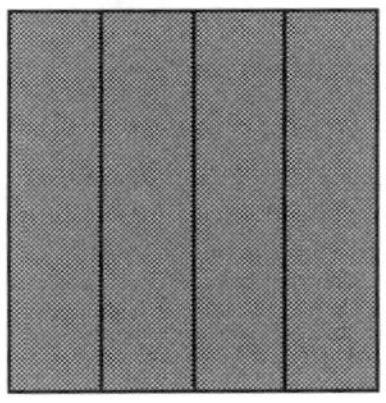

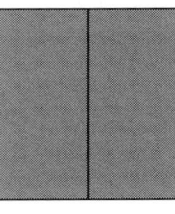

Halves v Quarters

Fraction	Shape	Fraction Name / Decimal	→	Fraction Name / Decimal	Shape	Fraction
$\dfrac{0}{2}$	(empty square, halves)	nothing / 0	=	nothing / 0	(empty square, quarters)	$\dfrac{0}{4}$
				one-quarter / 0.25	(one quarter shaded)	$\dfrac{1}{4}$
$\dfrac{1}{2}$	(top half shaded)	one-half / 0.50	=	two-quarters / 0.50	(two quarters shaded)	$\dfrac{2}{4}$
				three-quarters / 0.75	(three quarters shaded)	$\dfrac{3}{4}$
$\dfrac{2}{2}$	(fully shaded)	two-halves, one-whole / 1.00	=	four-quarters, one-whole / 1.00	(fully shaded)	$\dfrac{4}{4}$

Quarters v Eighths

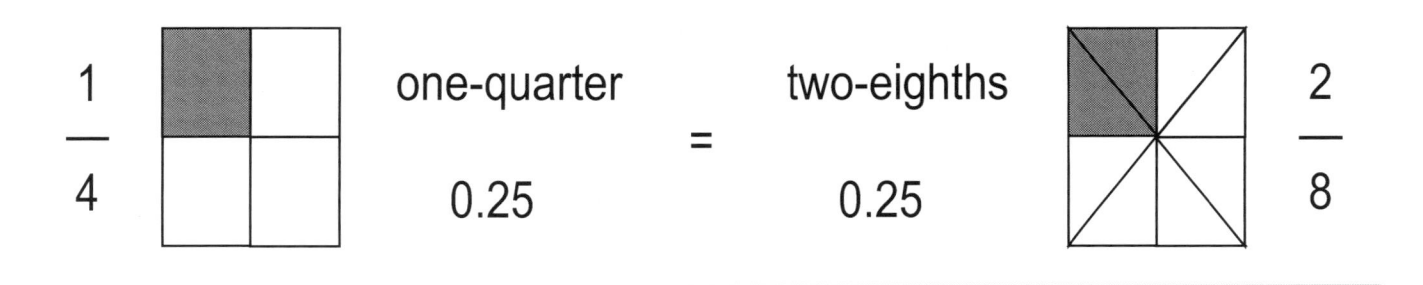

Fraction	Shape	Fraction Name / Decimal	→	Fraction Name / Decimal	Shape	Fraction
$\frac{0}{4}$		nothing 0	=	nothing 0	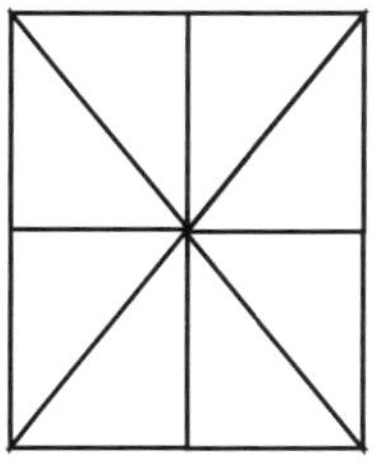	$\frac{0}{8}$
				one-eighth 0.125	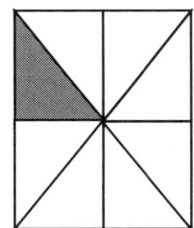	$\frac{1}{8}$
$\frac{1}{4}$		one-quarter 0.25	=	two-eighths 0.25		$\frac{2}{8}$
				three-eighths 0.375	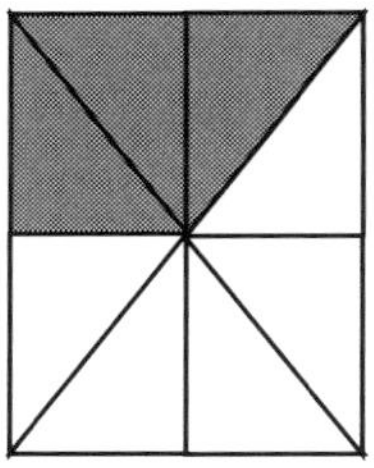	$\frac{3}{8}$
$\frac{2}{4}$	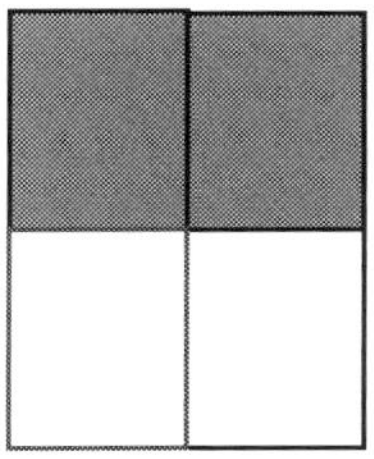	two-quarters 0.50	=	four-eighths 0.50	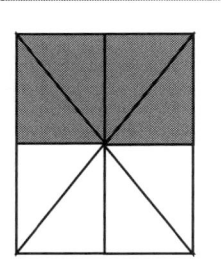	$\frac{4}{8}$

Quarters v Eighths

Fraction	Shape	Fraction Name / Decimal	→	Fraction Name / Decimal	Shape	Fraction
$\dfrac{2}{4}$		two-quarters 0.50	=	four-eighths 0.50		$\dfrac{4}{8}$
				five-eighths 0.625		$\dfrac{5}{8}$
$\dfrac{3}{4}$		three-quarters 0.75	=	six-eighths 0.75		$\dfrac{6}{8}$
				seven-eighths 0.875		$\dfrac{7}{8}$
$\dfrac{4}{4}$		four-quarters, one-whole 1.00	=	eight-eighths, one-whole 1.00		$\dfrac{8}{8}$

Halves v Quarters v Eighths

Fraction Shape	→	Fraction Shape	→	Fraction Shape	Decimal

$\dfrac{0}{2}$ = $\dfrac{0}{4}$ = $\dfrac{0}{8}$ = 0.00

$\dfrac{1}{8}$ = 0.125

$\dfrac{1}{4}$ = $\dfrac{2}{8}$ = 0.25

$\dfrac{3}{8}$ = 0.375

$\dfrac{1}{2}$ = $\dfrac{2}{4}$ = $\dfrac{4}{8}$ = 0.50

Halves ∨ Quarters ∨ Eighths

Fraction Shape	→	Fraction Shape	→	Fraction Shape	→	Decimal
$\frac{1}{2}$	=	$\frac{2}{4}$	=	$\frac{4}{8}$	=	0.50
				$\frac{5}{8}$	=	0.625
		$\frac{3}{4}$	=	$\frac{6}{8}$	=	0.75
				$\frac{7}{8}$	=	0.875
$\frac{2}{2}$	=	$\frac{4}{4}$	=	$\frac{8}{8}$	=	1.00

Fifths v Tenths

Fraction	Shape	Fraction Name / Decimal	→	Fraction Name / Decimal	Shape	Fraction
$\dfrac{0}{5}$		nothing 0	=	nothing 0		$\dfrac{0}{10}$
				one-tenth 0.10		$\dfrac{1}{10}$
$\dfrac{1}{5}$		one-fifth 0.20	=	two-tenths 0.20		$\dfrac{2}{10}$
				three-tenths 0.30		$\dfrac{3}{10}$

Fifths v Tenths

Fraction	Shape	Fraction Name / Decimal	→	Fraction Name / Decimal	Shape	Fraction

$\dfrac{2}{5}$ [shape] two-fifths 0.40 = four-tenths 0.40 [shape] $\dfrac{4}{10}$

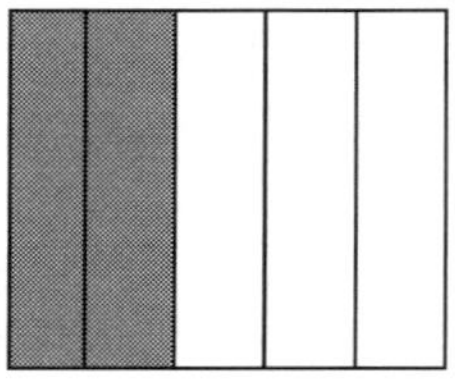

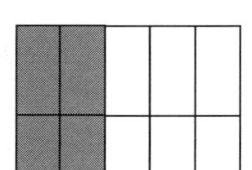

five-tenths 0.50 [shape] $\dfrac{5}{10}$

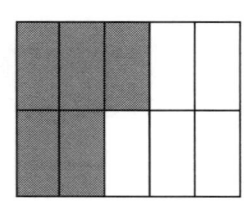

$\dfrac{3}{5}$ [shape] three-fifths 0.60 = six-tenths 0.60 [shape] $\dfrac{6}{10}$

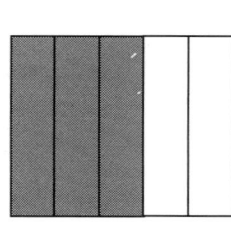

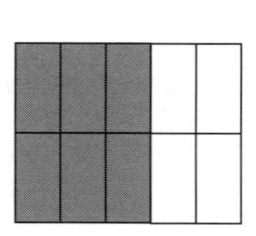

Fifths   v   Tenths

Fraction	Shape	Fraction Name / Decimal	→	Fraction Name / Decimal	Shape	Fraction

| | | | | seven-tenths 0.70 | 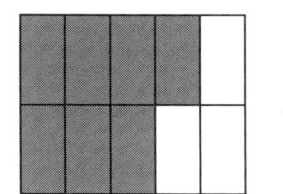 ▨ | $\dfrac{7}{10}$ |

| $\dfrac{4}{5}$ | 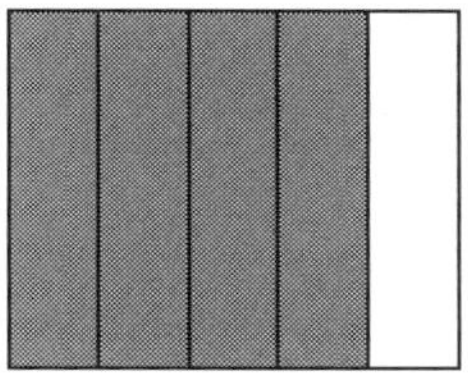 ▨ | four-fifths 0.80 | = | eight-tenths 0.80 | 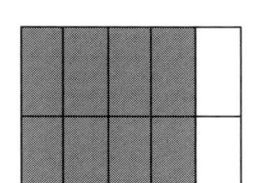 ▨ | $\dfrac{8}{10}$ |

| | | | | nine-tenths 0.90 | 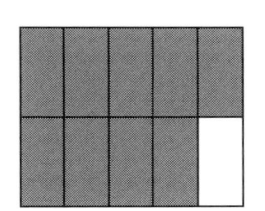 ▨ | $\dfrac{9}{10}$ |

| $\dfrac{5}{5}$ | 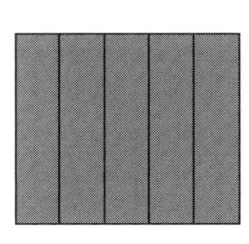 ▨ | five-fifths, one-whole 1.00 | = | ten-tenths, one-whole 1.00 | 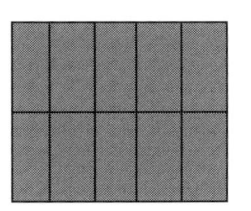 ▨ | $\dfrac{10}{10}$ |

Thirds   v   Sixths

Fraction	Shape	Fraction Name / Decimal	→	Fraction Name / Decimal	Shape	Fraction

$\dfrac{0}{3}$ nothing   0   =   nothing   0 $\dfrac{0}{6}$

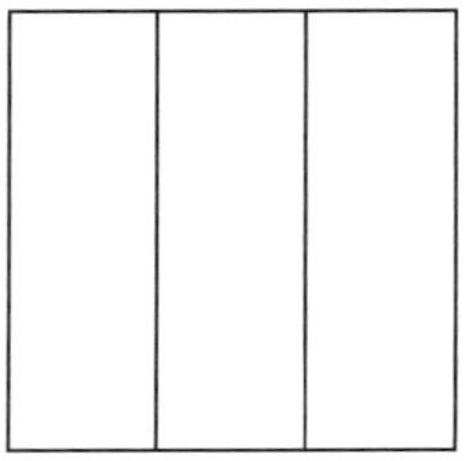

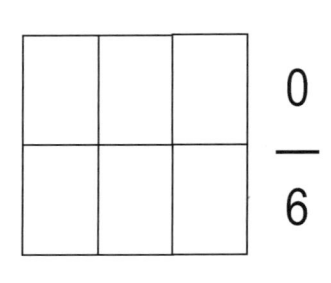

one-sixth   0.166 $\dfrac{1}{6}$

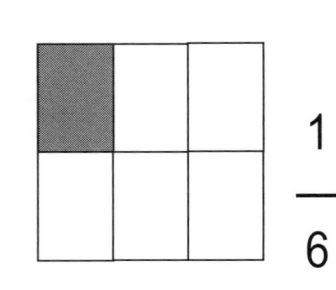

$\dfrac{1}{3}$ third   0.333   =   two-sixths   0.333 $\dfrac{2}{6}$

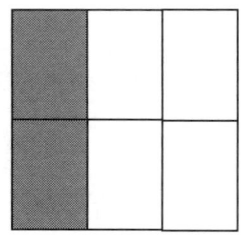

Thirds   v   Sixths

Fraction	Shape	Fraction Name / Decimal	→	Fraction Name / Decimal	Shape	Fraction
				three-sixths 0.50	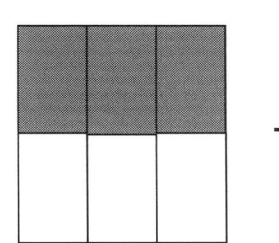	$\dfrac{3}{6}$
$\dfrac{2}{3}$	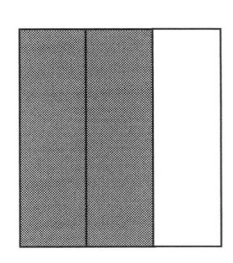	two-thirds 0.666	=	four-sixths 0.666	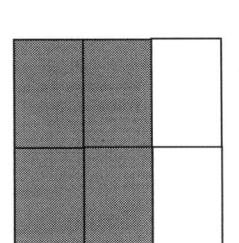	$\dfrac{4}{6}$
				five-sixths 0.833	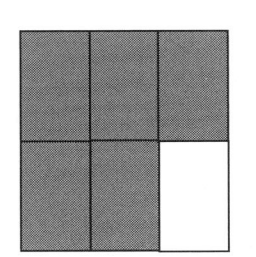	$\dfrac{5}{6}$
$\dfrac{3}{3}$	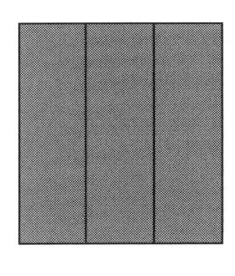	three-thirds, one-whole 1.00	=	six-sixths, one-whole 1.00	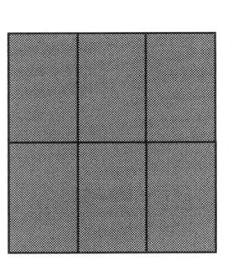	$\dfrac{6}{6}$

Sixths   v   Ninths

Fraction	Shape	Fraction Name / Decimal	→	Fraction Name / Decimal	Shape	Fraction
$\dfrac{0}{6}$		nothing 0	=	nothing 0		$\dfrac{0}{9}$
				one-ninth 0.111		$\dfrac{1}{9}$
				two-ninths 0.222		$\dfrac{2}{9}$
$\dfrac{2}{6}$		two-sixths 0.333	=	three-ninths 0.333		$\dfrac{3}{9}$
				four-ninths 0.444		$\dfrac{4}{9}$

Sixths   v   Ninths

Fraction	Shape	Fraction Name / Decimal	→	Fraction Name / Decimal	Shape	Fraction
				five-ninths 0.555		$\dfrac{5}{9}$
$\dfrac{4}{6}$		four-sixths 0.666	=	six-ninths 0.666		$\dfrac{6}{9}$
				seven-ninths 0.777		$\dfrac{7}{9}$
				eight-ninths 0.888		$\dfrac{8}{9}$
$\dfrac{6}{6}$		six-sixths one-whole 1.00	=	nine-ninths one-whole 1.00		$\dfrac{9}{9}$

Thirds v Sixths v Ninths

| Fraction / Shape → | Fraction / Shape → | Shape / Fraction | Decimal |

$\dfrac{0}{3}$ = $\dfrac{0}{6}$ = $\dfrac{0}{9}$ = 0

$\dfrac{1}{9}$ = 0.111

$\dfrac{2}{9}$ = 0.222

$\dfrac{1}{3}$ = $\dfrac{2}{6}$ = $\dfrac{3}{9}$ = 0.333

$\dfrac{4}{9}$ = 0.444

Thirds ∨ Sixths ∨ Ninths

Fraction Shape	→	Fraction Shape	→	Shape Fraction	Decimal

$\dfrac{5}{9}$ = 0.555

$\dfrac{2}{3}$ = $\dfrac{4}{6}$ = $\dfrac{6}{9}$ = 0.666

$\dfrac{7}{9}$ = 0.777

$\dfrac{8}{9}$ = 0.888

$\dfrac{3}{3}$ = $\dfrac{6}{6}$ = $\dfrac{9}{9}$ = 1.00

Thirds v Twelfths

$\dfrac{0}{3}$	nothing 0	=	nothing 0	$\dfrac{0}{12}$
$\dfrac{1}{3}$	one-third 0.333	=	four-twelfths 0.333	$\dfrac{4}{12}$
$\dfrac{2}{3}$	two-thirds 0.666	=	eight-twelfths 0.666	$\dfrac{8}{12}$
$\dfrac{3}{3}$	three-thirds, whole 1.00	=	twelve-twelfths, whole 1.00	$\dfrac{12}{12}$

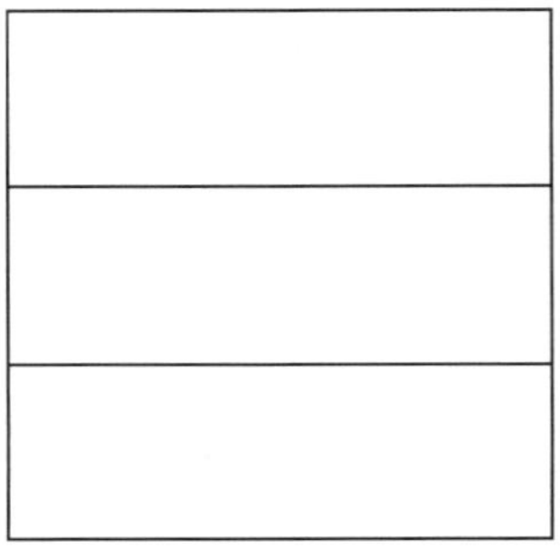

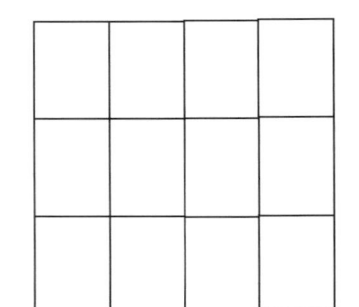

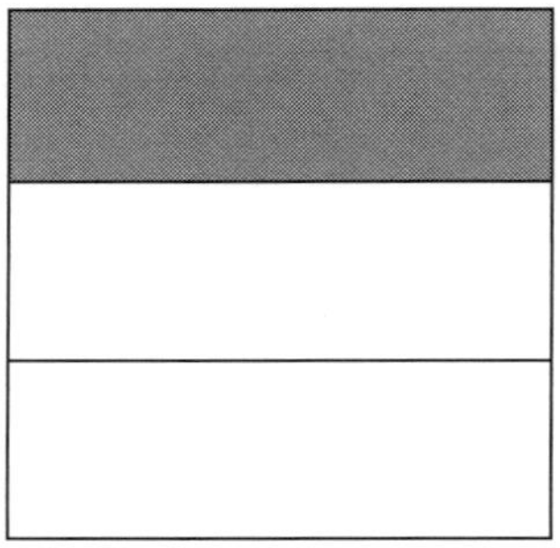

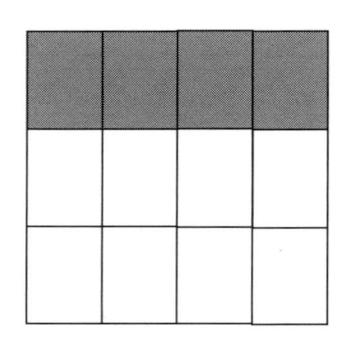

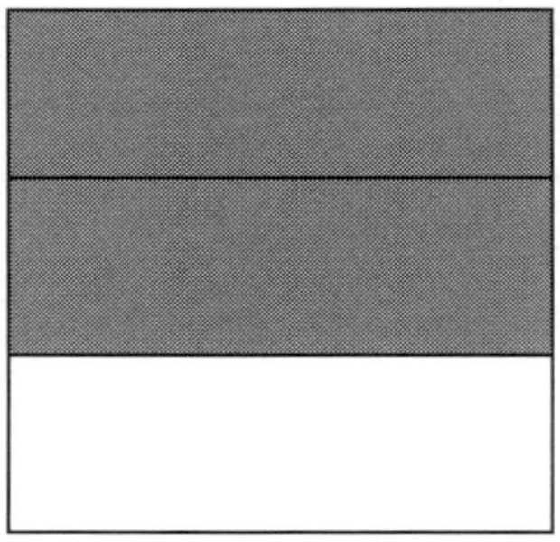

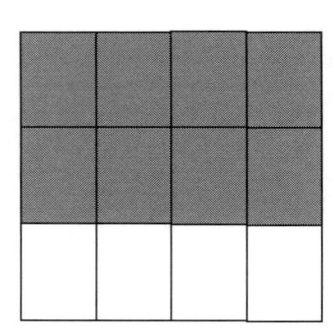

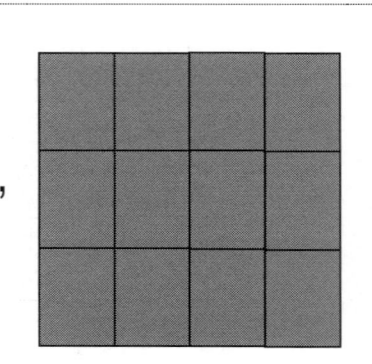

Quarters   v   Twelfths

$\dfrac{0}{4}$	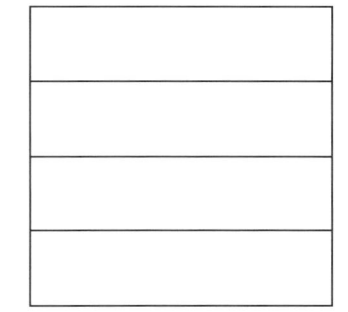	nothing 0	=	nothing 0	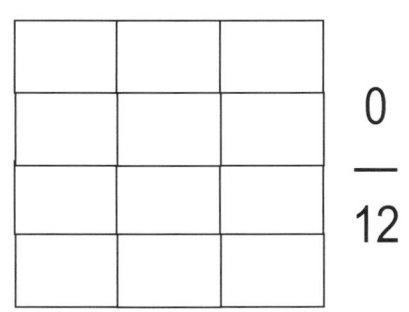	$\dfrac{0}{12}$

$\dfrac{1}{4}$ — one-quarter 0.25 = three-twelfths 0.25 — $\dfrac{3}{12}$

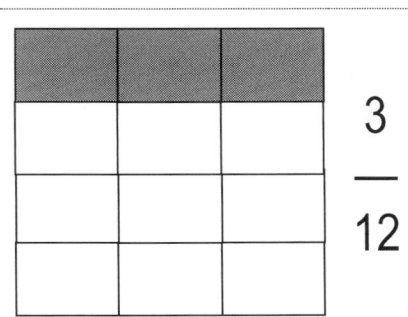

$\dfrac{2}{4}$ — two-quarters 0.50 = six-twelfths 0.50 — $\dfrac{6}{12}$

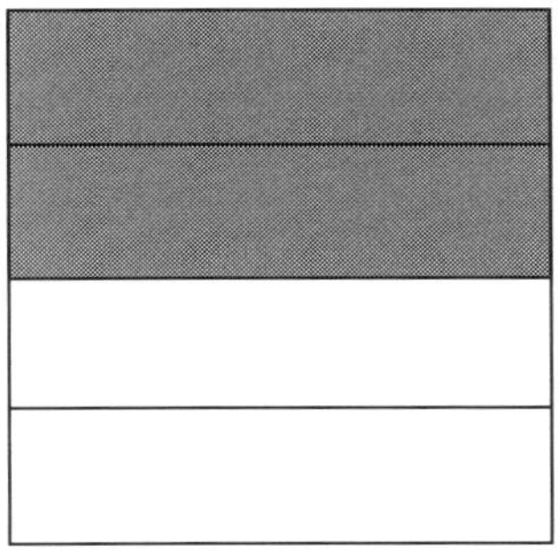

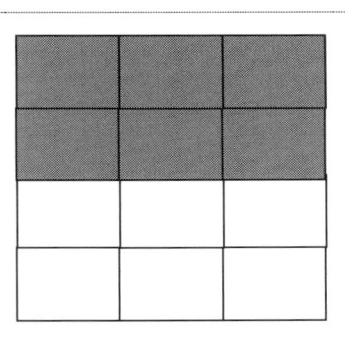

$\dfrac{3}{4}$ — three-quarters 0.75 = nine-twelfths 0.75 — $\dfrac{9}{12}$

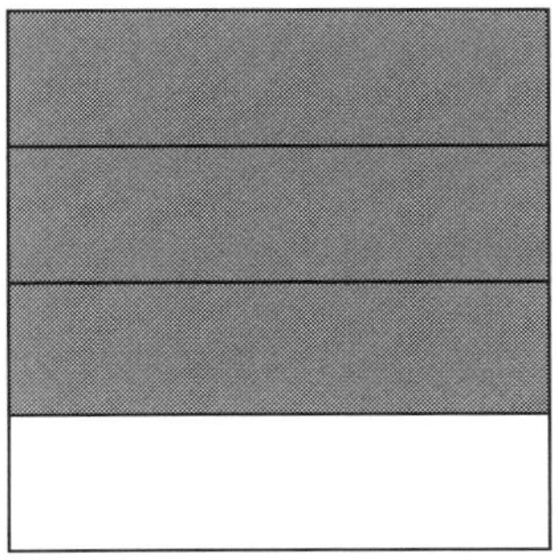

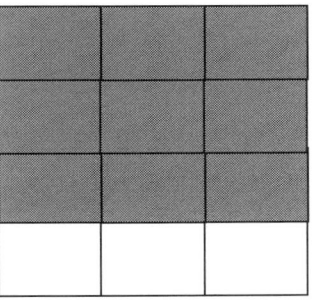

$\dfrac{4}{4}$ — four-quarters, whole 1.00 = twelve-twelfths, whole 1.00 — $\dfrac{12}{12}$

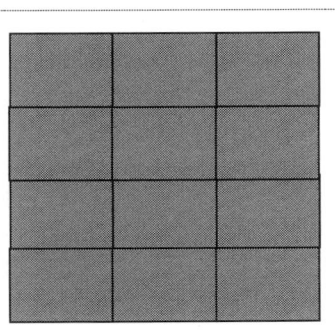

Sixths v Twelfths

Sixths			Twelfths
$\dfrac{0}{6}$	nothing 0	=	nothing 0	$\dfrac{0}{12}$
$\dfrac{1}{6}$	one-sixth 0.166	=	two-twelfths 0.166	$\dfrac{2}{12}$
$\dfrac{2}{6}$	two-sixths 0.333	=	four-twelfths 0.333	$\dfrac{4}{12}$
$\dfrac{3}{6}$	three-sixths 0.50	=	six-twelfths 0.50	$\dfrac{6}{12}$
$\dfrac{4}{6}$	four-sixths 0.666	=	eight-twelfths 0.666	$\dfrac{8}{12}$
$\dfrac{5}{6}$	five-sixths 0.833	=	ten-twelfths 0.833	$\dfrac{10}{12}$
$\dfrac{6}{6}$	six-sixths, whole 1.00	=	twelve-twelfths, whole 1.00	$\dfrac{12}{12}$

Equivalent Fractions and Decimals

These are fractions with the **same value** even though their **numerators** and **denominators** are **different**.

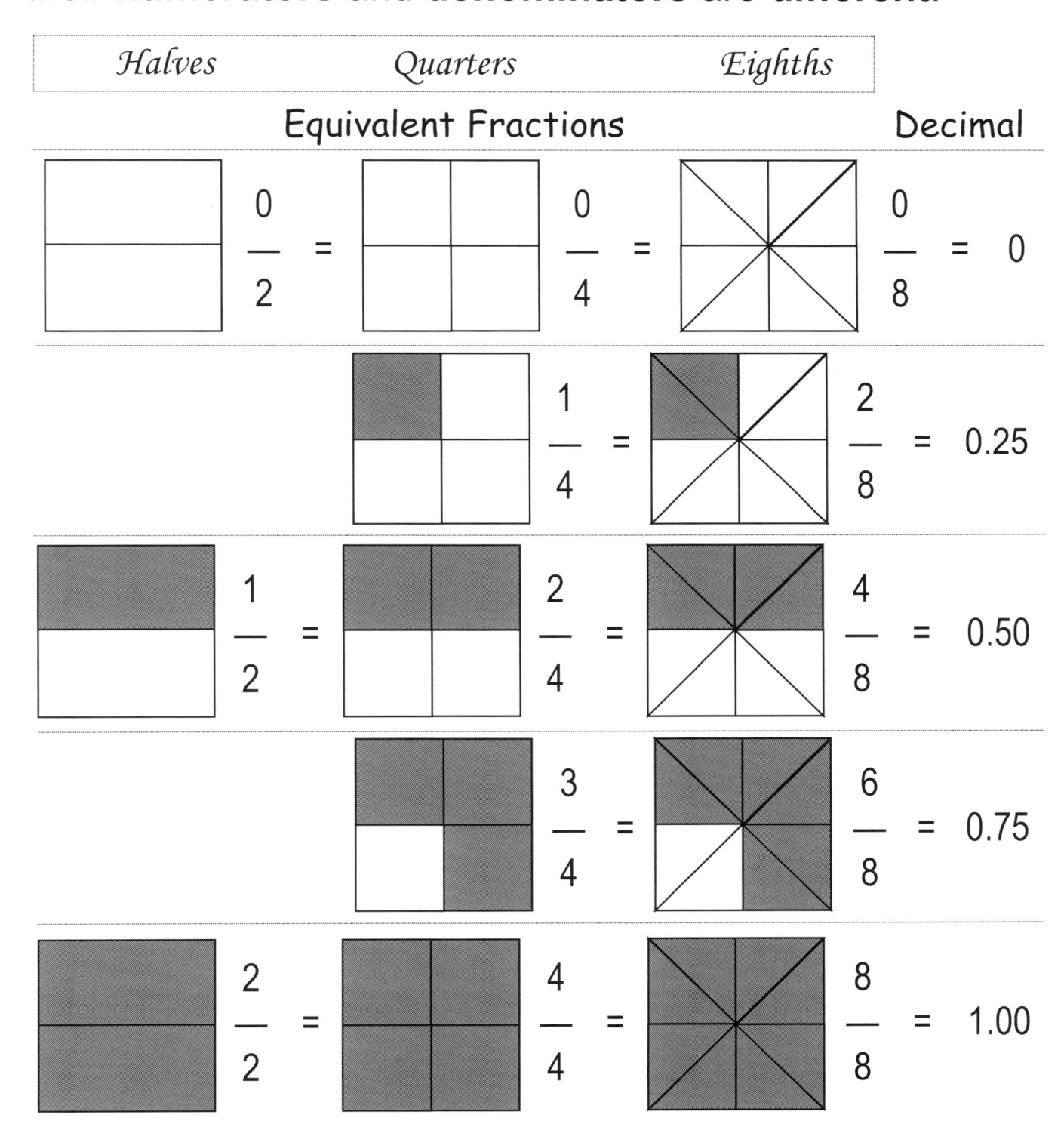

Halves   *Quarters*   *Eighths*

Equivalent Fractions   Decimal

$\dfrac{0}{2} = \dfrac{0}{4} = \dfrac{0}{8} = 0$

$\dfrac{1}{4} = \dfrac{2}{8} = 0.25$

$\dfrac{1}{2} = \dfrac{2}{4} = \dfrac{4}{8} = 0.50$

$\dfrac{3}{4} = \dfrac{6}{8} = 0.75$

$\dfrac{2}{2} = \dfrac{4}{4} = \dfrac{8}{8} = 1.00$

Equivalent Fractions and Decimals

Fifths		Tenths		
	Equivalent Fractions			Decimal

$\dfrac{0}{5} = \dfrac{0}{10} = 0$

$\dfrac{1}{5} = \dfrac{2}{10} = 0.20$

$\dfrac{2}{5} = \dfrac{4}{10} = 0.40$

$\dfrac{3}{5} = \dfrac{6}{10} = 0.60$

$\dfrac{4}{5} = \dfrac{8}{10} = 0.80$

$\dfrac{5}{5} = \dfrac{10}{10} = 1.00$

Equivalent Fractions and Decimals

| Thirds | Sixths | Ninths |

Equivalent Fractions　　　　　　Decimal

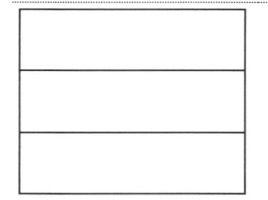

$\dfrac{0}{3} = \dfrac{0}{6} = \dfrac{0}{9} = 0$

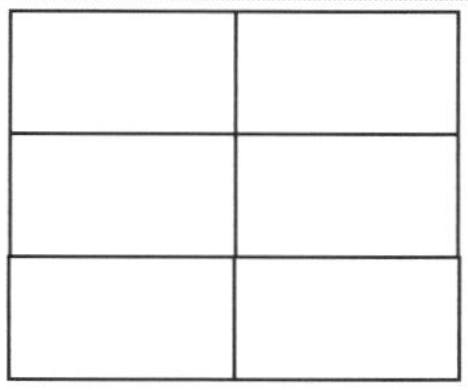

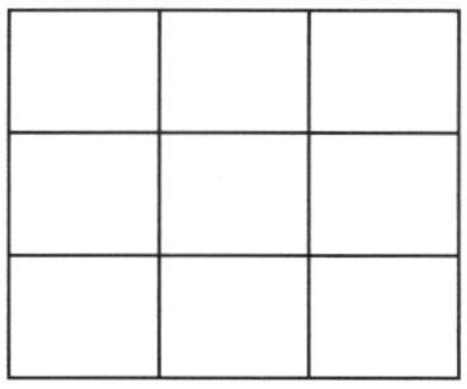

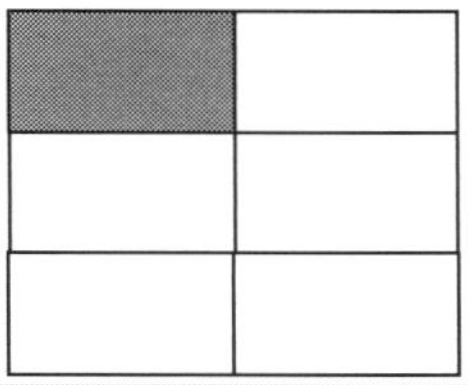

$\dfrac{1}{6} = 0.166$

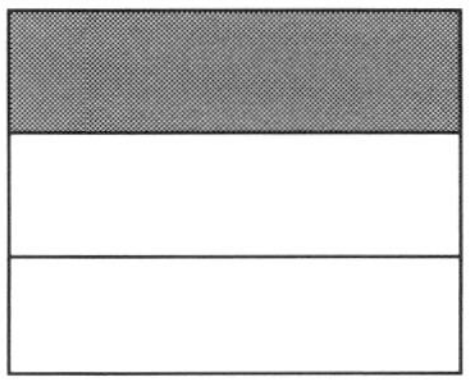

$\dfrac{1}{3} = \dfrac{2}{6} = \dfrac{3}{9} = 0.333$

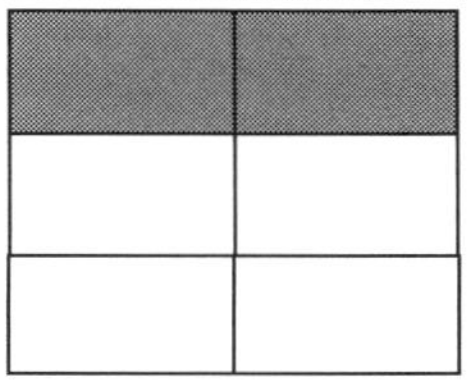

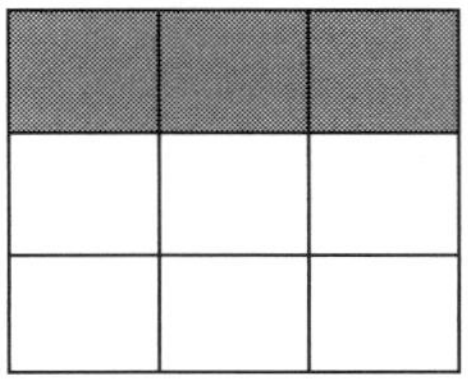

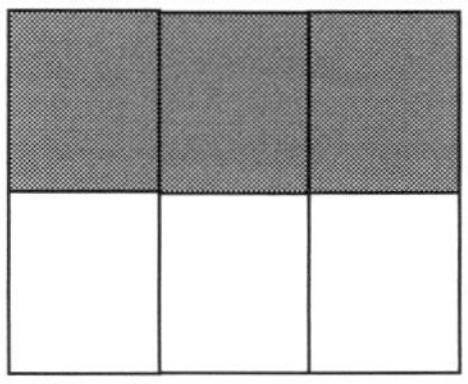

$\dfrac{3}{6} = 0.50$

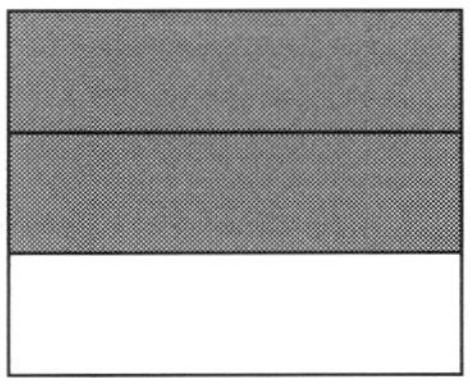

$\dfrac{2}{3} = \dfrac{4}{6} = \dfrac{6}{9} = 0.666$

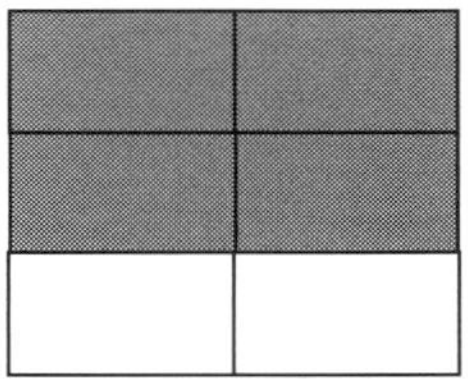

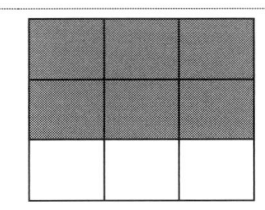

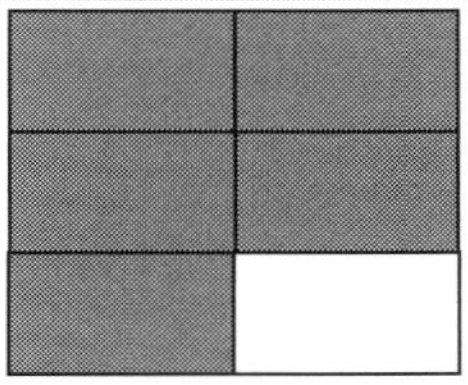

$\dfrac{5}{6} = 0.833$

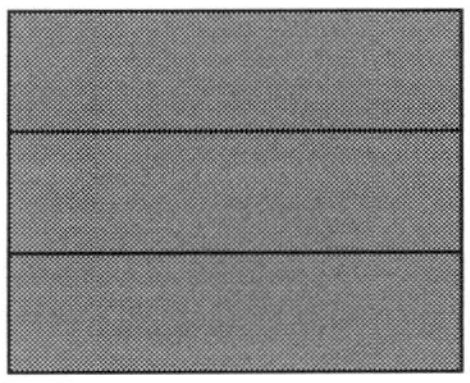

$\dfrac{3}{3} = \dfrac{6}{6} = \dfrac{9}{9} = 1.00$

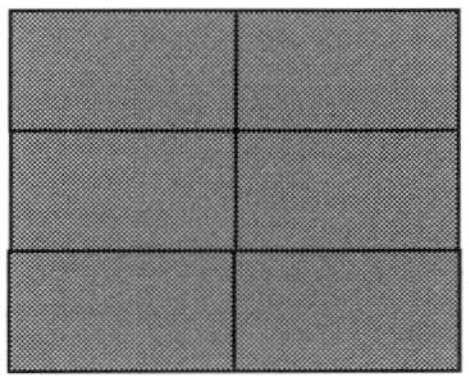

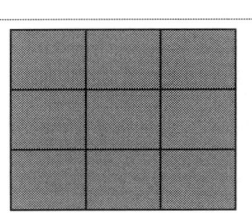

Equivalent Fractions and Decimals

| Halves | Quarters | Twelfths |

Equivalent Fractions　　　　　　　　Decimal

$\dfrac{0}{2}$ = $\dfrac{0}{4}$ = $\dfrac{0}{12}$ = 0

$\dfrac{1}{4}$ = $\dfrac{3}{12}$ = 0.25

$\dfrac{1}{2}$ = $\dfrac{2}{4}$ = $\dfrac{6}{12}$ = 0.50

$\dfrac{3}{4}$ = $\dfrac{9}{12}$ = 0.75

$\dfrac{2}{2}$ = $\dfrac{4}{4}$ = $\dfrac{12}{12}$ = 1.00

Equivalent Fractions and Decimals

| Thirds | Sixths | Twelfths |

Equivalent Fractions   Decimal

$\dfrac{0}{3} = \dfrac{0}{6} = \dfrac{0}{12} = 0$

$\dfrac{1}{6} = \dfrac{2}{12} = 0.166$

$\dfrac{1}{3} = \dfrac{2}{6} = \dfrac{4}{12} = 0.333$

$\dfrac{3}{6} = \dfrac{6}{12} = 0.50$

$\dfrac{2}{3} = \dfrac{4}{6} = \dfrac{8}{12} = 0.666$

$\dfrac{5}{6} = \dfrac{10}{12} = 0.833$

$\dfrac{3}{3} = \dfrac{6}{6} = \dfrac{12}{12} = 1.00$

Fractions, Decimals and Percentages

Halves	*Quarters*	*Eighths*		
Fraction or Equivalent Fractions			Decimal	Percentage

$$\frac{0}{2} = \frac{0}{4} = \frac{0}{8} = 0.00 = 0\%$$

$$\frac{1}{8} = 0.125 = 12.5\%$$

$$\frac{1}{4} = \frac{2}{8} = 0.25 = 25\%$$

$$\frac{3}{8} = 0.375 = 37.5\%$$

Fractions, Decimals and Percentages

Halves   Quarters   Eighths

Fraction or Equivalent Fractions	Decimal	Percentage
$\frac{1}{2} = \frac{2}{4} = \frac{4}{8}$ =	0.50 =	50%
$\frac{5}{8}$ =	0.625 =	62.5%
$\frac{3}{4} = \frac{6}{8}$ =	0.75 =	75%
$\frac{7}{8}$ =	0.875 =	87.5%
$\frac{2}{2} = \frac{4}{4} = \frac{8}{8}$ =	1.00 =	100%

Fractions, Decimals and Percentages

Fifths *Tenths*

Fraction or Equivalent Fractions			Decimal		Percentage
$\dfrac{0}{5}$	=	$\dfrac{0}{10}$	= 0.00	=	0%
		$\dfrac{1}{10}$	= 0.10	=	10%
$\dfrac{1}{5}$	=	$\dfrac{2}{10}$	= 0.20	=	20%
		$\dfrac{3}{10}$	= 0.30	=	30%
$\dfrac{2}{5}$	=	$\dfrac{4}{10}$	= 0.40	=	40%
		$\dfrac{5}{10}$	= 0.50	=	50%

Fractions, Decimals and Percentages

Fifths *Tenths*

Fraction or Equivalent Fractions	Decimal	Percentage
$\frac{3}{5}$ = $\frac{6}{10}$ =	0.60 =	60%
$\frac{7}{10}$ =	0.70 =	70%
$\frac{4}{5}$ = $\frac{8}{10}$ =	0.80 =	80%
$\frac{9}{10}$ =	0.90 =	90%
$\frac{5}{5}$ = $\frac{10}{10}$ =	1.00 =	100%

Fractions, Decimals and Percentages

Thirds   Sixths   Ninths

Fraction or Equivalent Fractions	Decimal	Percentage
$\dfrac{0}{3} = \dfrac{0}{6} = \dfrac{0}{9}$ =	0.00 =	0%
$\dfrac{1}{9}$ =	0.111˙ =	11.1˙%
$\dfrac{2}{9}$ =	0.222˙ =	22.2˙%
$\dfrac{1}{3} = \dfrac{2}{6} = \dfrac{3}{9}$ =	0.333˙ =	33.3˙%
$\dfrac{4}{9}$ =	0.444˙ =	44.4˙%

˙ means a **recurring** number; a number that keeps repeating forever.
Example, 0.111˙ = 0.11111…, 11.1˙ = 11.111…; 0.222˙ = 0.22222…, 22.2˙ = 22.222…; 0.333˙ = 0.33333…, 33.3˙ = 33.333…; 0.444˙ = 0.44444…, 44.4˙ = 44.444… etc.

Fractions, Decimals and Percentages

Thirds   Sixths   Ninths

Fraction or Equivalent Fractions	Decimal	Percentage
$\frac{5}{9}$	= 0.555˙	= 55.5˙%
$\frac{2}{3} = \frac{4}{6} = \frac{6}{9}$	= 0.666˙	= 66.6˙%
$\frac{7}{9}$	= 0.777˙	= 77.7˙%
$\frac{8}{9}$	= 0.888˙	= 88.8˙%
$\frac{3}{3} = \frac{6}{6} = \frac{9}{9}$	= 1.00	= 100%

˙ shows a **recurring** number, which keeps repeating forever!
Example, 0.555˙ = 0.55555…, 55.5˙ = 55.555…; 0.666˙ = 0.66666…, 66.6˙ = 66.666…; 0.777˙ = 0.77777…, 77.7˙ = 77.777…; 0.888˙ = 0.88888…, 88.8˙ = 88.888… and so on.

Fractions, Decimals and Percentages

| Halves | Quarters | Twelfths |

Fraction or Equivalent Fractions	Decimal	Percentage
$\dfrac{0}{2} = \dfrac{0}{4} = \dfrac{0}{12}$ =	0 =	0%
$\dfrac{1}{4} = \dfrac{3}{12}$ =	0.25 =	25%
$\dfrac{1}{2} = \dfrac{2}{4} = \dfrac{6}{12}$ =	0.50 =	50%
$\dfrac{3}{4} = \dfrac{9}{12}$ =	0.75 =	75%
$\dfrac{2}{2} = \dfrac{4}{4} = \dfrac{12}{12}$ =	1.00 =	100%

Fractions, Decimals and Percentages

| Thirds | Sixths | Twelfths |

Fraction or Equivalent Fractions	Decimal	Percentage
$\dfrac{0}{3} = \dfrac{0}{6} = \dfrac{0}{12}$	= 0	= 0%
$\dfrac{1}{6} = \dfrac{2}{12}$	= 0.166˙	= 16.6˙%
$\dfrac{1}{3} = \dfrac{2}{6} = \dfrac{4}{12}$	= 0.333˙	= 33.3˙%
$\dfrac{3}{6} = \dfrac{6}{12}$	= 0.50	= 50%

˙ means a **recurring** number that never ends, but keeps repeating forever.
Example, 0.166˙ = 0.16666…, 16.6˙ = 16.666…, 0.333˙ = 0.33333…, 33.3˙ = 33.333…
And so on.

Fractions, Decimals and Percentages

Thirds   Sixths   Twelfths

Fraction or Equivalent Fractions	Decimal	Percentage
$\frac{3}{6} = \frac{6}{12}$	0.50	50%
$\frac{2}{3} = \frac{4}{6} = \frac{8}{12}$	$0.666\dot{}$	$66.6\dot{}\%$
$\frac{5}{6} = \frac{10}{12}$	$0.833\dot{}$	$83.3\dot{}\%$
$\frac{3}{3} = \frac{6}{6} = \frac{12}{12}$	1.00	100%

$\dot{}$ indicates a **recurring** number that never ends, but keeps repeating forever. Example, $0.666\dot{} = 0.66666...$, $66.6\dot{} = 66.666...$, $0.833\dot{} = 0.83333...$, $83.3\dot{} = 83.333...$ And so on and so forth.

Answers and explanation from pages 9 to 10.

Why was the younger boy not happy?
  He thought his older brother had more pizza!

The younger boy had 1 big slice, $\frac{1}{3}$ of the whole pizza.

The older boy had 2 small slices – each half of the size of that of his younger brother. $\frac{1}{6} + \frac{1}{6} = \frac{2}{6} = \frac{1}{3}$ of the whole pizza.

The girl also got 1 big slice, $\frac{1}{3}$ of the whole pizza.

So, all the children had the same amount of pizza!

$\frac{1}{3} + \frac{1}{3} + \frac{1}{3} = \frac{3}{3} = 1$ whole pizza.

What could be the problem?
The younger boy did not understand fair sharing in fractions!
He had thought his older brother had more pizza; 2 small slices. ☹

The solution was to swap their shares of the pizza for the boys.
The younger boy still had the same amount of pizza, $\frac{1}{3}$ of the whole pizza. But he thought he got more pizza (from his older brother). ☺

Adding Like Fractions

Fractions with **same denominators** (like bottom numbers).

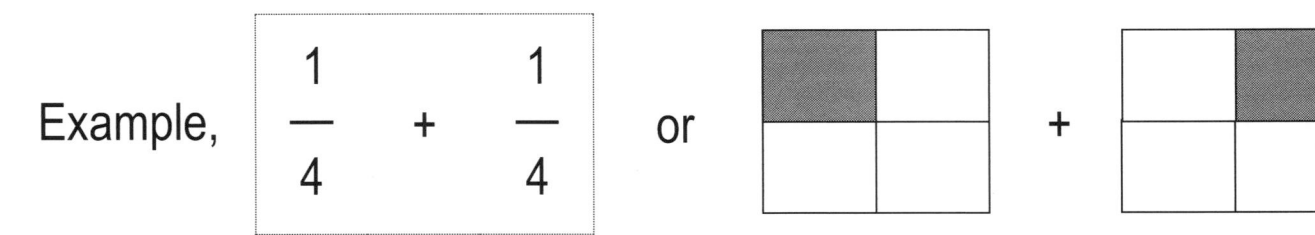

Example, $\dfrac{1}{4} + \dfrac{1}{4}$ or ▦ + ▦

i) Add numerators (top numbers) together.

$\dfrac{1}{} + \dfrac{1}{} = \dfrac{2}{}$ → ▦ + ▦ = ▦

ii) Use the **common** denominator (bottom number shared by fractions).

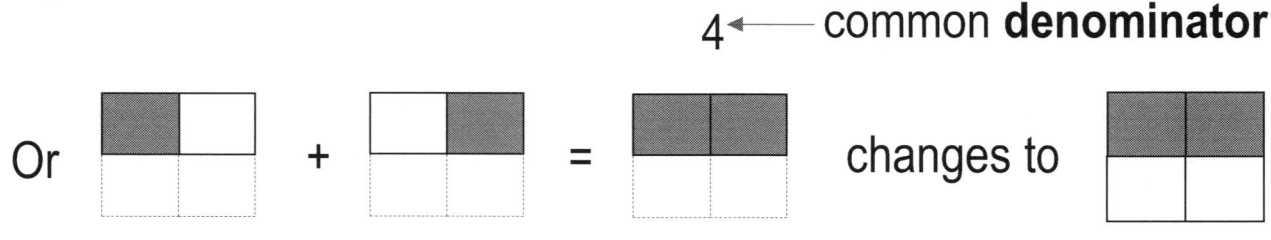

So, $\dfrac{1}{} + \dfrac{1}{} = \dfrac{2}{}$ becomes $\dfrac{2}{4}$ ← **numerators** added
← common **denominator**

Or ▦ + ▦ = ▦ changes to ▦

That's, the **denominator** stays the **same** – not added like numerators! The result is a fraction with the **same denominator** (bottom number).

iii) If possible, simplify the result by dividing both the numerator and denominator by the same **factor** (number). For instance,

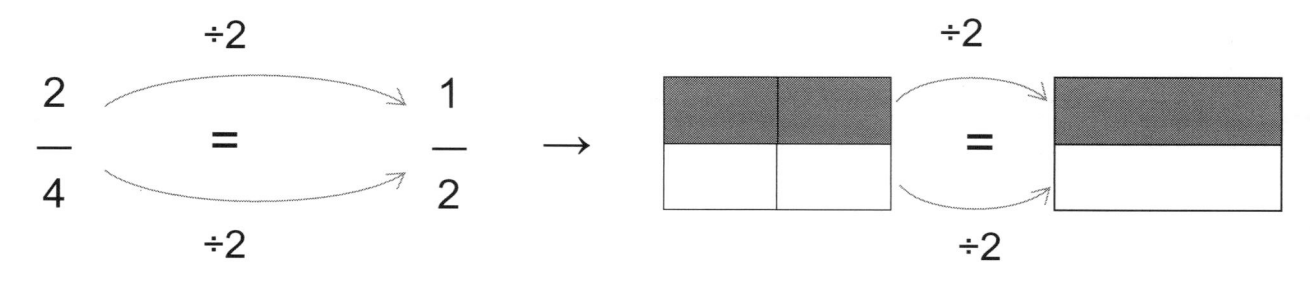

$\dfrac{2}{4} \xrightarrow{\div 2} = \xrightarrow{\div 2} \dfrac{1}{2}$ → ▦ = ▦

(÷2)

Simplifying Fractions

This means changing into equivalent fractions with the smallest numbers (simplest form) by diving the numerator and denominator by a common factor.

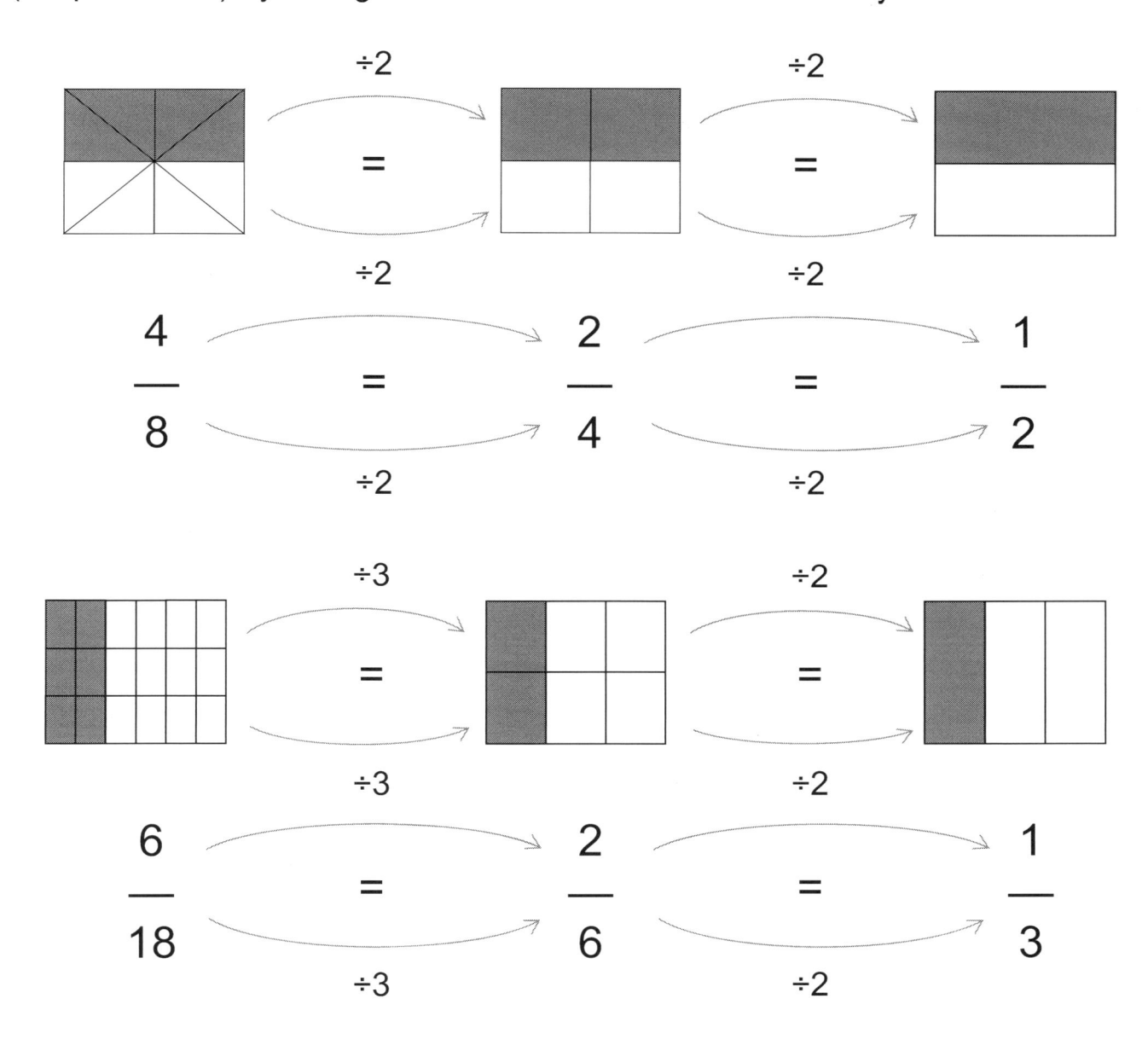

$$\frac{4}{8} \xrightarrow{\div 2} = \frac{2}{4} \xrightarrow{\div 2} = \frac{1}{2}$$

$$\frac{6}{18} \xrightarrow{\div 3} = \frac{2}{6} \xrightarrow{\div 2} = \frac{1}{3}$$

For instance,

$$\frac{1}{2} + \frac{1}{2} = \frac{2}{2} = 1$$

Adding **Halves**

[|] + [|] = [|] = [ ]

$$\frac{0}{2} + \frac{0}{2} = \frac{0}{2} = 0$$

nothing + nothing = nothing = nothing

0.0 + 0.0 = 0.0 = 0

Adding **Halves**

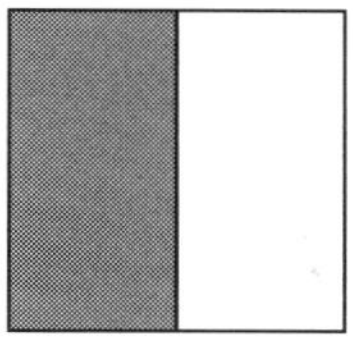

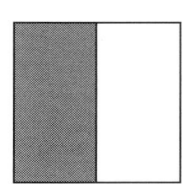

$$\frac{0}{2} + \frac{1}{2} = \frac{1}{2}$$

nothing + half = half

0.00 + 0.50 = 0.50

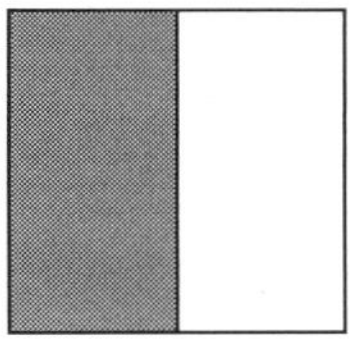

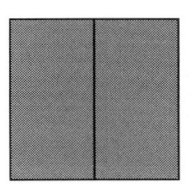

$$\frac{1}{2} + \frac{1}{2} = \frac{2}{2} = 1$$

half + half = two-halves = whole, one

0.50 + 0.50 = 1.00 = 1

Adding Quarters

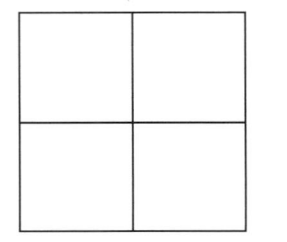

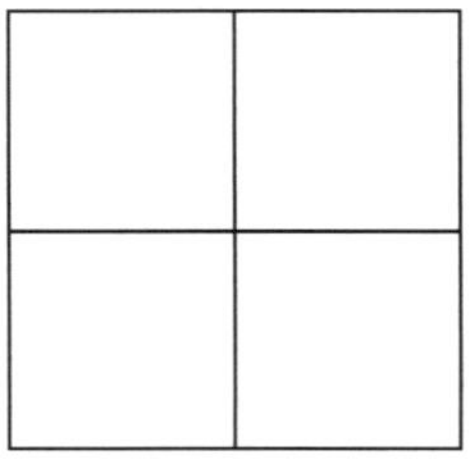

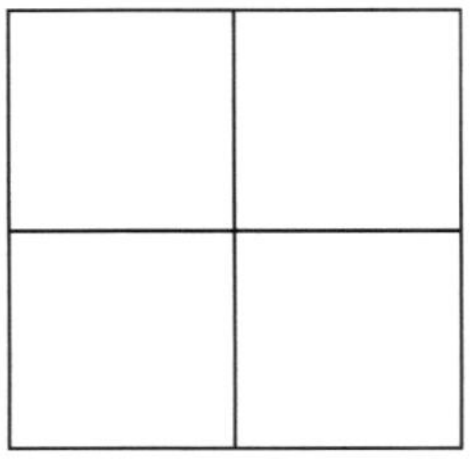

$$\frac{0}{4} + \frac{0}{4} = \frac{0}{4} = 0$$

nothing + nothing = nothing = nothing

0.0 + 0.0 = 0.0 = 0

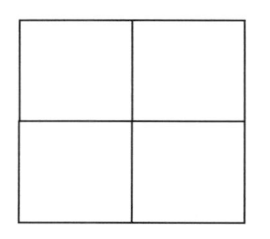

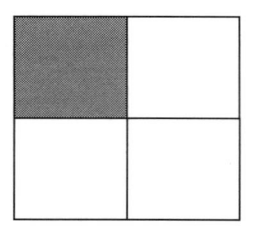

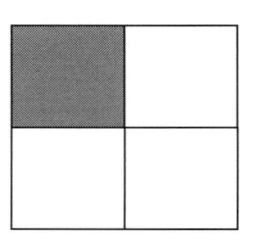

$$\frac{0}{4} + \frac{1}{4} = \frac{1}{4}$$

nothing + quarter = one-quarter

0.00 + 0.25 = 0.25

Adding Quarters

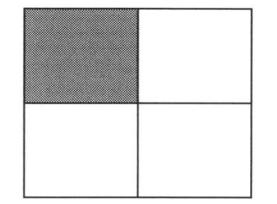

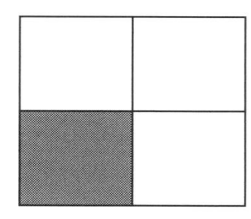

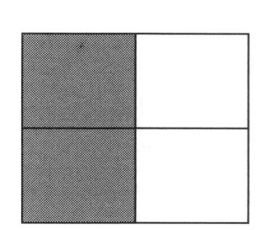

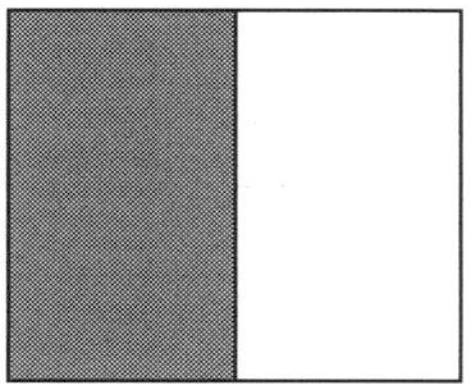

$$\frac{1}{4} + \frac{1}{4} = \frac{2}{4} = \frac{1}{2}$$

quarter + quarter = two-quarters = one-half

0.25 + 0.25 = 0.50 = 0.50

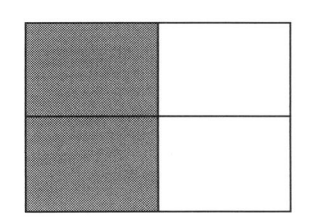

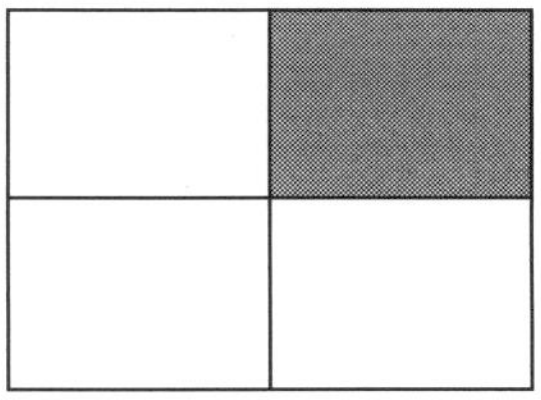

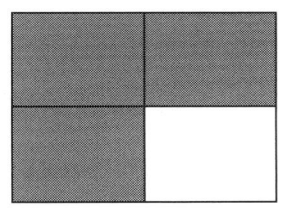

$$\frac{2}{4} + \frac{1}{4} = \frac{3}{4}$$

two-quarters + quarter = three-quarters

0.50 + 0.25 = 0.75

Adding Quarters

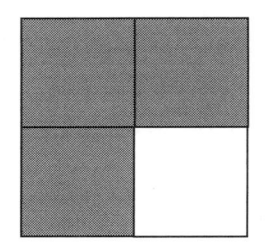

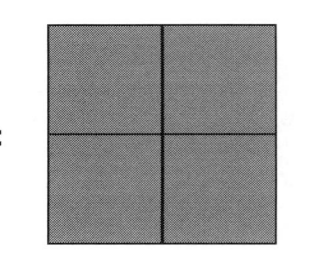

$$\frac{3}{4} \quad + \quad \frac{1}{4} \quad = \quad \frac{4}{4} \quad = \quad 1$$

three-quarters + quarter = four-quarters = one, whole

0.75 + 0.25 = 1.00 = 1

Adding Eighths

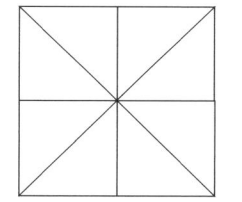

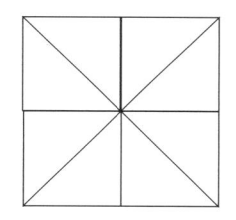

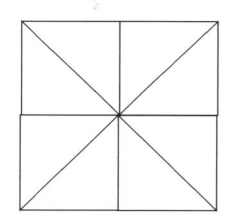

$$\frac{0}{8} + \frac{0}{8} = \frac{0}{8} = 0$$

nothing + nothing = nothing = nothing

0.00 + 0.00 = 0.00 = 0

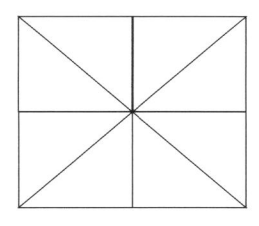

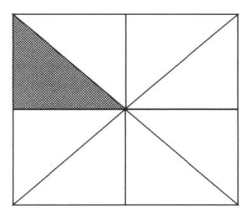

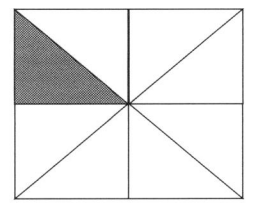

$$\frac{0}{8} + \frac{1}{8} = \frac{1}{8}$$

nothing + eighth = one-eighth

0.00 + 0.125 = 0.125

Adding **Eighths**

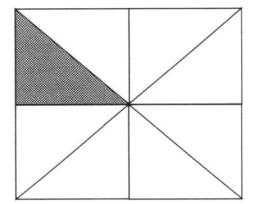

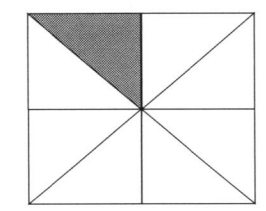

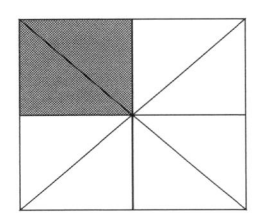

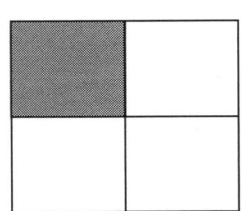

$$\frac{1}{8} + \frac{1}{8} = \frac{2}{8} = \frac{1}{4}$$

eighth + eighth = two-eighths = one-quarter

0.125 + 0.125 = 0.250 = 0.25

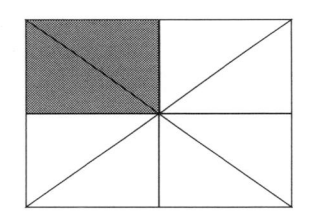

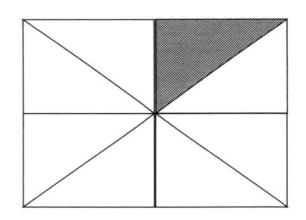

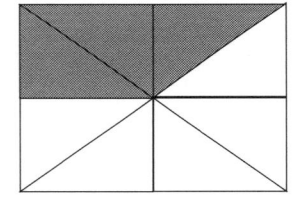

$$\frac{2}{8} + \frac{1}{8} = \frac{3}{8}$$

two-eighths + eighth = three-eighths

0.25 + 0.125 = 0.375

Adding **Eighths**

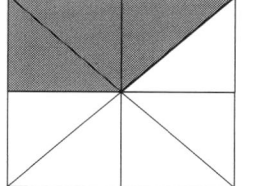

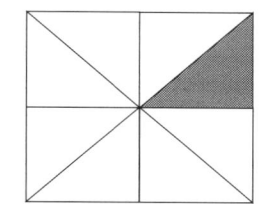

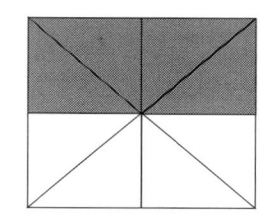

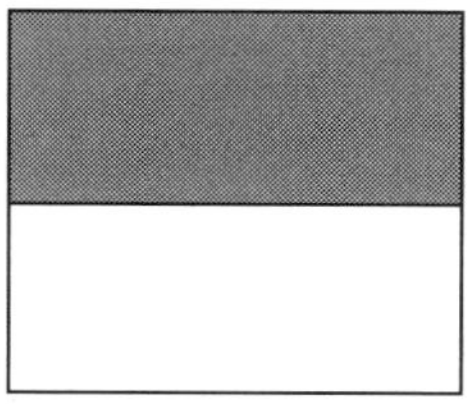

$$\frac{3}{8} + \frac{1}{8} = \frac{4}{8} = \frac{1}{2}$$

three-eighths + eighth = four-eighths = one-half

0.375 + 0.125 = 0.500 = 0.50

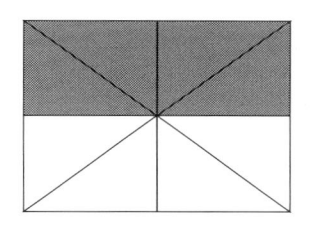

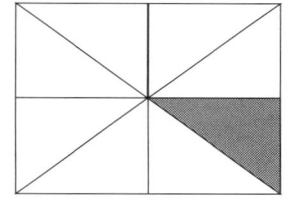

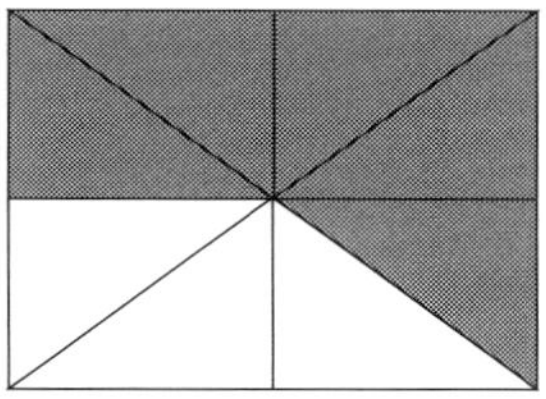

$$\frac{4}{8} + \frac{1}{8} = \frac{5}{8}$$

four-eighths + eighth = five-eighths

0.50 + 0.125 = 0.625

Adding **Eighths**

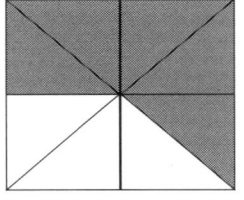

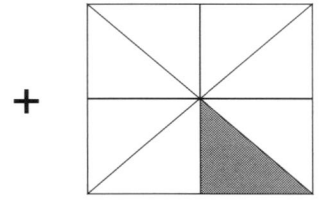

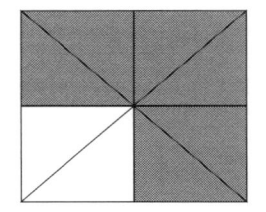

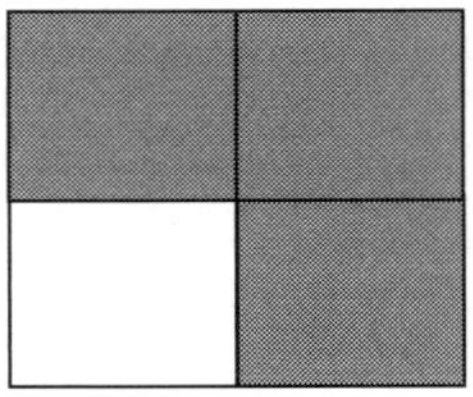

$$\frac{5}{8} + \frac{1}{8} = \frac{6}{8} = \frac{3}{4}$$

five-eighths + one eighth = six-eighths = three-quarters

0.625 + 0.125 = 0.750 = 0.75

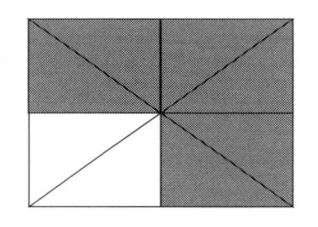

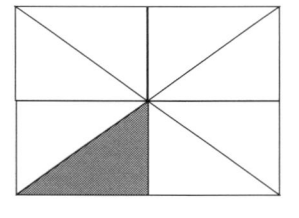

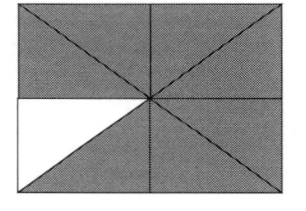

$$\frac{6}{8} + \frac{1}{8} = \frac{7}{8}$$

six-eighths + one eighth = seven-eighths

0.75 + 0.125 = 0.875

Adding **Eighths**

$$\frac{7}{8} + \frac{1}{8} = \frac{8}{8} = 1$$

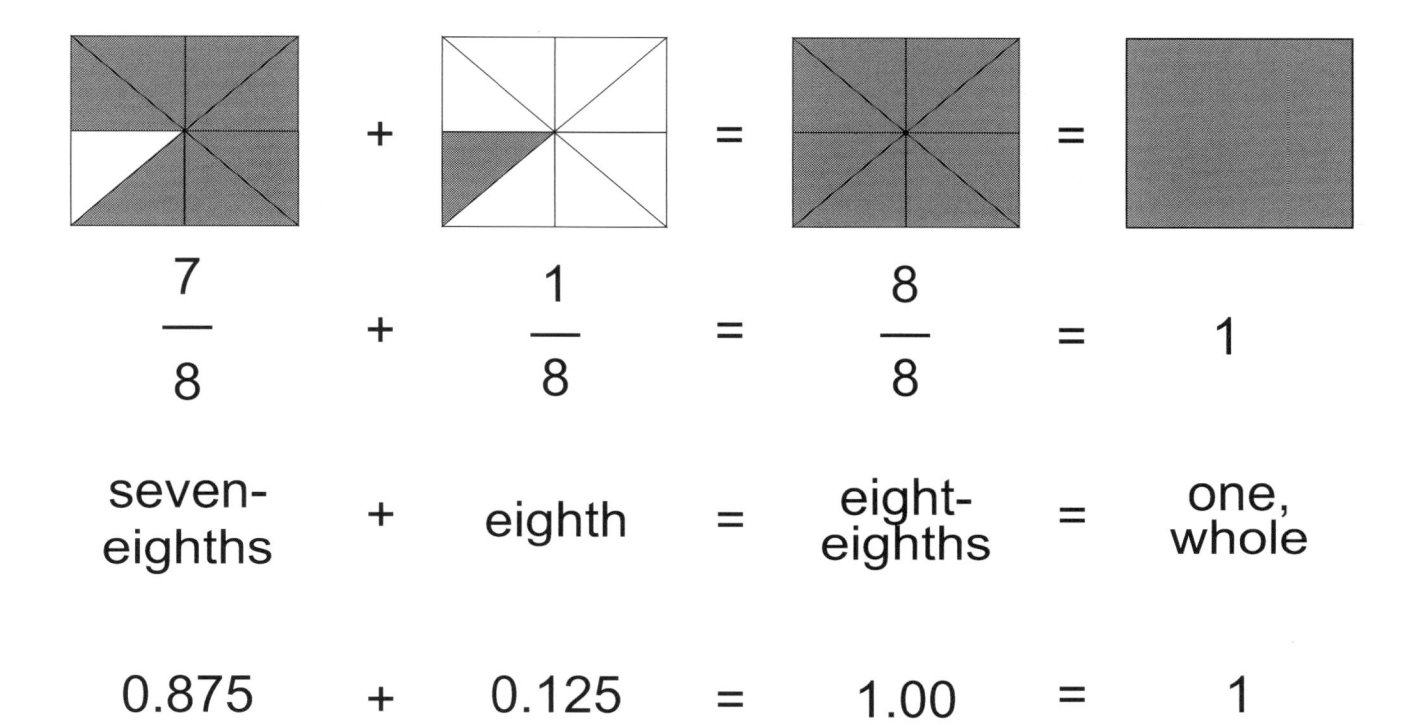

seven-eighths + eighth = eight-eighths = one, whole

0.875 + 0.125 = 1.00 = 1

Quiz 1

Match fractions with their sums (See example given)

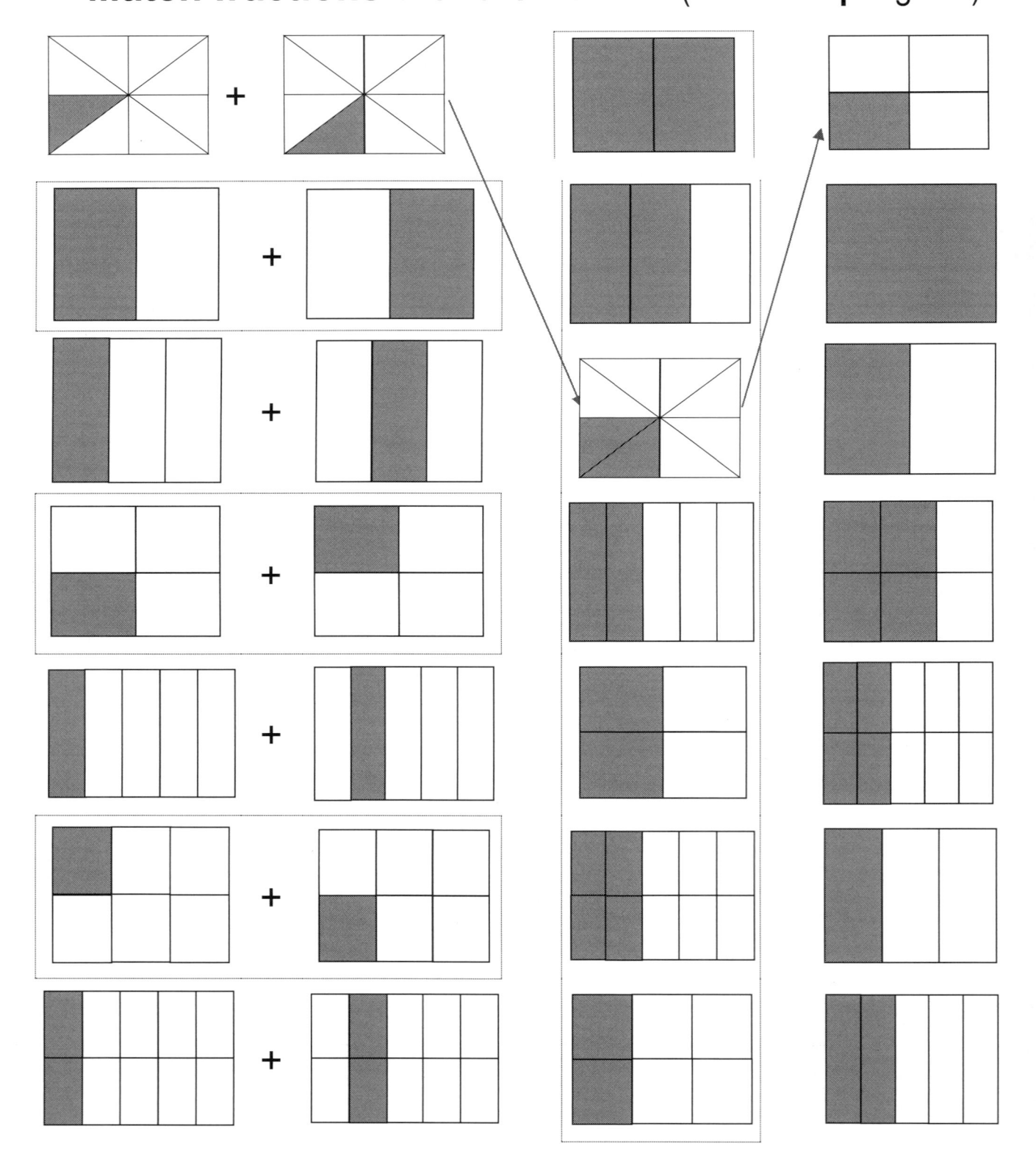

Adding Fifths

$$\frac{0}{5} + \frac{0}{5} = \frac{0}{5} = 0$$

nothing + nothing = nothing = nothing

0.0 + 0.0 = 0.0 = 0

$$\frac{0}{5} + \frac{1}{5} = \frac{1}{5}$$

nothing + fifth = one-fifth

0.00 + 0.20 = 0.20

Adding Fifths

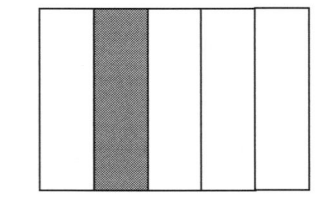

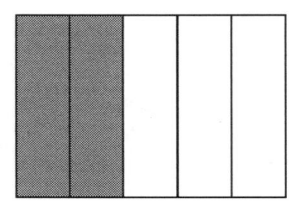

$\dfrac{1}{5}$ + $\dfrac{1}{5}$ = $\dfrac{2}{5}$

fifth + fifth = two-fifths

0.20 + 0.20 = 0.40

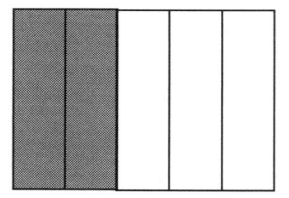

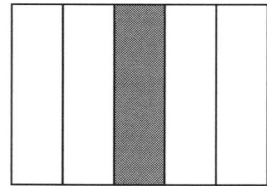

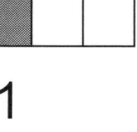

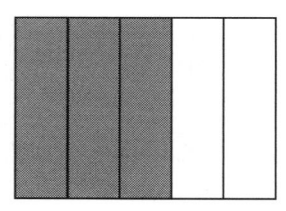

$\dfrac{2}{5}$ + $\dfrac{1}{5}$ = $\dfrac{3}{5}$

two-fifths + fifth = three-fifths

0.40 + 0.20 = 0.60

Adding **Fifths**

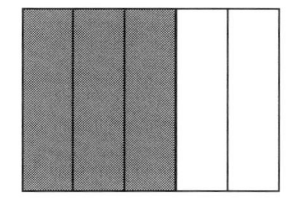

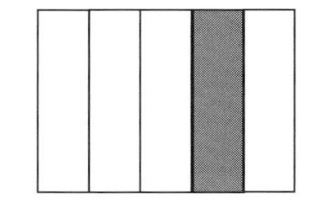

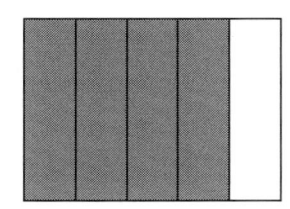

$$\frac{3}{5} + \frac{1}{5} = \frac{4}{5}$$

three-fifths + fifth = four-fifths

0.60 + 0.20 = 0.80

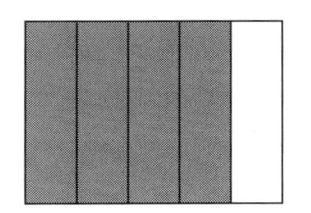

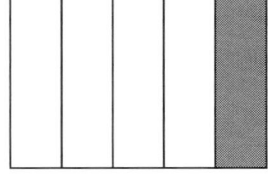

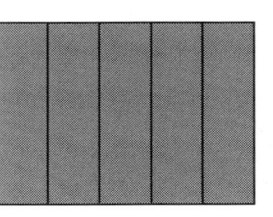

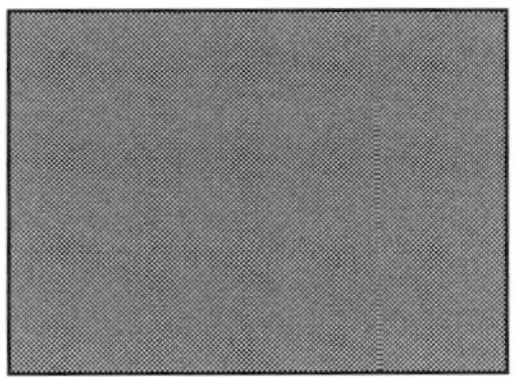

$$\frac{4}{5} + \frac{1}{5} = \frac{5}{5} = 1$$

four-fifths + fifth = five-fifths = one, whole

0.80 + 0.20 = 1.00 = 1

Adding Tenths

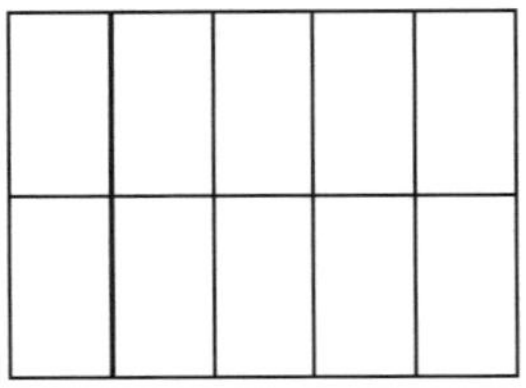

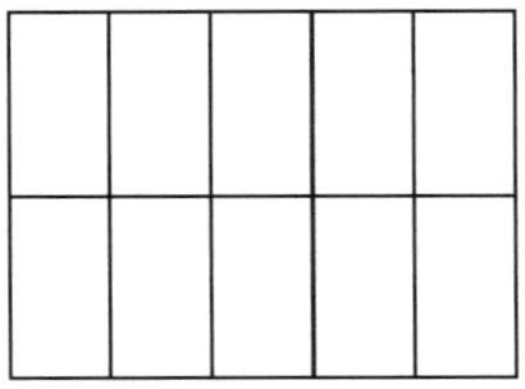

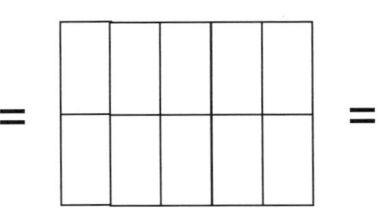

$$\frac{0}{10} + \frac{0}{10} = \frac{0}{10} = 0$$

nothing + nothing = nothing = nothing

0.0 + 0.0 = 0.0 = 0

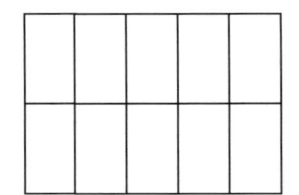

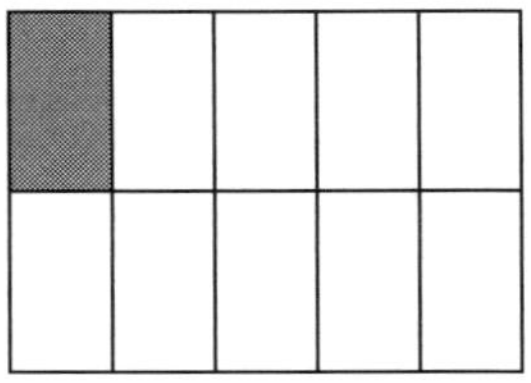

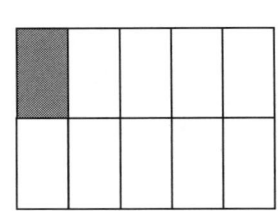

$$\frac{0}{10} + \frac{1}{10} = \frac{1}{10}$$

nothing + tenth = one-tenth

0.00 + 0.10 = 0.10

Adding Tenths

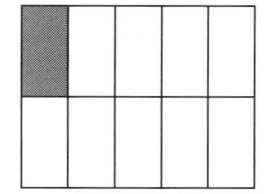

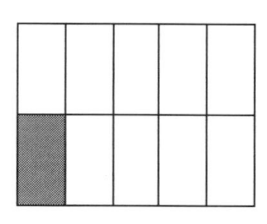

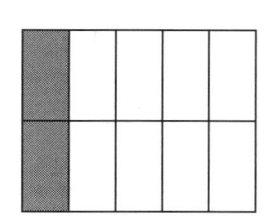

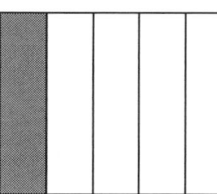

$\frac{1}{10}$ + $\frac{1}{10}$ = $\frac{2}{10}$ = $\frac{1}{5}$

tenth + tenth = two-tenths = one-fifth

0.10 + 0.10 = 0.20 = 0.20

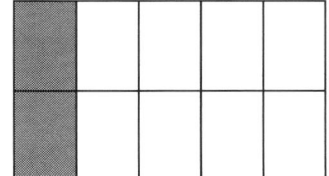

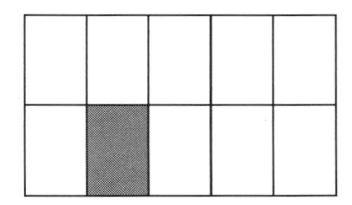

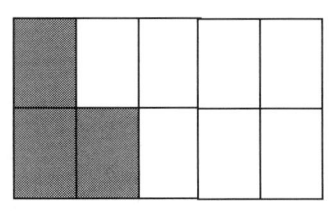

$\frac{2}{10}$ + $\frac{1}{10}$ = $\frac{3}{10}$

two-tenths + tenth = three-tenths

0.20 + 0.10 = 0.30

Adding Tenths

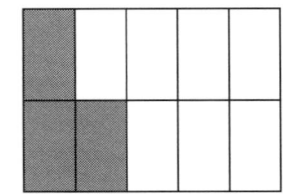

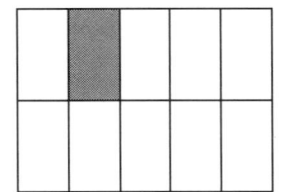

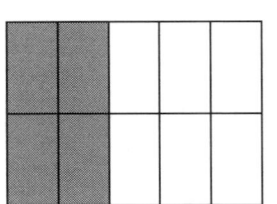

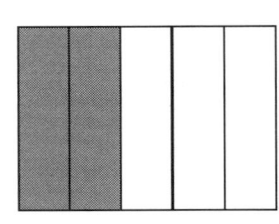

$\dfrac{3}{10}$ + $\dfrac{1}{10}$ = $\dfrac{4}{10}$ = $\dfrac{2}{5}$

three-tenths + tenth = four-tenths = two-fifths

0.30 + 0.10 = 0.40 = 0.40

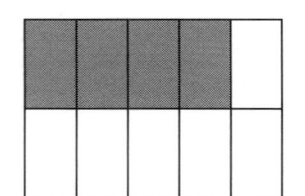

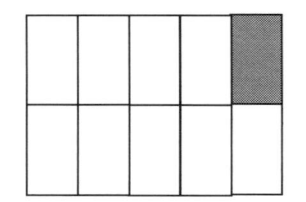

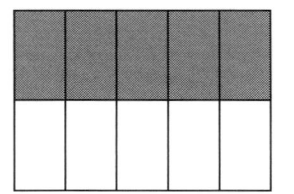

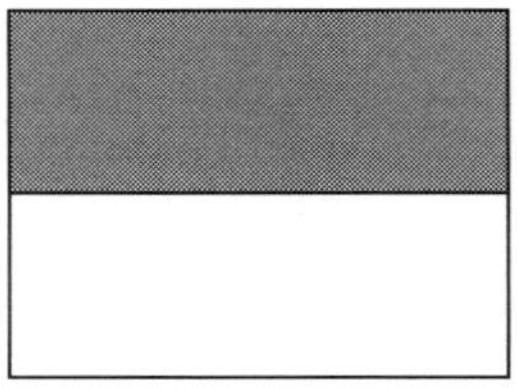

$\dfrac{4}{10}$ + $\dfrac{1}{10}$ = $\dfrac{5}{10}$ = $\dfrac{1}{2}$

four-tenths + tenth = five-tenths = one-half

0.40 + 0.10 = 0.50 = 0.50

Adding Tenths

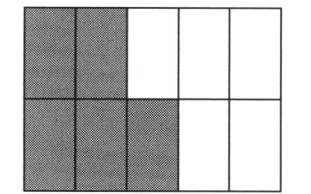

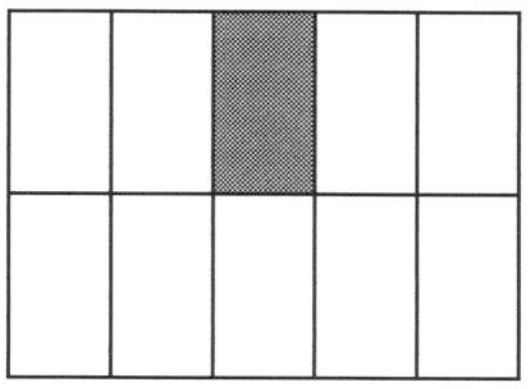

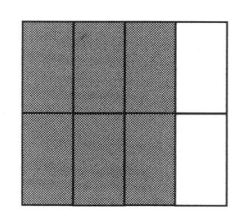

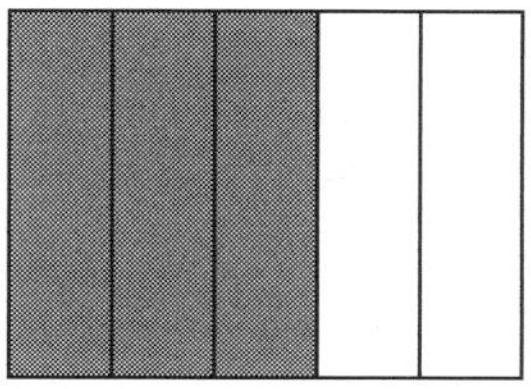

$\frac{5}{10}$ + $\frac{1}{10}$ = $\frac{6}{10}$ = $\frac{3}{5}$

five-tenths + tenth = six-tenths = three-fifths

0.50 + 0.10 = 0.60 = 0.60

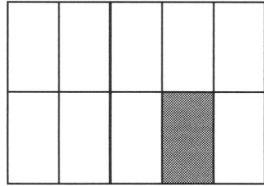

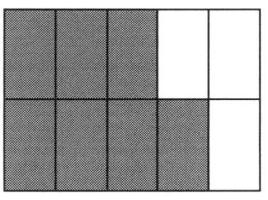

$\frac{6}{10}$ + $\frac{1}{10}$ = $\frac{7}{10}$

six-tenths + tenth = seven-tenths

0.60 + 0.10 = 0.70

Adding **Tenths**

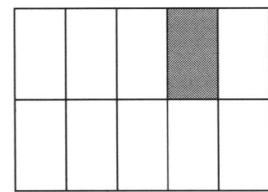

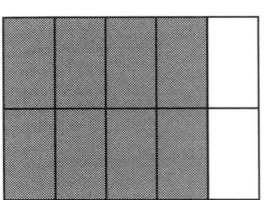

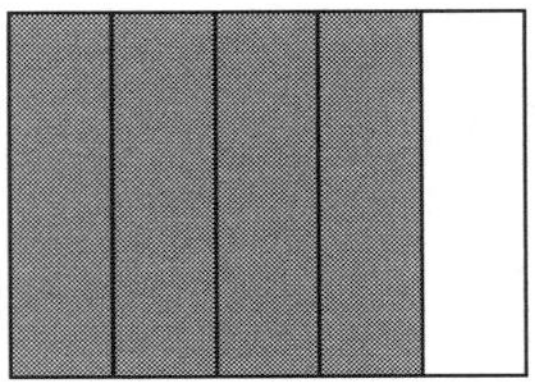

$$\frac{7}{10} + \frac{1}{10} = \frac{8}{10} = \frac{4}{5}$$

seven-tenths + tenth = eight-tenths = four-fifths

0.70 + 0.10 = 0.80 = 0.80

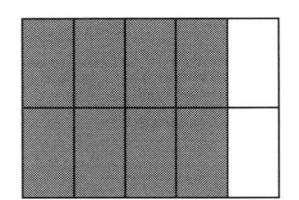

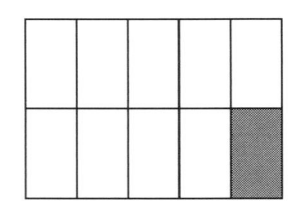

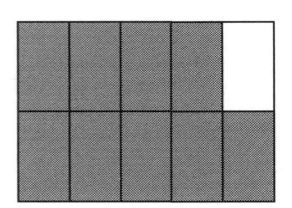

$$\frac{8}{10} + \frac{1}{10} = \frac{9}{10}$$

eight-tenths + tenth = nine-tenths

0.80 + 0.10 = 0.90

Adding Tenths

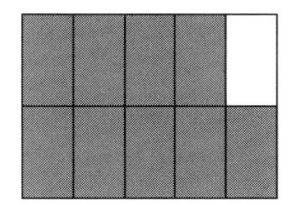

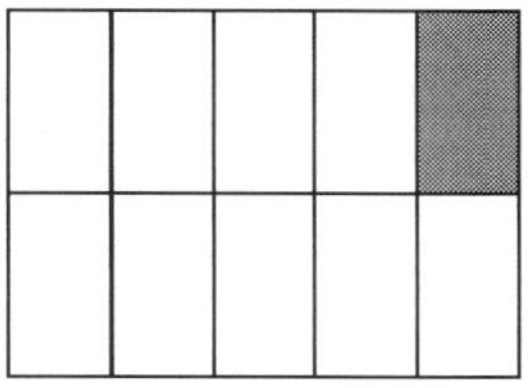

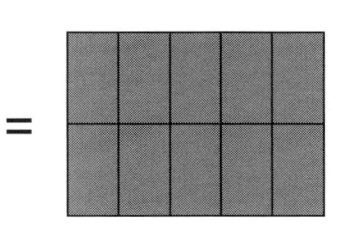

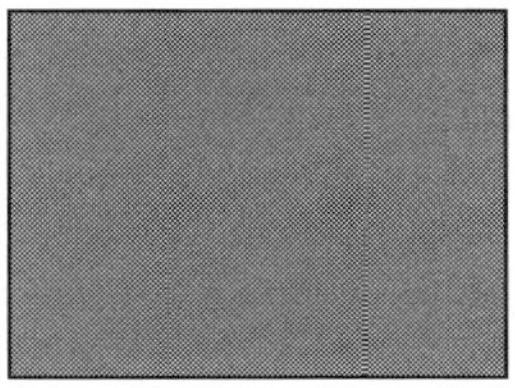

$\dfrac{9}{10}$ + $\dfrac{1}{10}$ = $\dfrac{10}{10}$ = 1

nine-tenths + tenth = ten-tenths = one, whole

0.90 + 0.10 = 1.00 = 1

Adding Thirds

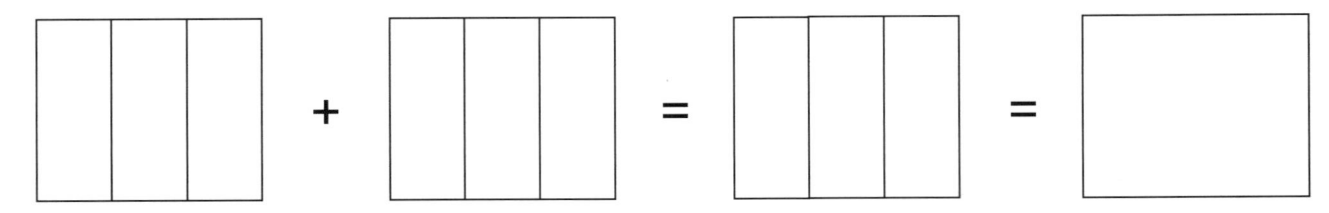

$\frac{0}{3}$ + $\frac{0}{3}$ = $\frac{0}{3}$ = 0

nothing + nothing = nothing = nothing

0.0 + 0.0 = 0.0 = 0

$\frac{0}{3}$ + $\frac{1}{3}$ = $\frac{1}{3}$

nothing + third = one-third

0.00 + 0.3˙ = 0.3˙

116

Adding Thirds

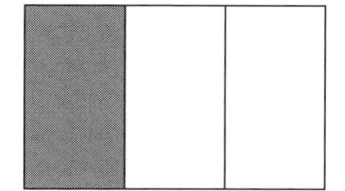

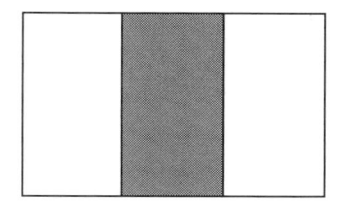

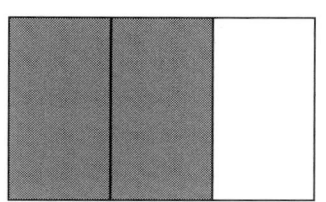

$\frac{1}{3}$ + $\frac{1}{3}$ = $\frac{2}{3}$

third + third = two-thirds

0.3˙ + 0.3˙ = 0.6˙

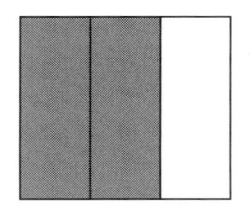

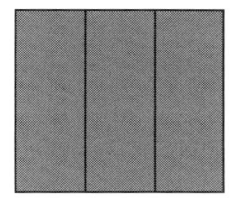

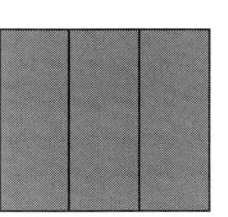

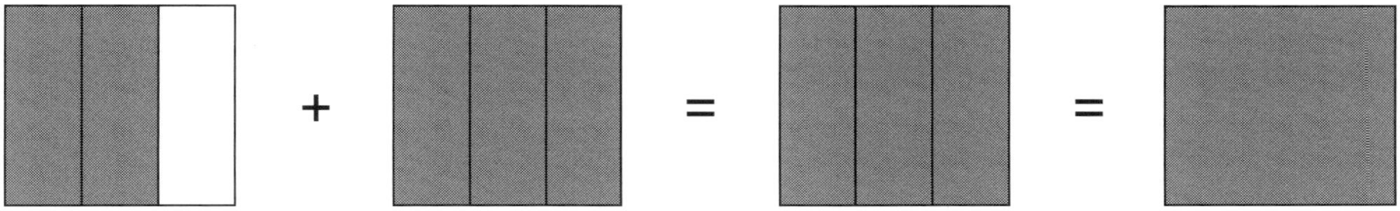

$\frac{2}{3}$ + $\frac{1}{3}$ = $\frac{3}{3}$ = 1

two-thirds + third = three-thirds = one, whole

0.6˙ + 0.3˙ = 1.00 = 1

Adding **Sixths**

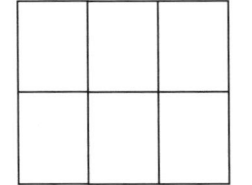

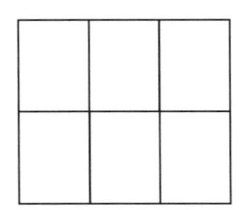

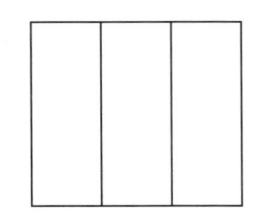

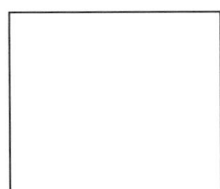

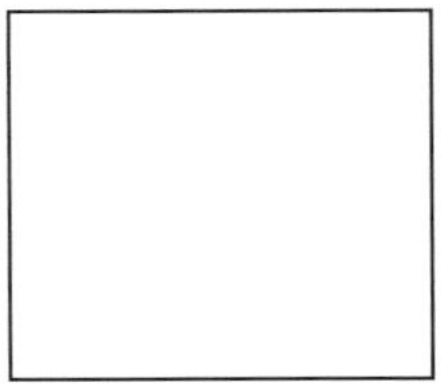

$$\frac{0}{6} + \frac{0}{6} = \frac{0}{3} = 0$$

nothing + nothing = nothing = nothing

0.00 + 0.00 = 0.00 = 0

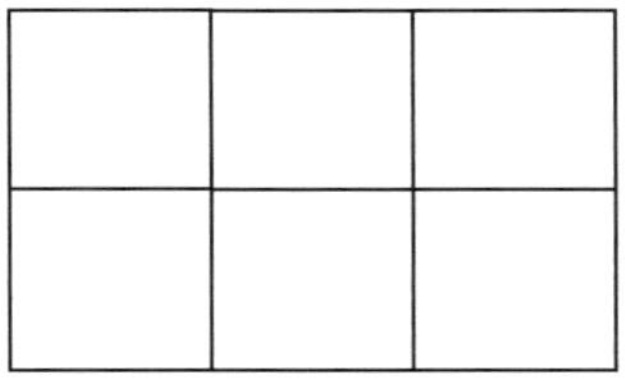

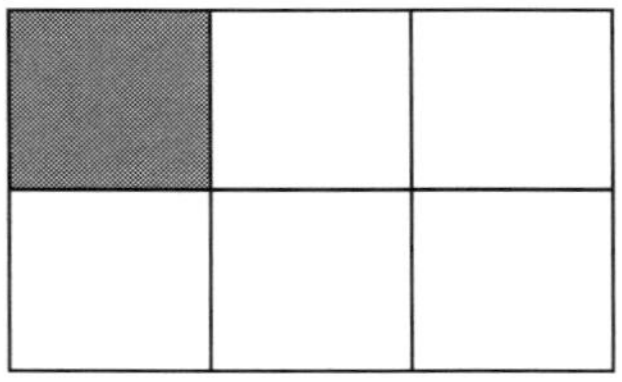

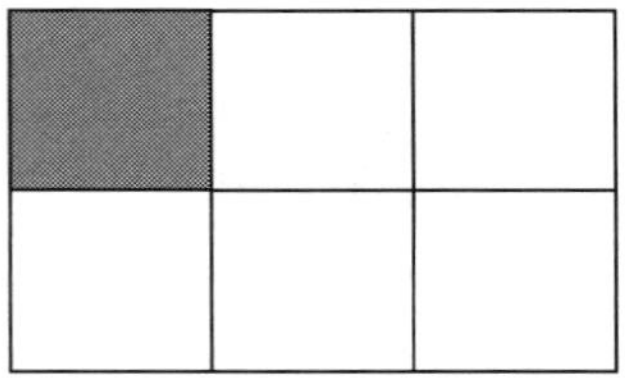

$$\frac{0}{6} + \frac{1}{6} = \frac{1}{6}$$

nothing + sixth = one-sixth

0.00 + 0.16˙ = 0.16˙

118

Adding **Sixths**

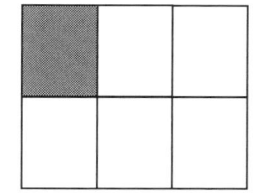

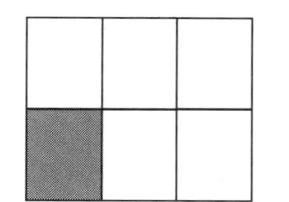

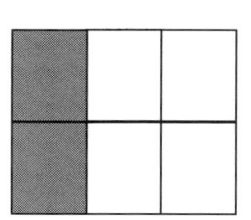

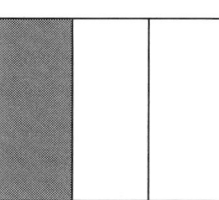

$$\frac{1}{6} + \frac{1}{6} = \frac{2}{6} = \frac{1}{3}$$

sixth + sixth = two-sixths = one-third

0.16˙ + 0.16˙ = 0.3˙ = 0.3˙

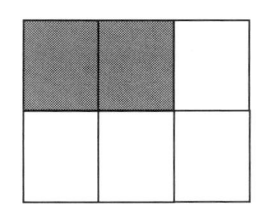

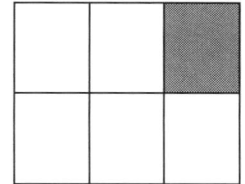

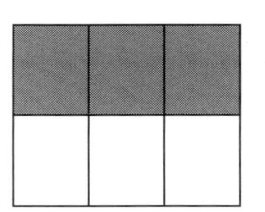

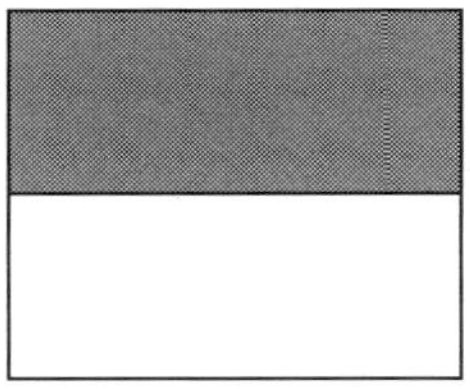

$$\frac{2}{6} + \frac{1}{6} = \frac{3}{6} = \frac{1}{2}$$

two-sixths + sixth = three-sixths = one-half

0.3˙ + 0.16˙ = 0.50 = 0.50

Adding Sixths

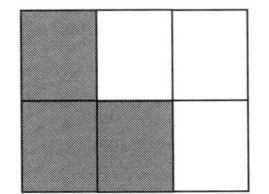

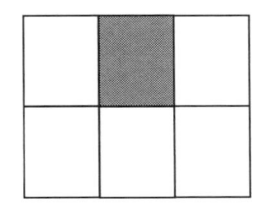

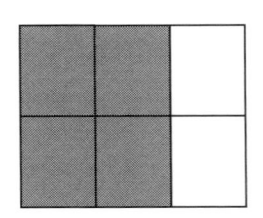

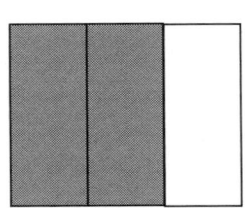

$$\frac{3}{6} + \frac{1}{6} = \frac{4}{6} = \frac{2}{3}$$

three-sixths + sixth = four-sixths = two-thirds

0.50 + 0.16˙ = 0.6˙ = 0.6˙

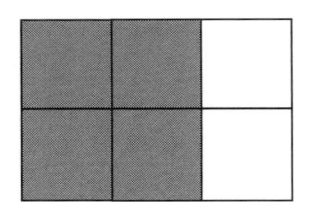

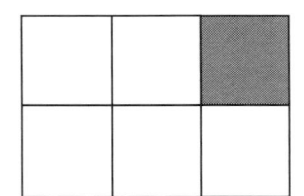

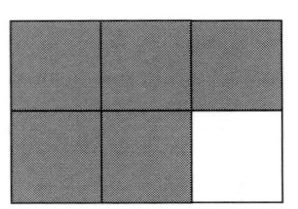

$$\frac{4}{6} + \frac{1}{6} = \frac{5}{6}$$

four-sixths + sixth = five-sixths

0.6˙ + 0.16˙ = 0.83˙

Adding **Sixths**

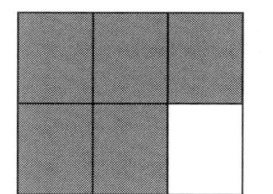

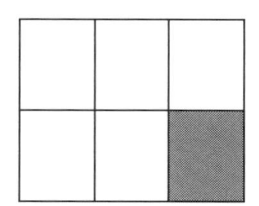

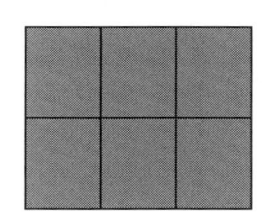

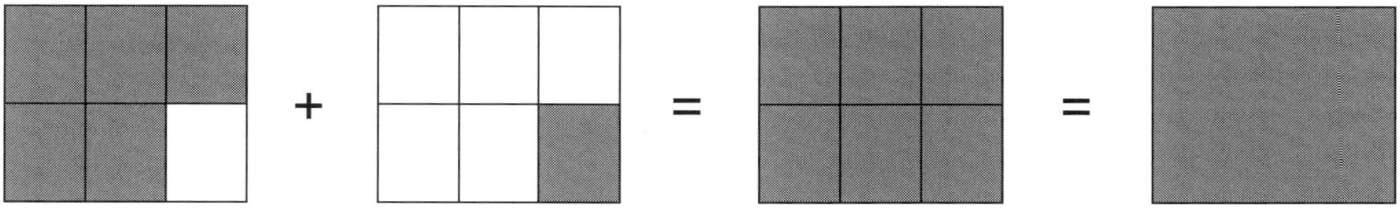

$$\frac{5}{6} + \frac{1}{6} = \frac{6}{6} = 1$$

five-sixths + sixth = six-sixths = one, whole

0.83˙ + 0.16˙ = 1.00 = 1

Adding **Ninths**

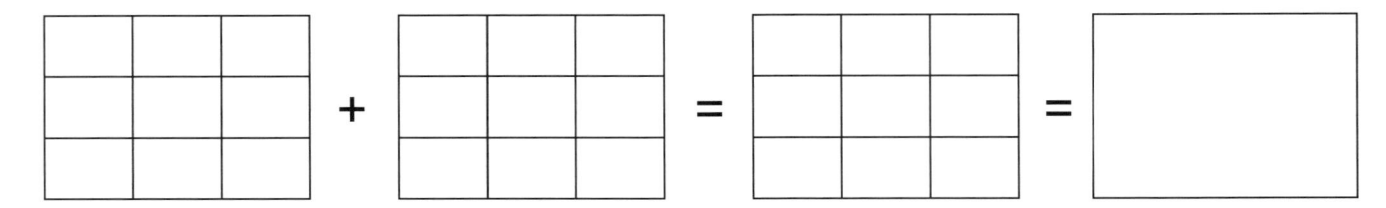

$$\frac{0}{9} + \frac{0}{9} = \frac{0}{9} = 0$$

nothing + nothing = nothing = nothing

0.00 + 0.00 = 0 = 0

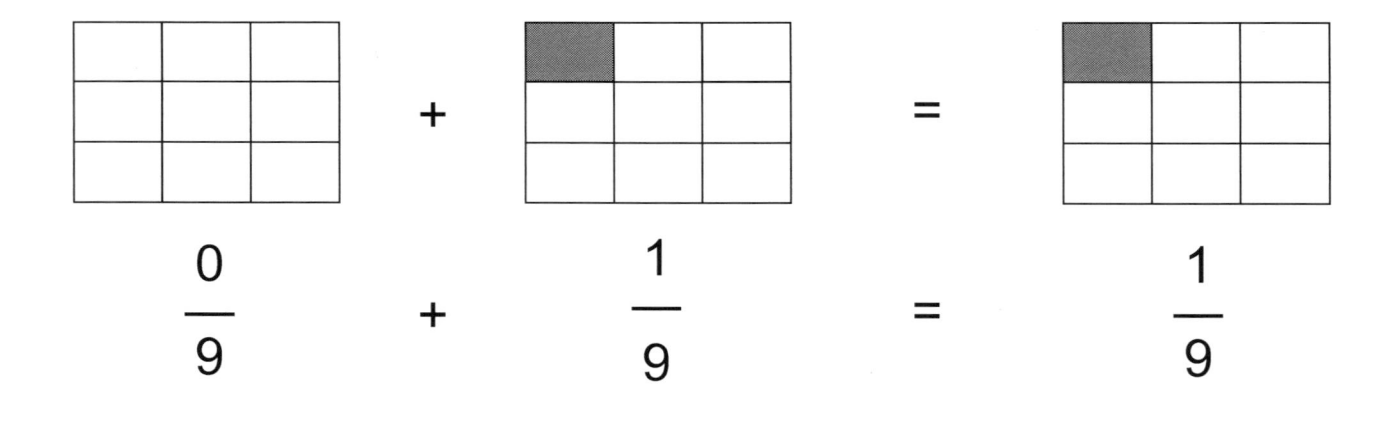

$$\frac{0}{9} + \frac{1}{9} = \frac{1}{9}$$

nothing + ninth = one-ninth

0.00 + 0.1˙ = 0.1˙

122

Adding **Ninths**

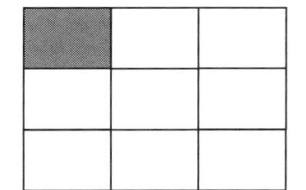

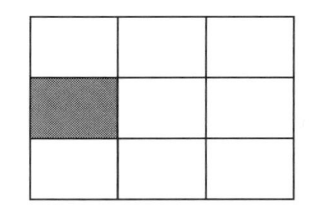

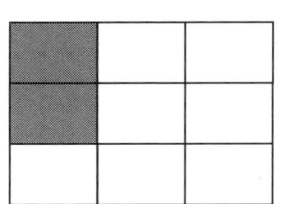

$$\frac{1}{9} + \frac{1}{9} = \frac{2}{9}$$

ninth + ninth = two-ninths

0.1˙ + 0.1˙ = 0.2˙

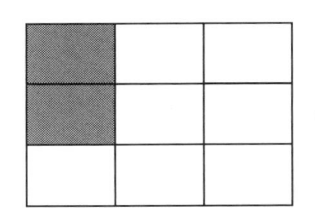

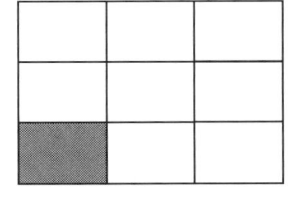

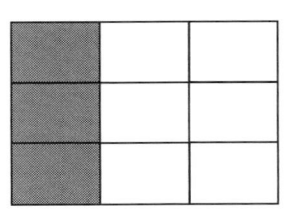

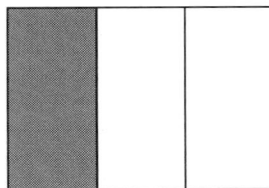

$$\frac{2}{9} + \frac{1}{9} = \frac{3}{9} = \frac{1}{3}$$

two-ninths + ninth = three-ninths = one-third

0.2˙ + 0.1˙ = 0.3˙ = 0.3˙

Adding **Ninths**

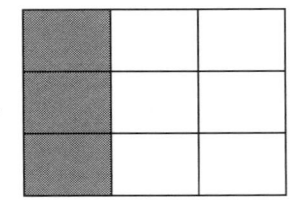

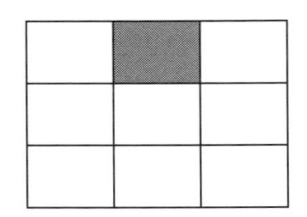

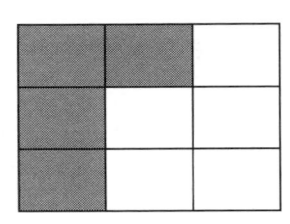

$$\frac{3}{9} + \frac{1}{9} = \frac{4}{9}$$

three-ninths + ninth = four-ninths

0.3˙ + 0.1˙ = 0.4˙

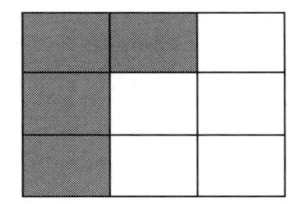

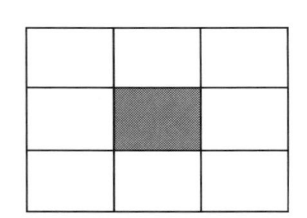

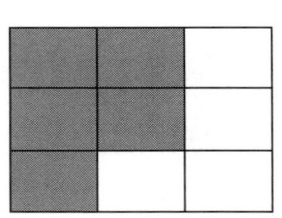

$$\frac{4}{9} + \frac{1}{9} = \frac{5}{9}$$

four-ninths + ninth = five-ninths

0.4˙ + 0.1˙ = 0.5˙

Adding **Ninths**

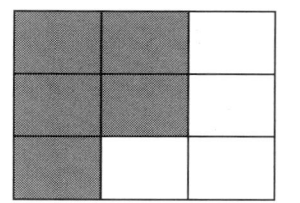

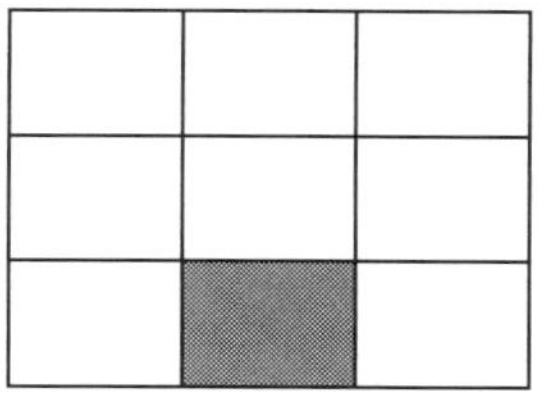

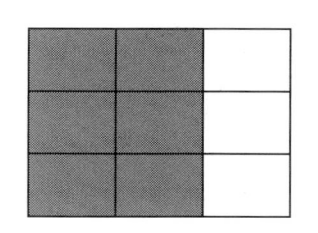

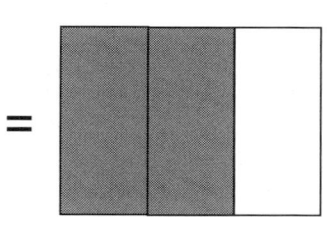

$$\frac{5}{9} + \frac{1}{9} = \frac{6}{9} = \frac{2}{3}$$

five-ninths + ninth = six-ninths = two-thirds

0.5˙ + 0.1˙ = 0.6˙ = 0.6˙

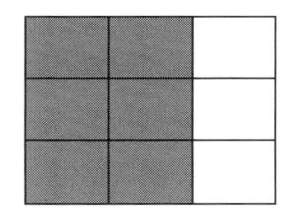

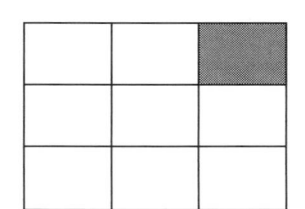

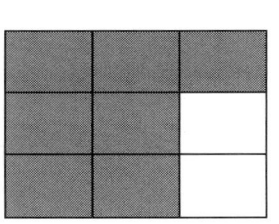

$$\frac{6}{9} + \frac{1}{9} = \frac{7}{9}$$

six-ninths + ninth = seven-ninths

0.6˙ + 0.1˙ = 0.7˙

Adding **Ninths**

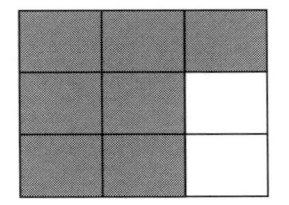

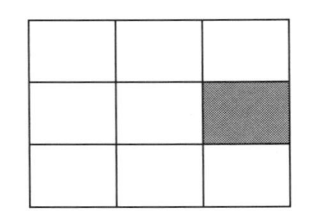

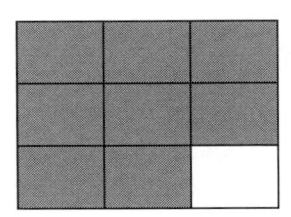

$$\frac{7}{9} + \frac{1}{9} = \frac{8}{9}$$

seven-ninths + ninth = eight-ninths

0.7˙ + 0.1˙ = 0.8˙

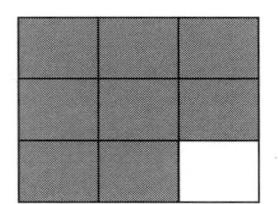

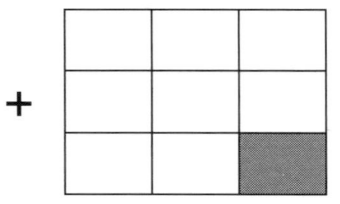

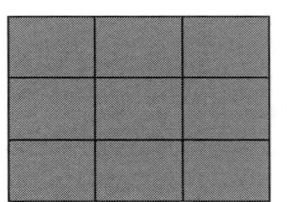

$$\frac{8}{9} + \frac{1}{9} = \frac{9}{9} = 1$$

eight-ninths + ninth = nine-ninths = one, whole

0.8˙ + 0.1˙ = 1.00 = 1

Adding Twelfths

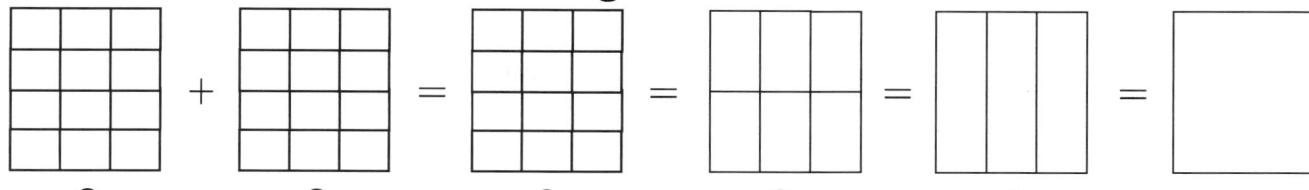

$\dfrac{0}{12}$ + $\dfrac{0}{12}$ = $\dfrac{0}{12}$ = $\dfrac{0}{6}$ = $\dfrac{0}{3}$ = 0

nothing + nothing = nothing = nothing = nothing = nothing

0.00 + 0.00 = 0.00 = 0.00 = 0.00 = 0

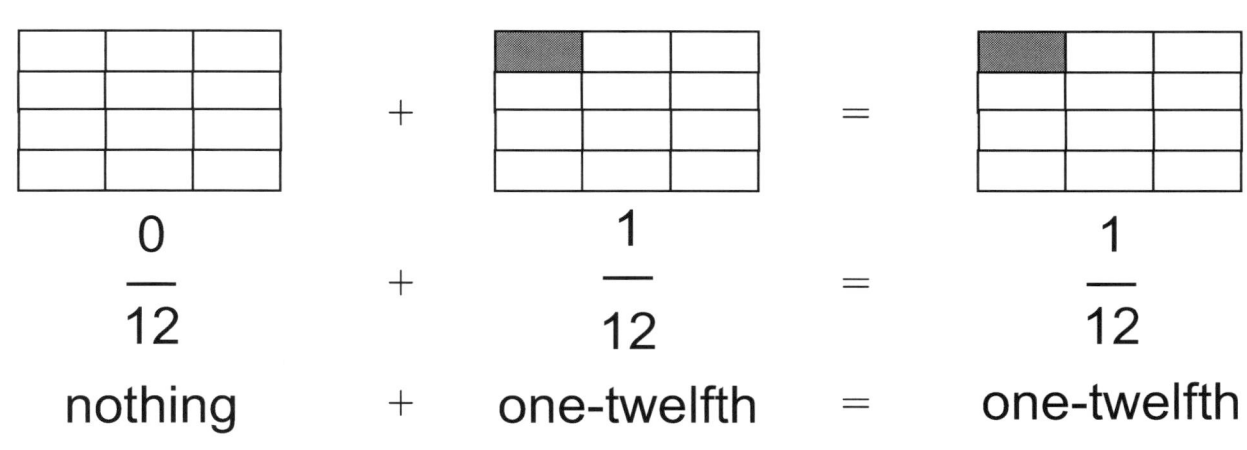

$\dfrac{0}{12}$ + $\dfrac{1}{12}$ = $\dfrac{1}{12}$

nothing + one-twelfth = one-twelfth

0.00 + 0.08333˙ = 0.08333˙

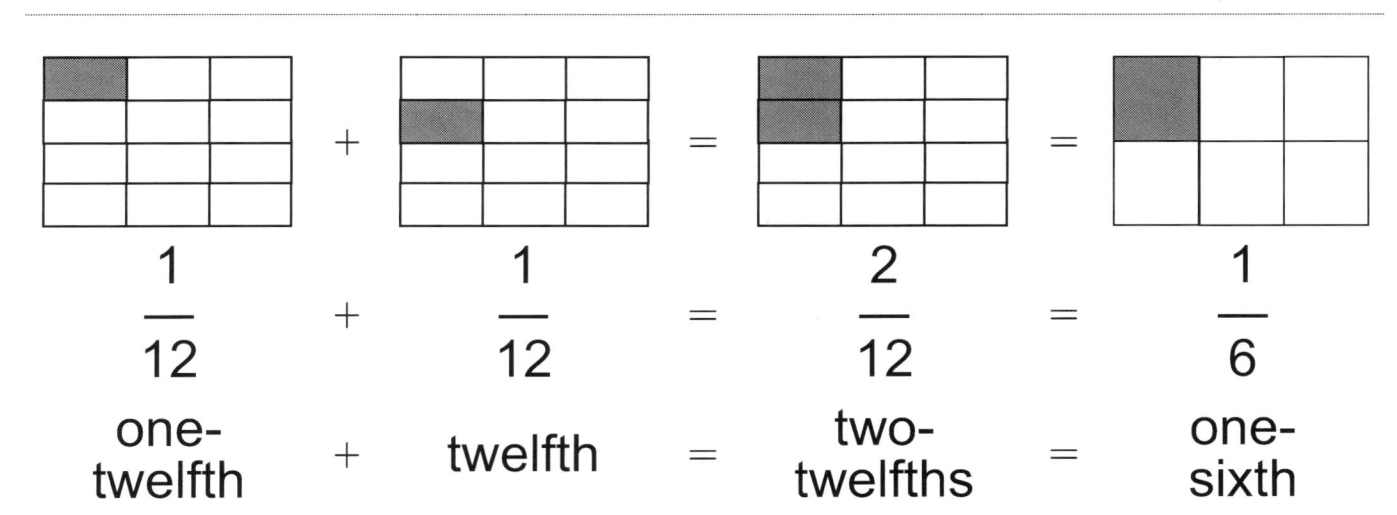

$\dfrac{1}{12}$ + $\dfrac{1}{12}$ = $\dfrac{2}{12}$ = $\dfrac{1}{6}$

one-twelfth + one-twelfth = two-twelfths = one-sixth

0.0833˙ + 0.0833˙ = 0.1666˙ = 0.1666˙

Adding Twelfths

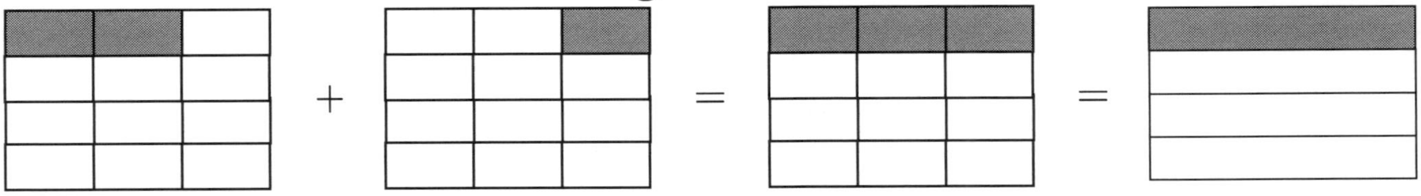

$\dfrac{2}{12}$ + $\dfrac{1}{12}$ = $\dfrac{3}{12}$ = $\dfrac{1}{4}$

two-twelfths + one-twelfth = three-twelfths = one-quarter

0.1666˙ + 0.0833˙ = 0.250 = 0.25

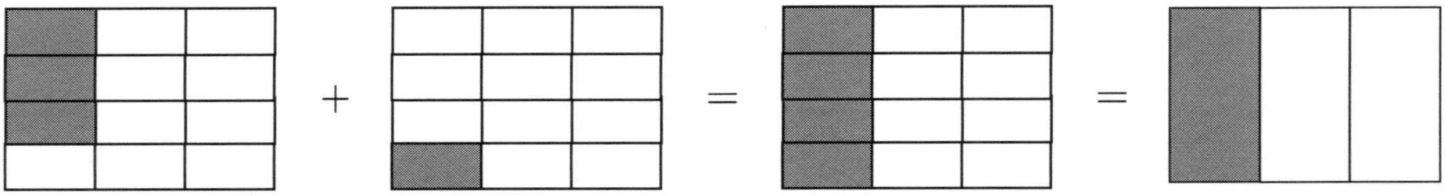

$\dfrac{3}{12}$ + $\dfrac{1}{12}$ = $\dfrac{4}{12}$ = $\dfrac{1}{3}$

three-twelfths + twelfth = four-twelfths = one-third

0.25 + 0.0833˙ = 0.333˙ = 0.333˙

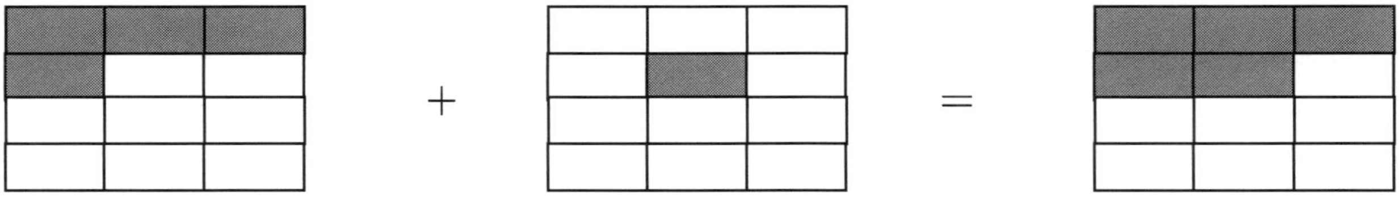

$\dfrac{4}{12}$ + $\dfrac{1}{12}$ = $\dfrac{5}{12}$

four-twelfths + one-twelfth = five-twelfths

0.333˙ + 0.08333˙ = 0.4166˙

Adding Twelfths

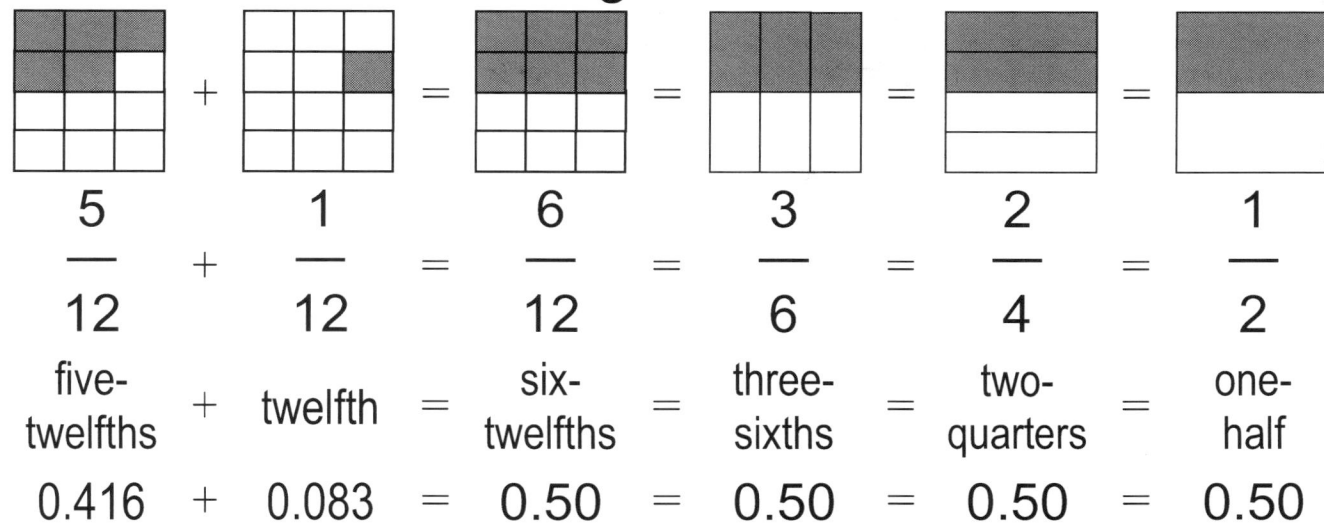

$$\frac{5}{12} + \frac{1}{12} = \frac{6}{12} = \frac{3}{6} = \frac{2}{4} = \frac{1}{2}$$

five-twelfths + twelfth = six-twelfths = three-sixths = two-quarters = one-half

0.416 + 0.083 = 0.50 = 0.50 = 0.50 = 0.50

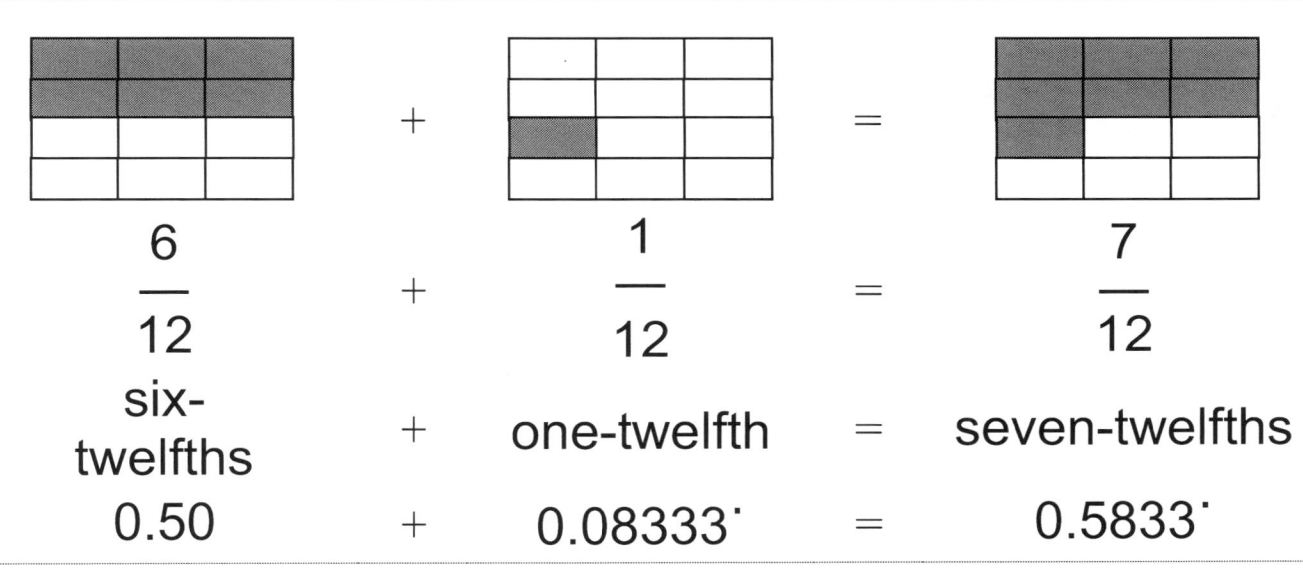

$$\frac{6}{12} + \frac{1}{12} = \frac{7}{12}$$

six-twelfths + one-twelfth = seven-twelfths

0.50 + 0.08333˙ = 0.5833˙

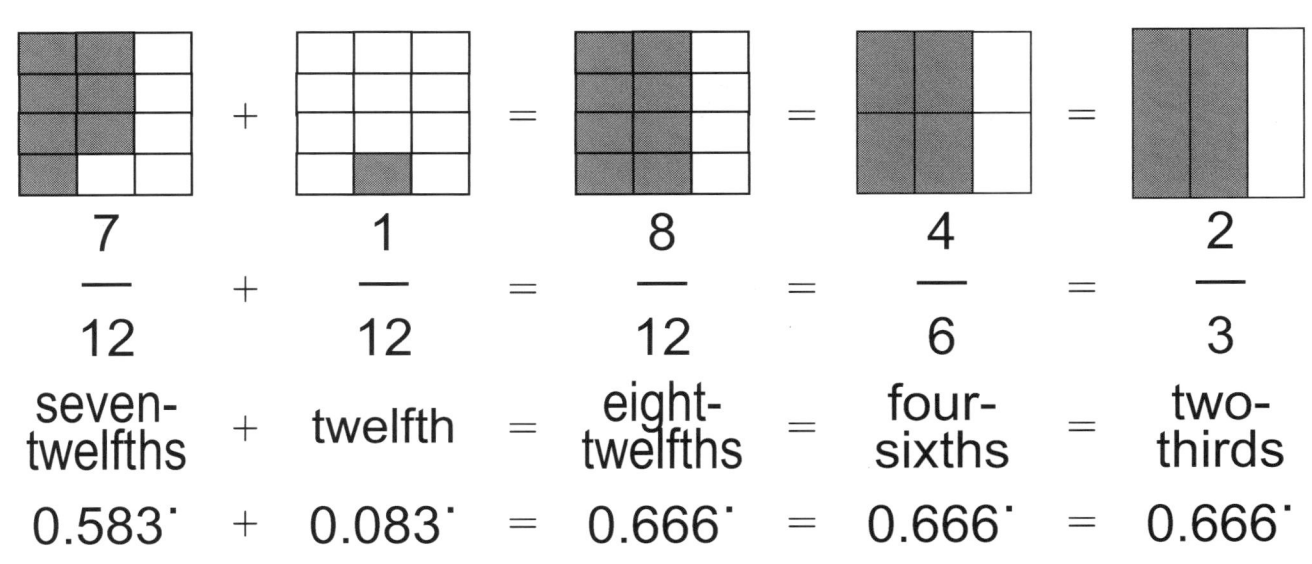

$$\frac{7}{12} + \frac{1}{12} = \frac{8}{12} = \frac{4}{6} = \frac{2}{3}$$

seven-twelfths + twelfth = eight-twelfths = four-sixths = two-thirds

0.583˙ + 0.083˙ = 0.666˙ = 0.666˙ = 0.666˙

Adding Twelfths

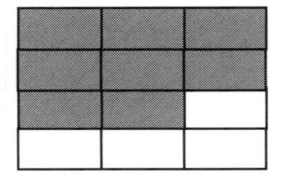

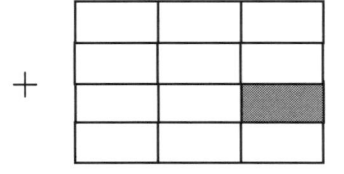

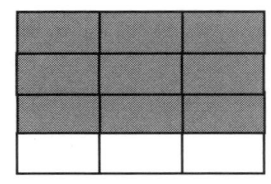

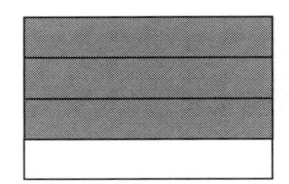

$\frac{8}{12}$ + $\frac{1}{12}$ = $\frac{9}{12}$ = $\frac{3}{4}$

eight-twelfths + twelfth = nine-twelfths = three-quarters

0.666˙ + 0.0833˙ = 0.750 = 0.75

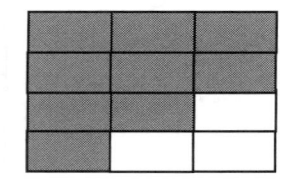

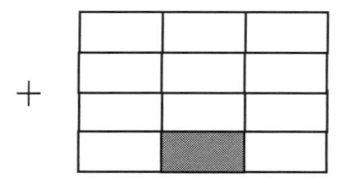

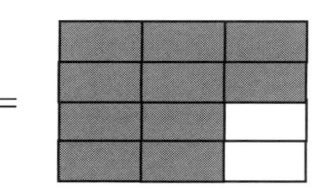

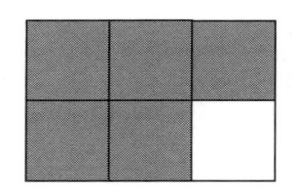

$\frac{9}{12}$ + $\frac{1}{12}$ = $\frac{10}{12}$ = $\frac{5}{6}$

nine-twelfths + twelfth = ten-twelfths = five-sixths

0.75 + 0.08333˙ = 0.8333˙ = 0.8333˙

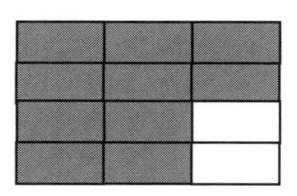

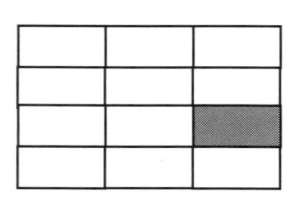

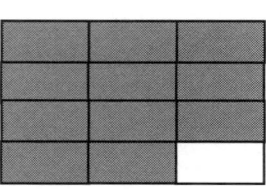

$\frac{10}{12}$ + $\frac{1}{12}$ = $\frac{11}{12}$

ten-twelfths + one-twelfth = eleven-twelfths

0.8333˙ + 0.08333˙ = 0.9166˙

Adding Twelfths

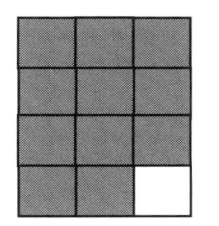

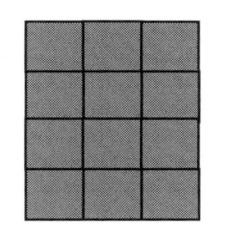

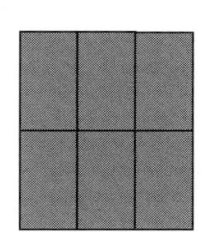

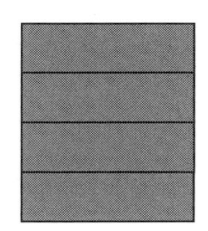

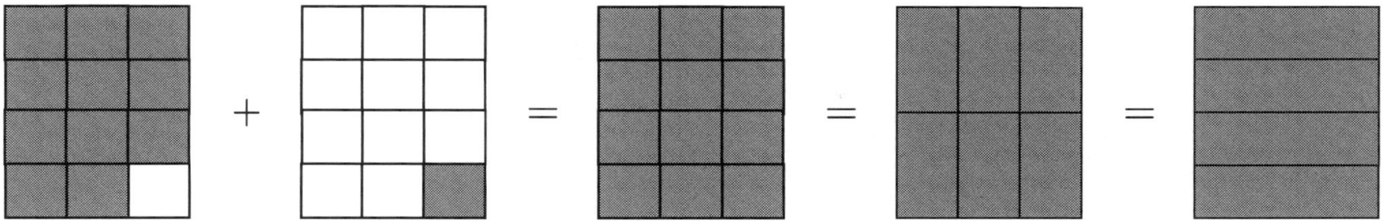

$\frac{11}{12}$ + $\frac{1}{12}$ = $\frac{12}{12}$ = $\frac{6}{6}$ = $\frac{4}{4}$

eleven-twelfths + twelfth = twelve-twelfths = six-sixths = four-quarters

0.916˙ + 0.083˙ = 1.00 = 1.00 = 1.00

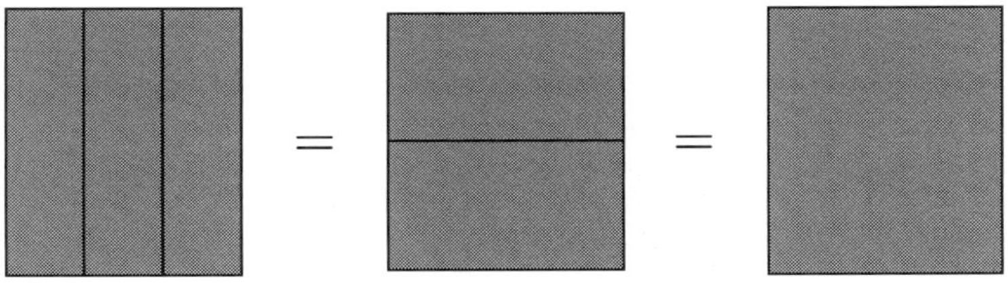

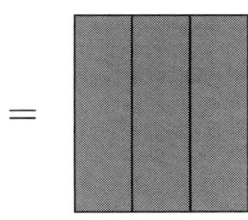

= $\frac{3}{3}$ = $\frac{2}{2}$ = 1

= three-thirds = two-halves = one, whole

= 1.00 = 1.00 = 1

131

Quiz 2

Match each fraction sum with its answers

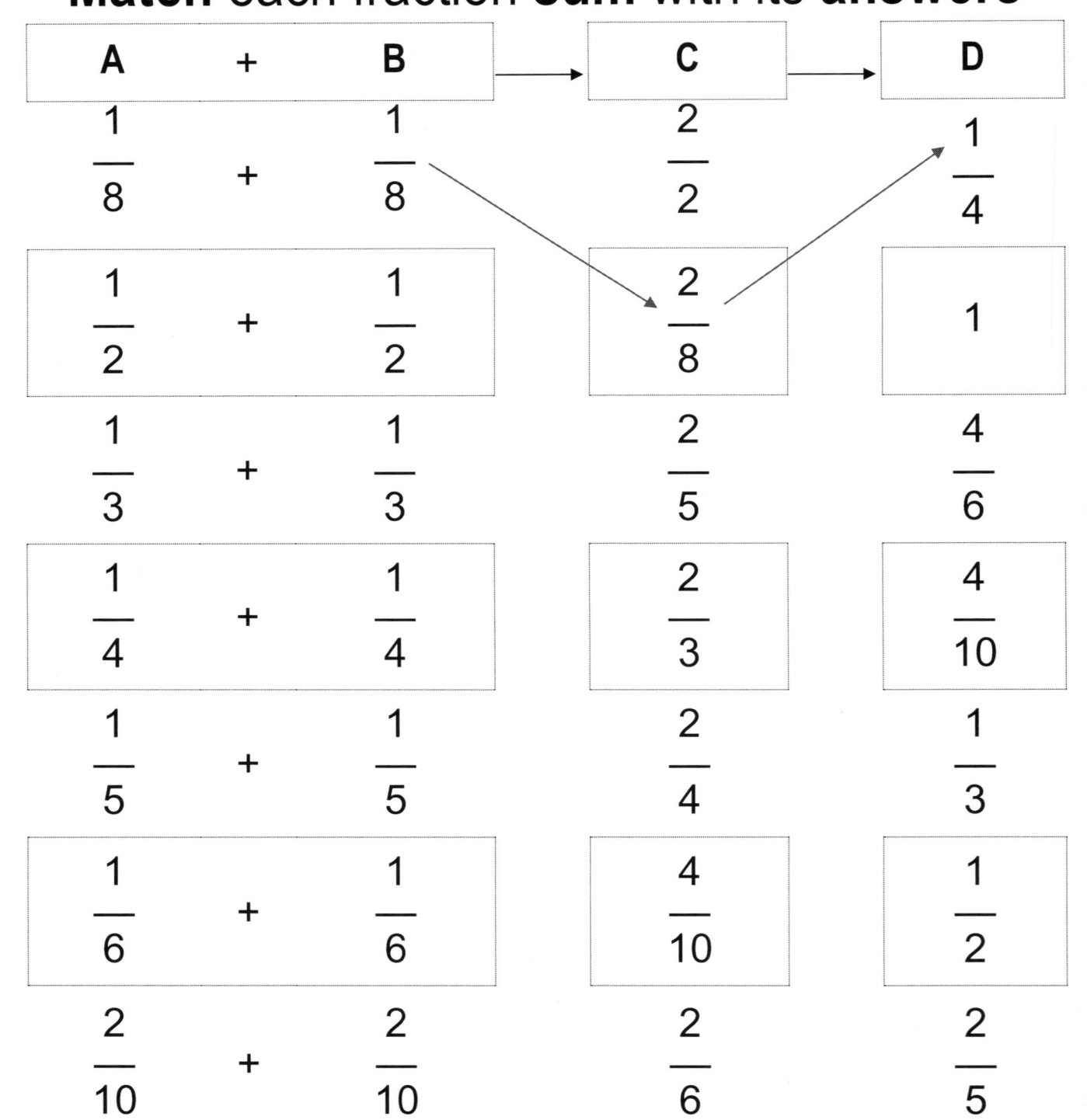

A	+	B	→ C	→ D
$\dfrac{1}{8}$	+	$\dfrac{1}{8}$	$\dfrac{2}{2}$	$\dfrac{1}{4}$
$\dfrac{1}{2}$	+	$\dfrac{1}{2}$	$\dfrac{2}{8}$	1
$\dfrac{1}{3}$	+	$\dfrac{1}{3}$	$\dfrac{2}{5}$	$\dfrac{4}{6}$
$\dfrac{1}{4}$	+	$\dfrac{1}{4}$	$\dfrac{2}{3}$	$\dfrac{4}{10}$
$\dfrac{1}{5}$	+	$\dfrac{1}{5}$	$\dfrac{2}{4}$	$\dfrac{1}{3}$
$\dfrac{1}{6}$	+	$\dfrac{1}{6}$	$\dfrac{4}{10}$	$\dfrac{1}{2}$
$\dfrac{2}{10}$	+	$\dfrac{2}{10}$	$\dfrac{2}{6}$	$\dfrac{2}{5}$

Adding Unlike Fractions

How to add fractions with **different denominators** or unlike bottom numbers. For example,

$$\frac{1}{2} + \frac{2}{4}$$ or

i) First, make the **denominators** (bottom numbers) same!

$$\frac{1}{2} + \frac{2}{4} = \frac{2}{4} + \frac{2}{4} \rightarrow$$

That is, find the **Lowest Common Multiple** (LCM) of the bottom numbers of the fractions to be added. LCM is the *smallest* whole number which each of the denominators will divide exactly into.

LCM can be found using times tables or **multiplication** lists.

Example **a**: Find the LCM of **2** and **4**.

| 2 times table | = | 0 , 2 , **4** , 6 , 8 ... |
| 4 times table | = | 0 , **4** , 8 ... |

4 appears in both 2 and 4 times tables or multiplication lists.
That means it is a **common multiple**.
4 is also the *first* or the **lowest** number to appear in both multiples.
Hence, the **Lowest Common Multiple** (LCM) of 2 and 4 is **4**.

Example **a**-1,

$$\frac{1}{2} + \frac{2}{4} \rightarrow \frac{2}{4} + \frac{2}{4} = \frac{4}{4} = 1.$$

Example **b**: Find the LCM of **4** and **8**.

| x4 table | is | 0 | , | 4 | , | **8** | , | 12 | , | 16 | ... |
| x8 table | is | 0 | , | | , | **8** | , | | , | 16 | ... |

8 is the lowest multiple in both x4 table and x8 table lists.
Therefore, **8** is the LCM of 4 and 8.

Example **b**-1,

$$\frac{1}{4} + \frac{5}{8} \rightarrow \frac{2}{8} + \frac{5}{8} = \frac{7}{8}$$

Example **c**: Find the LCM of **2**, **4** and **8**.

Multiples of 2	are	0	,	2	,	4	,	6	,	8	...
Multiples of 4	are	0	,		,	4	,		,	8	...
Multiples of 8	are	0	,		,		,		,	8	...

8 appears in all multiples of 2, 4 and 8. So, it's a common multiple.
As a result, the LCM of 2, 4 and 8 is **8**.

Example **c**-1,

$$\frac{1}{2} + \frac{1}{4} + \frac{1}{8} \rightarrow \frac{4}{8} + \frac{2}{8} + \frac{1}{8} = \frac{7}{8}$$

Example **d**: Find the LCM of **5** and **10**.

| Multiples of 5 | = | 0 , | 5 , | 10 ... |
| Multiples of 10 | = | 0 , | | 10 ... |

Both multiples of 5 and 10 contain **10**.
Thus, **10** is the Lowest Common Multiple (LCM) of 5 and 10.

Example **d**-1,

$$\frac{2}{5} + \frac{5}{10} \rightarrow \frac{4}{10} + \frac{5}{10} = \frac{9}{10}$$

In examples **a-**1, **b-**1, **c-**1 and **d-**1 the numerator (top number) and denominator (bottom number) of each fraction can be any number! But, for ease of understanding and simplicity, small numbers are used.

Likewise, the LCM of **3** and **6** can be shown to be **6**.
The LCM of **6** and **9** is **18**.
The LCM of **3**, **6** and **9** will be **18**.
And so on.

Example **e**: Find the LCM of **3** and **6**.

| 3 times table | = | 0 , | 3 , | 6 ... |
| 6 times table | = | 0 , | | 6 ... |

6 appears in both 3 and 6 times tables or multiplication lists.
Consequently, the LCM of 3 and 6 is **6**.

Example **e**-1,

$$\frac{1}{3} + \frac{2}{6} \rightarrow \frac{2}{6} + \frac{2}{6} = \frac{4}{6} = \frac{2}{3}$$

Example **f**: Find the LCM of **6** and **9**.

| Multiples of 6 are 0 , 6 , 12 , 18 ... |
| Multiples of 9 are 0 , 9 , 18 ... |

Multiples of 6 and multiples of 9 *first* meet at **18**.
Accordingly, **18** is the LCM of 6 and 9.

Example **f**-1,

$$\frac{1}{6} + \frac{2}{9} \rightarrow \frac{3}{18} + \frac{4}{18} = \frac{7}{18}$$

Example **g**: Find the LCM of **3**, **6** and **9**.

x3 table	is	0 ,	3 ,	6 ,	9 ,	12 ,	15 ,	18 ...
x6 table	is	0 ,		6 ,		12 ,		18 ...
x9 table	is	0 ,			9 ,			18 ...

18 is the first multiple to appear in all x3, x6 and x9 tables. Therefore, the LCM of 3, 6 and 9 is **18**.

Example **g**-1,

$$\frac{1}{3} + \frac{1}{6} + \frac{1}{9} \rightarrow \frac{6}{18} + \frac{3}{18} + \frac{2}{18} = \frac{11}{18}$$

In short;
When all numbers are in the same multiples list or times table, the bigger (or the biggest) number or multiple is their LCM.
For example, 2, 4, 8 all appear in the '2 times table'. LCM = **8**.
5 and 10 are in the 'Multiples of 5' list. LCM = **10**.
3 and 6 appear in the '3 times table'. LCM = **6**.

If, however, all numbers are not in the same times table, then, their LCM is the *first* number at which all their times tables meet.
Example, multiples of 6 and 9 first meet at 18. LCM = **18**.
x3 table, x6 table and x9 table first meet at 18. LCM = **18**.

And so on and so forth.

Adding Unlike Fractions continued

After making the denominators the same, the rest of the process becomes just like **Adding Like Fractions** with **same denominators** as in step i) previously on page 94.

That is converting addend fractions into their equivalent fractions.

ii) Add **numerators** and use the **common** denominator (LCM).

So, $\boxed{\dfrac{2}{4} + \dfrac{2}{4}}$ becomes $\dfrac{4}{4}$ ← **Numerators** addend
← Common **denominator**

i.e. + Changes to

iii) If possible, simplify the result.

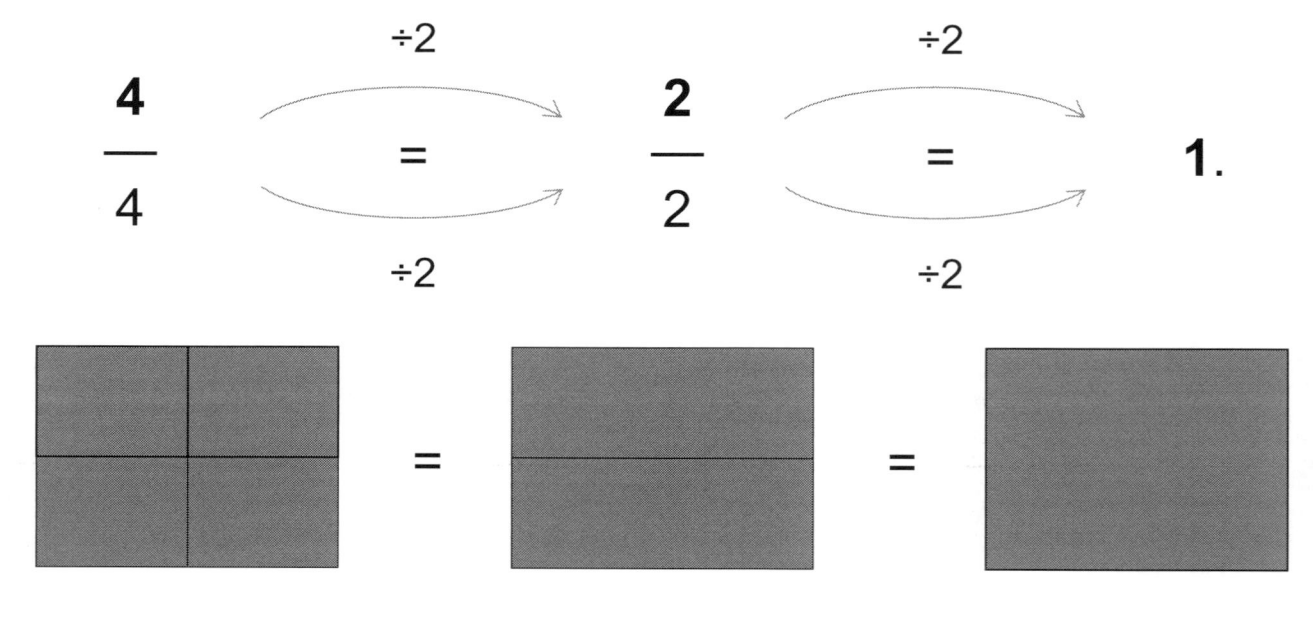

$$\dfrac{4}{4} \xrightarrow[\div 2]{\div 2} = \dfrac{2}{2} \xrightarrow[\div 2]{\div 2} = 1.$$

= =

138

Halves + Quarters

$$\frac{0}{2} + \frac{0}{4} = \frac{0}{4} + \frac{0}{4} = \frac{0}{4} = 0$$

0.00 + 0.00 = 0.00 + 0.00 = 0.00 = 0

$$\frac{1}{2} + \frac{1}{4} = \frac{2}{4} + \frac{1}{4} = \frac{3}{4}$$

0.50 + 0.25 = 0.50 + 0.25 = 0.75

$$\frac{1}{2} + \frac{2}{4} = \frac{2}{4} + \frac{2}{4} = \frac{4}{4} = 1$$

0.50 + 0.50 = 0.50 + 0.50 = 1.00 = 1

Halves + Eighths

$$\frac{0}{2} + \frac{0}{8} = \frac{0}{8} + \frac{0}{8} = \frac{0}{8} = 0$$

0.00 + 0.00 = 0.00 + 0.00 = 0.00 = 0

$$\frac{1}{2} + \frac{1}{8} = \frac{4}{8} + \frac{1}{8} = \frac{5}{8}$$

0.50 + 0.125 = 0.50 + 0.125 = 0.625

$$\frac{1}{2} + \frac{2}{8} = \frac{4}{8} + \frac{2}{8} = \frac{6}{8} = \frac{3}{4}$$

0.50 + 0.25 = 0.50 + 0.25 = 0.75 = 0.75

Halves + Eighths

$$\frac{1}{2} + \frac{3}{8} = \frac{4}{8} + \frac{3}{8} = \frac{7}{8}$$

0.50 + 0.375 = 0.50 + 0.375 = 0.875

$$\frac{1}{2} + \frac{4}{8} = \frac{4}{8} + \frac{4}{8} = \frac{8}{8} = 1$$

0.50 + 0.50 = 0.50 + 0.50 = 1.00 = 1

Quarters + Eighths

$$\frac{1}{4} + \frac{1}{8} = \frac{2}{8} + \frac{1}{8} = \frac{3}{8}$$

0.25 + 0.125 = 0.25 + 0.125 = 0.375

$$\frac{1}{4} + \frac{2}{8} = \frac{2}{8} + \frac{2}{8} = \frac{4}{8} = \frac{2}{4}$$

0.25 + 0.25 = 0.25 + 0.25 = 0.50 = 0.50

$$\frac{1}{4} + \frac{3}{8} = \frac{2}{8} + \frac{3}{8} = \frac{5}{8}$$

0.25 + 0.375 = 0.25 + 0.375 = 0.625

Quarters + Eighths

$$\frac{2}{4} + \frac{1}{8} = \frac{4}{8} + \frac{1}{8} = \frac{5}{8}$$

0.50 + 0.125 = 0.50 + 0.125 = 0.625

$$\frac{1}{4} + \frac{4}{8} = \frac{2}{8} + \frac{4}{8} = \frac{6}{8} = \frac{3}{4}$$

0.25 + 0.50 = 0.25 + 0.50 = 0.75 = 0.75

$$\frac{2}{4} + \frac{2}{8} = \frac{4}{8} + \frac{2}{8} = \frac{6}{8} = \frac{3}{4}$$

0.50 + 0.25 = 0.50 + 0.25 = 0.75 = 0.75

Quarters + Eighths

$$\frac{1}{4} + \frac{5}{8} = \frac{2}{8} + \frac{5}{8} = \frac{7}{8}$$

0.25 + 0.625 = 0.25 + 0.625 = 0.875

$$\frac{2}{4} + \frac{3}{8} = \frac{4}{8} + \frac{3}{8} = \frac{7}{8}$$

0.50 + 0.375 = 0.50 + 0.375 = 0.875

$$\frac{3}{4} + \frac{1}{8} = \frac{6}{8} + \frac{1}{8} = \frac{7}{8}$$

0.75 + 0.125 = 0.75 + 0.125 = 0.875

Quarters + Eighths

$$\frac{1}{4} + \frac{6}{8} = \frac{2}{8} + \frac{6}{8} = \frac{8}{8} = 1$$

0.25 + 0.75 = 0.25 + 0.75 = 1.00 = 1

$$\frac{2}{4} + \frac{4}{8} = \frac{4}{8} + \frac{4}{8} = \frac{8}{8} = 1$$

0.50 + 0.50 = 0.50 + 0.50 = 1.00 = 1

$$\frac{3}{4} + \frac{2}{8} = \frac{6}{8} + \frac{2}{8} = \frac{8}{8} = 1$$

0.75 + 0.25 = 0.75 + 0.25 = 1.00 = 1

Halves + Quarters + Eighths

$$\frac{0}{2} + \frac{0}{4} + \frac{0}{8} = \frac{0}{8} + \frac{0}{8} + \frac{0}{8} = \frac{0}{8}$$

0.00 + 0.00 + 0.00 = 0.00 + 0.00 + 0.00 = 0

$$\frac{1}{2} + \frac{1}{4} + \frac{1}{8} = \frac{4}{8} + \frac{2}{8} + \frac{1}{8} = \frac{7}{8}$$

0.50 + 0.25 + 0.125 = 0.50 + 0.25 + 0.125 = 0.875

$$\frac{1}{2} + \frac{1}{4} + \frac{2}{8} = \frac{4}{8} + \frac{2}{8} + \frac{2}{8} = \frac{8}{8} = 1$$

0.50 + 0.25 + 0.25 = 0.50 + 0.25 + 0.25 = 1.00 = 1

Fifths + Tenths

$$\frac{0}{5} + \frac{0}{10} = \frac{0}{10} + \frac{0}{10} = \frac{0}{10} = 0$$

0.00 + 0.00 = 0.00 + 0.00 = 0.00 = 0

$$\frac{1}{5} + \frac{1}{10} = \frac{2}{10} + \frac{1}{10} = \frac{3}{10}$$

0.20 + 0.10 = 0.20 + 0.10 = 0.30

$$\frac{1}{5} + \frac{2}{10} = \frac{2}{10} + \frac{2}{10} = \frac{4}{10} = \frac{2}{5}$$

0.20 + 0.20 = 0.20 + 0.20 = 0.40 = 0.40

Fifths + Tenths

$$\frac{1}{5} + \frac{3}{10} = \frac{2}{10} + \frac{3}{10} = \frac{5}{10} = \frac{1}{2}$$

0.20 + 0.30 = 0.20 + 0.30 = 0.50 = 0.50

$$\frac{2}{5} + \frac{1}{10} = \frac{4}{10} + \frac{1}{10} = \frac{5}{10} = \frac{1}{2}$$

0.40 + 0.10 = 0.40 + 0.10 = 0.50 = 0.50

$$\frac{1}{5} + \frac{4}{10} = \frac{2}{10} + \frac{4}{10} = \frac{6}{10} = \frac{3}{5}$$

0.20 + 0.40 = 0.20 + 0.40 = 0.60 = 0.60

Fifths + Tenths

$$\frac{2}{5} + \frac{2}{10} = \frac{4}{10} + \frac{2}{10} = \frac{6}{10} = \frac{3}{5}$$

0.40 + 0.20 = 0.40 + 0.20 = 0.60 = 0.60

$$\frac{1}{5} + \frac{5}{10} = \frac{2}{10} + \frac{5}{10} = \frac{7}{10}$$

0.20 + 0.50 = 0.20 + 0.50 = 0.70

$$\frac{2}{5} + \frac{3}{10} = \frac{4}{10} + \frac{3}{10} = \frac{7}{10}$$

0.40 + 0.30 = 0.40 + 0.30 = 0.70

149

Fifths + Tenths

$$\frac{3}{5} + \frac{1}{10} = \frac{6}{10} + \frac{1}{10} = \frac{7}{10}$$

0.60 + 0.10 = 0.60 + 0.10 = 0.70

$$\frac{1}{5} + \frac{6}{10} = \frac{2}{10} + \frac{6}{10} = \frac{8}{10} = \frac{4}{5}$$

0.20 + 0.60 = 0.20 + 0.60 = 0.80 = 0.80

$$\frac{2}{5} + \frac{4}{10} = \frac{4}{10} + \frac{4}{10} = \frac{8}{10} = \frac{4}{5}$$

0.40 + 0.40 = 0.40 + 0.40 = 0.80 = 0.80

Fifths + Tenths

$\dfrac{3}{5} + \dfrac{2}{10} = \dfrac{6}{10} + \dfrac{2}{10} = \dfrac{8}{10} = \dfrac{4}{5}$

0.60 + 0.20 = 0.60 + 0.20 = 0.80 = 0.80

$\dfrac{1}{5} + \dfrac{7}{10} = \dfrac{2}{10} + \dfrac{7}{10} = \dfrac{9}{10}$

0.20 + 0.70 = 0.20 + 0.70 = 0.90

$\dfrac{2}{5} + \dfrac{5}{10} = \dfrac{4}{10} + \dfrac{5}{10} = \dfrac{9}{10}$

0.40 + 0.50 = 0.40 + 0.50 = 0.90

Fifths + Tenths

$\frac{3}{5}$ + $\frac{3}{10}$ = $\frac{6}{10}$ + $\frac{3}{10}$ = $\frac{9}{10}$

0.60 + 0.30 = 0.60 + 0.30 = 0.90

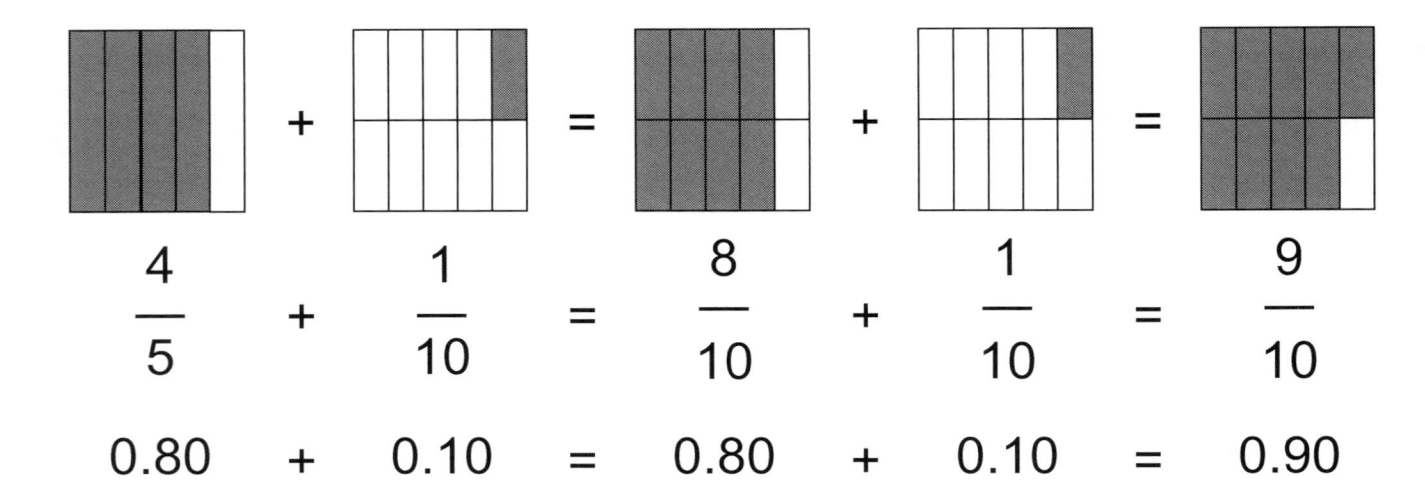

$\frac{4}{5}$ + $\frac{1}{10}$ = $\frac{8}{10}$ + $\frac{1}{10}$ = $\frac{9}{10}$

0.80 + 0.10 = 0.80 + 0.10 = 0.90

$\frac{1}{5}$ + $\frac{8}{10}$ = $\frac{2}{10}$ + $\frac{8}{10}$ = $\frac{10}{10}$ = 1

0.20 + 0.80 = 0.20 + 0.80 = 1.00 = 1

Fifths + Tenths

$\dfrac{2}{5} + \dfrac{6}{10} = \dfrac{4}{10} + \dfrac{6}{10} = \dfrac{10}{10} = 1$

0.40 + 0.60 = 0.40 + 0.60 = 1.00 = 1

$\dfrac{3}{5} + \dfrac{4}{10} = \dfrac{6}{10} + \dfrac{4}{10} = \dfrac{10}{10} = 1$

0.60 + 0.40 = 0.60 + 0.40 = 1.00 = 1

$\dfrac{4}{5} + \dfrac{2}{10} = \dfrac{8}{10} + \dfrac{2}{10} = \dfrac{10}{10} = 1$

0.80 + 0.20 = 0.80 + 0.20 = 1.00 = 1

Thirds + Sixths

$$\frac{1}{3} + \frac{1}{6} = \frac{2}{6} + \frac{1}{6} = \frac{3}{6} = \frac{1}{2}$$

$$0.\dot{3} + 0.1\dot{6} = 0.\dot{3} + 0.1\dot{6} = 0.50 = 0.50$$

$$\frac{1}{3} + \frac{2}{6} = \frac{2}{6} + \frac{2}{6} = \frac{4}{6} = \frac{2}{3}$$

$$0.\dot{3} + 0.\dot{3} = 0.\dot{3} + 0.\dot{3} = 0.\dot{6} = 0.\dot{6}$$

Thirds + Sixths

$$\frac{1}{3} + \frac{3}{6} = \frac{2}{6} + \frac{3}{6} = \frac{5}{6}$$

0.3˙ + 0.50 = 0.3˙ + 0.50 = 0.83˙

$$\frac{2}{3} + \frac{1}{6} = \frac{4}{6} + \frac{1}{6} = \frac{5}{6}$$

0.6˙ + 0.16˙ = 0.6˙ + 0.16˙ = 0.83˙

Thirds + Sixths

$$\frac{1}{3} + \frac{4}{6} = \frac{2}{6} + \frac{4}{6} = \frac{6}{6} = 1$$

$$0.3\dot{} + 0.6\dot{} = 0.3\dot{} + 0.6\dot{} = 1.00 = 1$$

$$\frac{2}{3} + \frac{2}{6} = \frac{4}{6} + \frac{2}{6} = \frac{6}{6} = 1$$

$$0.6\dot{} + 0.3\dot{} = 0.6\dot{} + 0.3\dot{} = 1.00 = 1$$

Thirds + Ninths

$$\frac{0}{3} + \frac{0}{9} = \frac{0}{9} + \frac{0}{9} = \frac{0}{9} = 0$$

0.00 + 0.00 = 0.00 + 0.00 = 0.00 = 0

$$\frac{1}{3} + \frac{1}{9} = \frac{3}{9} + \frac{1}{9} = \frac{4}{9}$$

0.3˙ + 0.1˙ = 0.3˙ + 0.1˙ = 0.4˙

157

Thirds + Ninths

$$\frac{1}{3} + \frac{2}{9} = \frac{3}{9} + \frac{2}{9} = \frac{5}{9}$$

0.3˙ + 0.2˙ = 0.3˙ + 0.2˙ = 0.5˙

$$\frac{1}{3} + \frac{3}{9} = \frac{3}{9} + \frac{3}{9} = \frac{6}{9} = \frac{2}{3}$$

0.3˙ + 0.3˙ = 0.3˙ + 0.3˙ = 0.6˙ = 0.6˙

Thirds + Ninths

$$\frac{1}{3} + \frac{4}{9} = \frac{3}{9} + \frac{4}{9} = \frac{7}{9}$$

$$0.\dot{3} + 0.\dot{4} = 0.\dot{3} + 0.\dot{4} = 0.\dot{7}$$

$$\frac{2}{3} + \frac{1}{9} = \frac{6}{9} + \frac{1}{9} = \frac{7}{9}$$

$$0.\dot{6} + 0.\dot{1} = 0.\dot{6} + 0.\dot{1} = 0.\dot{7}$$

Thirds + Ninths

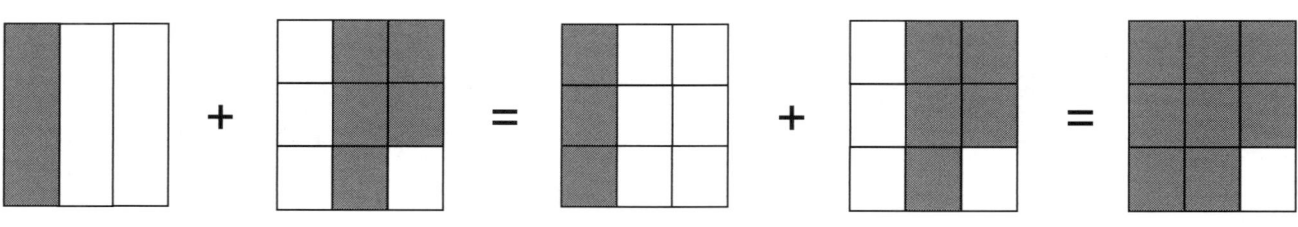

$$\frac{1}{3} + \frac{5}{9} = \frac{3}{9} + \frac{5}{9} = \frac{8}{9}$$

0.3˙ + 0.5˙ = 0.3˙ + 0.5˙ = 0.8˙

$$\frac{2}{3} + \frac{2}{9} = \frac{6}{9} + \frac{2}{9} = \frac{8}{9}$$

0.6˙ + 0.2˙ = 0.6˙ + 0.2˙ = 0.8˙

Thirds + Ninths

$$\frac{1}{3} + \frac{6}{9} = \frac{3}{9} + \frac{6}{9} = \frac{9}{9} = 1$$

$$0.\dot{3} + 0.\dot{6} = 0.\dot{3} + 0.\dot{6} = 1.00 = 1$$

$$\frac{2}{3} + \frac{3}{9} = \frac{6}{9} + \frac{3}{9} = \frac{9}{9} = 1$$

$$0.\dot{6} + 0.\dot{3} = 0.\dot{6} + 0.\dot{3} = 1.00 = 1$$

Sixths + Ninths

$$\frac{0}{6} + \frac{0}{9} = \frac{0}{18} + \frac{0}{18} = \frac{0}{18} = 0$$

0.00 + 0.00 = 0.00 + 0.00 = 0.00 = 0

$$\frac{1}{6} + \frac{1}{9} = \frac{3}{18} + \frac{2}{18} = \frac{5}{18}$$

0.16˙ + 0.1˙ = 0.16˙ + 0.1˙ = 0.27˙

Sixths + Ninths

$$\frac{1}{6} + \frac{2}{9} = \frac{3}{18} + \frac{4}{18} = \frac{7}{18}$$

$$0.1\dot{6} \;+\; 0.\dot{2} \;=\; 0.1\dot{6} \;+\; 0.\dot{2} \;=\; 0.3\dot{8}$$

$$\frac{2}{6} + \frac{1}{9} = \frac{6}{18} + \frac{2}{18} = \frac{8}{18} = \frac{4}{9}$$

$$0.\dot{3} \;+\; 0.\dot{1} \;=\; 0.\dot{3} \;+\; 0.\dot{1} \;=\; 0.\dot{4} \;=\; 0.\dot{4}$$

Sixths + Ninths

$$\frac{1}{6} + \frac{3}{9} = \frac{3}{18} + \frac{6}{18} = \frac{9}{18} = \frac{1}{2}$$

$$0.1\dot{6} + 0.\dot{3} = 0.1\dot{6} + 0.\dot{3} = 0.50 = 0.50$$

$$\frac{2}{6} + \frac{2}{9} = \frac{6}{18} + \frac{4}{18} = \frac{10}{18} = \frac{5}{9}$$

$$0.\dot{3} + 0.\dot{2} = 0.\dot{3} + 0.\dot{2} = 0.\dot{5} = 0.\dot{5}$$

Sixths + Ninths

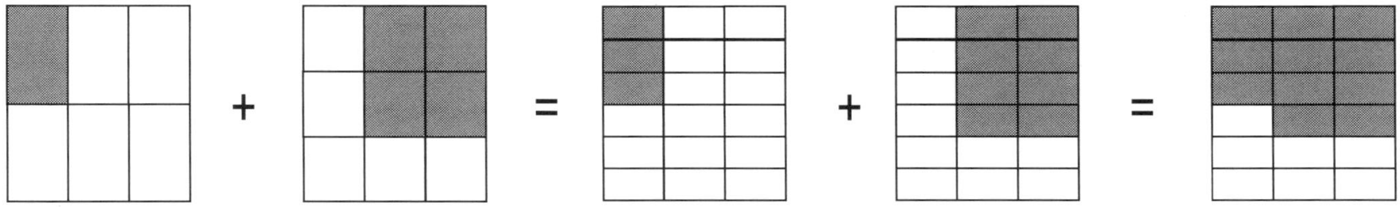

$$\frac{1}{6} + \frac{4}{9} = \frac{3}{18} + \frac{8}{18} = \frac{11}{18}$$

$$0.16\dot{} \;+\; 0.\dot{4} \;=\; 0.16\dot{} \;+\; 0.\dot{4} \;=\; 0.6\dot{1}$$

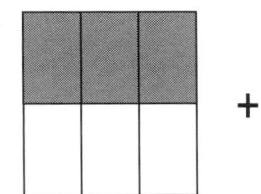

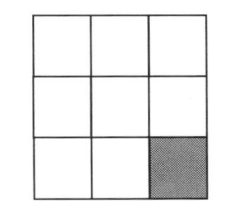

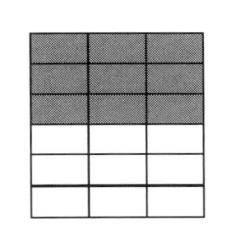

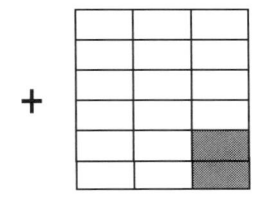

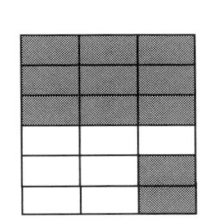

$$\frac{3}{6} + \frac{1}{9} = \frac{9}{18} + \frac{2}{18} = \frac{11}{18}$$

$$0.50 \;+\; 0.\dot{1} \;=\; 0.50 \;+\; 0.\dot{1} \;=\; 0.6\dot{1}$$

Sixths + Ninths

$$\frac{2}{6} + \frac{3}{9} = \frac{6}{18} + \frac{6}{18} = \frac{12}{18} = \frac{2}{3}$$

0.3˙ + 0.3˙ = 0.3˙ + 0.3˙ = 0.6˙ = 0.6˙

$$\frac{1}{6} + \frac{5}{9} = \frac{3}{18} + \frac{10}{18} = \frac{13}{18}$$

0.16˙ + 0.5˙ = 0.16˙ + 0.5˙ = 0.72˙

Sixths + Ninths

$$\frac{3}{6} + \frac{2}{9} = \frac{9}{18} + \frac{4}{18} = \frac{13}{18}$$

0.50 + 0.2˙ = 0.50 + 0.2˙ = 0.72˙

$$\frac{2}{6} + \frac{4}{9} = \frac{6}{18} + \frac{8}{18} = \frac{14}{18} = \frac{7}{9}$$

0.3˙ + 0.4˙ = 0.3˙ + 0.4˙ = 0.7˙ = 0.7˙

Sixths + Ninths

$$\frac{4}{6} + \frac{1}{9} = \frac{12}{18} + \frac{2}{18} = \frac{14}{18} = \frac{7}{9}$$

$$0.\dot{6} + 0.\dot{1} = 0.\dot{6} + 0.\dot{1} = 0.\dot{7} = 0.\dot{7}$$

$$\frac{1}{6} + \frac{6}{9} = \frac{3}{18} + \frac{12}{18} = \frac{15}{18} = \frac{5}{6}$$

$$0.1\dot{6} + 0.\dot{6} = 0.1\dot{6} + 0.\dot{6} = 0.8\dot{3} = 0.8\dot{3}$$

Sixths + Ninths

$$\frac{3}{6} + \frac{3}{9} = \frac{9}{18} + \frac{6}{18} = \frac{15}{18} = \frac{5}{6}$$

0.50 + 0.3˙ = 0.50 + 0.3˙ = 0.83˙ = 0.83˙

$$\frac{2}{6} + \frac{5}{9} = \frac{6}{18} + \frac{10}{18} = \frac{16}{18} = \frac{8}{9}$$

0.3˙ + 0.5˙ = 0.3˙ + 0.5˙ = 0.8˙ = 0.8˙

Sixths + Ninths

$$\frac{4}{6} + \frac{2}{9} = \frac{12}{18} + \frac{4}{18} = \frac{16}{18} = \frac{8}{9}$$

0.6˙ + 0.2˙ = 0.6˙ + 0.2˙ = 0.8˙ = 0.8˙

$$\frac{1}{6} + \frac{7}{9} = \frac{3}{18} + \frac{14}{18} = \frac{17}{18}$$

0.16˙ + 0.7˙ = 0.16˙ + 0.7˙ = 0.94˙

Sixths + Ninths

$$\frac{3}{6} + \frac{4}{9} = \frac{9}{18} + \frac{8}{18} = \frac{17}{18}$$

$$0.50 \;+\; 0.\dot{4} \;=\; 0.50 \;+\; 0.\dot{4} \;=\; 0.9\dot{4}$$

$$\frac{5}{6} + \frac{1}{9} = \frac{15}{18} + \frac{2}{18} = \frac{17}{18}$$

$$0.8\dot{3} \;+\; 0.\dot{1} \;=\; 0.8\dot{3} \;+\; 0.\dot{1} \;=\; 0.9\dot{4}$$

Sixths + Ninths

$$\frac{2}{6} + \frac{6}{9} = \frac{6}{18} + \frac{12}{18} = \frac{18}{18} = 1$$

$$0.\dot{3} + 0.\dot{6} = 0.\dot{3} + 0.\dot{6} = 1.00 = 1$$

$$\frac{4}{6} + \frac{3}{9} = \frac{12}{18} + \frac{6}{18} = \frac{18}{18} = 1$$

$$0.\dot{6} + 0.\dot{3} = 0.\dot{6} + 0.\dot{3} = 1.00 = 1$$

Thirds + Sixths + Ninths

$$\frac{0}{3} + \frac{0}{6} + \frac{0}{9} = \frac{0}{18} + \frac{0}{18} + \frac{0}{18} = \frac{0}{18} = 0$$

$$0.00 + 0.00 + 0.00 = 0.00 + 0.00 + 0.00 = 0.00 = 0.00$$

$$\frac{1}{3} + \frac{1}{6} + \frac{1}{9} = \frac{6}{18} + \frac{3}{18} + \frac{2}{18} = \frac{11}{18}$$

$$0.\dot{3} + 0.1\dot{6} + 0.\dot{1} = 0.\dot{3} + 0.1\dot{6} + 0.\dot{1} = 0.6\dot{1}$$

173

Thirds + Sixths + Ninths

$$\frac{1}{3} + \frac{1}{6} + \frac{2}{9} = \frac{6}{18} + \frac{3}{18} + \frac{4}{18} = \frac{13}{18}$$

$$0.\dot{3} + 0.1\dot{6} + 0.\dot{2} = 0.\dot{3} + 0.1\dot{6} + 0.\dot{2} = 0.7\dot{2}$$

$$\frac{1}{3} + \frac{2}{6} + \frac{1}{9} = \frac{6}{18} + \frac{6}{18} + \frac{2}{18} = \frac{14}{18} = \frac{7}{9}$$

$$0.\dot{3} + 0.\dot{3} + 0.\dot{1} = 0.\dot{3} + 0.\dot{3} + 0.\dot{1} = 0.\dot{7} = 0.\dot{7}$$

Thirds + Sixths + Ninths

$$\frac{1}{3} + \frac{1}{6} + \frac{3}{9} = \frac{6}{18} + \frac{3}{18} + \frac{6}{18} = \frac{15}{18} = \frac{5}{6}$$

$$0.\dot{3} + 0.1\dot{6} + 0.\dot{3} = 0.\dot{3} + 0.1\dot{6} + 0.\dot{3} = 0.8\dot{3} = 0.8\dot{3}$$

$$\frac{1}{3} + \frac{2}{6} + \frac{2}{9} = \frac{6}{18} + \frac{6}{18} + \frac{4}{18} = \frac{16}{18} = \frac{8}{9}$$

$$0.\dot{3} + 0.\dot{3} + 0.\dot{2} = 0.\dot{3} + 0.\dot{3} + 0.\dot{2} = 0.\dot{8} = 0.\dot{8}$$

Thirds + Sixths + Ninths

$$\frac{1}{3} + \frac{1}{6} + \frac{4}{9} = \frac{6}{18} + \frac{3}{18} + \frac{8}{18} = \frac{17}{18}$$

$$0.\overline{3} + 0.1\overline{6} + 0.\overline{4} = 0.\overline{3} + 0.1\overline{6} + 0.\overline{4} = 0.9\overline{4}$$

$$\frac{1}{3} + \frac{3}{6} + \frac{1}{9} = \frac{6}{18} + \frac{9}{18} + \frac{2}{18} = \frac{17}{18}$$

$$0.\overline{3} + 0.50 + 0.\overline{1} = 0.\overline{3} + 0.50 + 0.\overline{1} = 0.9\overline{4}$$

Thirds + Sixths + Ninths

$$\frac{2}{3} + \frac{1}{6} + \frac{1}{9} = \frac{12}{18} + \frac{3}{18} + \frac{2}{18} = \frac{17}{18}$$

$$0.\dot{6} + 0.1\dot{6} + 0.\dot{1} = 0.\dot{6} + 0.1\dot{6} + 0.\dot{1} = 0.9\dot{4}$$

$$\frac{1}{3} + \frac{2}{6} + \frac{3}{9} = \frac{6}{18} + \frac{6}{18} + \frac{6}{18} = \frac{18}{18} = 1$$

$$0.\dot{3} + 0.\dot{3} + 0.\dot{3} = 0.\dot{3} + 0.\dot{3} + 0.\dot{3} = 1.00 = 1$$

Halves + Thirds + Sixths

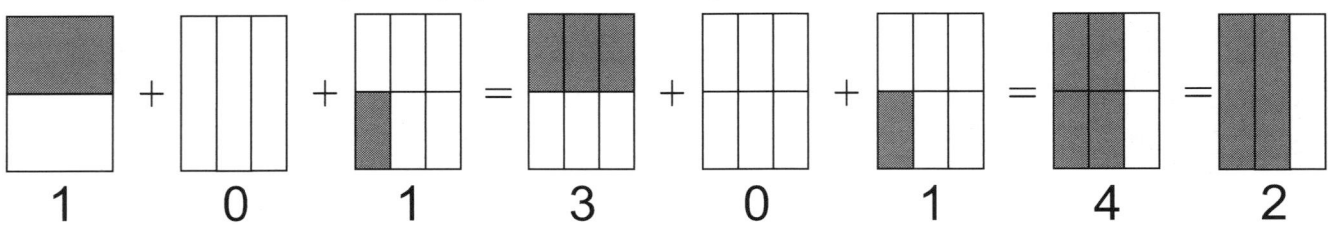

$$\frac{1}{2} + \frac{0}{3} + \frac{1}{6} = \frac{3}{6} + \frac{0}{6} + \frac{1}{6} = \frac{4}{6} = \frac{2}{3}$$

0.50 + 0.00 + 0.16 = 0.50 + 0.00 + 0.16 = 0.66 = 0.66

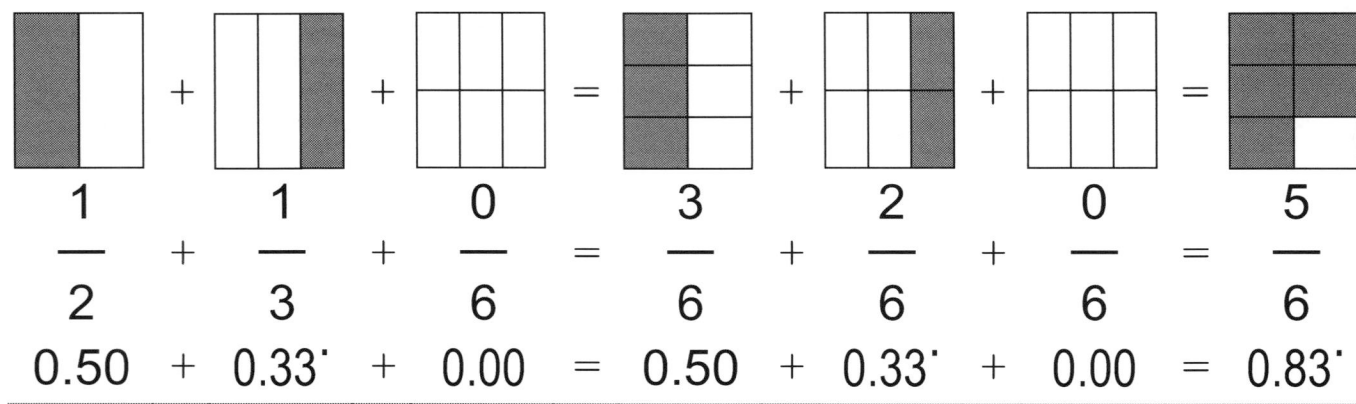

$$\frac{1}{2} + \frac{1}{3} + \frac{0}{6} = \frac{3}{6} + \frac{2}{6} + \frac{0}{6} = \frac{5}{6}$$

0.50 + 0.33˙ + 0.00 = 0.50 + 0.33˙ + 0.00 = 0.83˙

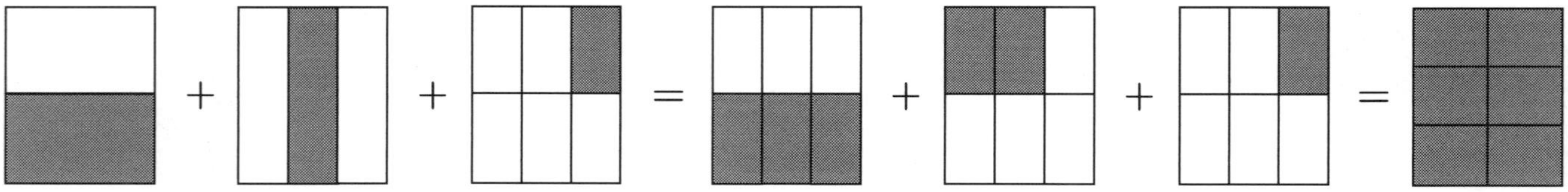

$$\frac{1}{2} + \frac{1}{3} + \frac{1}{6} = \frac{3}{6} + \frac{2}{6} + \frac{1}{6} = \frac{6}{6}$$

0.50 + 0.33˙ + 0.16˙ = 0.50 + 0.33˙ + 0.16˙ = 1.00

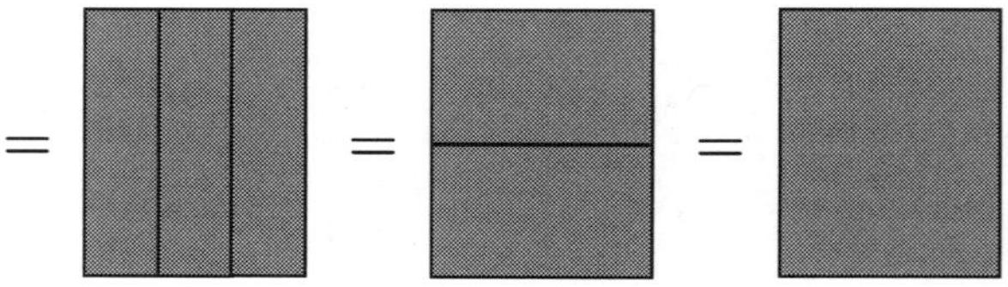

$$= \frac{3}{3} = \frac{2}{2} = 1$$

= 1.00 = 1.00 = 1.00

Halves + Quarters + Twelfths

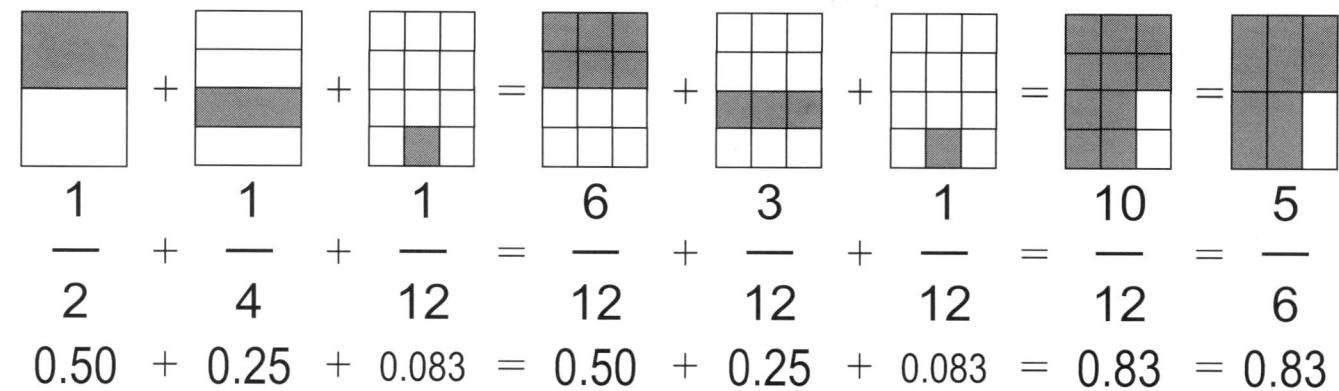

$$\frac{1}{2} + \frac{1}{4} + \frac{1}{12} = \frac{6}{12} + \frac{3}{12} + \frac{1}{12} = \frac{10}{12} = \frac{5}{6}$$

$$0.50 + 0.25 + 0.083 = 0.50 + 0.25 + 0.083 = 0.83 = 0.83$$

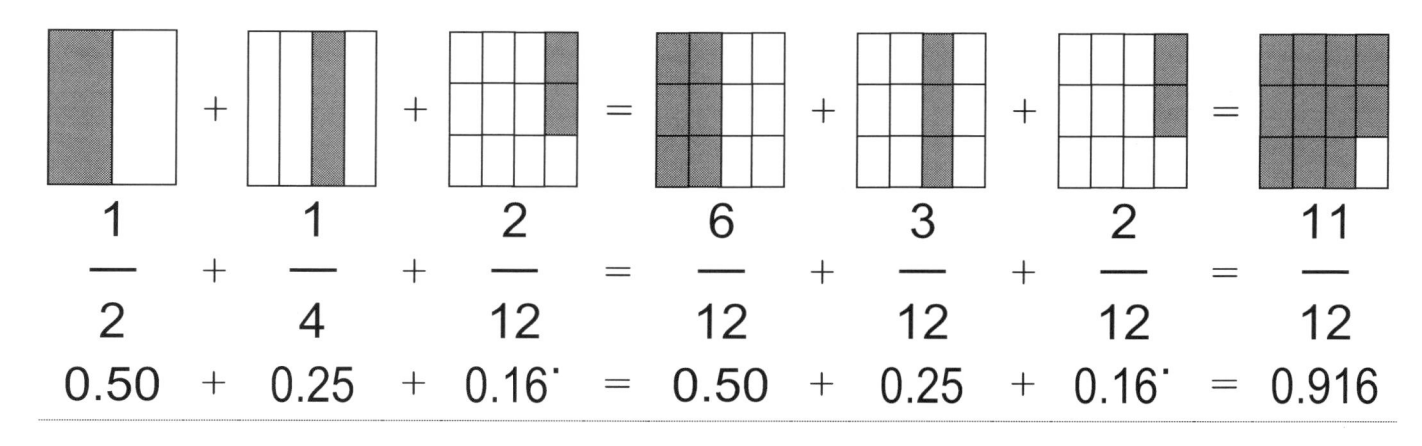

$$\frac{1}{2} + \frac{1}{4} + \frac{2}{12} = \frac{6}{12} + \frac{3}{12} + \frac{2}{12} = \frac{11}{12}$$

$$0.50 + 0.25 + 0.16\dot{} = 0.50 + 0.25 + 0.16\dot{} = 0.916$$

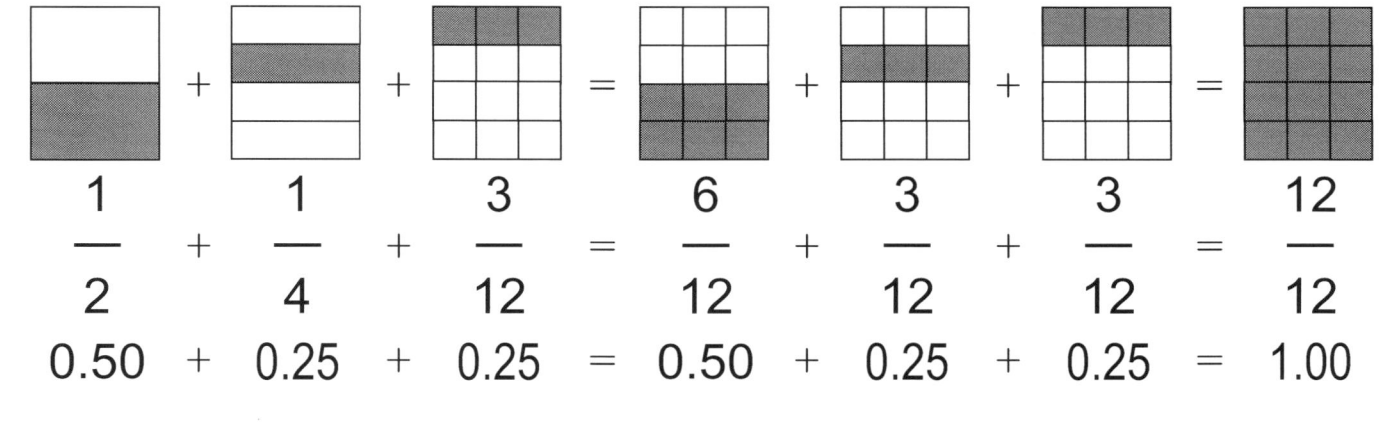

$$\frac{1}{2} + \frac{1}{4} + \frac{3}{12} = \frac{6}{12} + \frac{3}{12} + \frac{3}{12} = \frac{12}{12}$$

$$0.50 + 0.25 + 0.25 = 0.50 + 0.25 + 0.25 = 1.00$$

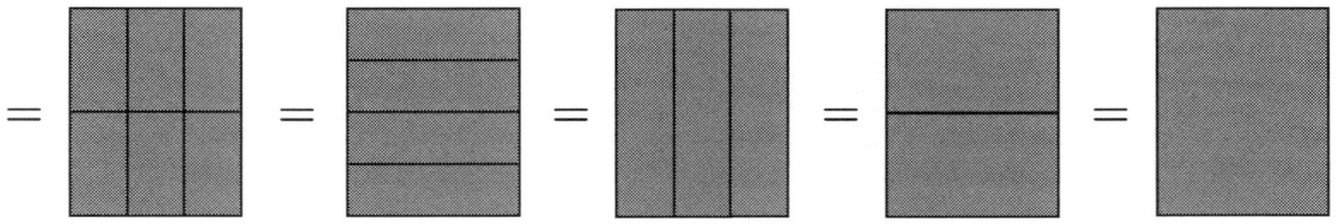

$$= \frac{6}{6} = \frac{4}{4} = \frac{3}{3} = \frac{2}{2} = 1$$

$$= 1.00 = 1.00 = 1.00 = 1.00 = 1$$

Thirds + Sixths + Twelfths

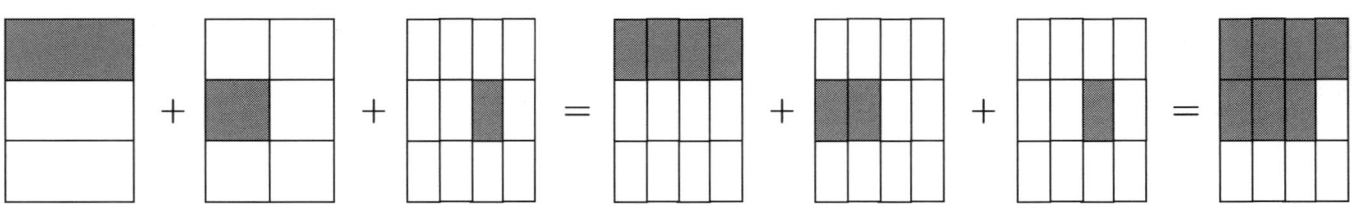

$$\frac{1}{3} + \frac{1}{6} + \frac{1}{12} = \frac{4}{12} + \frac{2}{12} + \frac{1}{12} = \frac{7}{12}$$

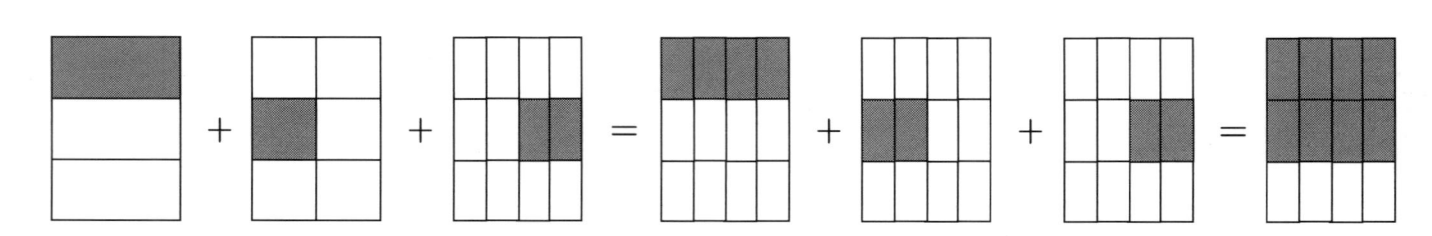

$$0.33\dot{} + 0.16\dot{} + 0.083 = 0.33\dot{} + 0.16\dot{} + 0.083 = 0.583$$

$$\frac{1}{3} + \frac{1}{6} + \frac{2}{12} = \frac{4}{12} + \frac{2}{12} + \frac{2}{12} = \frac{8}{12}$$

$$0.33\dot{} + 0.16\dot{} + 0.16\dot{} = 0.33\dot{} + 0.16\dot{} + 0.16\dot{} = 0.66\dot{}$$

$$= \frac{4}{6} = \frac{2}{3}$$

$$= 0.66\dot{} = 0.66\dot{}$$

Thirds + Sixths + Twelfth

$$\frac{1}{3} + \frac{1}{6} + \frac{3}{12} = \frac{4}{12} + \frac{2}{12} + \frac{3}{12} = \frac{9}{12} = \frac{3}{4}$$

$0.3˙ + 0.16 + 0.25 = 0.3˙ + 0.16 + 0.25 = 0.75 = 0.75$

$$\frac{1}{3} + \frac{2}{6} + \frac{1}{12} = \frac{4}{12} + \frac{4}{12} + \frac{1}{12} = \frac{9}{12} = \frac{3}{4}$$

$0.3˙ + 0.3˙ + 0.083 = 0.3˙ + 0.3˙ + 0.083 = 0.75 = 0.75$

$$\frac{1}{3} + \frac{1}{6} + \frac{4}{12} = \frac{4}{12} + \frac{2}{12} + \frac{4}{12} = \frac{10}{12} = \frac{5}{8}$$

$0.3˙ + 0.16 + 0.3˙ = 0.3˙ + 0.16 + 0.3˙ = 0.83 = 0.83$

Thirds + Sixths + Twelfth

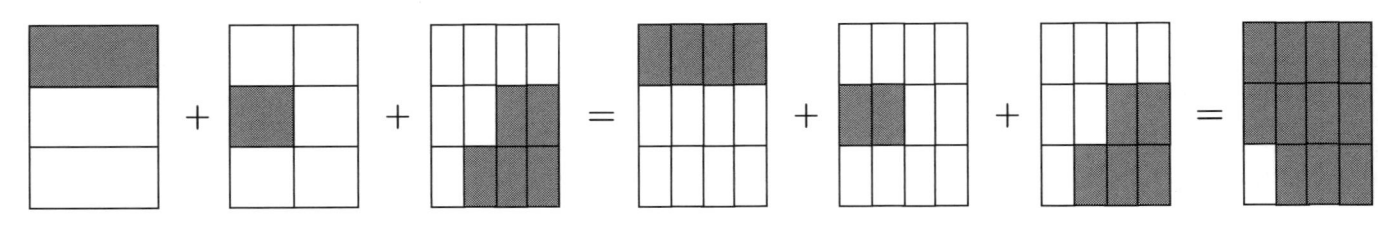

$$\frac{1}{3} + \frac{1}{6} + \frac{5}{12} = \frac{4}{12} + \frac{2}{12} + \frac{5}{12} = \frac{11}{12}$$

0.33˙ + 0.16˙ + 0.416 = 0.33˙ + 0.16˙ + 0.416 = 0.916

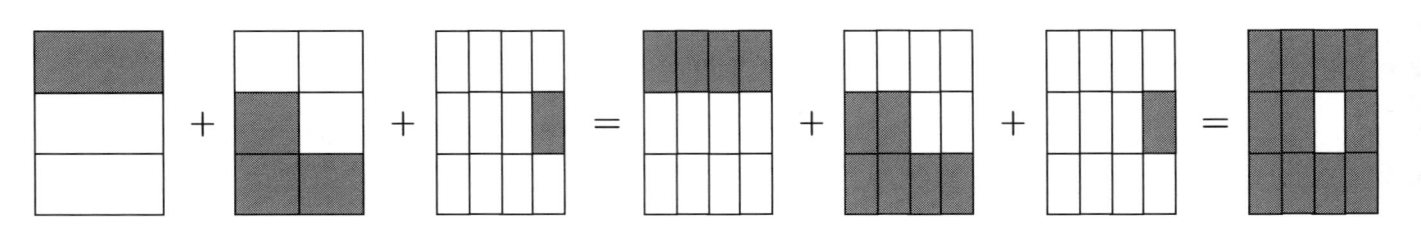

$$\frac{1}{3} + \frac{3}{6} + \frac{1}{12} = \frac{4}{12} + \frac{6}{12} + \frac{1}{12} = \frac{11}{12}$$

0.33˙ + 0.50 + 0.083 = 0.33˙ + 0.50 + 0.083 = 0.916

$$\frac{2}{3} + \frac{1}{6} + \frac{1}{12} = \frac{8}{12} + \frac{2}{12} + \frac{1}{12} = \frac{11}{12}$$

0.66˙ + 0.16˙ + 0.083 = 0.66˙ + 0.16˙ + 0.083 = 0.916

Thirds + Sixths + Twelfth

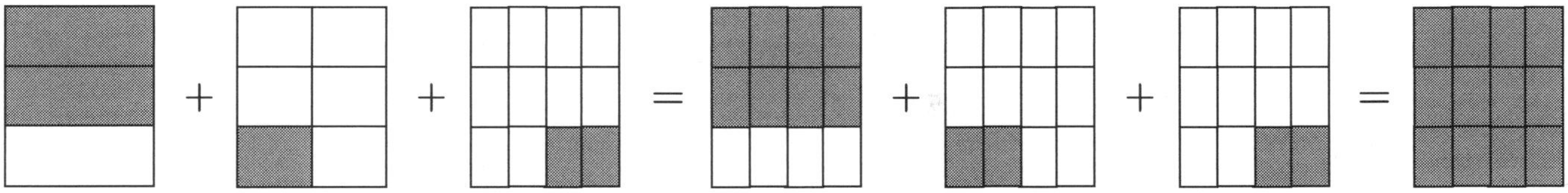

$$\frac{2}{3} + \frac{1}{6} + \frac{2}{12} = \frac{8}{12} + \frac{2}{12} + \frac{2}{12} = \frac{12}{12}$$

0.66˙ + 0.16˙ + 0.16˙ = 0.66˙ + 0.16˙ + 0.16˙ = 1.00

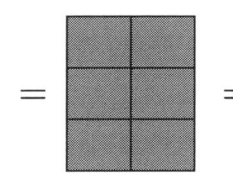

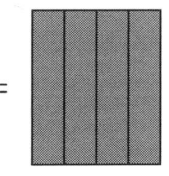

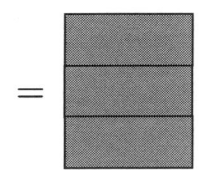

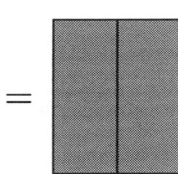

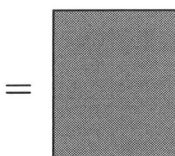

$$= \frac{6}{6} = \frac{4}{4} = \frac{3}{3} = \frac{2}{2} = 1$$

= 1.00 = 1.00 = 1.00 = 1.00 = 1

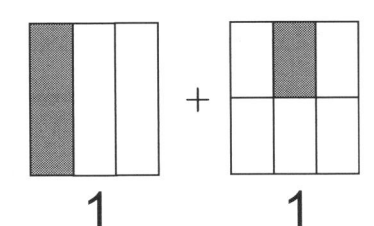

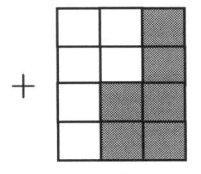

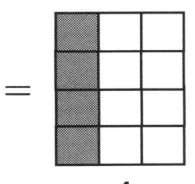

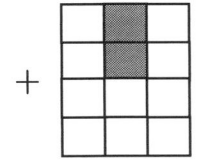

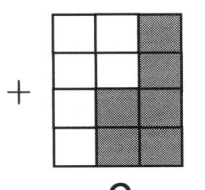

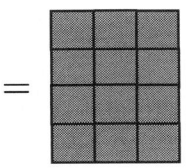

$$\frac{1}{3} + \frac{1}{6} + \frac{6}{12} = \frac{4}{12} + \frac{2}{12} + \frac{6}{12} = \frac{12}{12}$$

0.33˙ + 0.16˙ + 0.50 = 0.33˙ + 0.16˙ + 0.50 = 1.00

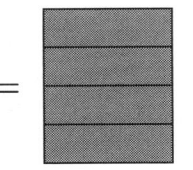

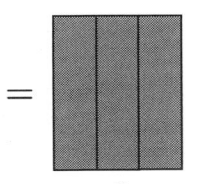

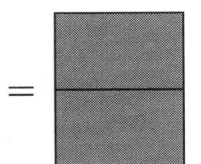

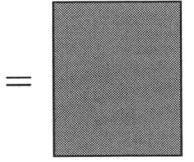

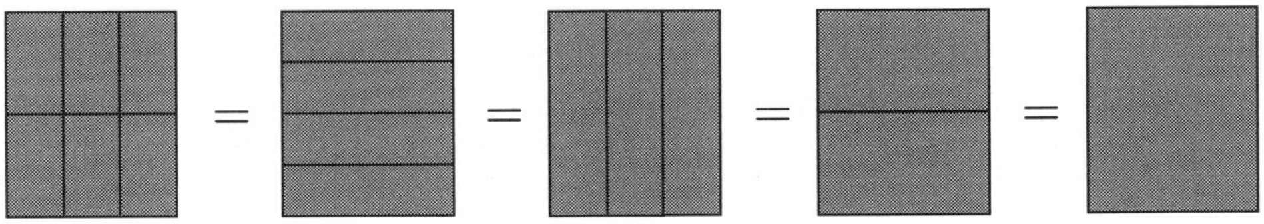

$$= \frac{6}{6} = \frac{4}{4} = \frac{3}{3} = \frac{2}{2} = 1$$

= 1.00 = 1.00 = 1.00 = 1.00 = 1

Subtracting Fractions Visually

Subtracting Like Fractions

How to subtract fractions with **same denominators**:

Example, $\dfrac{3}{4} - \dfrac{1}{4}$ or ▢ − ▢

i) Subtract numerators as normal.

$\dfrac{3}{-} - \dfrac{1}{-} = \dfrac{2}{-}$ → ▢ − ▢ = ▢

ii) Use the **common** denominator which the fractions share.

So, $\dfrac{3}{-} - \dfrac{1}{-} = \dfrac{2}{-}$ becomes $\dfrac{2}{4}$ ← **numerators** subtrahend
← common **denominator**

$\dfrac{3}{4} - \dfrac{1}{4} = \dfrac{2}{4}$ → ▢ − ▢ = ▢

The **denominator** stays the **same** - not subtracted like numerators!
The result is a fraction with the **same denominator** as the original fractions.

iii) If possible, simplify the result by dividing both the numerator and denominator by the same **factor** (number). For instance,

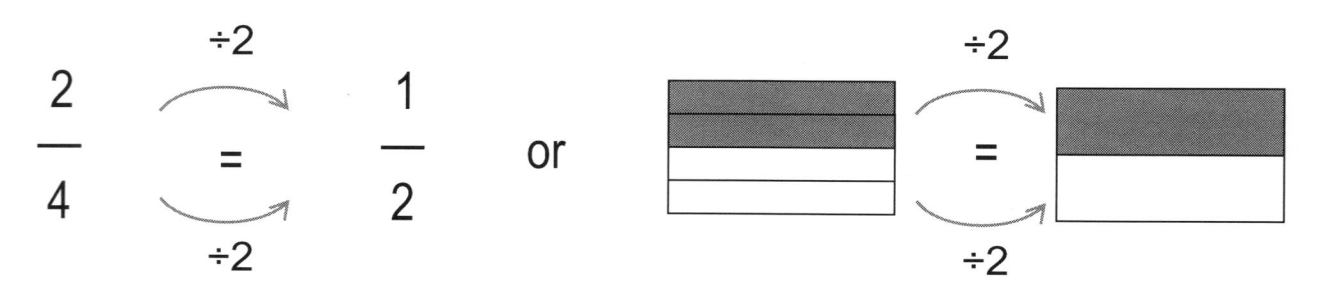

$\dfrac{2}{4} = \dfrac{1}{2}$ (÷2 / ÷2) or ▢ = ▢ (÷2 / ÷2)

Subtracting Halves

$\dfrac{2}{2}$ − $\dfrac{0}{2}$ = $\dfrac{2}{2}$ = 1

two-halves − nothing = two-halves = one-whole

1.00 − 0.00 = 1.00 = 1

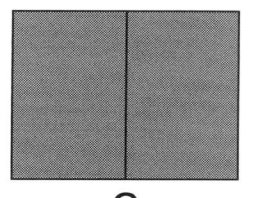

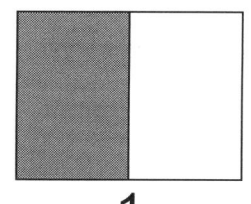

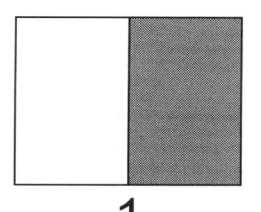

$\dfrac{2}{2}$ − $\dfrac{1}{2}$ = $\dfrac{1}{2}$

two-halves − one-half = one-half

1.00 − 0.50 = 0.50

$\dfrac{1}{2}$ − $\dfrac{1}{2}$ = $\dfrac{0}{2}$ = $\dfrac{0}{1}$

half − half = nothing = nothing

0.50 − 0.50 = 0.00 = 0

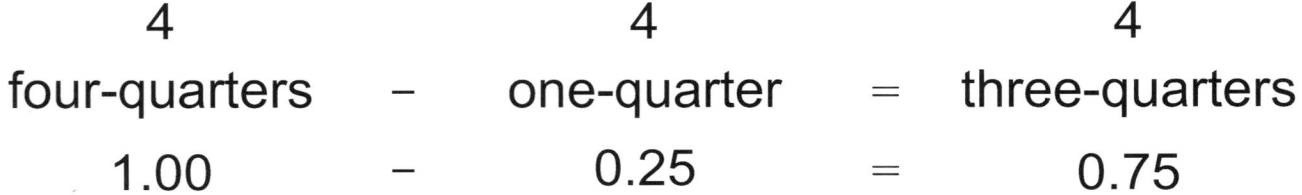

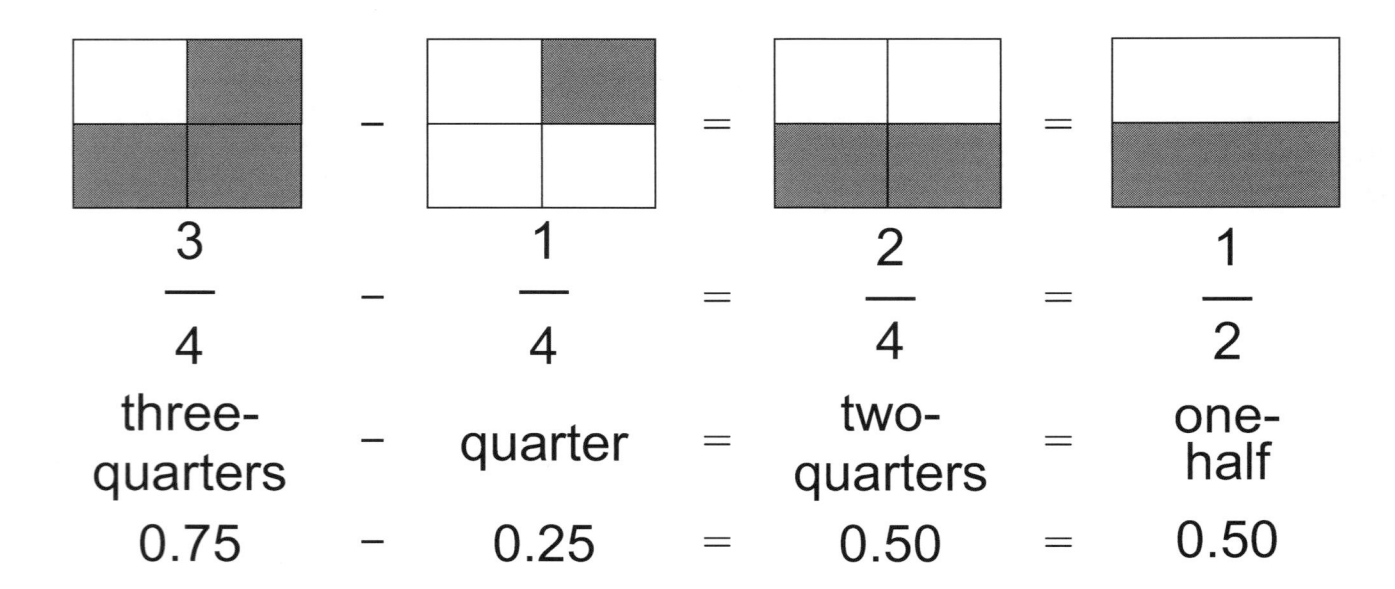

Subtracting **Quarters**

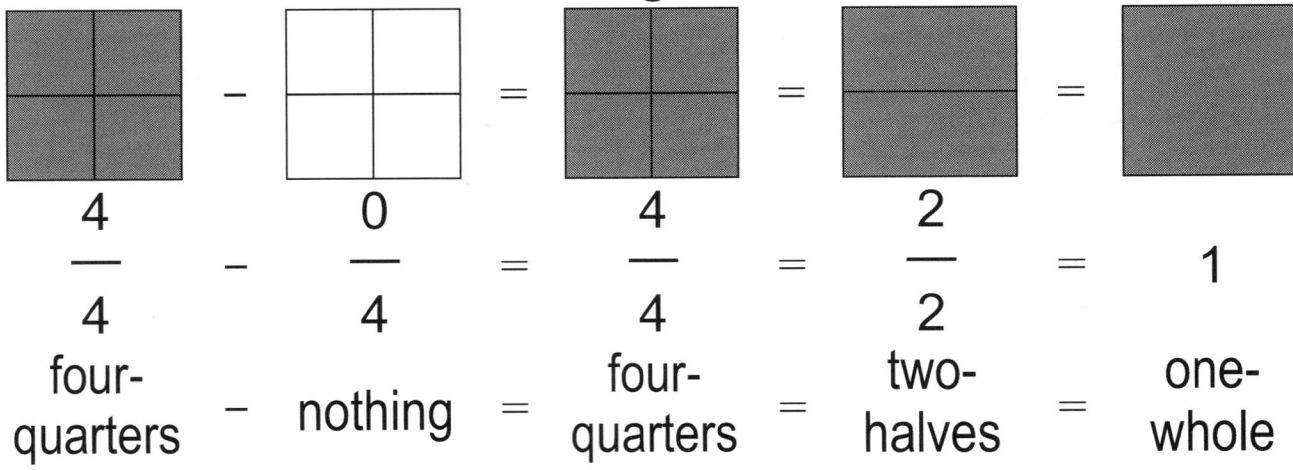

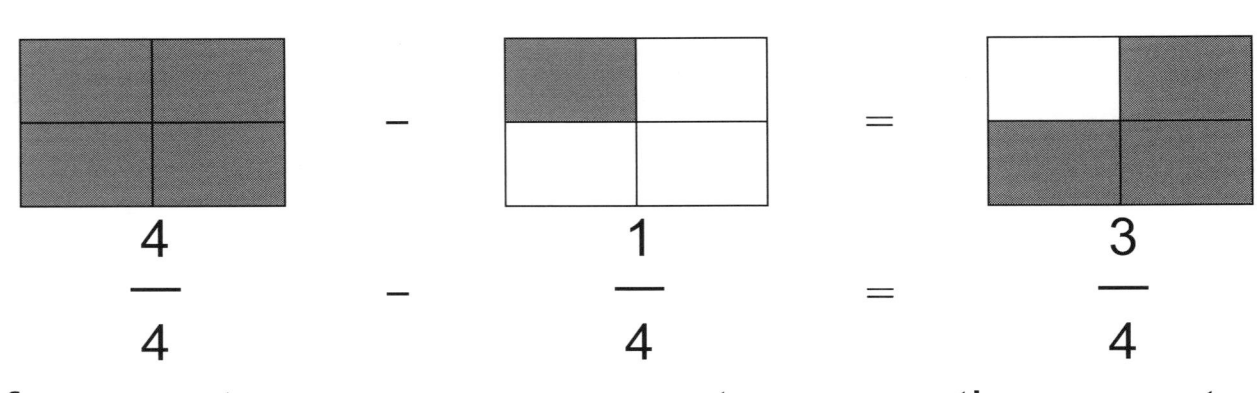

$$\frac{4}{4} - \frac{0}{4} = \frac{4}{4} = \frac{2}{2} = 1$$

four-quarters − nothing = four-quarters = two-halves = one-whole

1.00 − 0.00 = 1.00 = 1.00 = 1

$$\frac{4}{4} - \frac{1}{4} = \frac{3}{4}$$

four-quarters − one-quarter = three-quarters

1.00 − 0.25 = 0.75

$$\frac{3}{4} - \frac{1}{4} = \frac{2}{4} = \frac{1}{2}$$

three-quarters − quarter = two-quarters = one-half

0.75 − 0.25 = 0.50 = 0.50

186

Subtracting **Quarters**

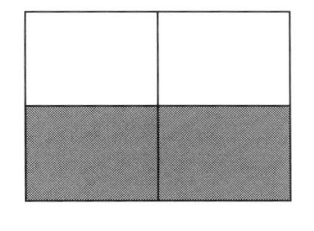

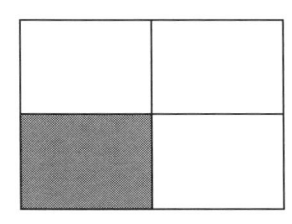

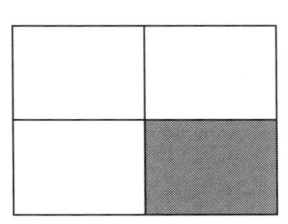

$$\frac{2}{4} - \frac{1}{4} = \frac{1}{4}$$

two-quarters − one-quarter = one-quarter

0.50 − 0.25 = 0.25

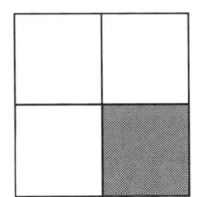

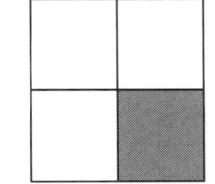

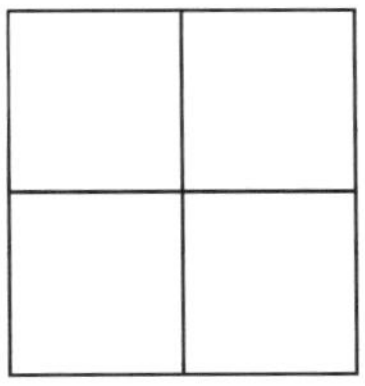

$$\frac{1}{4} - \frac{1}{4} = \frac{0}{4} = \frac{0}{2} = 0$$

quarter − quarter = nothing = nothing = nothing

0.25 − 0.25 = 0.00 = 0.00 = 0

Subtracting **Eighths**

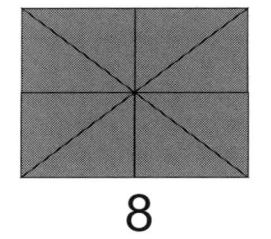

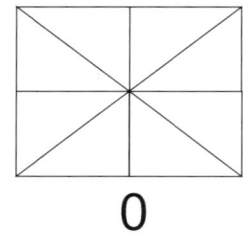

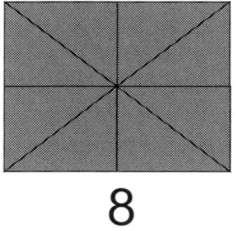

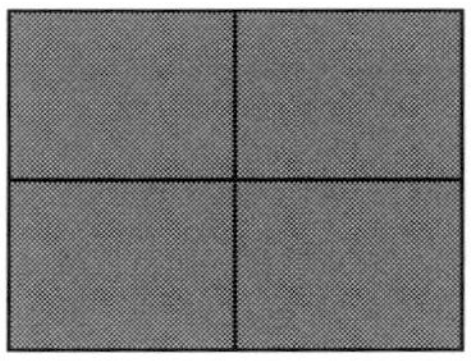

$$\frac{8}{8} - \frac{0}{8} = \frac{8}{8} = \frac{4}{4}$$

eight-eighths − nothing = eight-eighths = four-quarters

1.00 − 0.00 = 1.00 = 1.00

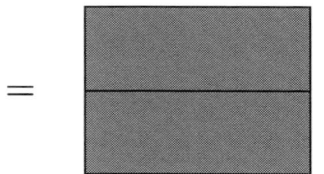

$$= \frac{2}{2} = 1$$

= two-halves = one-whole

= 1.00 = 1

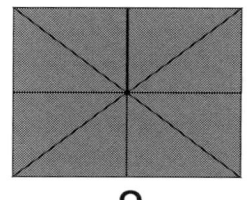

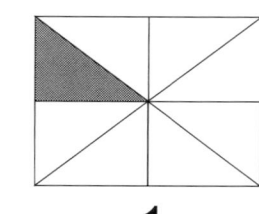

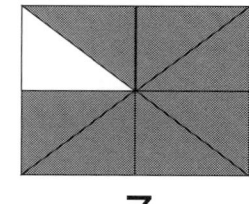

$$\frac{8}{8} - \frac{1}{8} = \frac{7}{8}$$

eight-eighths − one-eighth = seven-eighths

1.00 − 0.125 = 0.875

Subtracting Eighths

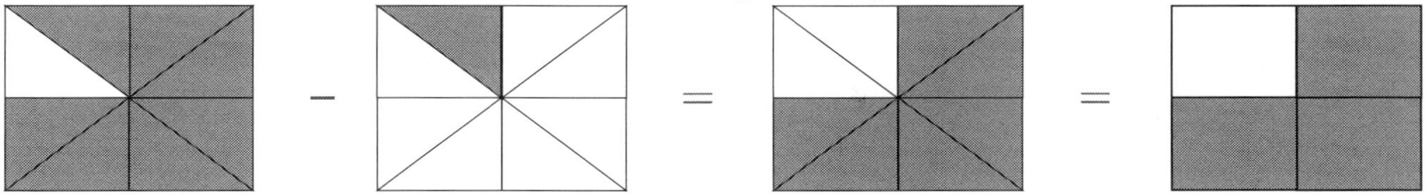

$$\frac{7}{8} - \frac{1}{8} = \frac{6}{8} = \frac{3}{4}$$

seven-eighths − eighth = six-eighths = three-quarters

0.875 − 0.125 = 0.750 = 0.75

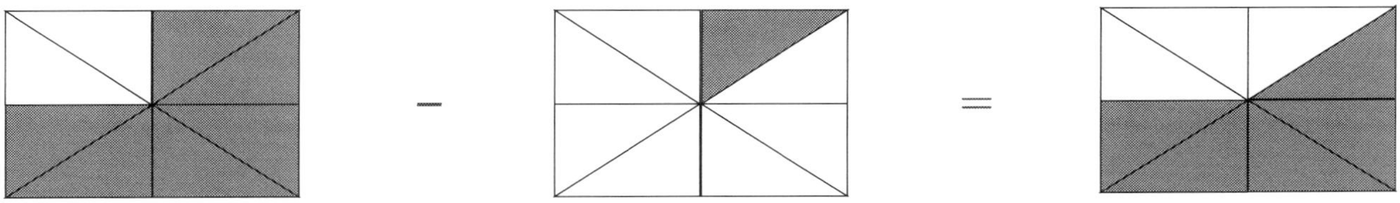

$$\frac{6}{8} - \frac{1}{8} = \frac{5}{8}$$

six-eighths − one-eighth = five-eighths

0.750 − 0.125 = 0.625

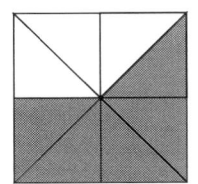

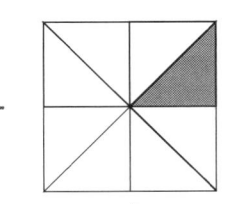

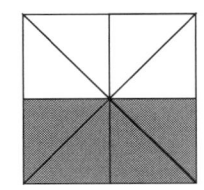

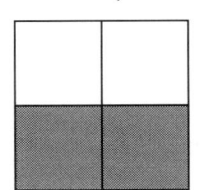

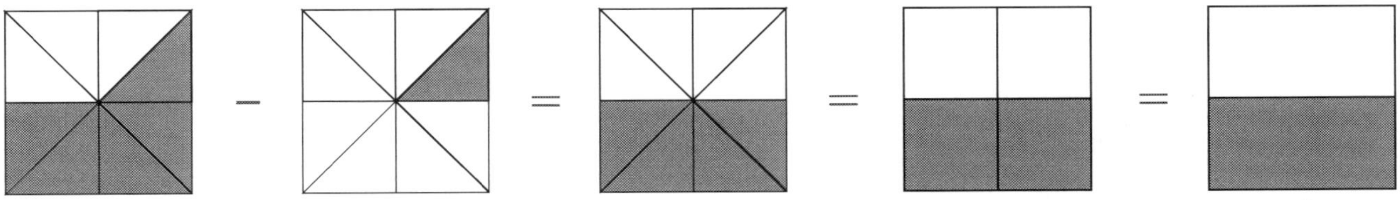

$$\frac{5}{8} - \frac{1}{8} = \frac{4}{8} = \frac{2}{4} = \frac{1}{2}$$

five-eighths − eighth = four-eighths = two-quarters = one-half

0.625 − 0.125 = 0.500 = 0.50 = 0.50

Subtracting Eighths

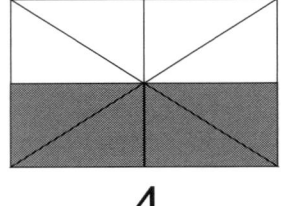

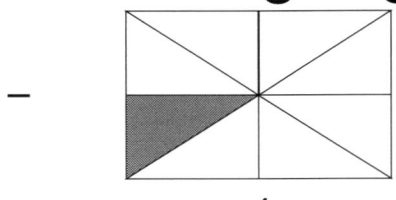

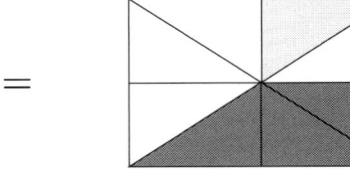

$$\frac{4}{8} - \frac{1}{8} = \frac{3}{8}$$

four-eighths − one-eighth = three-eighths

0.50 − 0.125 = 0.375

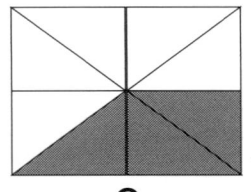

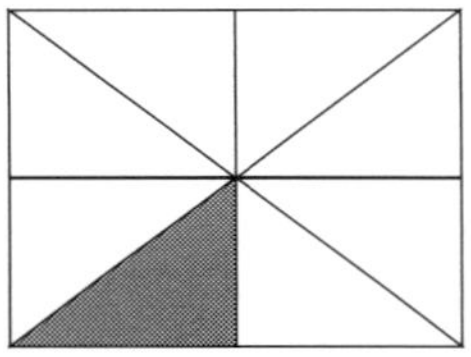

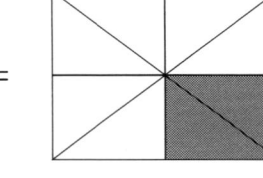

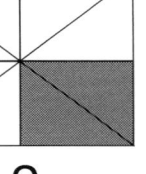

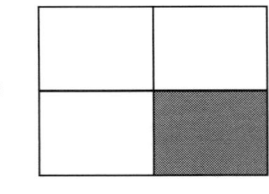

$$\frac{3}{8} - \frac{1}{8} = \frac{2}{8} = \frac{1}{4}$$

three-eighths − eighth = two-eighths = one-quarter

0.375 − 0.125 = 0.250 = 0.25

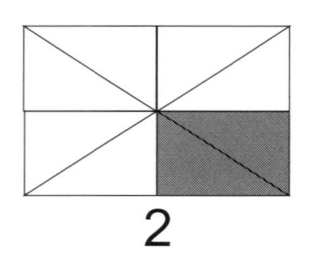

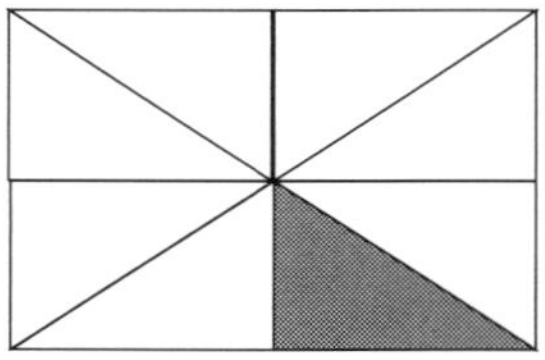

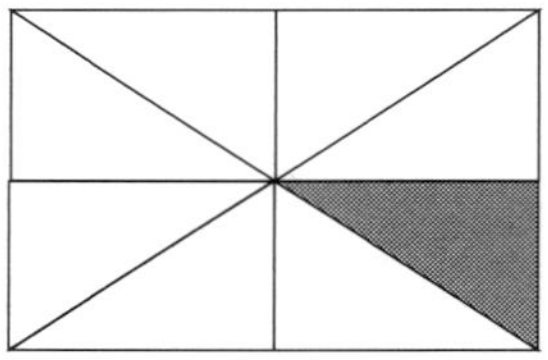

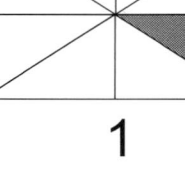

$$\frac{2}{8} - \frac{1}{8} = \frac{1}{8}$$

two-eighths − one-eighth = one-eighth

0.250 − 0.125 = 0.125

Subtracting Eighths

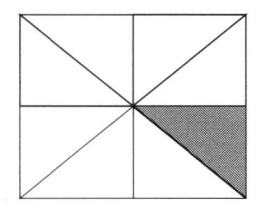

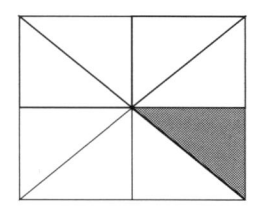

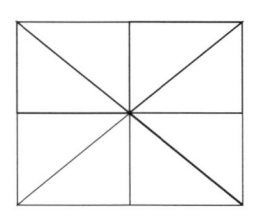

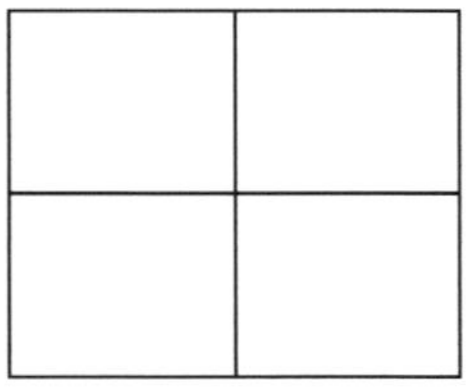

$$\frac{1}{8} - \frac{1}{8} = \frac{0}{8} = \frac{0}{4}$$

eighth − eighth = nothing = nothing

0.125 − 0.125 = 0.00 = 0.00

$$= \frac{0}{2} = 0$$

= nothing = nothing

= 0.00 = 0

Subtracting Fifths

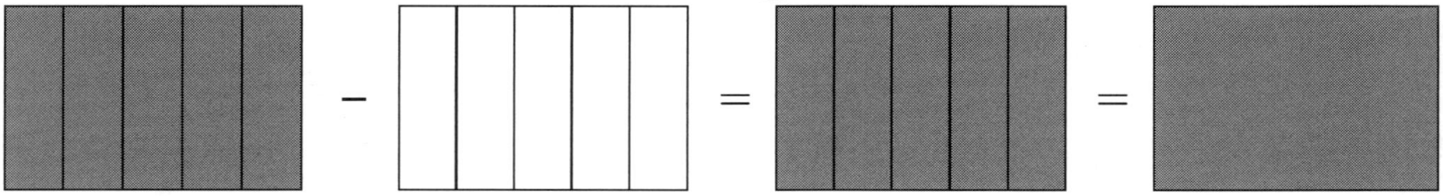

$$\frac{5}{5} - \frac{0}{5} = \frac{0}{5} = 1$$

five-fifths − nothing = five-fifths = one-whole

1.00 − 0.00 = 1.00 = 1.00

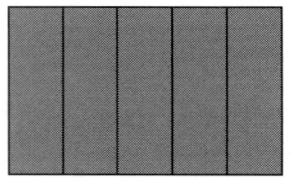

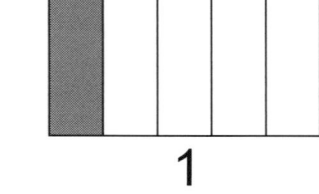

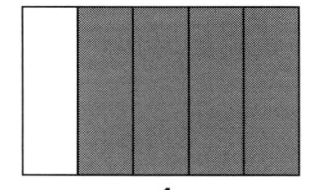

$$\frac{5}{5} - \frac{1}{5} = \frac{4}{5}$$

five-fifths − one-fifth = four-fifths

1.00 − 0.20 = 0.80

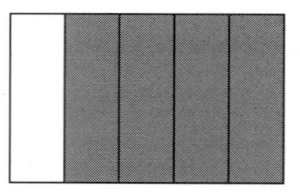

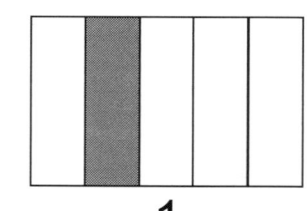

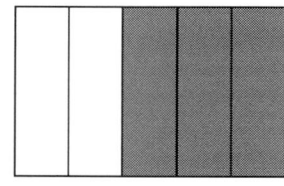

$$\frac{4}{5} - \frac{1}{5} = \frac{3}{5}$$

four-fifths − fifth = three-fifths

0.80 − 0.20 = 0.60

Subtracting Fifths

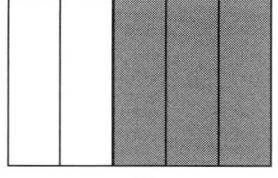

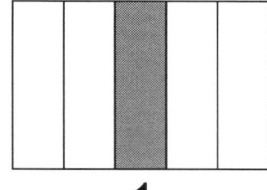

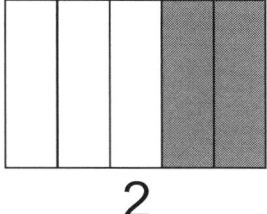

$$\frac{3}{5} - \frac{1}{5} = \frac{2}{5}$$

three-fifths − one-fifth = two-fifths

0.60 − 0.20 = 0.40

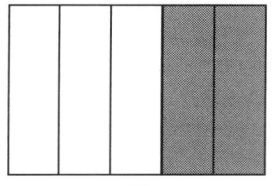

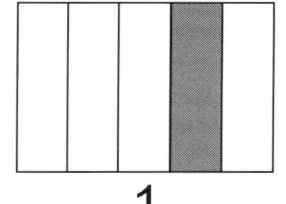

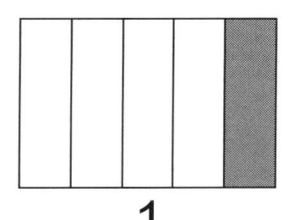

$$\frac{2}{5} - \frac{1}{5} = \frac{1}{5}$$

two-fifths − fifth = one-fifth

0.40 − 0.20 = 0.20

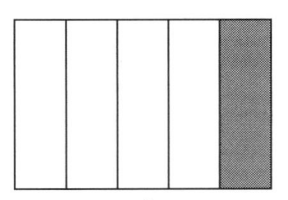

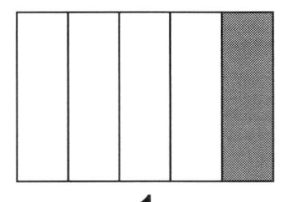

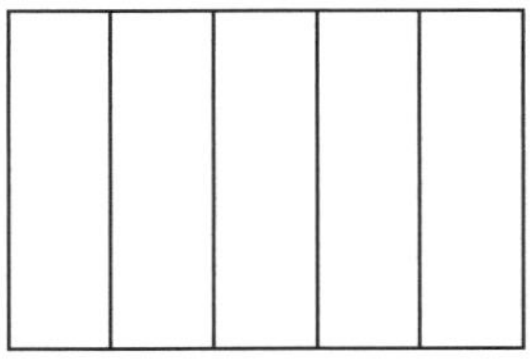

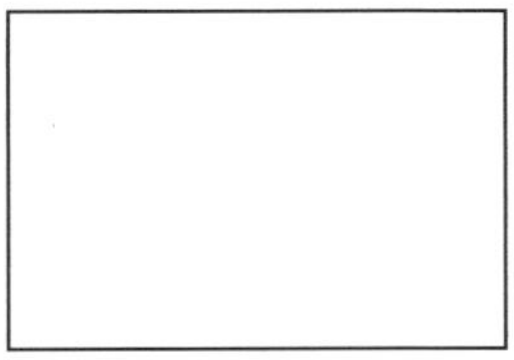

$$\frac{1}{5} - \frac{1}{5} = \frac{0}{5} = 0$$

fifth − one-fifth = nothing = nothing

0.20 − 0.20 = 0.00 = 0

Subtracting Tenths

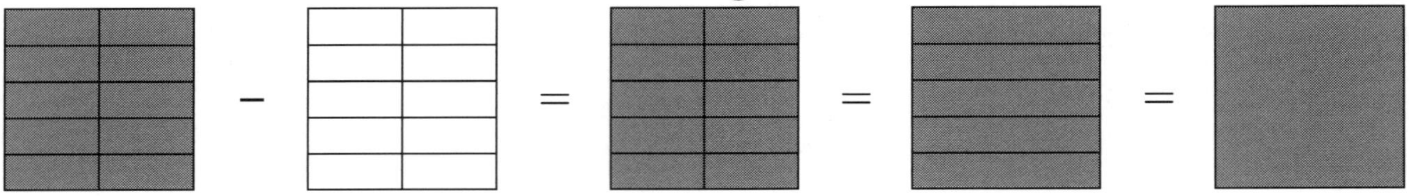

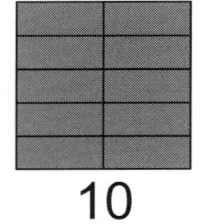

$$\frac{10}{10} - \frac{0}{10} = \frac{10}{10} = \frac{5}{5} = 1$$

ten-tenths − nothing = ten-tenths = five-fifths = one-whole

1.00 − 0.00 = 1.00 = 1.00 = 1.00

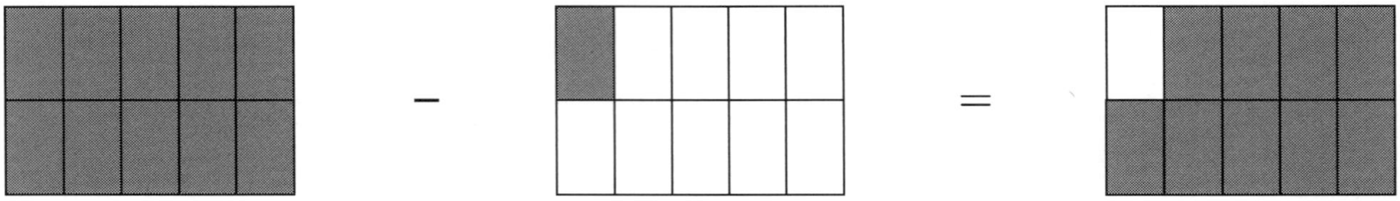

$$\frac{10}{10} - \frac{1}{10} = \frac{9}{10}$$

ten-tenths − one-tenth = nine-tenths

1.00 − 0.10 = 0.90

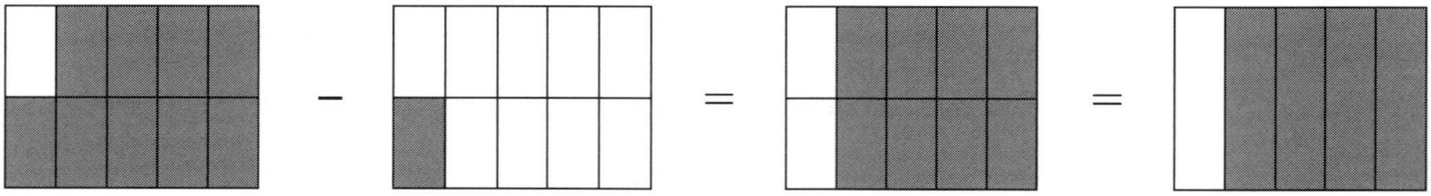

$$\frac{9}{10} - \frac{1}{10} = \frac{8}{10} = \frac{4}{5}$$

nine-tenths − tenth = eight-tenths = four-fifths

0.90 − 0.10 = 0.80 = 0.80

Subtracting Tenths

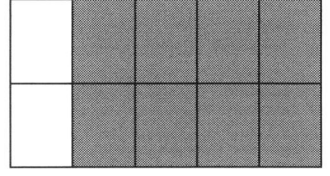

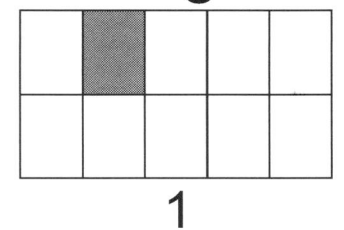

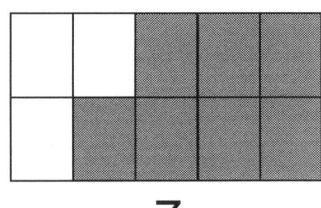

$$\frac{8}{10} - \frac{1}{10} = \frac{7}{10}$$

eight-tenths − one-tenth = seven-tenths

0.80 − 0.10 = 0.70

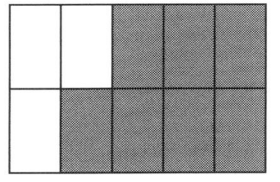

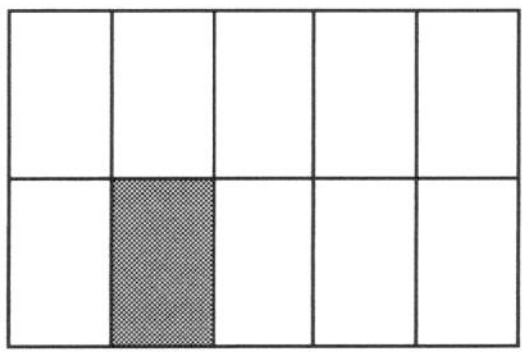

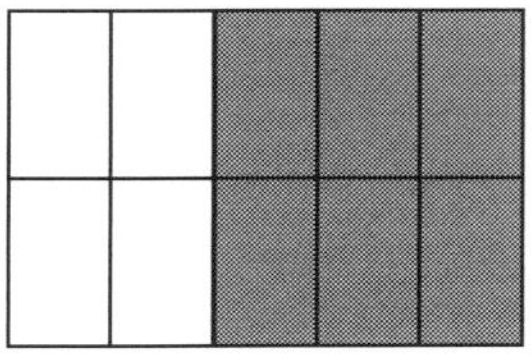

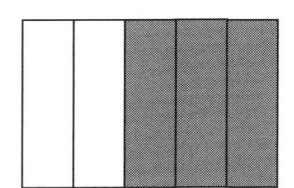

$$\frac{7}{10} - \frac{1}{10} = \frac{6}{10} = \frac{3}{5}$$

seven-tenths − tenth = six-tenths = three-fifths

0.70 − 0.10 = 0.60 = 0.60

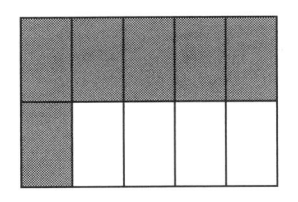

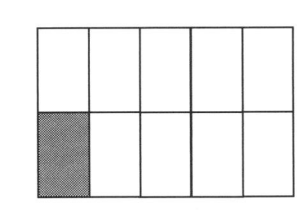

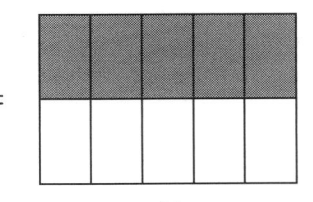

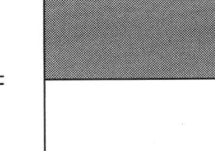

$$\frac{6}{10} - \frac{1}{10} = \frac{5}{10} = \frac{1}{2}$$

six-tenths − one-tenth = five-tenths = one-half

0.60 − 0.10 = 0.50 = 0.50

Subtracting Tenths

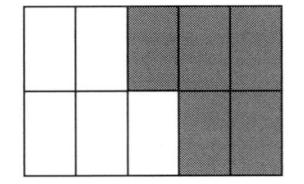

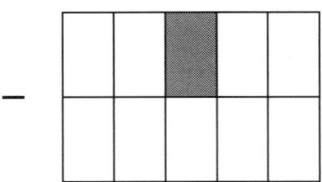

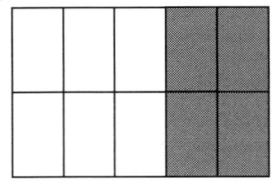

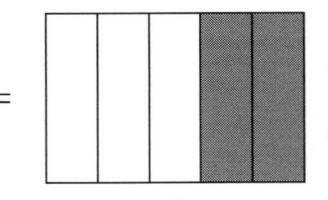

$$\frac{5}{10} - \frac{1}{10} = \frac{4}{10} = \frac{2}{5}$$

five-tenths − tenth = four-tenths = two-fifths

0.50 − 0.10 = 0.40 = 0.40

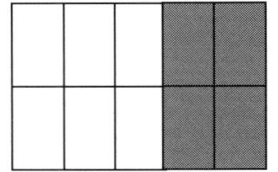

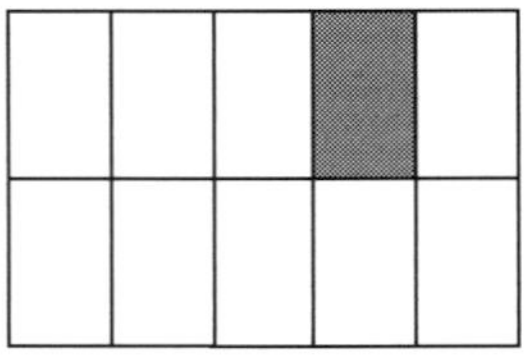

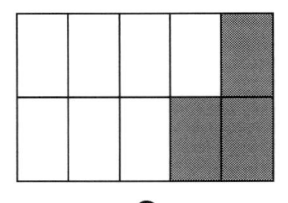

$$\frac{4}{10} - \frac{1}{10} = \frac{3}{10}$$

four-tenths − one-tenth = three-tenths

0.40 − 0.10 = 0.30

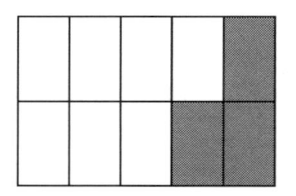

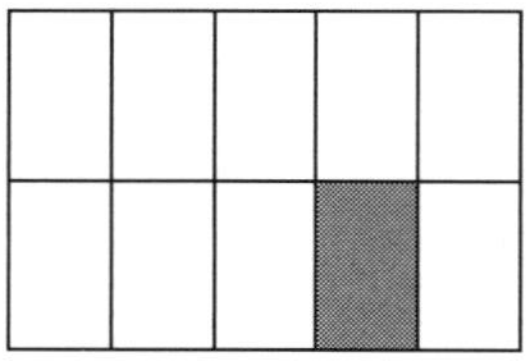

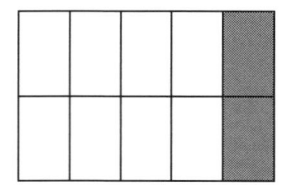

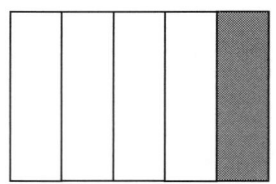

$$\frac{3}{10} - \frac{1}{10} = \frac{2}{10} = \frac{1}{5}$$

three-tenths − tenth = two-tenths = one-fifth

0.30 − 0.10 = 0.20 = 0.20

Subtracting Tenths

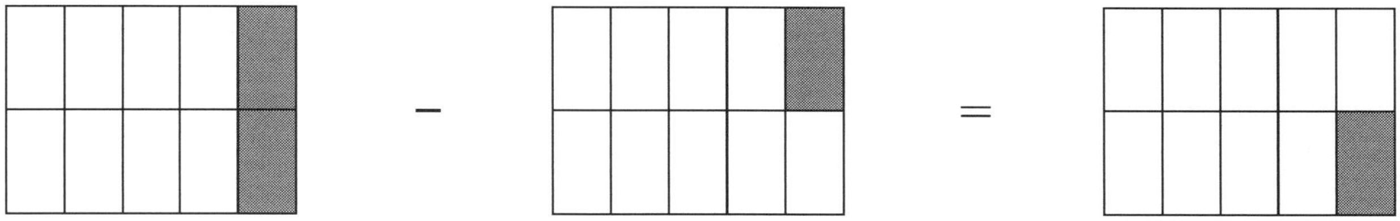

$$\frac{2}{10} - \frac{1}{10} = \frac{1}{10}$$

two-tenths   −   one-tenth   =   one-tenth

0.20   −   0.10   =   0.10

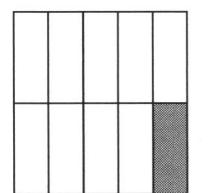

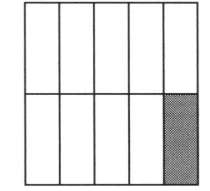

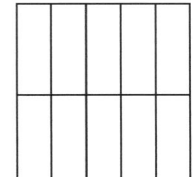

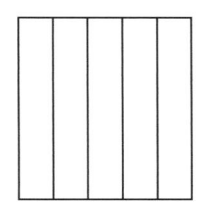

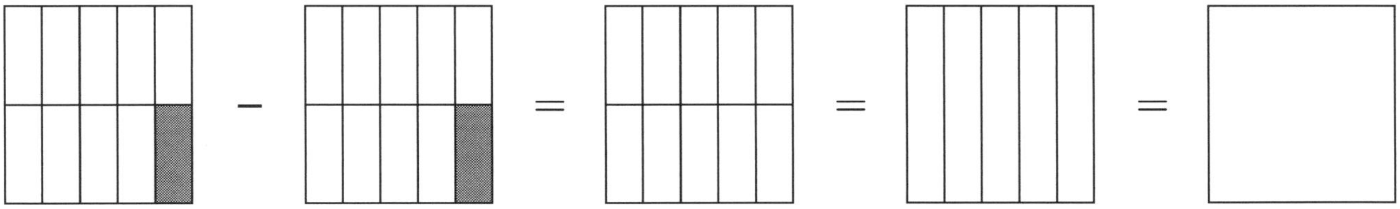

$$\frac{1}{10} - \frac{1}{10} = \frac{0}{10} = \frac{0}{5} = 0$$

tenth − tenth nothing = nothing = nothing

0.10 − 0.10 = 0.00 = 0.00 = 0

Subtracting **Thirds**

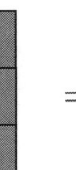

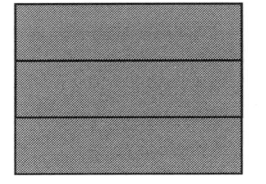

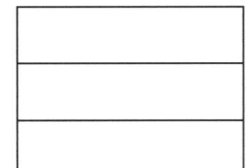

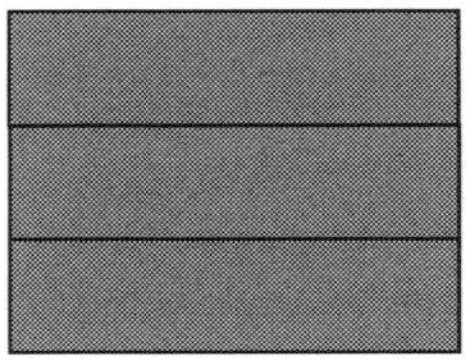

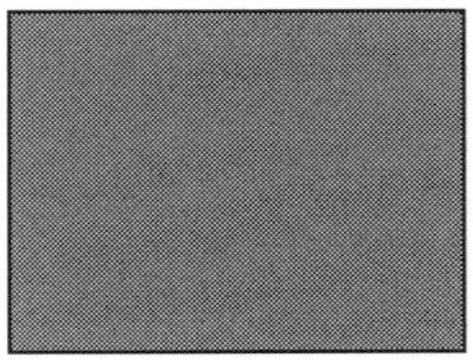

$$\frac{3}{3} - \frac{0}{3} = \frac{3}{3} = 1$$

three-thirds − nothing = three-thirds = one-whole

1.00 − 0.00 = 1.00 = 1.00

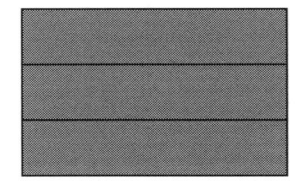

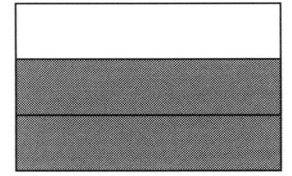

$$\frac{3}{3} - \frac{1}{3} = \frac{2}{3}$$

three-thirds − one-third = two-thirds

1.00 − 0.333˙ = 0.666˙

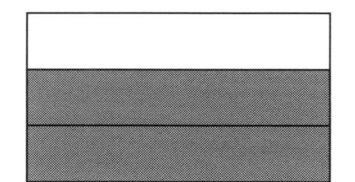

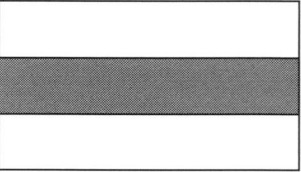

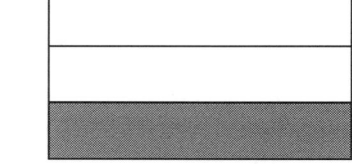

$$\frac{2}{3} - \frac{1}{3} = \frac{1}{3}$$

two-thirds − third = one-third

0.666˙ − 0.333˙ = 0.333˙

Subtracting Thirds

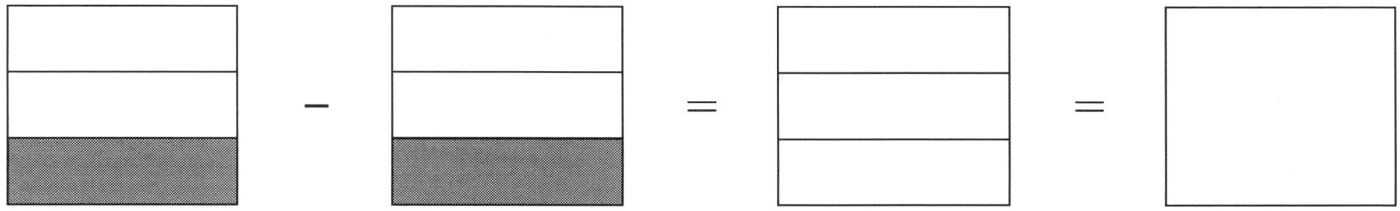

$$\frac{1}{3} - \frac{1}{3} = \frac{0}{3} = \frac{0}{1}$$

third   −   one-third   =   nothing   =   nothing

0.333˙   −   0.333˙   =   0.00   =   0.00

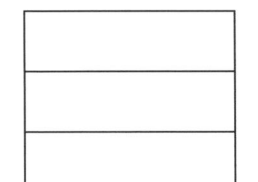

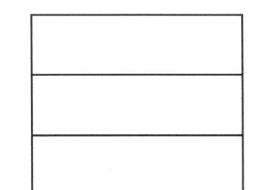

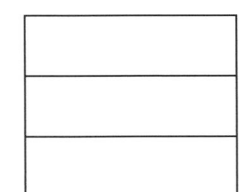

$$\frac{0}{3} - \frac{0}{3} = \frac{0}{3} = 0$$

nothing   −   nothing   =   nothing   =   nothing

0.00   −   0.00   =   0.00   =   0

Subtracting **Sixths**

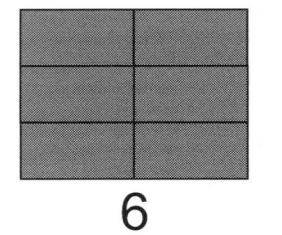

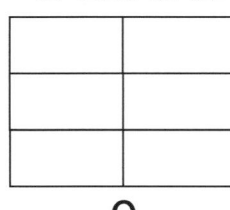

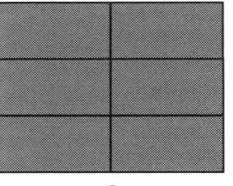

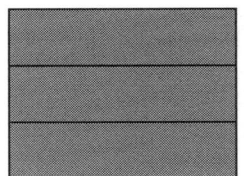

$$\frac{6}{6} - \frac{0}{6} = \frac{6}{6} = \frac{3}{3}$$

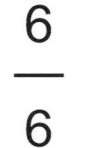

six-sixths − nothing = six-sixths = three-thirds

1.00 − 0.00 = 1.00 = 1.00

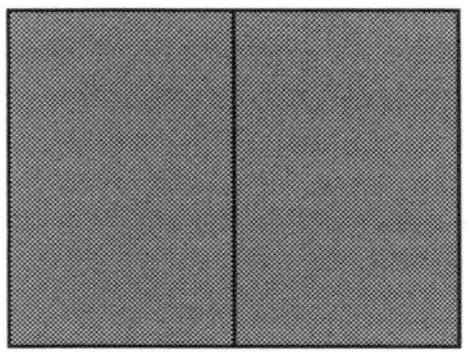

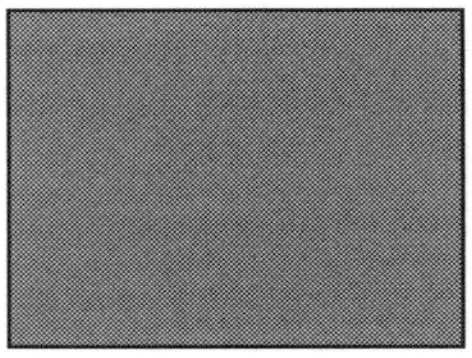

$$= \frac{2}{2} = 1$$

= two-halves = one-whole

= 1.00 = 1.00

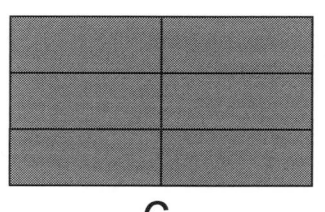

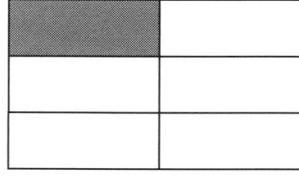

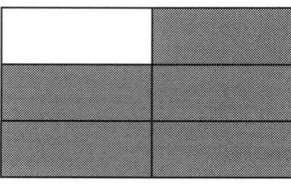

$$\frac{6}{6} - \frac{1}{6} = \frac{5}{6}$$

six-sixths − one-sixth = five-sixths

1.00 − 0.166˙ = 0.833˙

200

Subtracting Sixths

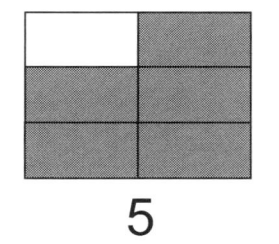

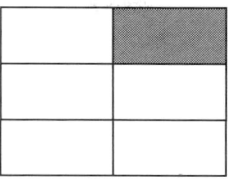

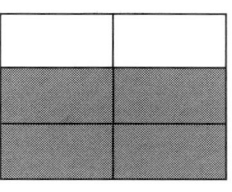

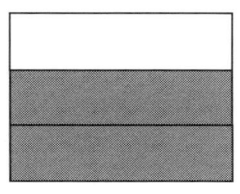

$$\frac{5}{6} - \frac{1}{6} = \frac{4}{6} = \frac{2}{3}$$

five-sixths − sixth = four-sixths = two-thirds

0.833˙ − 0.166˙ = 0.666˙ = 0.666˙

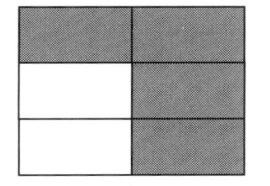

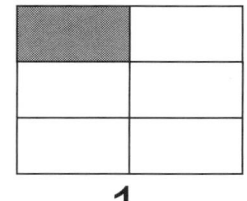

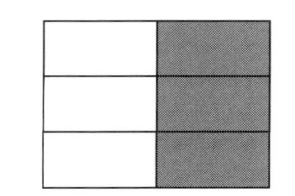

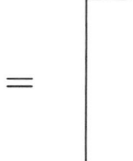

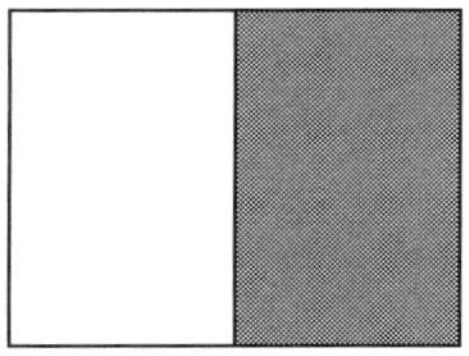

$$\frac{4}{6} - \frac{1}{6} = \frac{3}{6} = \frac{1}{2}$$

four-sixths − one-sixth = three-sixths = one-half

0.666˙ − 0.166˙ = 0.50 = 0.50

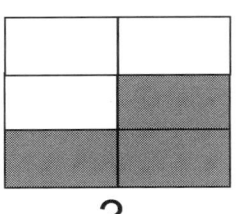

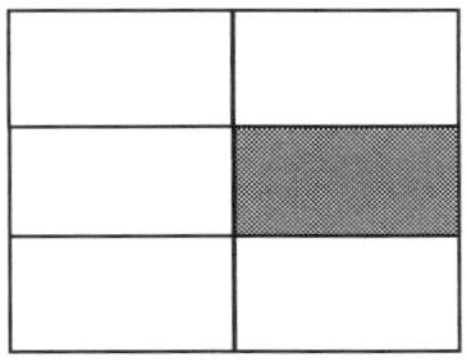

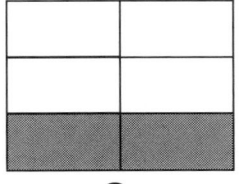

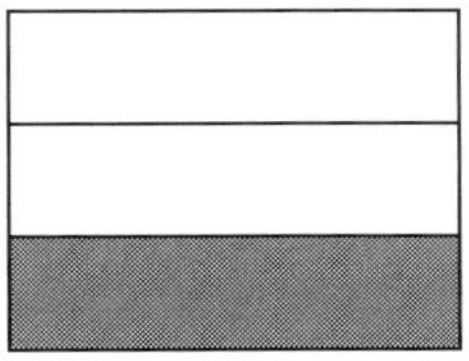

$$\frac{3}{6} - \frac{1}{6} = \frac{2}{6} = \frac{1}{3}$$

three-sixths − sixth = two-sixths = one-third

0.50 − 0.166˙ = 0.333˙ = 0.333˙

Subtracting Sixths

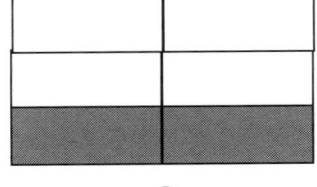

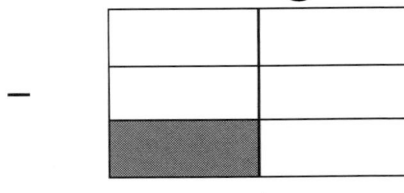

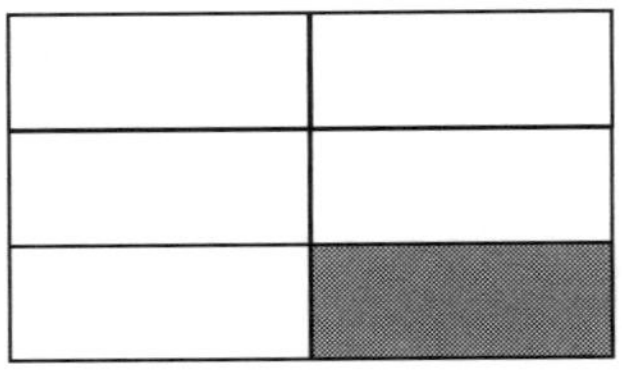

$$\frac{2}{6} - \frac{1}{6} = \frac{1}{6}$$

two-sixths − one-sixth = sixth

0.333˙ − 0.166˙ = 0.166˙

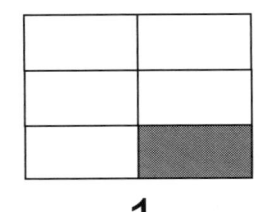

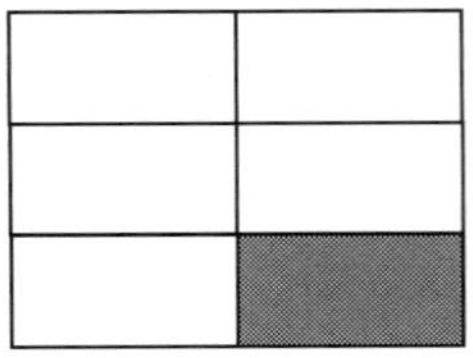

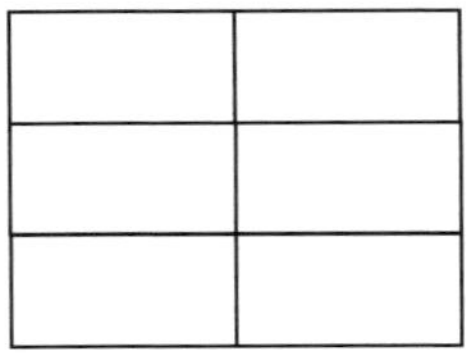

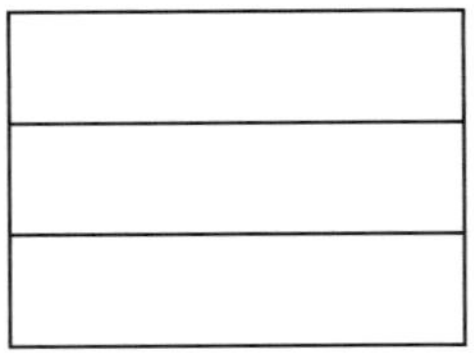

$$\frac{1}{6} - \frac{1}{6} = \frac{0}{6} = \frac{0}{3}$$

one-sixth − sixth = nothing = nothing

0.166˙ − 0.166˙ = 0.00 = 0.00

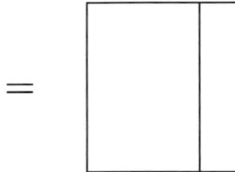

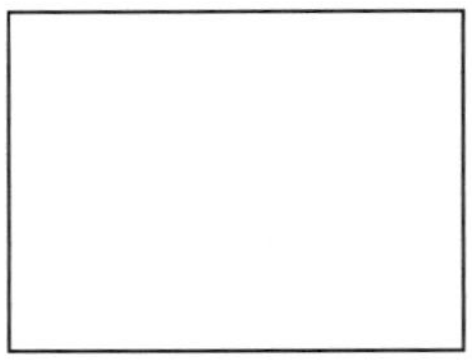

$$= \frac{0}{2} = 0$$

= nothing = nothing

= 0.00 = 0.00

202

Quiz 1

Match fractions with their answers (See example given)

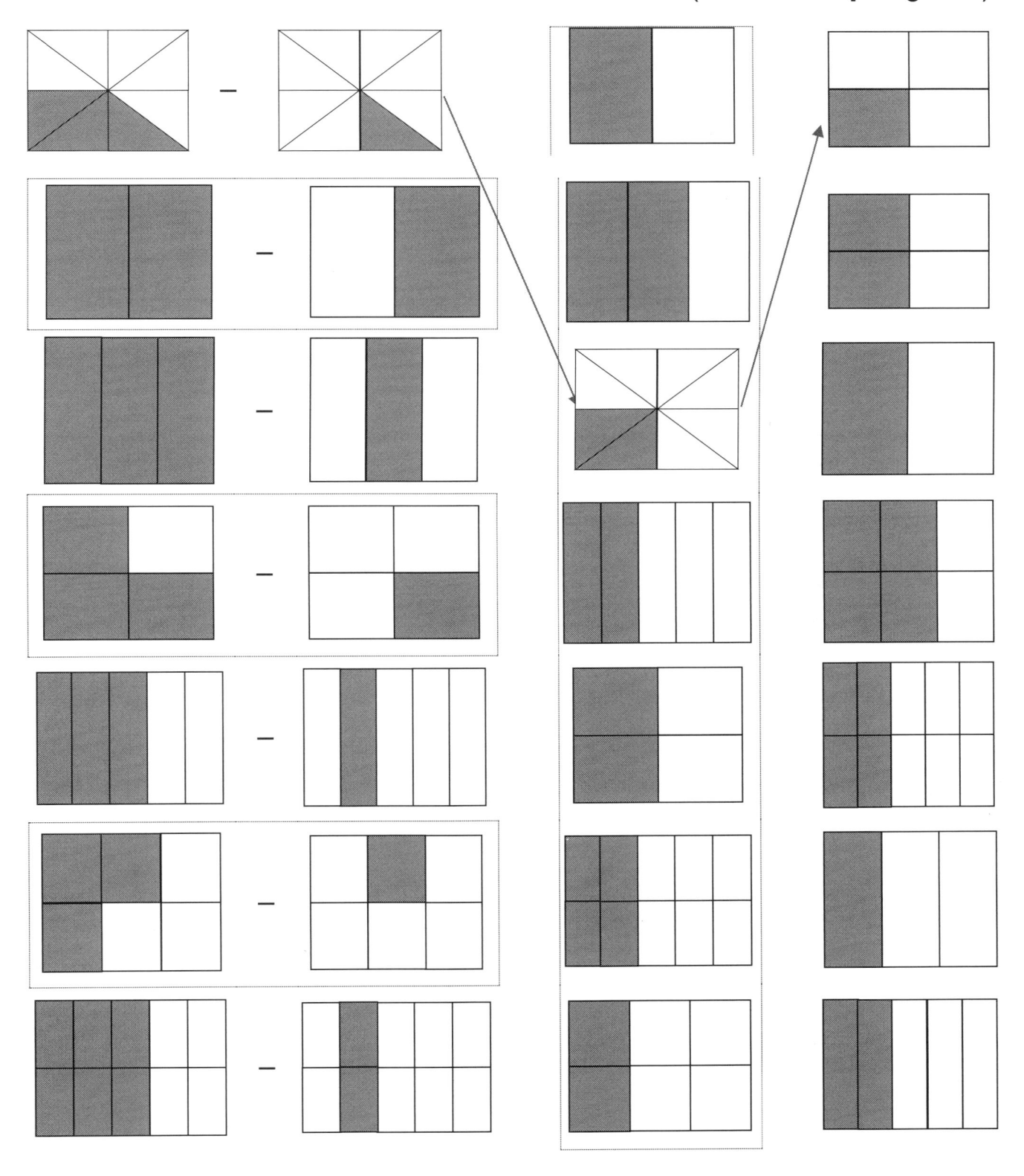

Subtracting Ninths

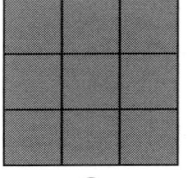

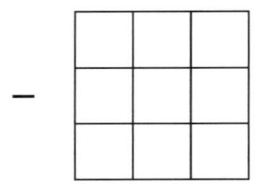

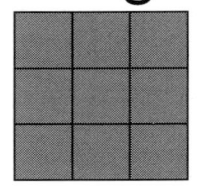

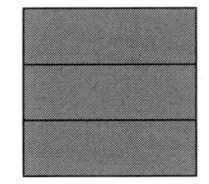

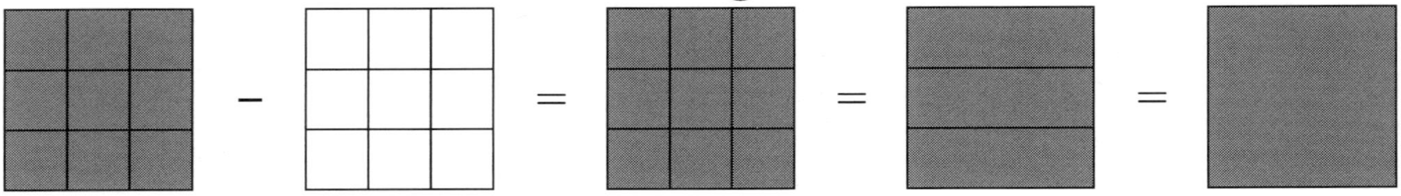

$$\frac{9}{9} - \frac{0}{9} = \frac{9}{9} = \frac{3}{3} = 1$$

nine-ninths − nothing = nine-ninths = three-thirds = one-whole

1.00 − 0.00 = 1.00 = 1.00 = 1.00

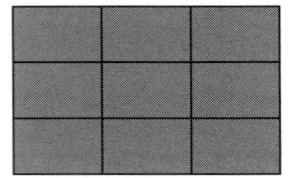

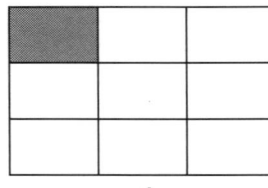

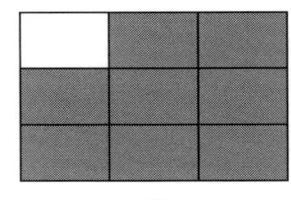

$$\frac{9}{9} - \frac{1}{9} = \frac{8}{9}$$

nine-ninths − ninth = eight-ninths

1.00 − 0.111˙ = 0.888˙

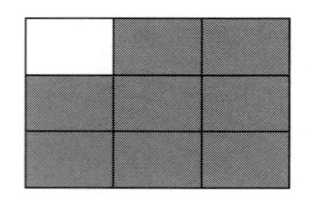

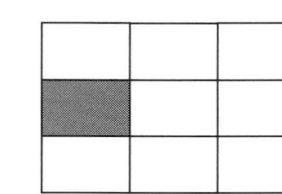

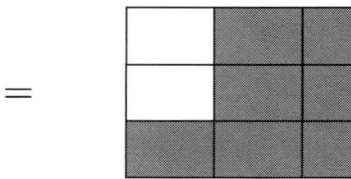

$$\frac{8}{9} - \frac{1}{9} = \frac{7}{9}$$

eight-ninths − one-ninth = seven-ninths

0.888˙ − 0.111˙ = 0.777˙

Subtracting Ninths

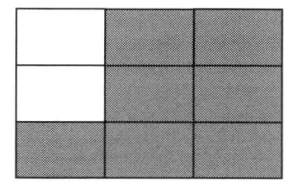

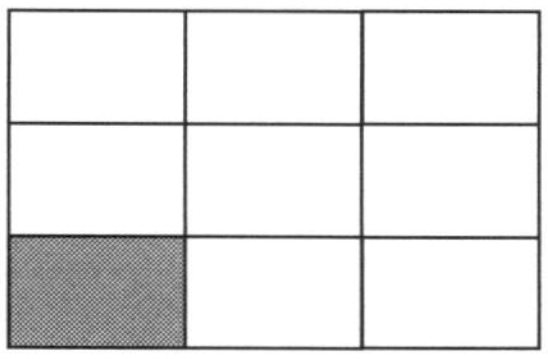

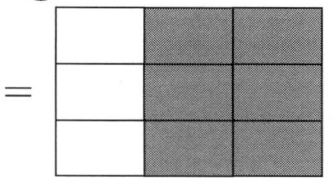

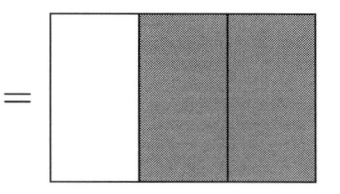

$$\frac{7}{9} - \frac{1}{9} = \frac{6}{9} = \frac{2}{3}$$

seven-ninths − ninth = six-ninths = two-thirds

0.777˙ − 0.111˙ = 0.666˙ = 0.666˙

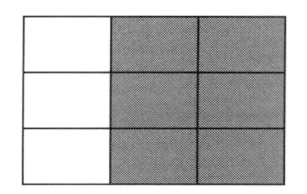

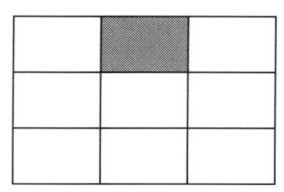

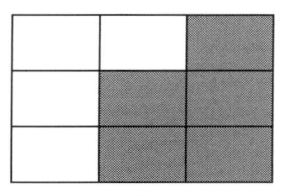

$$\frac{6}{9} - \frac{1}{9} = \frac{5}{9}$$

six-ninths − one-ninth = five-ninths

0.666˙ − 0.111˙ = 0.555˙

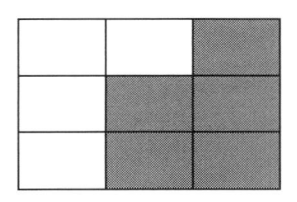

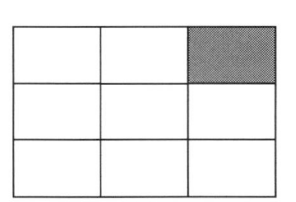

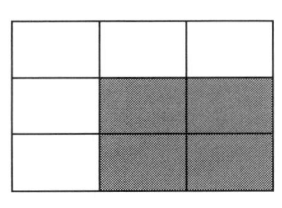

$$\frac{5}{9} - \frac{1}{9} = \frac{4}{9}$$

five-ninths − ninth = four-ninths

0.555˙ − 0.111˙ = 0.444˙

Subtracting Ninths

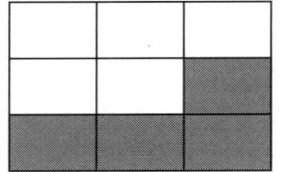

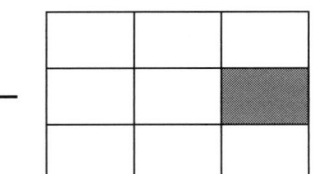

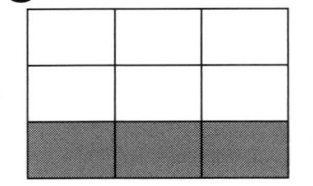

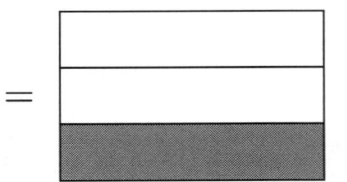

$$\frac{4}{9} - \frac{1}{9} = \frac{3}{9} = \frac{1}{3}$$

four-ninths − one-ninth = three-ninths = one-third

0.444˙ − 0.111˙ = 0.333˙ = 0.333˙

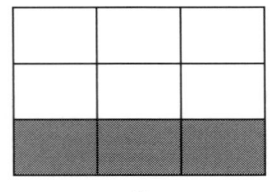

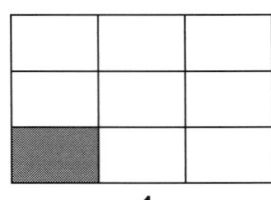

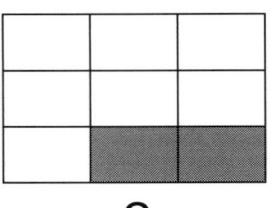

$$\frac{3}{9} - \frac{1}{9} = \frac{2}{9}$$

three-ninths − one-ninth = two-ninths

0.333˙ − 0.111˙ = 0.222˙

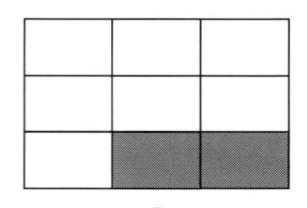

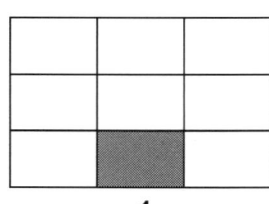

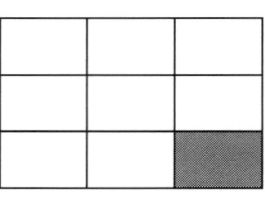

$$\frac{2}{9} - \frac{1}{9} = \frac{1}{9}$$

two-ninths − one-ninth = one-ninth

0.222˙ − 0.111˙ = 0.111˙

Subtracting **Ninths**

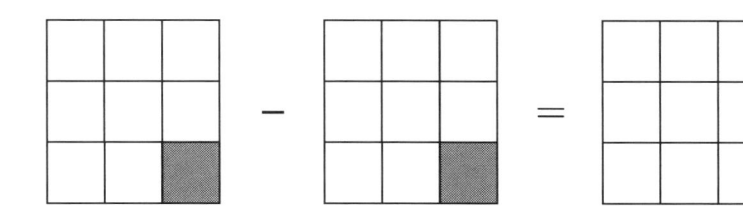

$$\frac{1}{9} - \frac{1}{9} = \frac{0}{9} = \frac{0}{3} = \frac{0}{1}$$

ninth − ninth = nothing = nothing = nothing

0.111˙ − 0.111˙ = 0.00 = 0.00 = 0.00

$$\frac{0}{9} - \frac{0}{9} = \frac{0}{9} = \frac{0}{3} = 0$$

nothing − nothing = nothing = nothing = nothing

0.00 − 0.00 = 0.00 = 0.00 = 0

207

Subtracting Twelfths

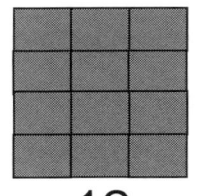

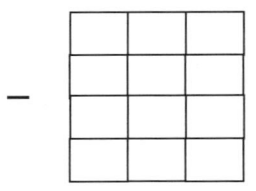

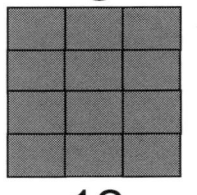

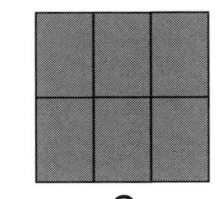

$$\frac{12}{12} - \frac{0}{12} = \frac{12}{12} = \frac{6}{6} = 1$$

twelve-twelfths − nothing = twelve-twelfths = six-sixths = one-whole

1.00 − 0.00 = 1.00 = 1.00 = 1.00

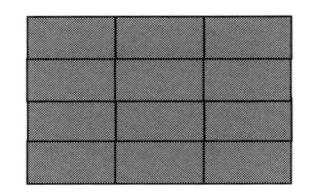

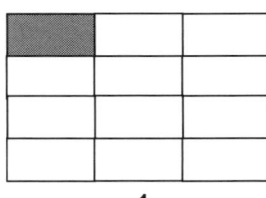

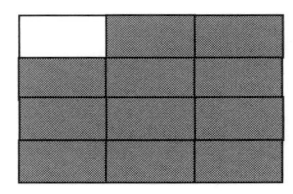

$$\frac{12}{12} - \frac{1}{12} = \frac{11}{12}$$

twelve-twelfths − one-twelfth = eleven-twelfths

1.00 − 0.083˙ = 0.916˙

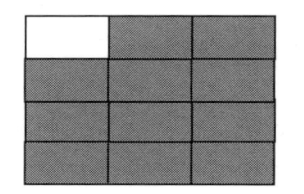

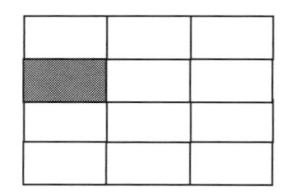

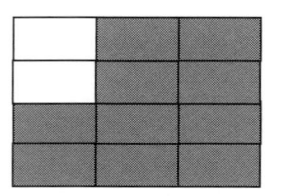

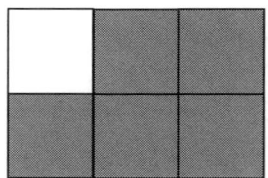

$$\frac{11}{12} - \frac{1}{12} = \frac{10}{12} = \frac{5}{6}$$

eleven-twelfths − twelfth = ten-twelfths = five-sixths

0.916˙ − 0.083˙ = 0.833˙ = 0.833˙

208

Subtracting Twelfths

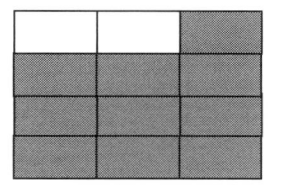

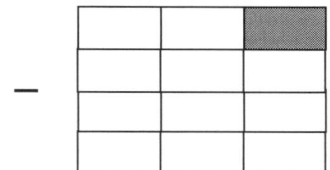

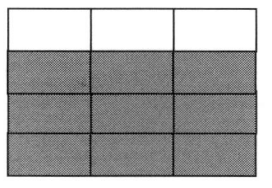

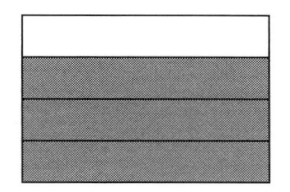

$$\frac{10}{12} - \frac{1}{12} = \frac{9}{12} = \frac{3}{4}$$

ten-twelfths − twelfth = nine-twelfths = three-quarters

0.833˙ − 0.083˙ = 0.750 = 0.75

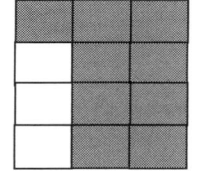

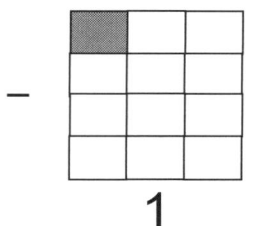

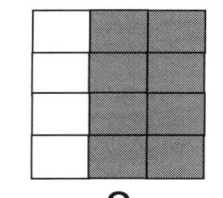

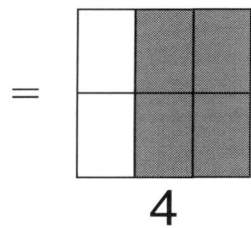

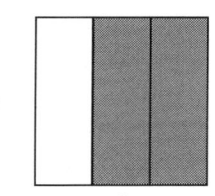

$$\frac{9}{12} - \frac{1}{12} = \frac{8}{12} = \frac{4}{6} = \frac{2}{3}$$

nine-twelfths − one-twelfth = eight-twelfths = four-sixths = two-thirds

0.750 − 0.083˙ = 0.666˙ = 0.666˙ = 0.666˙

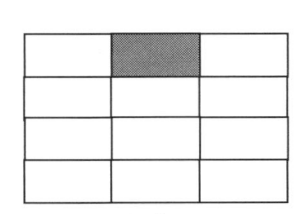

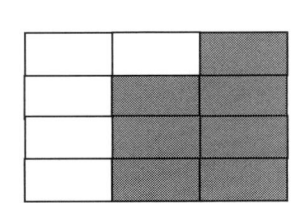

$$\frac{8}{12} - \frac{1}{12} = \frac{7}{12}$$

eight-twelfths − one-twelfth = seven-twelfths

0.666˙ − 0.083˙ = 0.583˙

Subtracting Twelfths

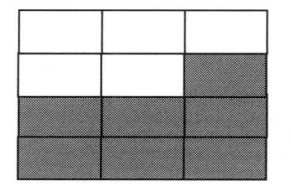

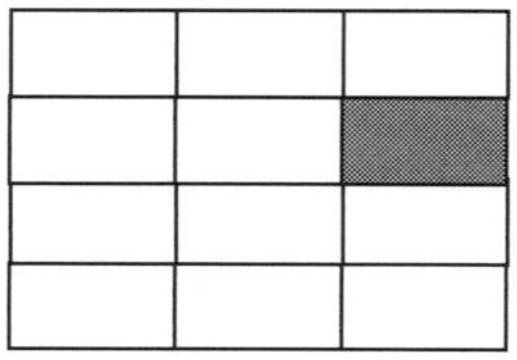

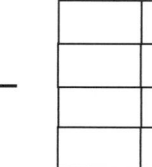

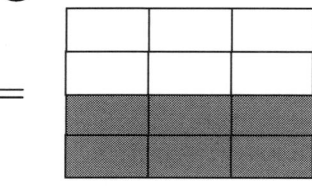

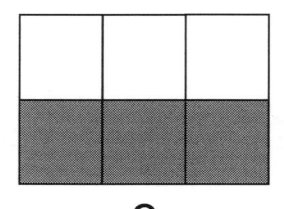

$$\frac{7}{12} - \frac{1}{12} = \frac{6}{12} = \frac{3}{6}$$

seven-twelfths − twelfth = six-twelfths = three-sixths

0.583˙ − 0.083˙ = 0.50 = 0.50

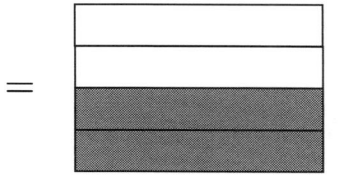

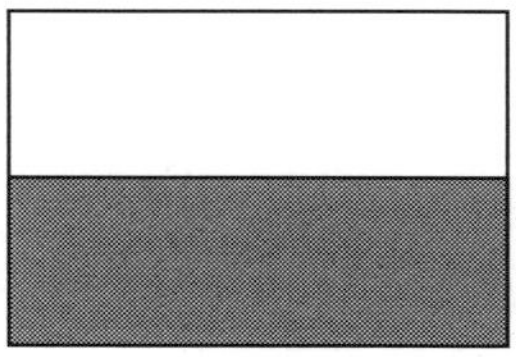

$$= \frac{2}{4} = \frac{1}{2}$$

= two-quarters = one-half

= 0.50 = 0.50

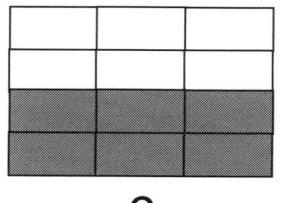

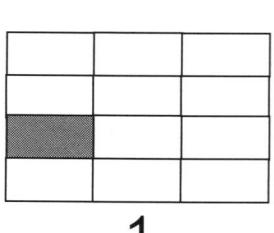

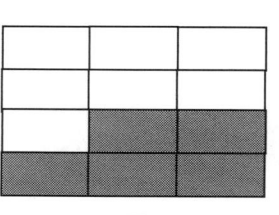

$$\frac{6}{12} - \frac{1}{12} = \frac{5}{12}$$

six-twelfths − one-twelfth = five-twelfths

0.500 − 0.083˙ = 0.416˙

Subtracting Twelfths

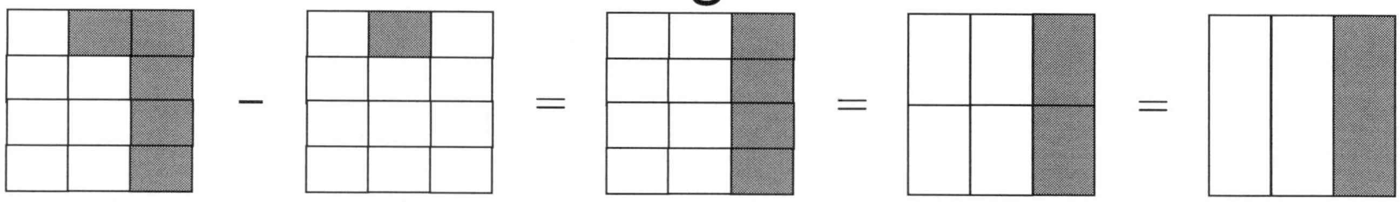

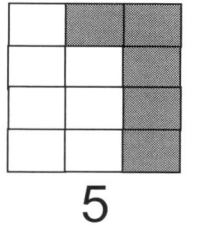

$$\frac{5}{12} - \frac{1}{12} = \frac{4}{12} = \frac{2}{6} = \frac{1}{3}$$

five-twelfths − twelfth = four-twelfths = two-sixths = one-third

0.416˙ − 0.083˙ = 0.333˙ = 0.333˙ = 0.333˙

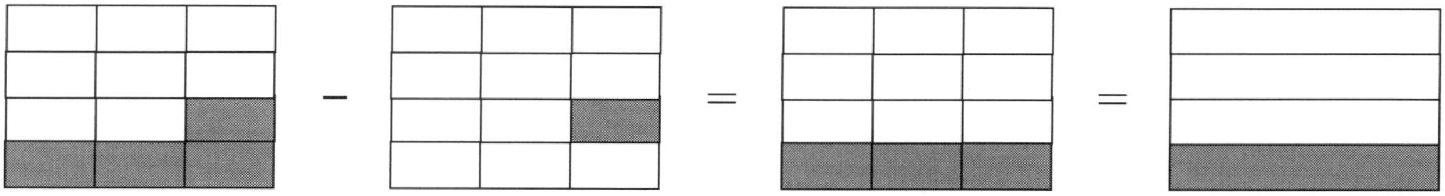

$$\frac{4}{12} - \frac{1}{12} = \frac{3}{12} = \frac{1}{4}$$

four-twelfths − one-twelfth = three-twelfths = one-quarter

0.333˙ − 0.083˙ = 0.250 = 0.25

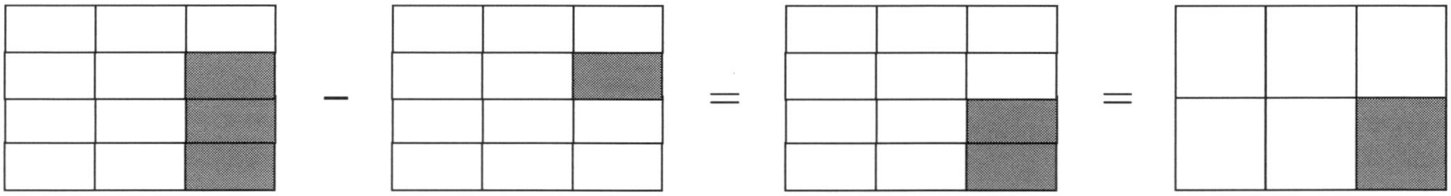

$$\frac{3}{12} - \frac{1}{12} = \frac{2}{12} = \frac{1}{6}$$

three-twelfths − twelfth = two-twelfths = one-sixth

0.250 − 0.083˙ = 0.166˙ = 0.166˙

Subtracting **Twelfths**

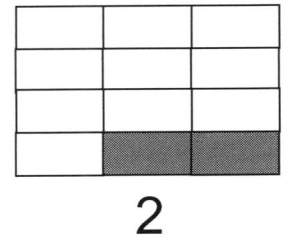

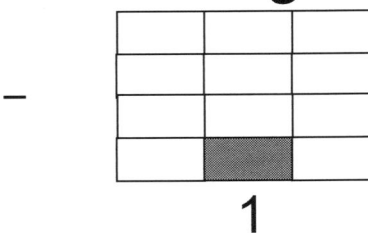

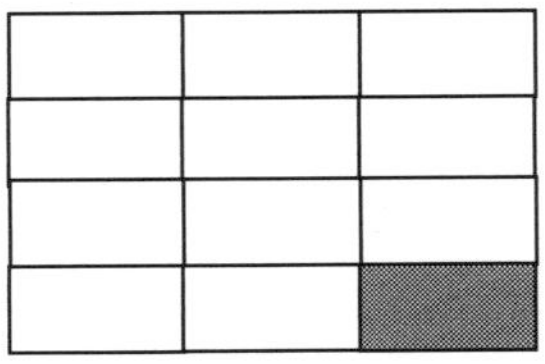

$$\frac{2}{12} - \frac{1}{12} = \frac{1}{12}$$

two-twelfths − one-twelfth = one-twelfth

0.166˙ − 0.083˙ = 0.083˙

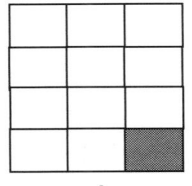

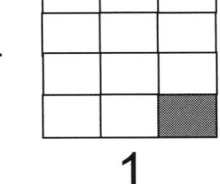

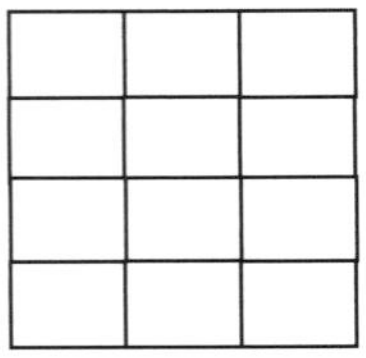

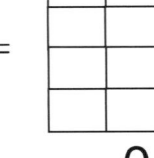

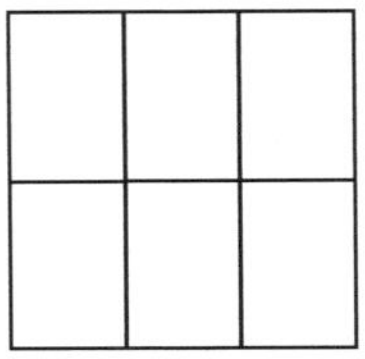

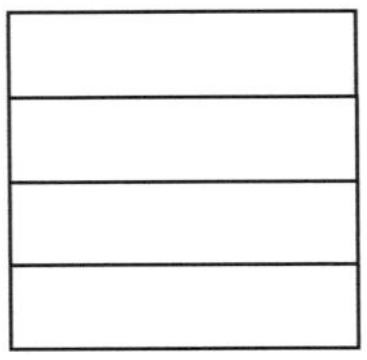

$$\frac{1}{12} - \frac{1}{12} = \frac{0}{12} = \frac{0}{6} = \frac{0}{4}$$

twelfth − twelfth = nothing = nothing = nothing

0.083˙ − 0.083˙ = 0.00 = 0.00 = 0

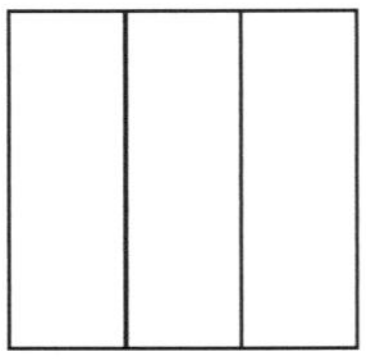

$$= \frac{0}{3} = \frac{0}{2} = 0$$

= nothing = nothing = nothing

= 0.00 = 0.00 = 0

212

Subtracting Unlike Fractions

How to subtract fractions with **different denominators**, for example,

$$\frac{1}{2}-\frac{1}{4}, \quad \frac{1}{2}-\frac{1}{4}-\frac{1}{8}, \quad \frac{3}{5}-\frac{2}{10}, \quad \frac{2}{3}-\frac{2}{6}, \quad \frac{1}{3}-\frac{1}{6}-\frac{1}{9} \ldots$$

i) First, make the fractions **denominators'** same!

$$\frac{2}{4}-\frac{2}{8} \rightarrow \frac{4}{8}-\frac{2}{8} \quad \text{or}$$

To summarise, a common denominator (the Lowest Common Multiple or LCM) can be found using times tables or **multiplication** lists.

2 times table = 0 , 2 , **4** , 6 , **8** …

4 times table = 0 , **4** , **8** …

8 times table = 0 , **8** …

The LCM is the first (*lowest*) number that appears in both times tables (for 2 & 4, and for 4 & 8) or in all tables (for 2, 4 and 8).

Therefore, the LCM of 2 and 4 is **4** (first common multiple).

The LCM of 2 and 8 is **8**.

The LCM of 4 and 8 is **8** (lowest multiple in both times tables).

The LCM of 2, 4 and 8 is **8** (common multiple in all tables).

× table of 5   is 0 , 5 , **10** , 15 ...
× table of 10   is 0 ,   **10**   ...

Therefore, the LCM of 5 and 10 is **10**.

Multiples of 3 are 0 , 3 , **6** , 9 , 12 , 15 , **18** ...
Multiples of 6 are 0 ,   **6** ,   12 ,   **18** ...
Multiples of 9 are 0 ,   9   ,   **18** ...

The LCM of 3 and 6 is **6**.

The LCM of 3 and 9 is **9**.

The LCM of 6 and 9 is **18** (first common multiple in ×6 and ×9 tables).

The LCM of 3, 6 and 9 is **18** (new common multiple in all three tables).

Likewise,

2 times table is 0 , 2 , **4** , **6** , 8 , 10 , **12** , 14 ...
3 times table = 0 , 3 , **6** , 9 , **12**   ...
4 times table is 0 ,   **4** ,   8 ,   **12**   ...
6 times table = 0 ,   **6** ,   **12**   ...
12 times table is 0 ,   **12**   ...

Therefore, the LCM of 2 and 3 is **6**.

The LCM of 2 and 4 is **4**.

The LCM of 2 and 6 is **6**.

The LCM of 2 and 12 is **12**.

In addition, the LCM of 3 and 4 is **12**.

              The LCM of 3 and 6 is **6**.

              The LCM of 3 and 12 is **12**.

Finally, the LCM of   4 and 6 is **12**.

      The LCM of   4 and 12 is **12**.

      The LCM of   6 and 12 is **12**.

      The LCM of   2, 3 and 6 is **6**.

      The LCM of   2, 3 and 4 is **12**.

      The LCM of   3, 4, 6 and 12 is **12**.

      The LCM of   2, 3, 4, 6 and 12 is **12**.

For detailed instructions on how to find the common denominator (LCM), please, refer back to **Adding Unlike Fractions**, *How to add fractions with **different** denominators* section on pages 133 – 138.

After making the denominators the same, the rest of the process becomes just like **Subtracting Like Fractions**, *How to subtract fractions with **same denominators**…* as before (page 184).

That is, converting subtrahend fractions into their equivalent fractions.

So, $\quad \boxed{\dfrac{2}{4} - \dfrac{2}{8}} \quad$ changes to $\quad \boxed{\dfrac{4}{8} - \dfrac{2}{8}}$

Subtracting Unlike Fractions *continued*

ii) Subtract the **numerators** and use their **common** denominator.

$$\frac{4}{8} - \frac{2}{8} = \frac{2}{8}$$

The **denominator** stays the **same** - not subtracted like numerators!
The result is a fraction with the **same denominator** as the subtracted fractions.

iii) If possible, simplify the result.

$$\frac{2}{8} \overset{\div 2}{\underset{\div 2}{=}} \frac{1}{4}$$ or

The full solution with the final answer in its *simplest form* is

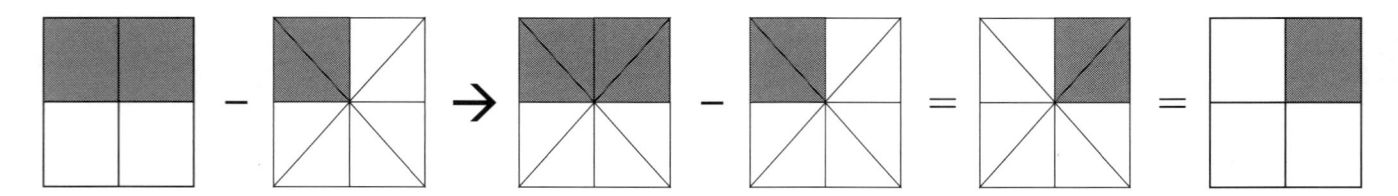

$$\frac{2}{4} - \frac{2}{8} \rightarrow \frac{4}{8} - \frac{2}{8} = \frac{4-2}{8} = \frac{2}{8} = \frac{1}{4}$$

Another similar example,

$$\frac{1}{2} - \frac{1}{4} \rightarrow \frac{2}{4} - \frac{1}{4} = \frac{2-1}{4} = \frac{1}{4}$$

More examples;

$$\frac{1}{2} - \frac{1}{4} - \frac{1}{8} \rightarrow \frac{4}{8} - \frac{2}{8} - \frac{1}{8} = \frac{4-2-1}{8} = \frac{1}{8}$$

$$\frac{3}{5} - \frac{2}{10} \rightarrow \frac{6}{10} - \frac{2}{10} = \frac{6-2}{10} = \frac{4}{10} = \frac{2}{5}$$

$$\frac{2}{3} - \frac{2}{6} \rightarrow \frac{4}{6} - \frac{2}{6} = \frac{4-2}{6} = \frac{2}{6} = \frac{1}{3}$$

$$\frac{1}{6} - \frac{1}{9} \rightarrow \frac{3}{18} - \frac{2}{18} = \frac{3-2}{18} = \frac{1}{18}$$

$$\frac{1}{3} - \frac{1}{6} - \frac{1}{9} \rightarrow \frac{6}{18} - \frac{3}{18} - \frac{2}{18} = \frac{6-3-2}{18} = \frac{1}{18}$$

Summary

When both or all denominators are in the same times table, the bigger (or the biggest) number is their LCM. Example, 2, 4 (= 4), 8 (= 8) etc.

If both or all denominators are not in the same multiple table, their LCM is the *first* (or lowest) number at which all their times tables meet. For instance, 3 × 6 = 18 would be a common denominator that works fine for 3 and 6. But their times tables share (as common) **6**; hence a smaller LCM of **6** for 3 and 6.

Halves – Quarters

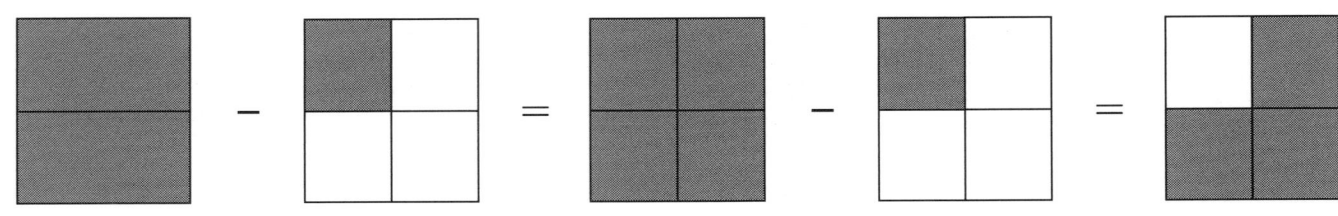

$$\frac{2}{2} - \frac{1}{4} = \frac{4}{4} - \frac{1}{4} = \frac{3}{4}$$

1.00 − 0.25 = 1.00 − 0.25 = 0.75

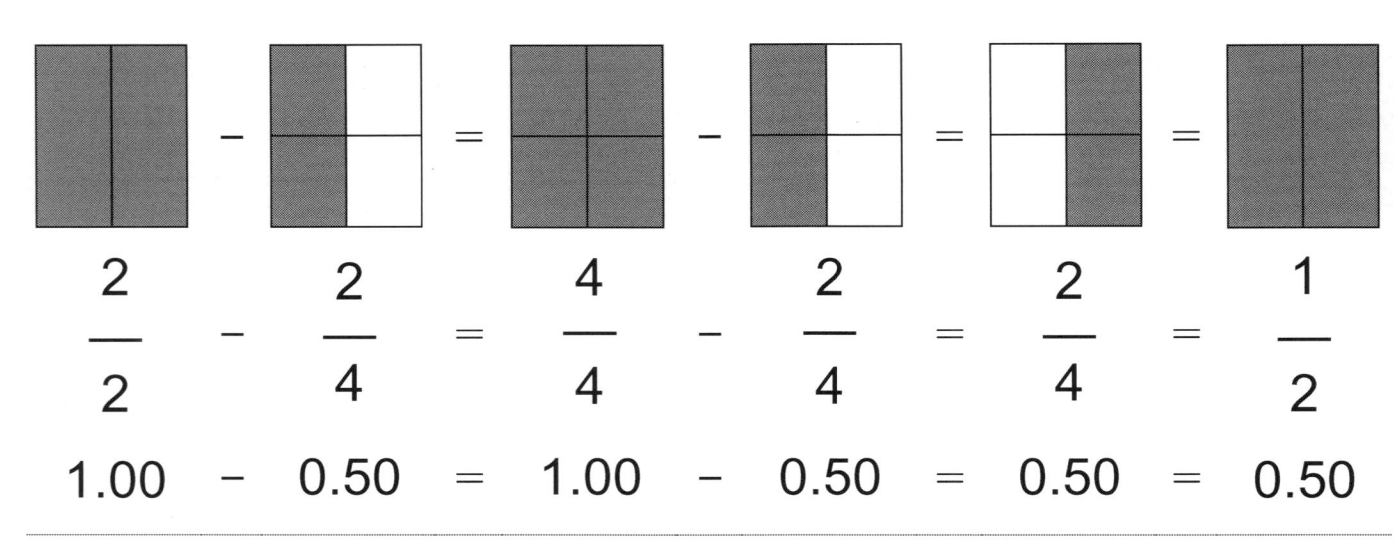

$$\frac{2}{2} - \frac{2}{4} = \frac{4}{4} - \frac{2}{4} = \frac{2}{4} = \frac{1}{2}$$

1.00 − 0.50 = 1.00 − 0.50 = 0.50 = 0.50

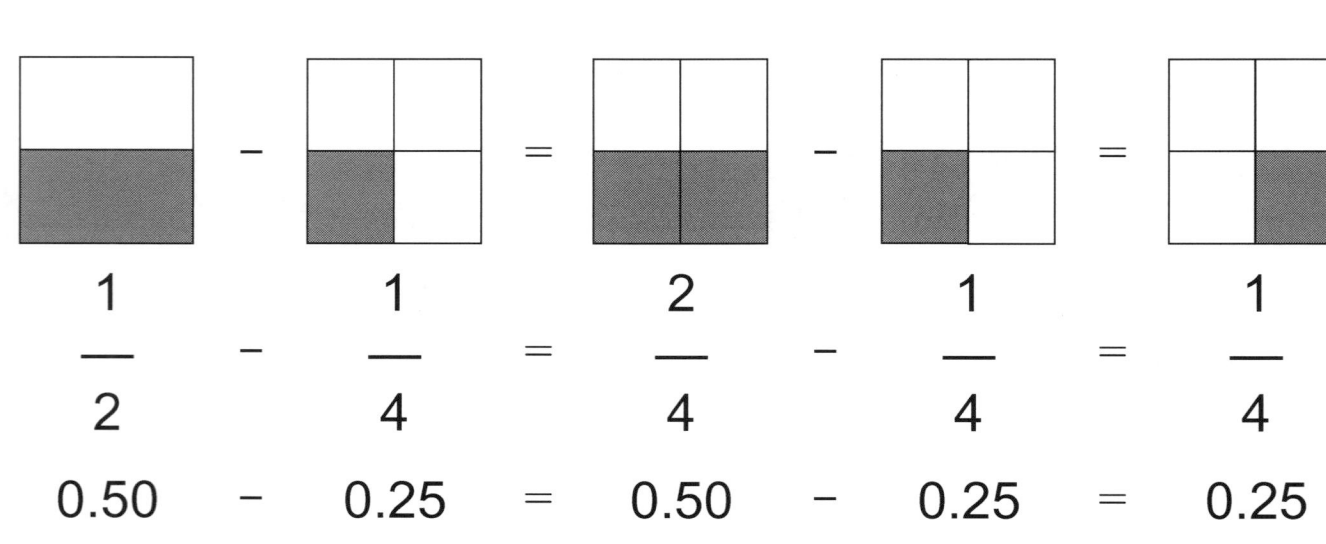

$$\frac{1}{2} - \frac{1}{4} = \frac{2}{4} - \frac{1}{4} = \frac{1}{4}$$

0.50 − 0.25 = 0.50 − 0.25 = 0.25

Halves − Quarters

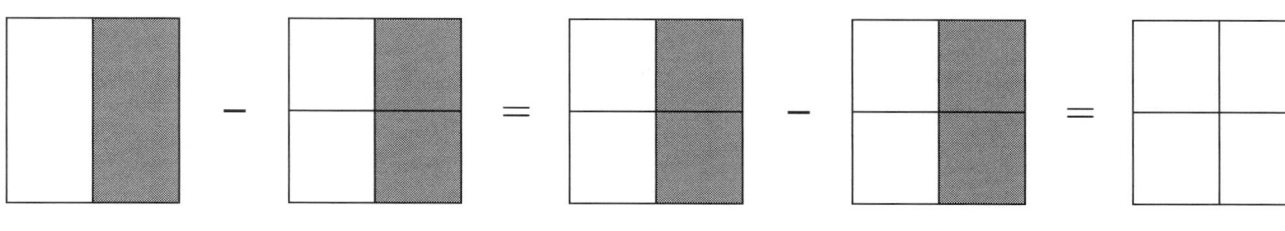

$$\frac{1}{2} - \frac{2}{4} = \frac{2}{4} - \frac{2}{4} = \frac{0}{4}$$

0.50 − 0.50 = 0.50 − 0.50 = 0.00

$$= \frac{0}{2} = 0$$

= 0.00 = 0

Halves – Eighths

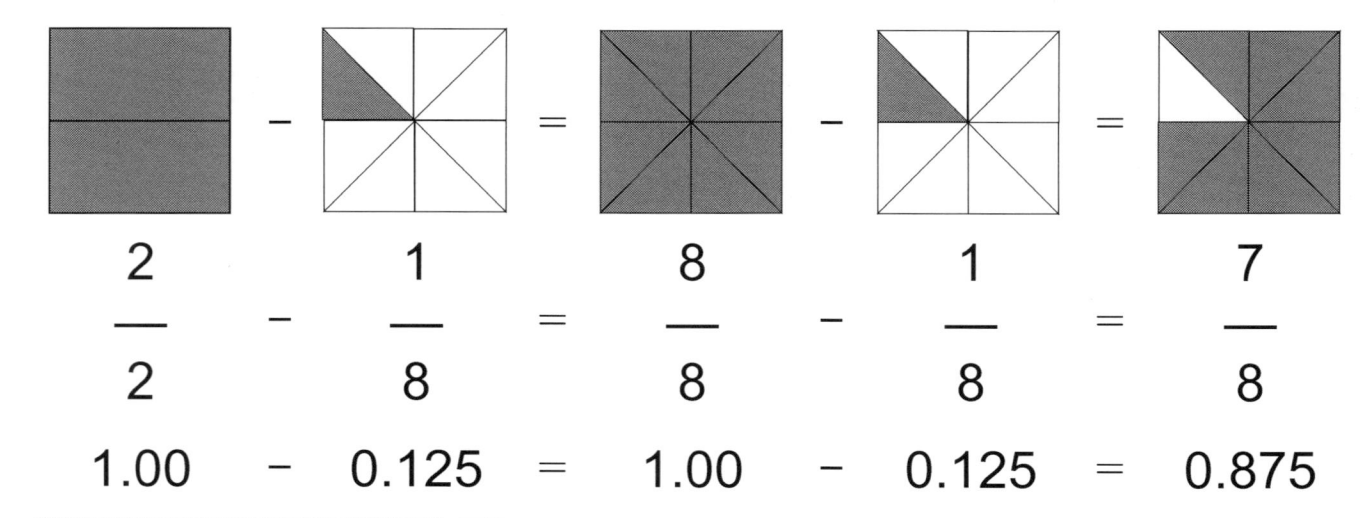

$$\frac{2}{2} - \frac{1}{8} = \frac{8}{8} - \frac{1}{8} = \frac{7}{8}$$

$$1.00 - 0.125 = 1.00 - 0.125 = 0.875$$

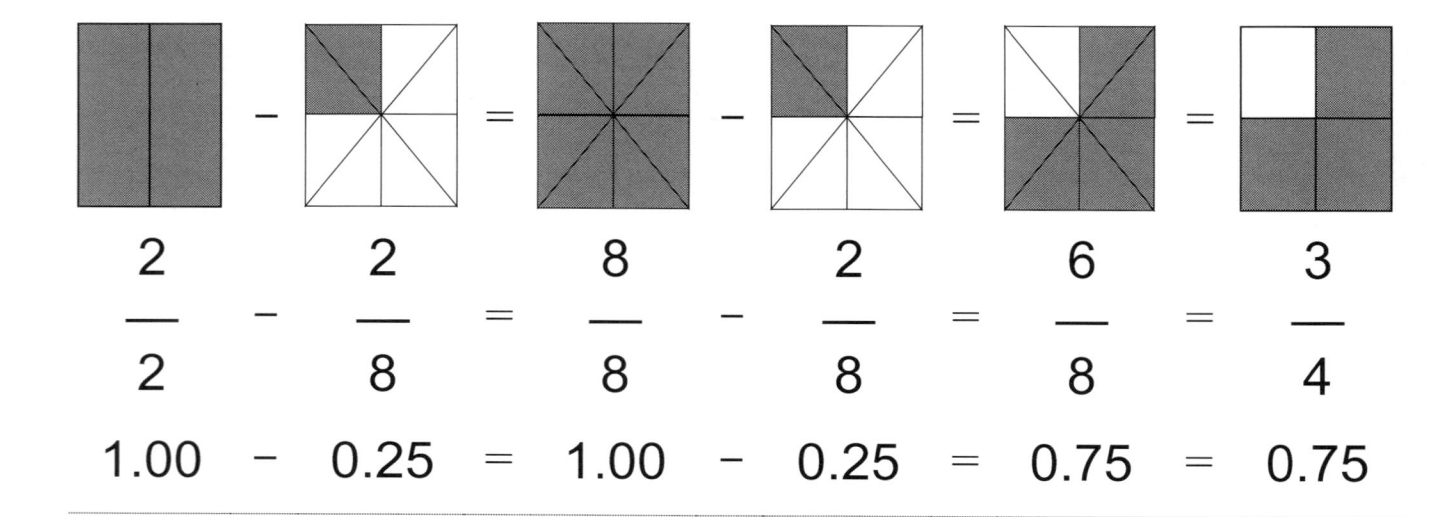

$$\frac{2}{2} - \frac{2}{8} = \frac{8}{8} - \frac{2}{8} = \frac{6}{8} = \frac{3}{4}$$

$$1.00 - 0.25 = 1.00 - 0.25 = 0.75 = 0.75$$

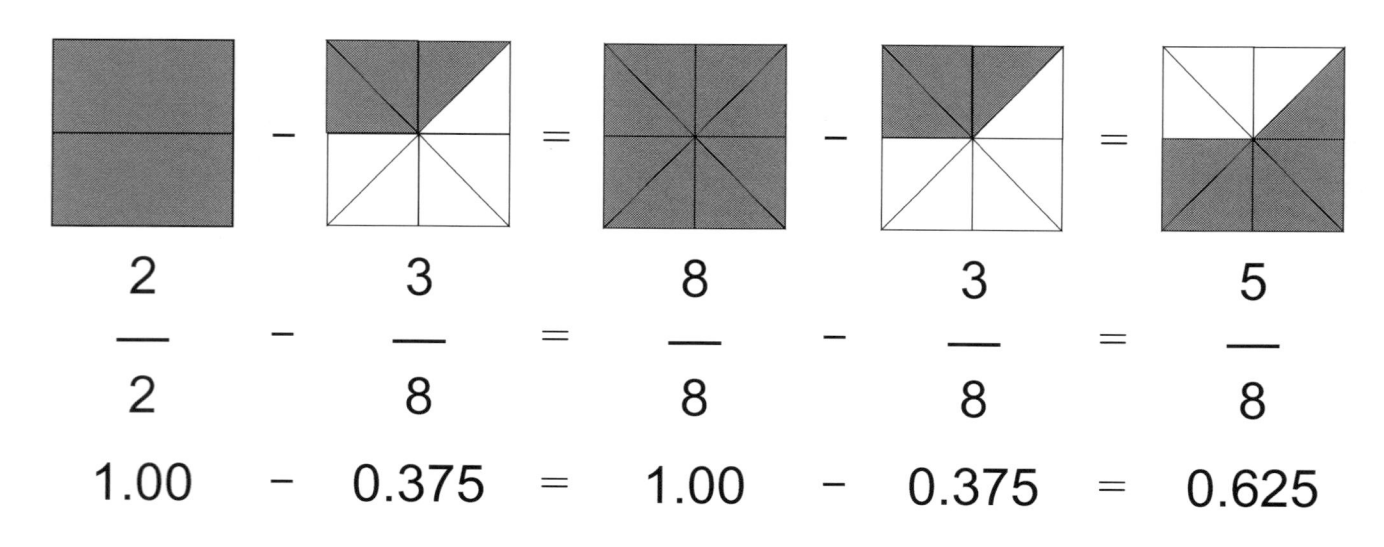

$$\frac{2}{2} - \frac{3}{8} = \frac{8}{8} - \frac{3}{8} = \frac{5}{8}$$

$$1.00 - 0.375 = 1.00 - 0.375 = 0.625$$

220

Halves – Eighths

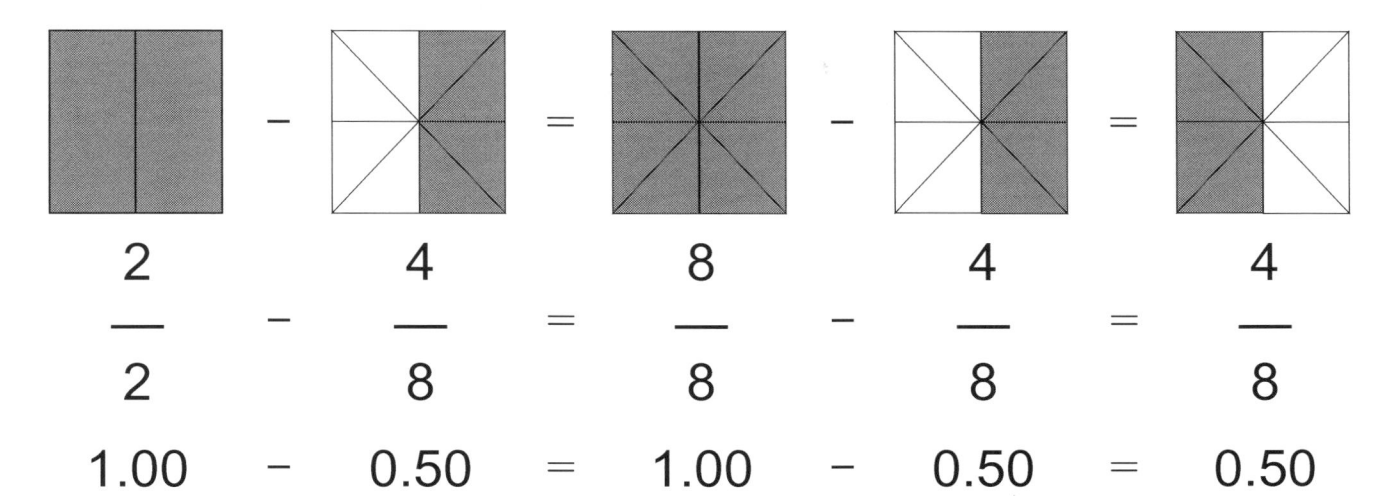

$$\frac{2}{2} - \frac{4}{8} = \frac{8}{8} - \frac{4}{8} = \frac{4}{8}$$

$$1.00 - 0.50 = 1.00 - 0.50 = 0.50$$

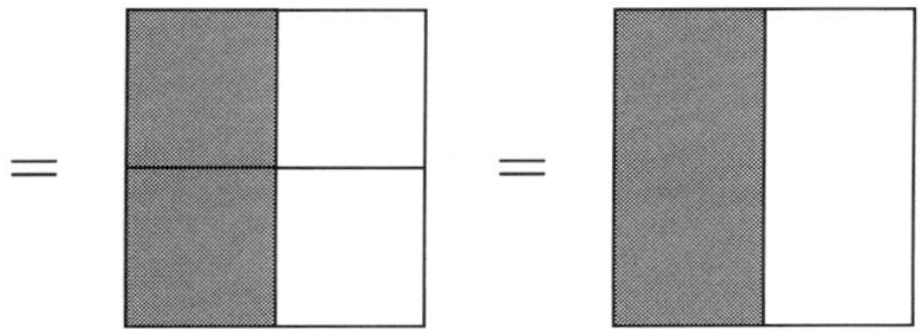

$$= \frac{2}{4} = \frac{1}{2}$$

$$= 0.50 = 0.50$$

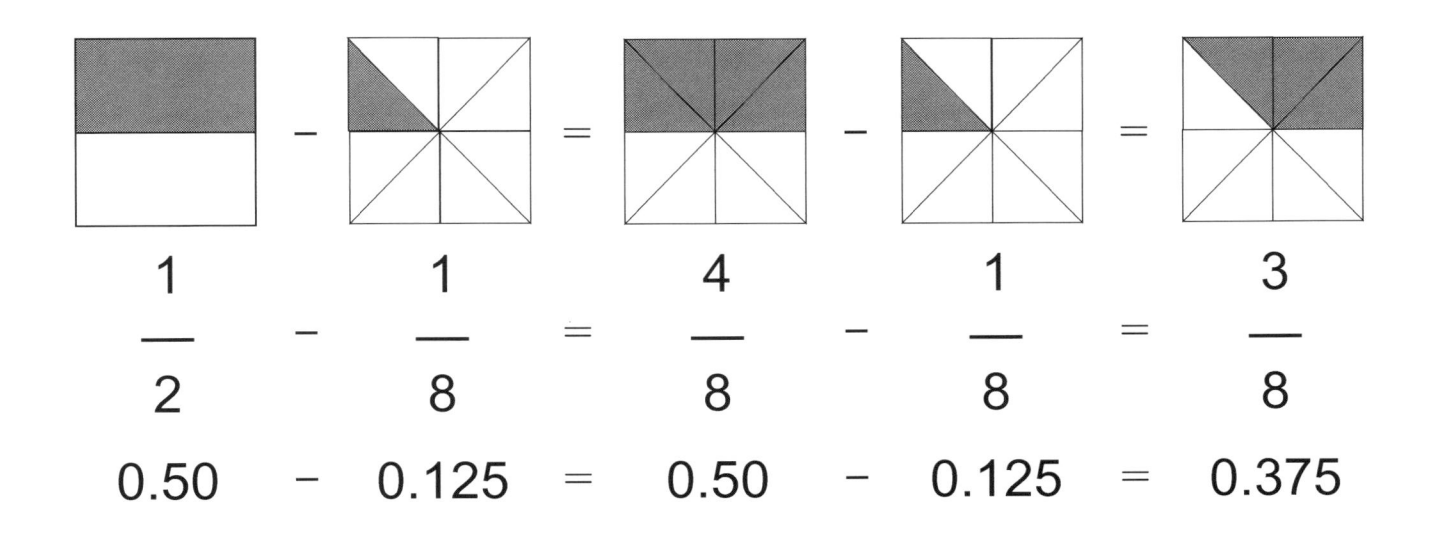

$$\frac{1}{2} - \frac{1}{8} = \frac{4}{8} - \frac{1}{8} = \frac{3}{8}$$

$$0.50 - 0.125 = 0.50 - 0.125 = 0.375$$

Halves – Eighths

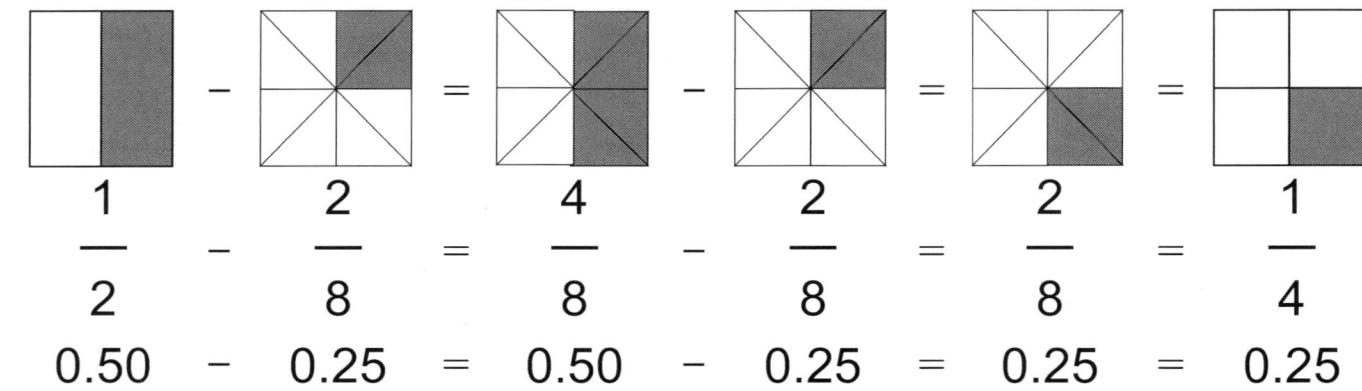

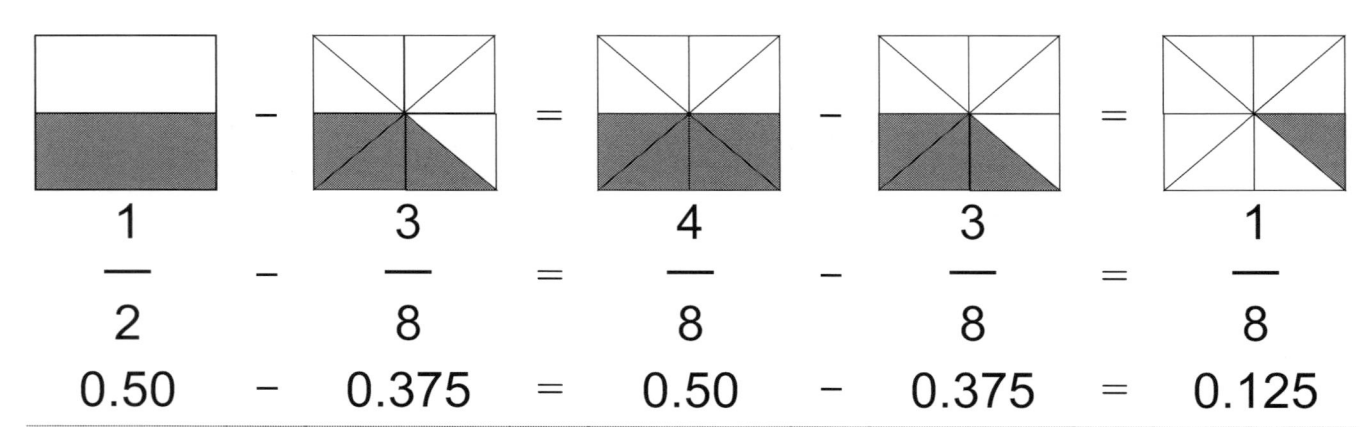

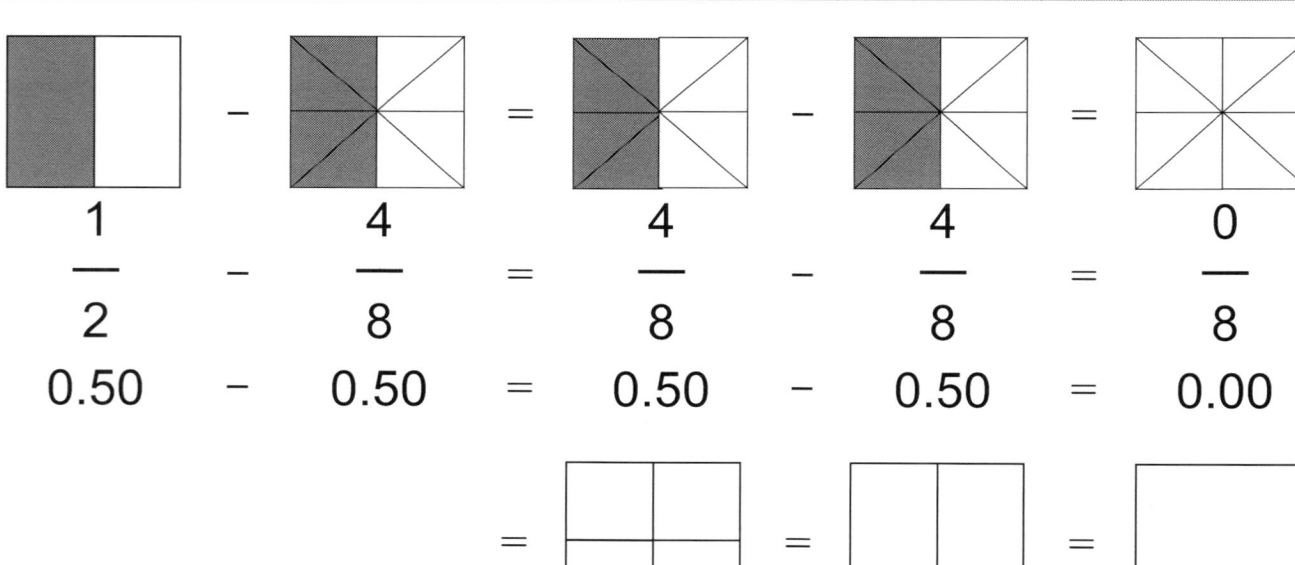

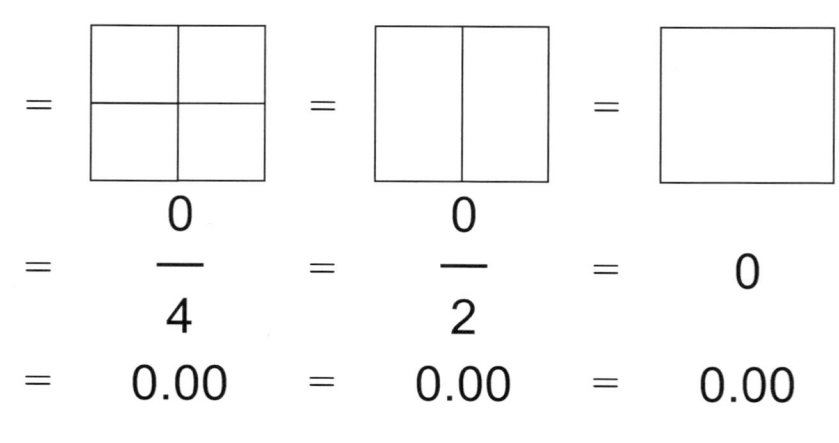

$$\frac{1}{2} - \frac{2}{8} = \frac{4}{8} - \frac{2}{8} = \frac{2}{8} = \frac{1}{4}$$

0.50 − 0.25 = 0.50 − 0.25 = 0.25 = 0.25

$$\frac{1}{2} - \frac{3}{8} = \frac{4}{8} - \frac{3}{8} = \frac{1}{8}$$

0.50 − 0.375 = 0.50 − 0.375 = 0.125

$$\frac{1}{2} - \frac{4}{8} = \frac{4}{8} - \frac{4}{8} = \frac{0}{8}$$

0.50 − 0.50 = 0.50 − 0.50 = 0.00

$$= \frac{0}{4} = \frac{0}{2} = 0$$

= 0.00 = 0.00 = 0.00

Quarters – Halves

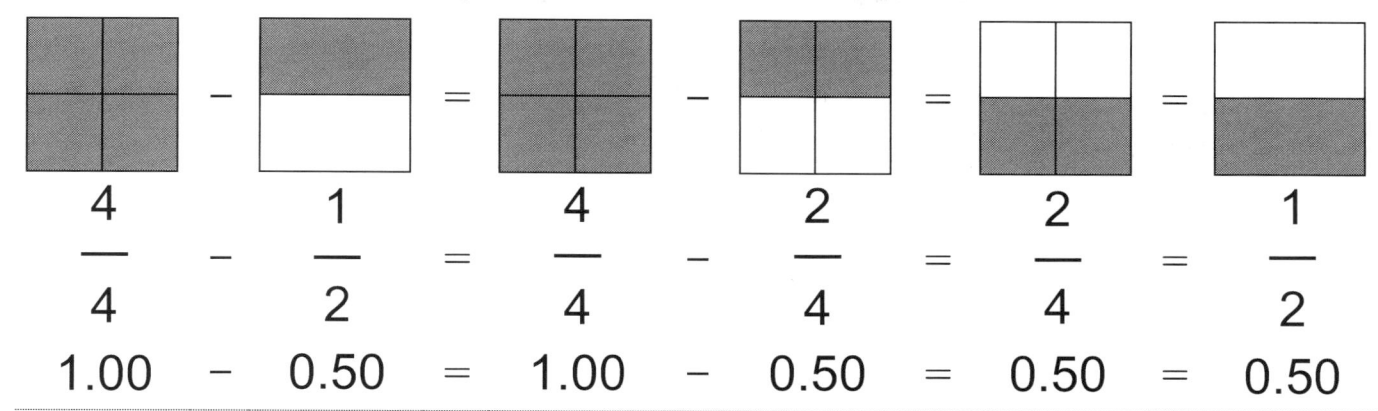

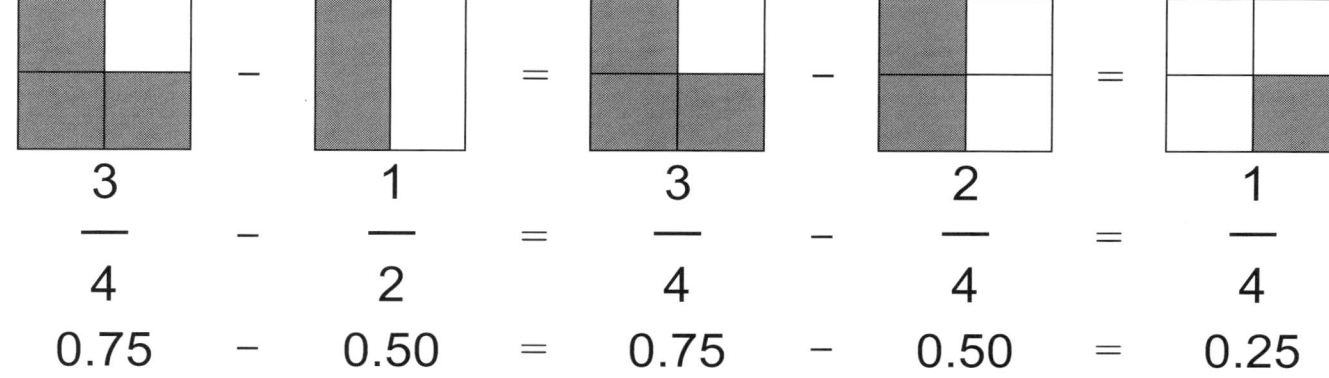

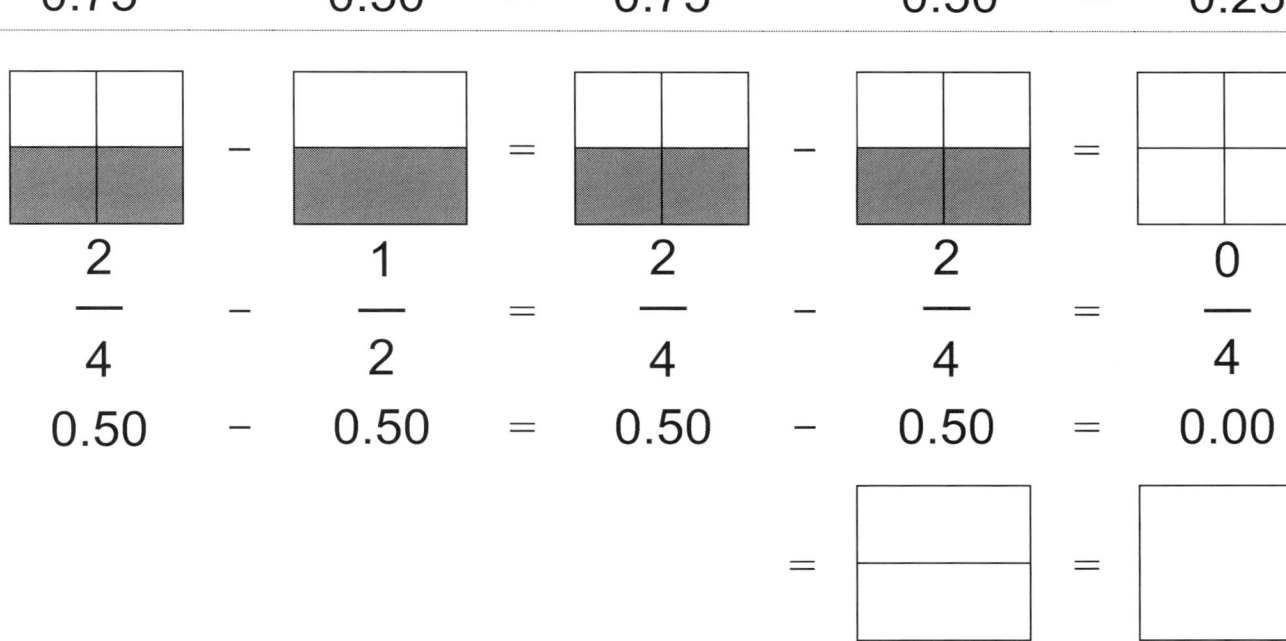

$$\frac{4}{4} - \frac{1}{2} = \frac{4}{4} - \frac{2}{4} = \frac{2}{4} = \frac{1}{2}$$

$$1.00 - 0.50 = 1.00 - 0.50 = 0.50 = 0.50$$

$$\frac{3}{4} - \frac{1}{2} = \frac{3}{4} - \frac{2}{4} = \frac{1}{4}$$

$$0.75 - 0.50 = 0.75 - 0.50 = 0.25$$

$$\frac{2}{4} - \frac{1}{2} = \frac{2}{4} - \frac{2}{4} = \frac{0}{4}$$

$$0.50 - 0.50 = 0.50 - 0.50 = 0.00$$

$$= \frac{0}{2} = 0$$

$$= 0.00 = 0$$

Quarters − Eighths

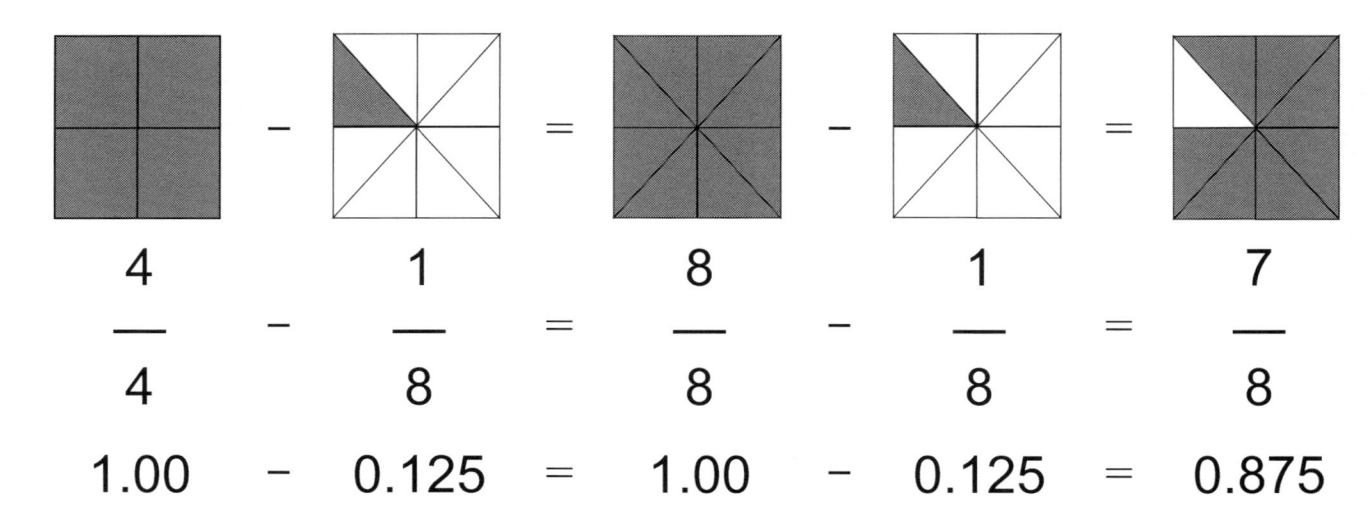

$$\frac{4}{4} - \frac{1}{8} = \frac{8}{8} - \frac{1}{8} = \frac{7}{8}$$

1.00 − 0.125 = 1.00 − 0.125 = 0.875

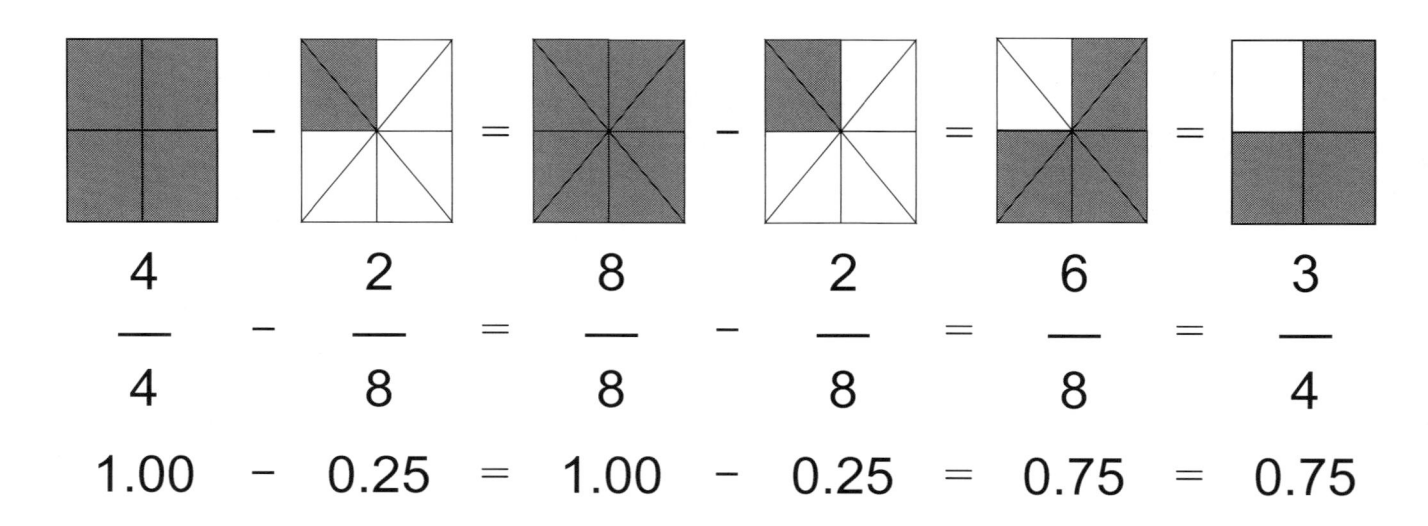

$$\frac{4}{4} - \frac{2}{8} = \frac{8}{8} - \frac{2}{8} = \frac{6}{8} = \frac{3}{4}$$

1.00 − 0.25 = 1.00 − 0.25 = 0.75 = 0.75

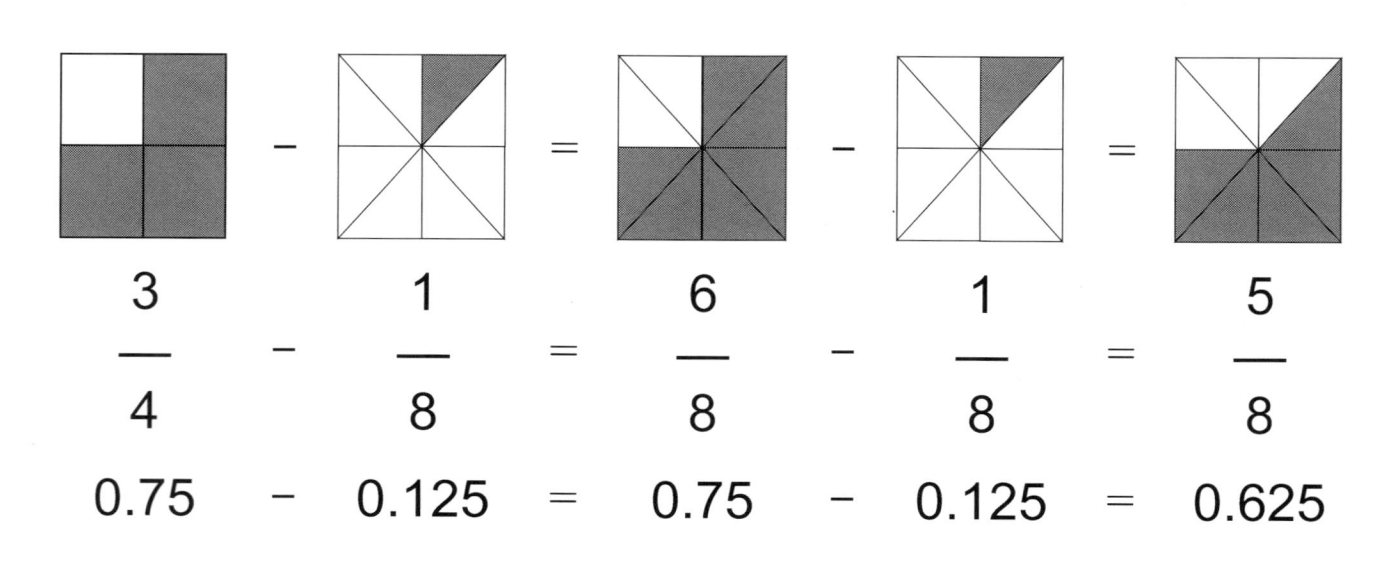

$$\frac{3}{4} - \frac{1}{8} = \frac{6}{8} - \frac{1}{8} = \frac{5}{8}$$

0.75 − 0.125 = 0.75 − 0.125 = 0.625

Quarters − Eighths

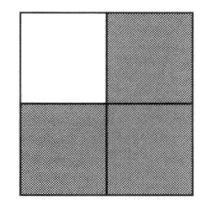

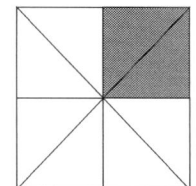

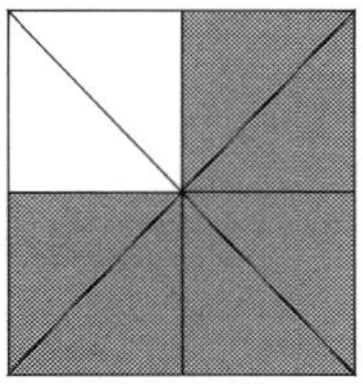

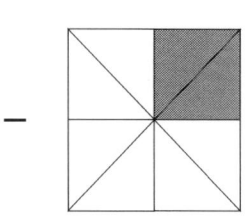

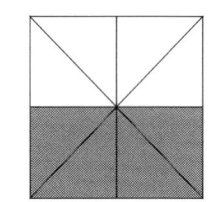

$$\frac{3}{4} - \frac{2}{8} = \frac{6}{8} - \frac{2}{8} = \frac{4}{8}$$

0.75 − 0.25 = 0.75 − 0.25 = 0.50

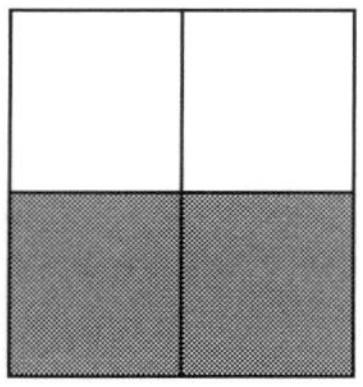

$$= \frac{2}{4} = \frac{1}{2}$$

= 0.50 = 0.50

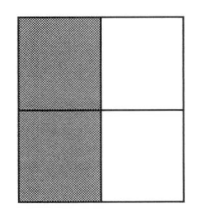

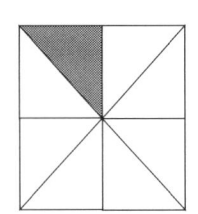

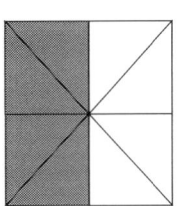

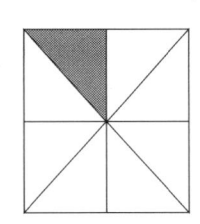

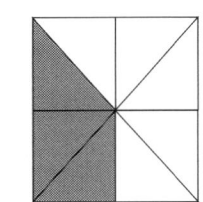

$$\frac{2}{4} - \frac{1}{8} = \frac{4}{8} - \frac{1}{8} = \frac{3}{8}$$

0.50 − 0.125 = 0.50 − 0.125 = 0.375

225

Quarters − Eighths

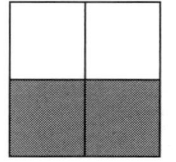

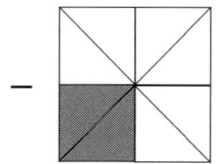

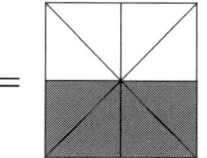

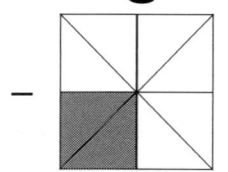

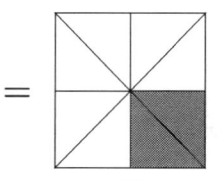

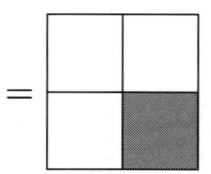

$$\frac{2}{4} - \frac{2}{8} = \frac{4}{8} - \frac{2}{8} = \frac{2}{8} = \frac{1}{4}$$

0.50 − 0.25 = 0.50 − 0.25 = 0.25 = 0.25

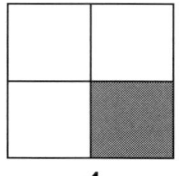

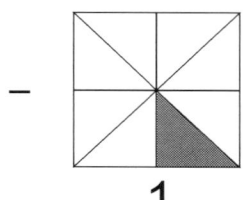

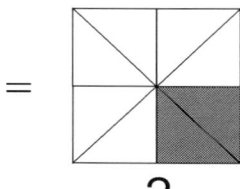

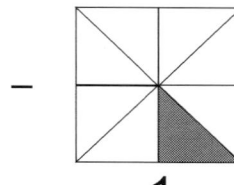

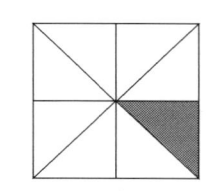

$$\frac{1}{4} - \frac{1}{8} = \frac{2}{8} - \frac{1}{8} = \frac{1}{8}$$

0.25 − 0.125 = 0.25 − 0.125 = 0.125

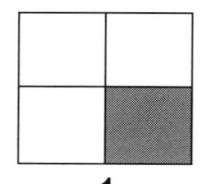

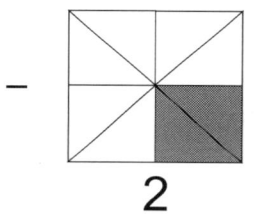

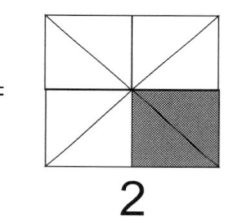

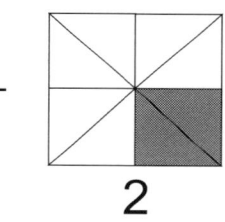

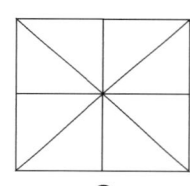

$$\frac{1}{4} - \frac{2}{8} = \frac{2}{8} - \frac{2}{8} = \frac{0}{8}$$

0.25 − 0.25 = 0.25 − 0.25 = 0.00

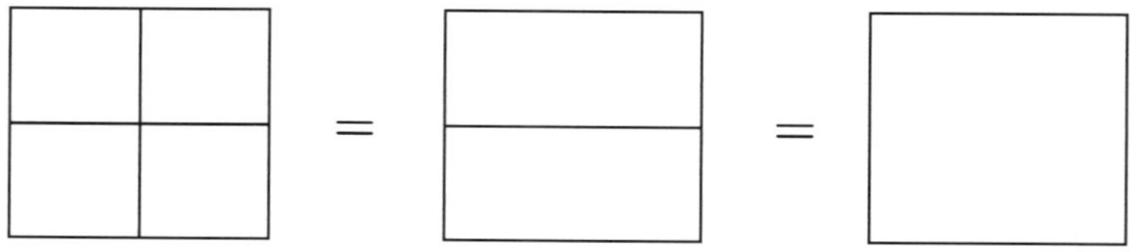

$$= \frac{0}{4} = \frac{0}{2} = 0$$

= 0.00 = 0.00 = 0

226

Eighths − Halves

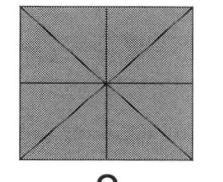

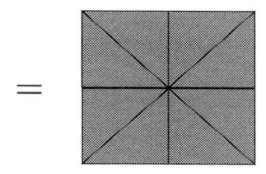

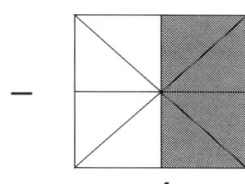

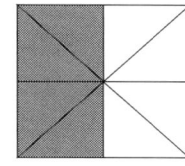

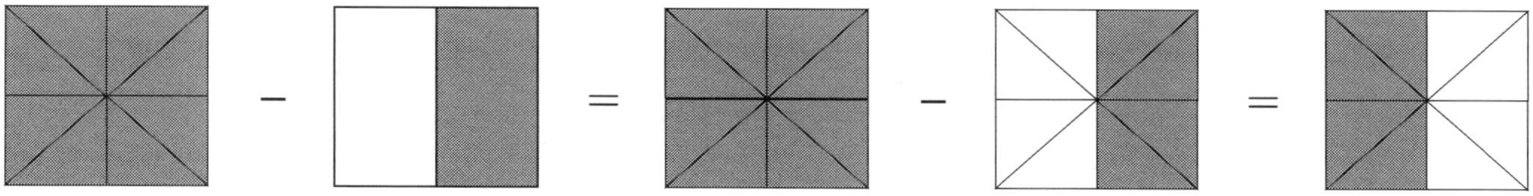

$$\frac{8}{8} - \frac{1}{2} = \frac{8}{8} - \frac{4}{8} = \frac{4}{8}$$
$$1.00 - 0.50 = 1.00 - 0.50 = 0.50$$ 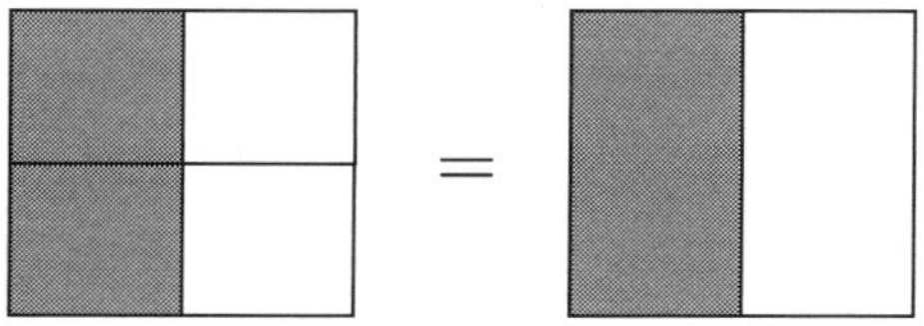
$$= \frac{2}{4} = \frac{1}{2}$$
$$= 0.50 = 0.50$$

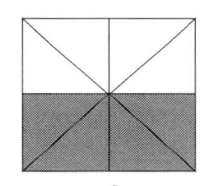

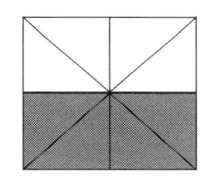

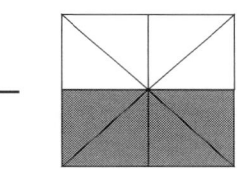

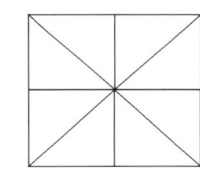

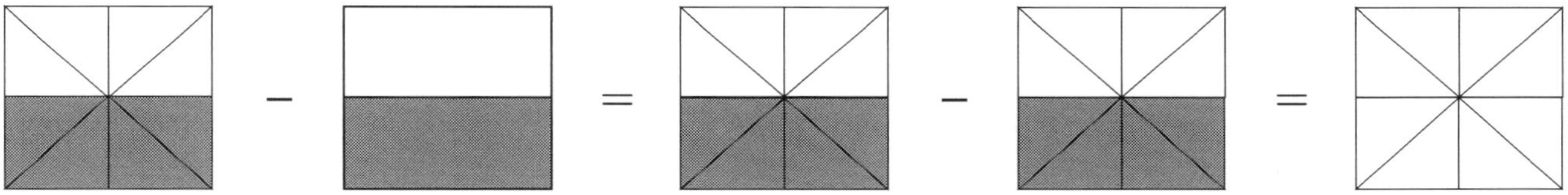

$$\frac{4}{8} - \frac{1}{2} = \frac{4}{8} - \frac{4}{8} = \frac{0}{8}$$
$$0.50 - 0.50 = 0.50 - 0.50 = 0.00$$
$$= \frac{0}{4} = \frac{0}{2} = 0$$ 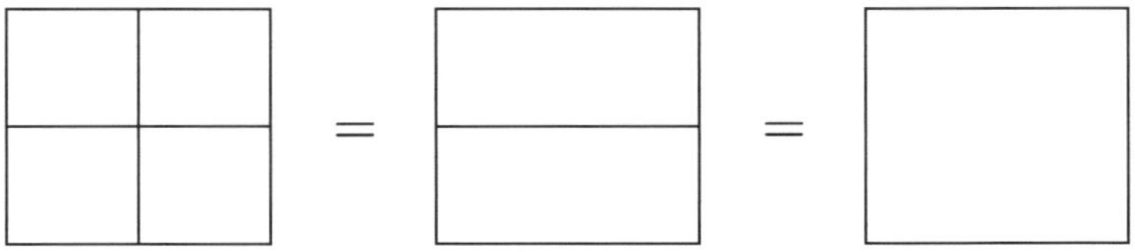
$$= 0.00 = 0.00 = 0$$

Eighths – Quarters

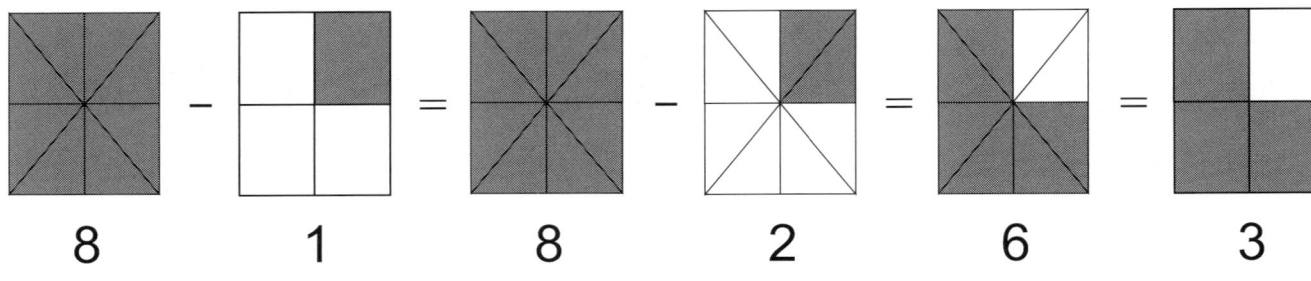

$$\frac{8}{8} - \frac{1}{4} = \frac{8}{8} - \frac{2}{8} = \frac{6}{8} = \frac{3}{4}$$

$$1.00 - 0.25 = 1.00 - 0.25 = 0.75 = 0.75$$

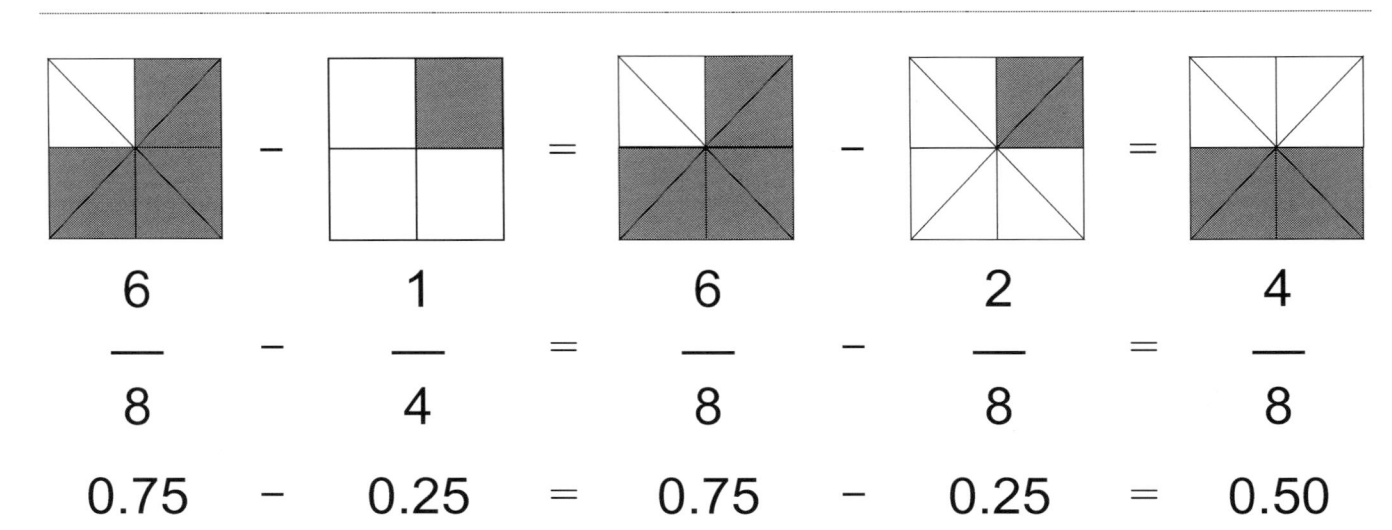

$$\frac{6}{8} - \frac{1}{4} = \frac{6}{8} - \frac{2}{8} = \frac{4}{8}$$

$$0.75 - 0.25 = 0.75 - 0.25 = 0.50$$

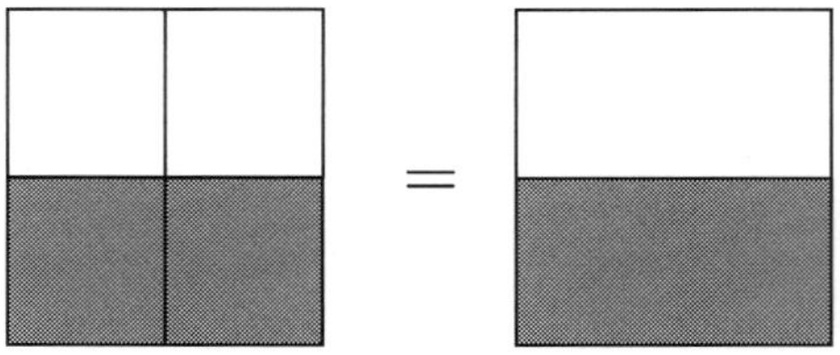

$$= \frac{2}{4} = \frac{1}{2}$$

$$= 0.50 = 0.50$$

Eighths – Quarters

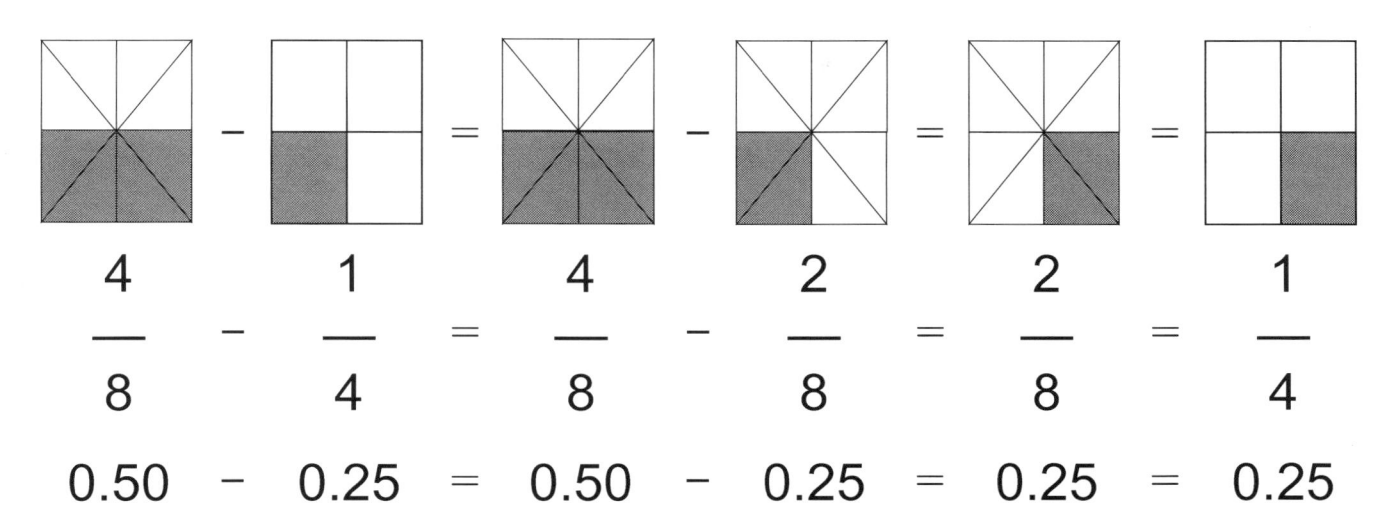

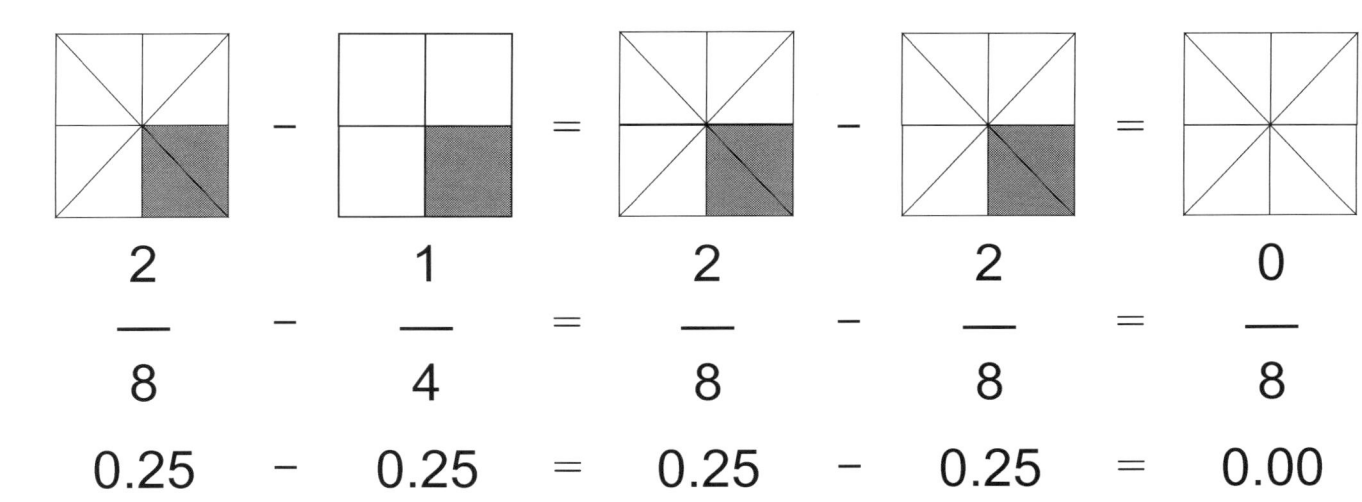

$$\frac{4}{8} - \frac{1}{4} = \frac{4}{8} - \frac{2}{8} = \frac{2}{8} = \frac{1}{4}$$

0.50 − 0.25 = 0.50 − 0.25 = 0.25 = 0.25

$$\frac{2}{8} - \frac{1}{4} = \frac{2}{8} - \frac{2}{8} = \frac{0}{8}$$

0.25 − 0.25 = 0.25 − 0.25 = 0.00

$$= \frac{0}{4} = \frac{0}{2} = 0$$

= 0.00 = 0.00 = 0

229

Halves – Quarters – Eighths

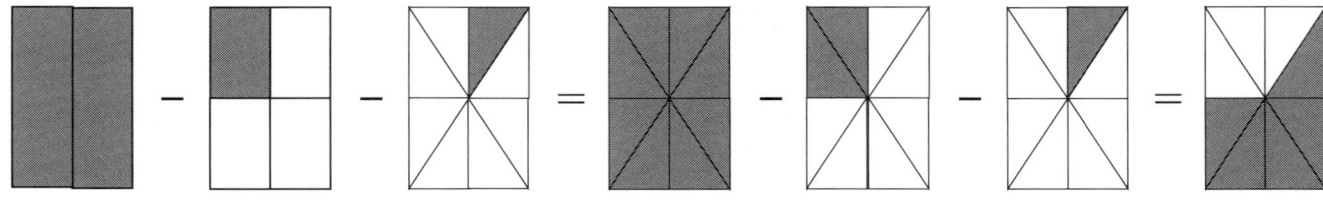

$$\frac{2}{2} - \frac{1}{4} - \frac{1}{8} = \frac{8}{8} - \frac{2}{8} - \frac{1}{8} = \frac{5}{8}$$

$$1.00 - 0.25 - 0.125 = 1.00 - 0.25 - 0.125 = 0.625$$

$$\frac{2}{2} - \frac{1}{4} - \frac{2}{8} = \frac{8}{8} - \frac{2}{8} - \frac{2}{8} = \frac{4}{8}$$

$$1.00 - 0.25 - 0.25 = 1.00 - 0.25 - 0.25 = 0.50$$

$$= \frac{2}{4} = \frac{1}{2}$$

$$= 0.50 = 0.50$$

Halves – Quarters – Eighths

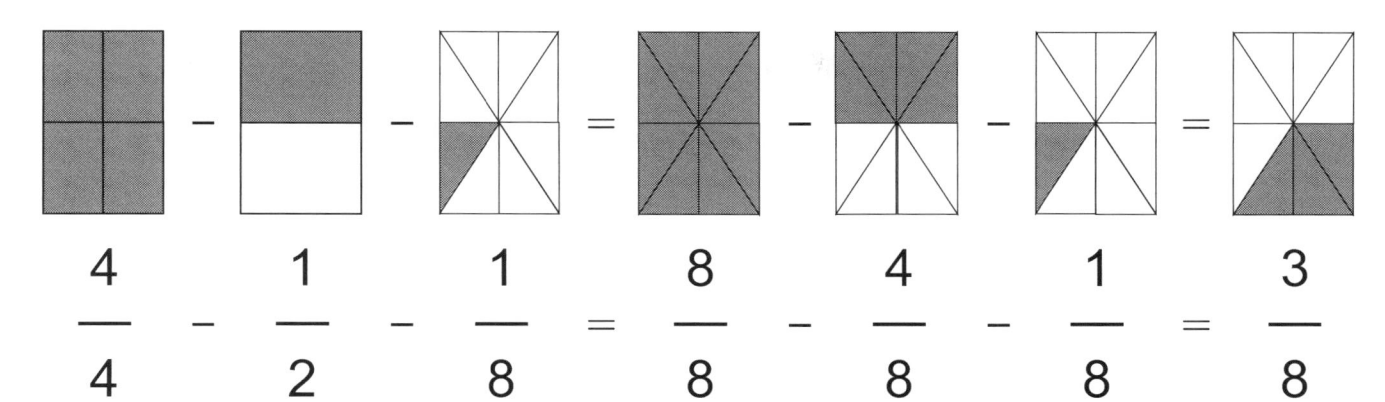

$$\frac{4}{4} - \frac{1}{2} - \frac{1}{8} = \frac{8}{8} - \frac{4}{8} - \frac{1}{8} = \frac{3}{8}$$

$$1.00 - 0.50 - 0.125 = 1.00 - 0.50 - 0.125 = 0.375$$

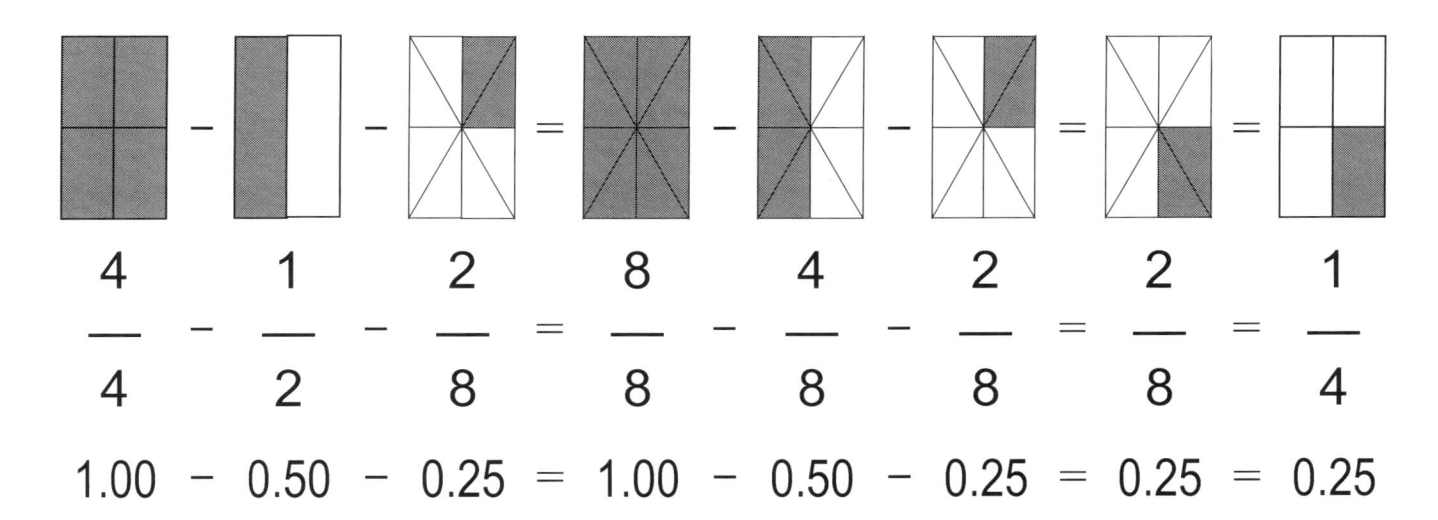

$$\frac{4}{4} - \frac{1}{2} - \frac{2}{8} = \frac{8}{8} - \frac{4}{8} - \frac{2}{8} = \frac{2}{8} = \frac{1}{4}$$

$$1.00 - 0.50 - 0.25 = 1.00 - 0.50 - 0.25 = 0.25 = 0.25$$

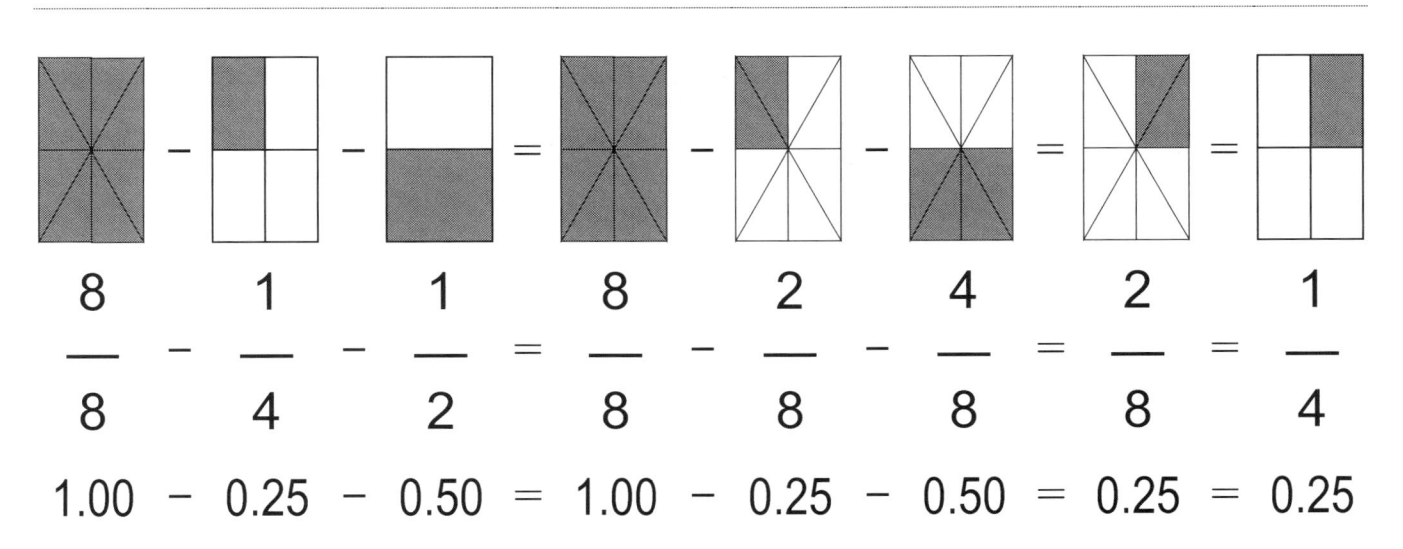

$$\frac{8}{8} - \frac{1}{4} - \frac{1}{2} = \frac{8}{8} - \frac{2}{8} - \frac{4}{8} = \frac{2}{8} = \frac{1}{4}$$

$$1.00 - 0.25 - 0.50 = 1.00 - 0.25 - 0.50 = 0.25 = 0.25$$

Halves – Quarters – Eighths

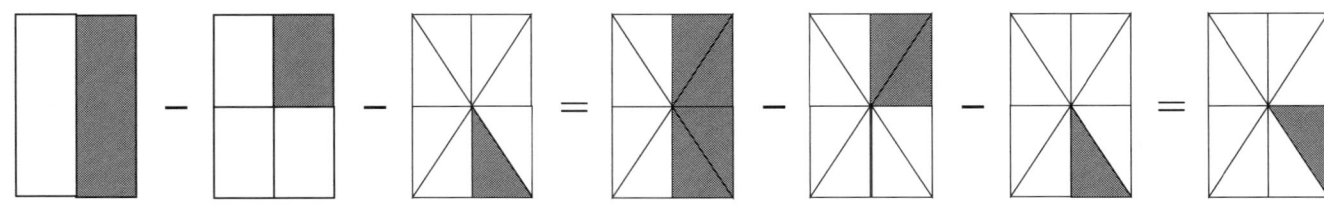

$$\frac{1}{2} - \frac{1}{4} - \frac{1}{8} = \frac{4}{8} - \frac{2}{8} - \frac{1}{8} = \frac{1}{8}$$

$$0.50 - 0.25 - 0.125 = 0.50 - 0.25 - 0.125 = 0.125$$

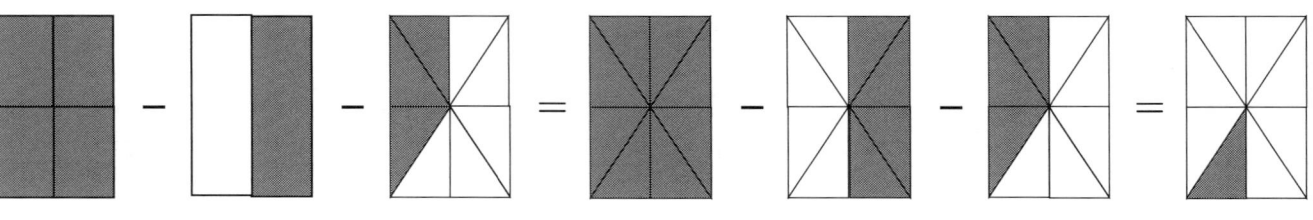

$$\frac{4}{4} - \frac{1}{2} - \frac{3}{8} = \frac{8}{8} - \frac{4}{8} - \frac{3}{8} = \frac{1}{8}$$

$$1.00 - 0.50 - 0.375 = 1.00 - 0.50 - 0.375 = 0.125$$

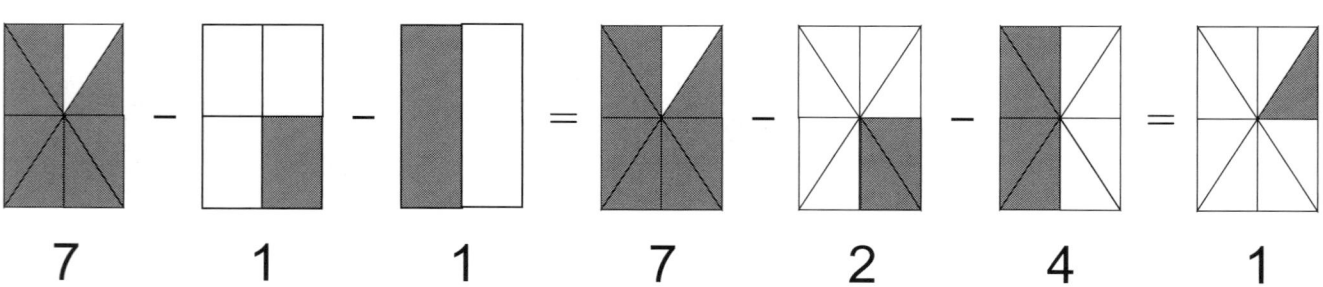

$$\frac{7}{8} - \frac{1}{4} - \frac{1}{2} = \frac{7}{8} - \frac{2}{8} - \frac{4}{8} = \frac{1}{8}$$

$$0.875 - 0.25 - 0.50 = 0.875 - 0.25 - 0.50 = 0.125$$

Halves – Quarters – Eighths

$$\frac{6}{8} - \frac{1}{4} - \frac{1}{2} = \frac{6}{8} - \frac{2}{8} - \frac{4}{8} = \frac{0}{8}$$

$$0.75 - 0.25 - 0.50 = 0.75 - 0.25 - 0.50 = 0.00$$

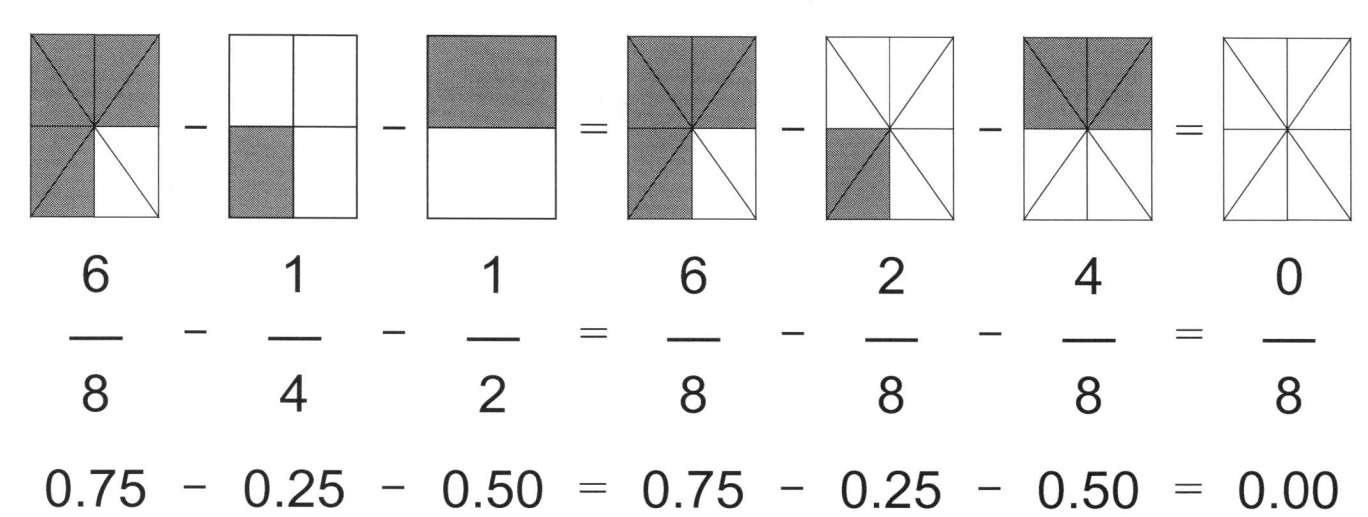

$$= \frac{0}{4} = \frac{0}{2} = 0$$

$$= 0.00 = 0.00 = 0$$

Fifths – Tenths

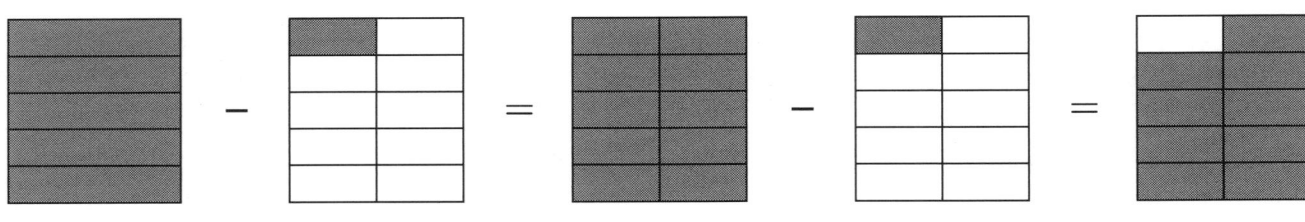

$$\frac{5}{5} - \frac{1}{10} = \frac{10}{10} - \frac{1}{10} = \frac{9}{10}$$

1.00 − 0.10 = 1.00 − 0.10 = 0.90

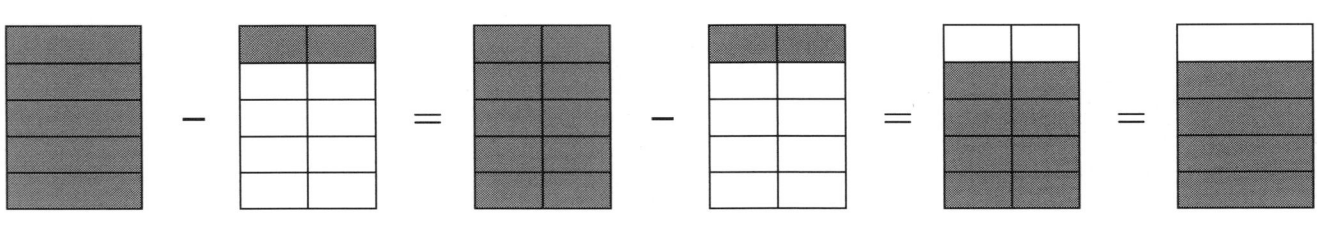

$$\frac{5}{5} - \frac{2}{10} = \frac{10}{10} - \frac{2}{10} = \frac{8}{10} = \frac{4}{5}$$

1.00 − 0.20 = 1.00 − 0.20 = 0.80 = 0.80

$$\frac{4}{5} - \frac{1}{10} = \frac{8}{10} - \frac{1}{10} = \frac{7}{10}$$

0.80 − 0.10 = 0.80 − 0.10 = 0.70

Fifths − Tenths

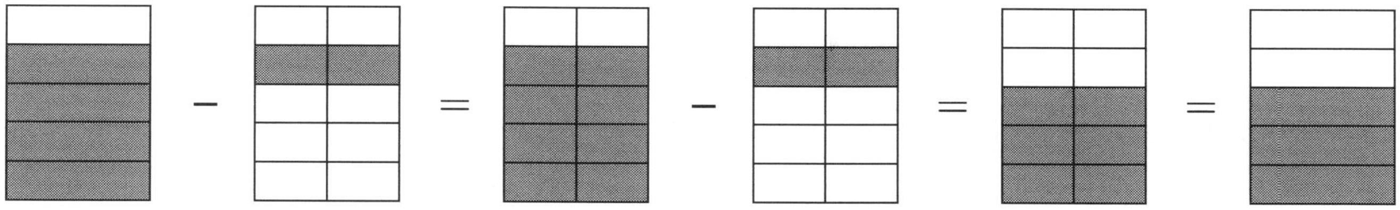

$$\frac{4}{5} - \frac{2}{10} = \frac{8}{10} - \frac{2}{10} = \frac{6}{10} = \frac{3}{5}$$

0.80 − 0.20 = 0.80 − 0.20 = 0.60 = 0.60

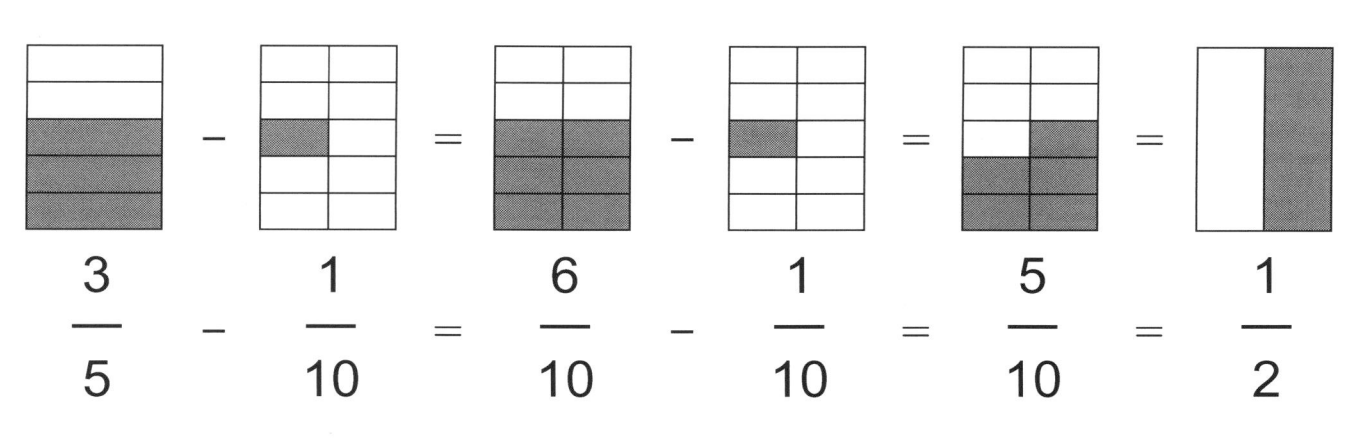

$$\frac{3}{5} - \frac{1}{10} = \frac{6}{10} - \frac{1}{10} = \frac{5}{10} = \frac{1}{2}$$

0.60 − 0.10 = 0.60 − 0.10 = 0.50 = 0.50

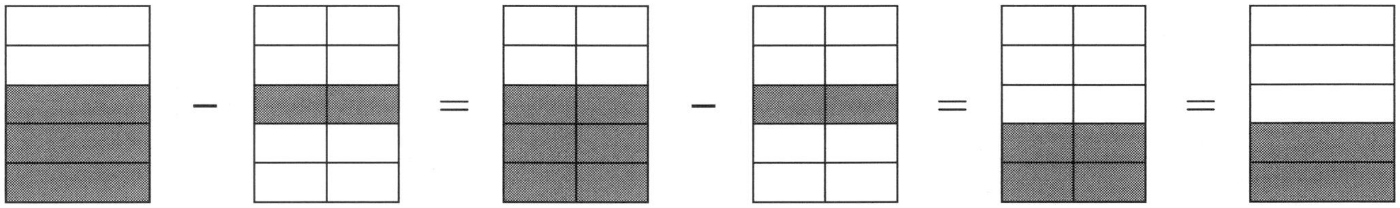

$$\frac{3}{5} - \frac{2}{10} = \frac{6}{10} - \frac{2}{10} = \frac{4}{10} = \frac{2}{5}$$

0.60 − 0.20 = 0.60 − 0.20 = 0.40 = 0.40

Fifths – Tenths

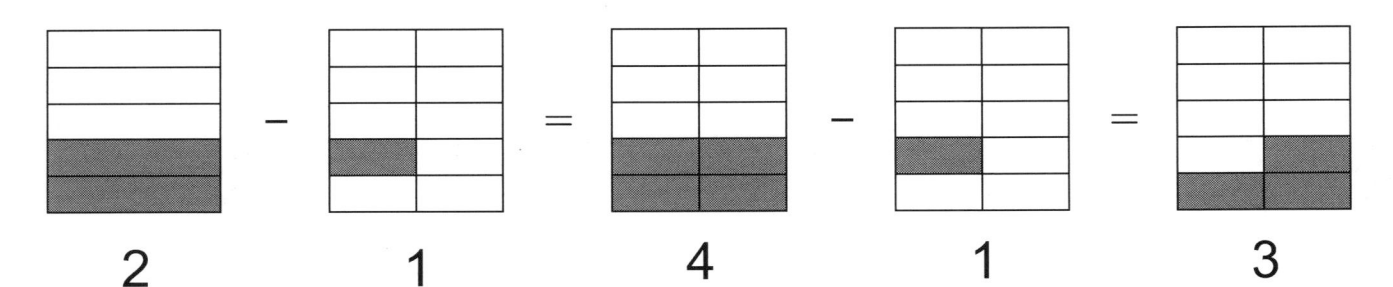

$$\frac{2}{5} - \frac{1}{10} = \frac{4}{10} - \frac{1}{10} = \frac{3}{10}$$

0.40 − 0.10 = 0.40 − 0.10 = 0.30

$$\frac{2}{5} - \frac{2}{10} = \frac{4}{10} - \frac{2}{10} = \frac{2}{10} = \frac{1}{5}$$

0.40 − 0.20 = 0.40 − 0.20 = 0.20 = 0.20

$$\frac{1}{5} - \frac{1}{10} = \frac{2}{10} - \frac{1}{10} = \frac{1}{10}$$

0.20 − 0.10 = 0.20 − 0.10 = 0.10

Fifths – Tenths

$$\frac{1}{5} - \frac{2}{10} = \frac{2}{10} - \frac{2}{10} = \frac{0}{10}$$

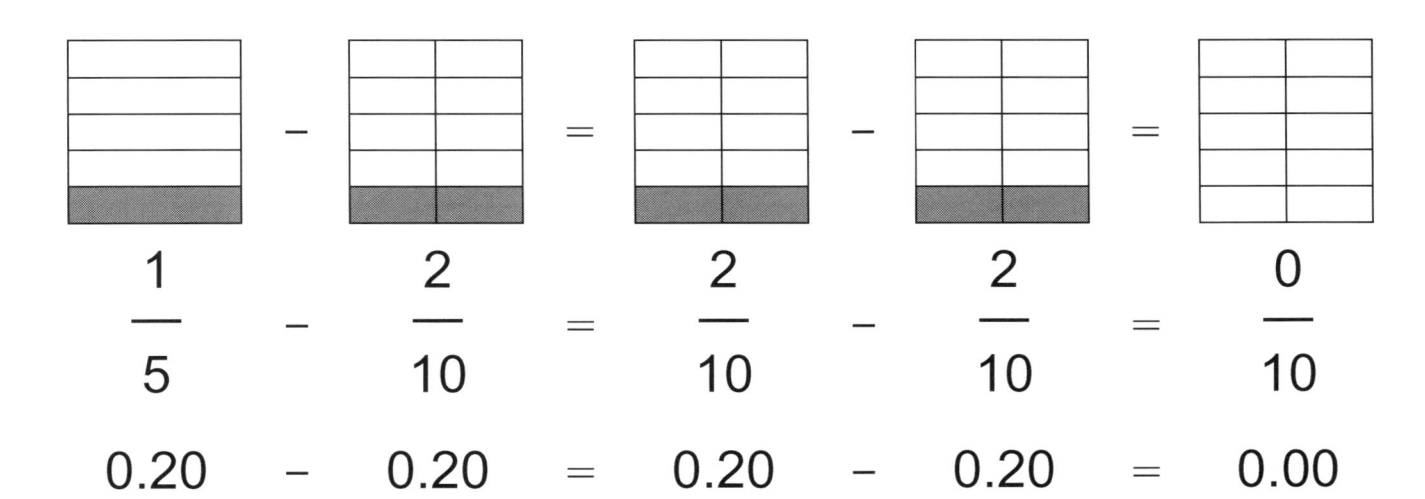

$$0.20 - 0.20 = 0.20 - 0.20 = 0.00$$

$$= \frac{0}{5} = 0$$

$$= 0.00 = 0$$

Tenths − Fifths

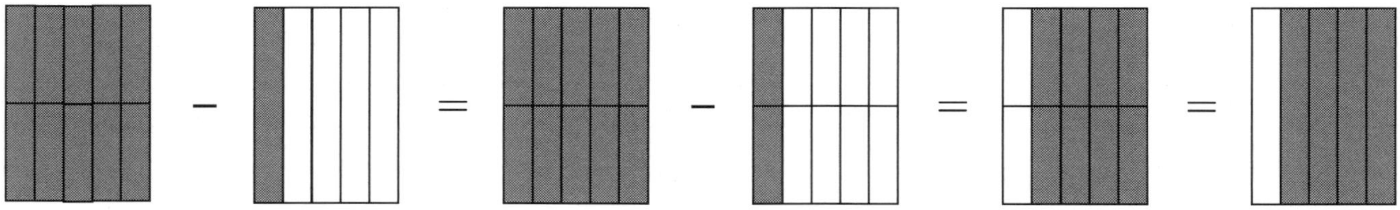

$$\frac{10}{10} - \frac{1}{5} = \frac{10}{10} - \frac{2}{10} = \frac{8}{10} = \frac{4}{5}$$

1.00 − 0.20 = 1.00 − 0.20 = 0.80 = 0.80

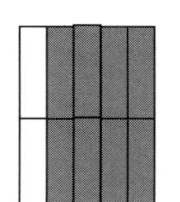

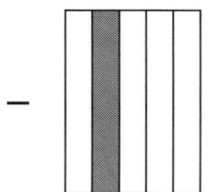

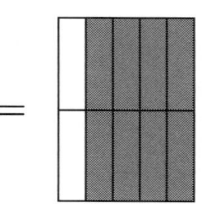

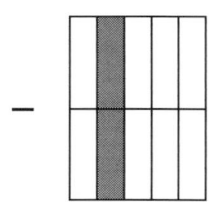

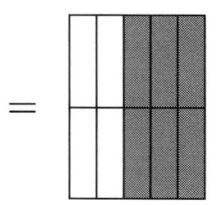

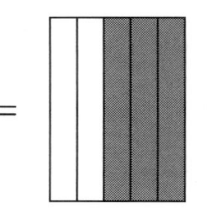

$$\frac{8}{10} - \frac{1}{5} = \frac{8}{10} - \frac{2}{10} = \frac{6}{10} = \frac{3}{5}$$

0.80 − 0.20 = 0.80 − 0.20 = 0.60 = 0.60

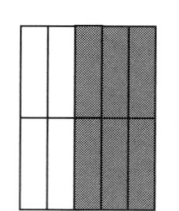

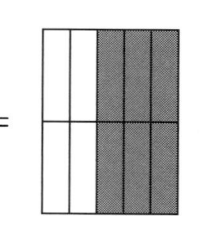

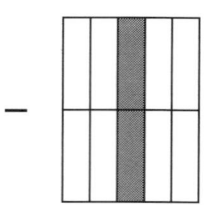

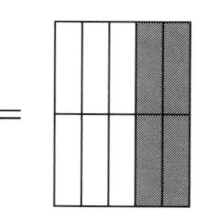

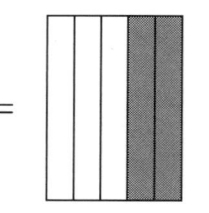

$$\frac{6}{10} - \frac{1}{5} = \frac{6}{10} - \frac{2}{10} = \frac{4}{10} = \frac{2}{5}$$

0.60 − 0.20 = 0.60 − 0.20 = 0.40 = 0.40

Tenths − Fifths

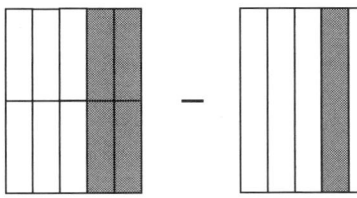

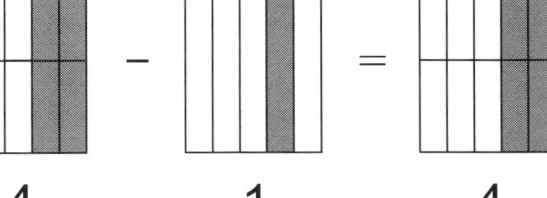

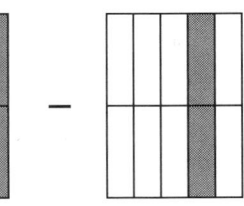

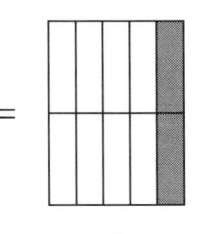

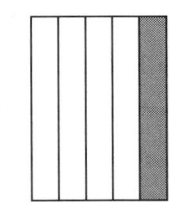

$$\frac{4}{10} - \frac{1}{5} = \frac{4}{10} - \frac{2}{10} = \frac{2}{10} = \frac{1}{5}$$

$$0.40 - 0.20 = 0.40 - 0.20 = 0.20 = 0.20$$

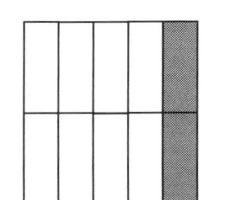

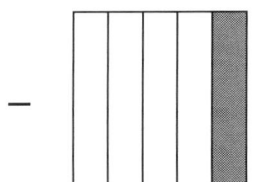

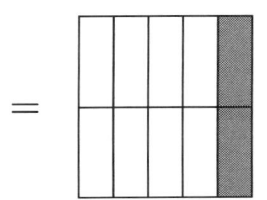

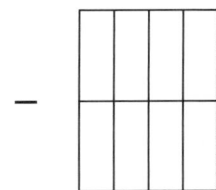

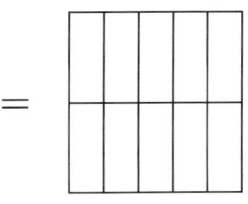

$$\frac{2}{10} - \frac{1}{5} = \frac{2}{10} - \frac{2}{10} = \frac{0}{10}$$

$$0.20 - 0.20 = 0.20 - 0.20 = 0.00$$

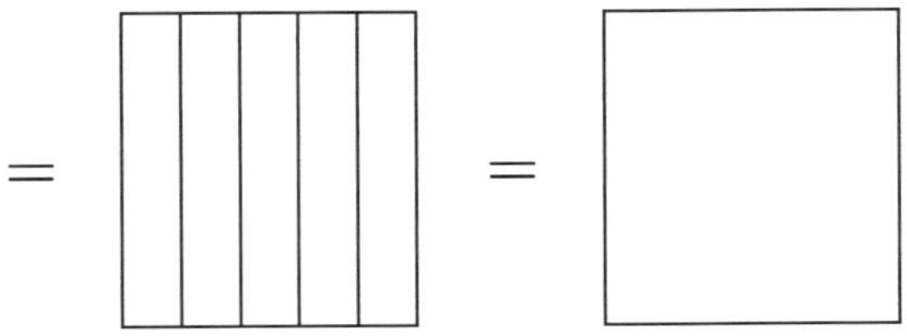

$$= \frac{0}{5} = 0$$

$$= 0.00 = 0$$

Thirds – Sixths

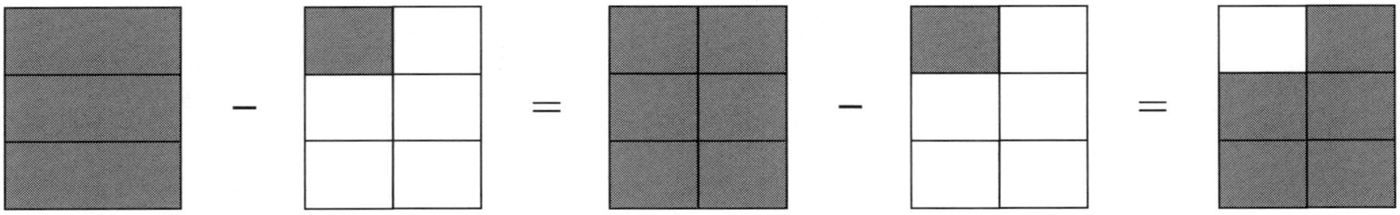

$$\frac{3}{3} - \frac{1}{6} = \frac{6}{6} - \frac{1}{6} = \frac{5}{6}$$

$$1.00 - 0.166^{\cdot} = 1.00 - 0.166^{\cdot} = 0.833^{\cdot}$$

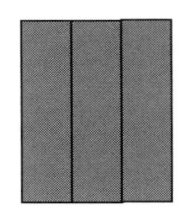

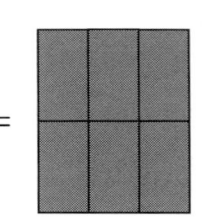

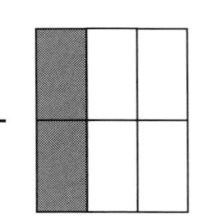

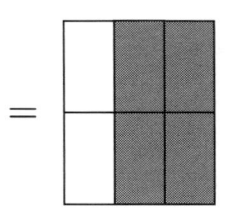

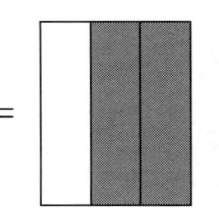

$$\frac{3}{3} - \frac{2}{6} = \frac{6}{6} - \frac{2}{6} = \frac{4}{6} = \frac{2}{3}$$

$$1.00 - 0.333^{\cdot} = 1.00 - 0.333^{\cdot} = 0.666^{\cdot} = 0.666^{\cdot}$$

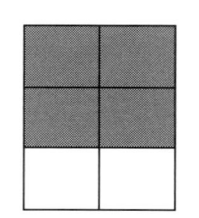

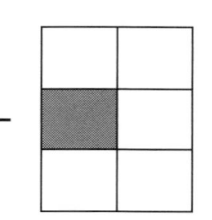

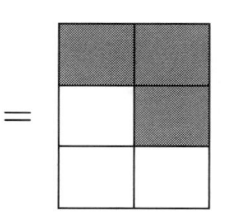

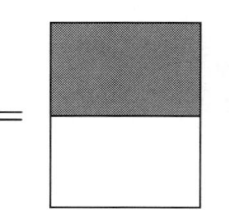

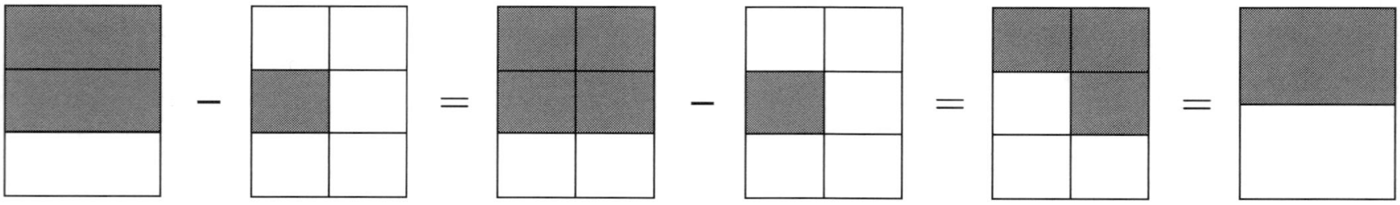

$$\frac{2}{3} - \frac{1}{6} = \frac{4}{6} - \frac{1}{6} = \frac{3}{6} = \frac{1}{2}$$

$$0.666^{\cdot} - 0.166^{\cdot} = 0.666^{\cdot} - 0.166^{\cdot} = 0.50 = 0.50$$

Thirds – Sixths

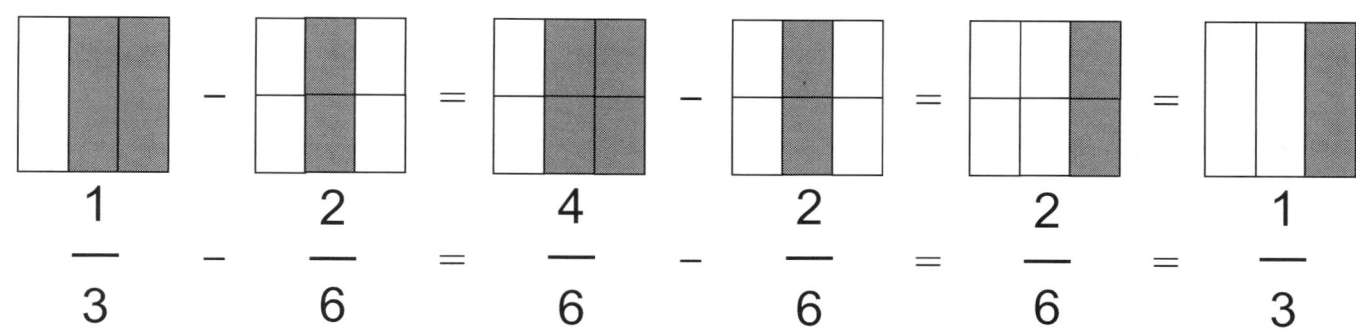

$$\frac{1}{3} - \frac{2}{6} = \frac{4}{6} - \frac{2}{6} = \frac{2}{6} = \frac{1}{3}$$

$$0.666˙ - 0.333˙ = 0.666˙ - 0.333˙ = 0.333˙ = 0.333˙$$

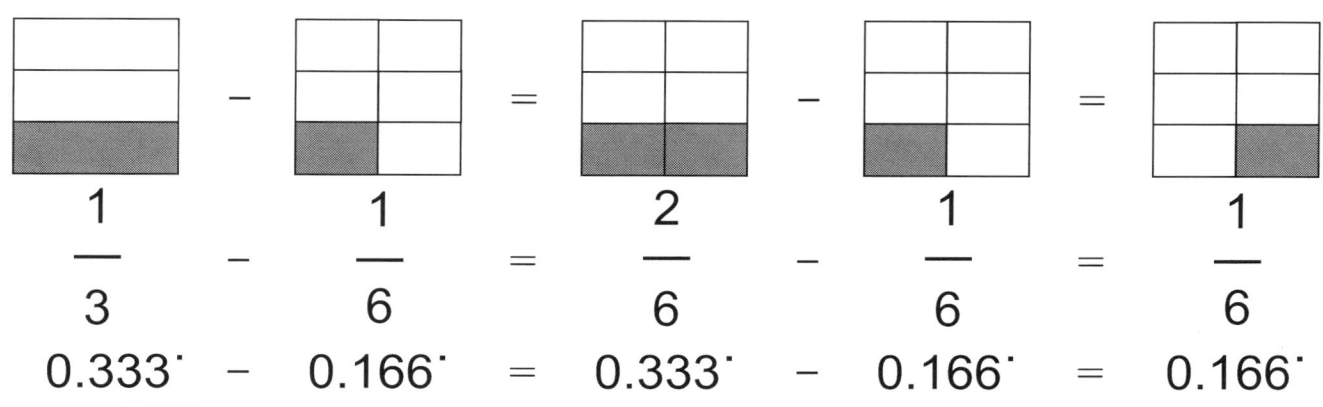

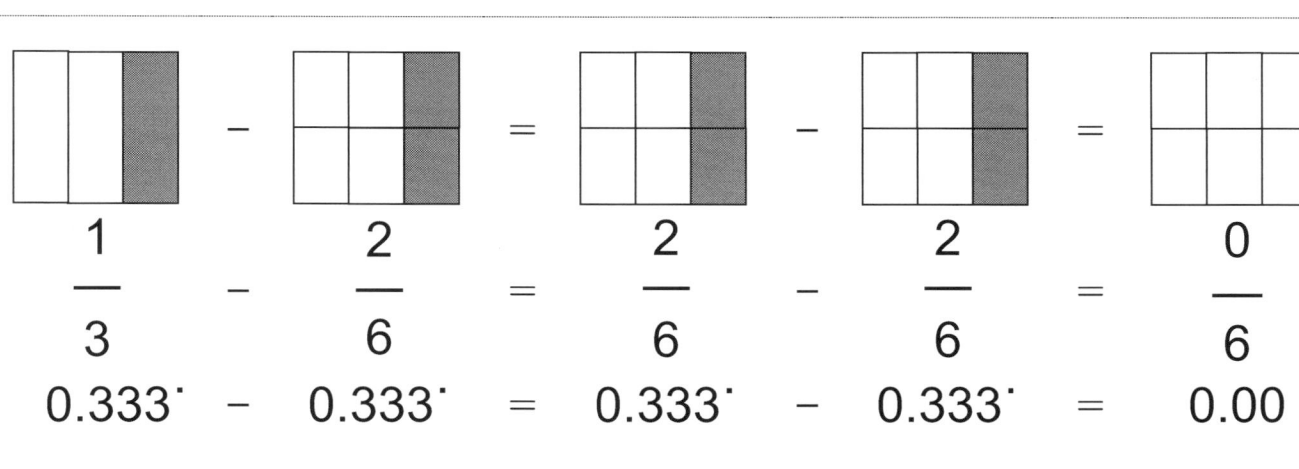

$$\frac{1}{3} - \frac{1}{6} = \frac{2}{6} - \frac{1}{6} = \frac{1}{6}$$

$$0.333˙ - 0.166˙ = 0.333˙ - 0.166˙ = 0.166˙$$

$$\frac{1}{3} - \frac{2}{6} = \frac{2}{6} - \frac{2}{6} = \frac{0}{6}$$

$$0.333˙ - 0.333˙ = 0.333˙ - 0.333˙ = 0.00$$

$$= \frac{0}{3} = \frac{0}{2} = 0$$

$$= 0.00 = 0.00 = 0.00$$

Thirds – Ninths

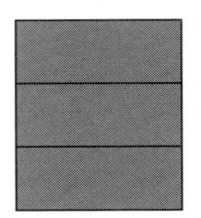

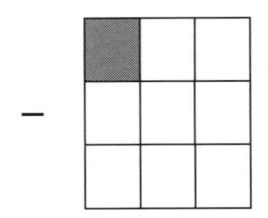

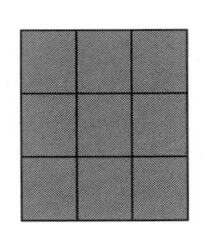

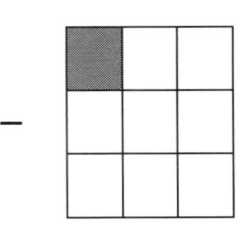

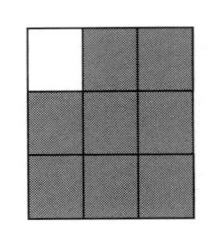

$$\frac{3}{3} - \frac{1}{9} = \frac{9}{9} - \frac{1}{9} = \frac{8}{9}$$

$$1.00 - 0.111^{\cdot} = 1.00 - 0.111^{\cdot} = 0.888^{\cdot}$$

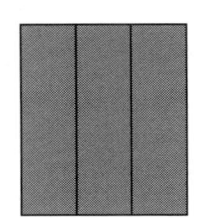

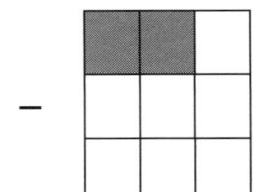

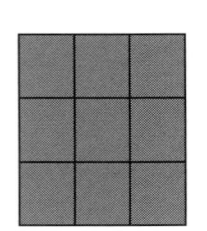

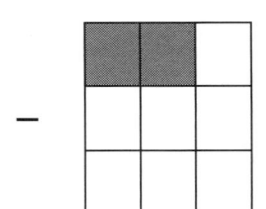

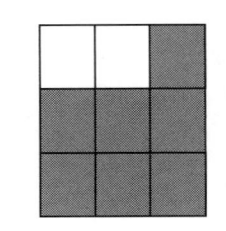

$$\frac{3}{3} - \frac{2}{9} = \frac{9}{9} - \frac{2}{9} = \frac{7}{9}$$

$$1.00 - 0.222^{\cdot} = 1.00 - 0.222^{\cdot} = 0.777^{\cdot}$$

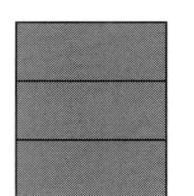

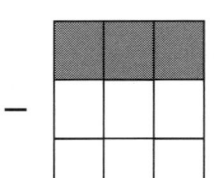

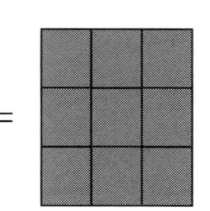

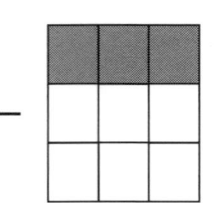

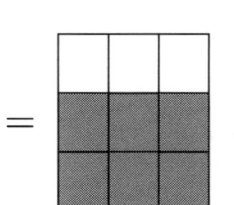

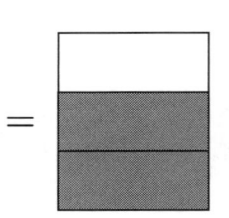

$$\frac{3}{3} - \frac{3}{9} = \frac{9}{9} - \frac{3}{9} = \frac{6}{9} = \frac{2}{3}$$

$$1.00 - 0.333^{\cdot} = 1.00 - 0.333^{\cdot} = 0.666^{\cdot} = 0.666^{\cdot}$$

Thirds − Ninths

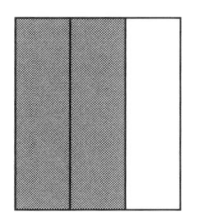

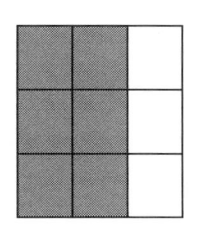

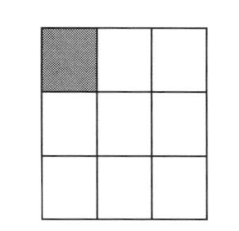

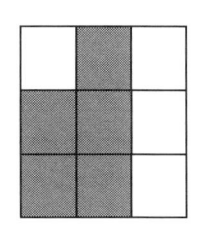

$$\frac{2}{3} - \frac{1}{9} = \frac{6}{9} - \frac{1}{9} = \frac{5}{9}$$

$$0.666˙ - 0.111˙ = 0.666˙ - 0.111˙ = 0.555˙$$

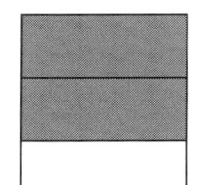

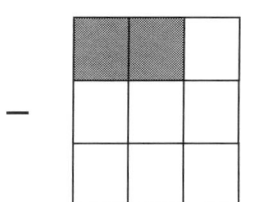

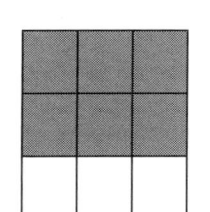

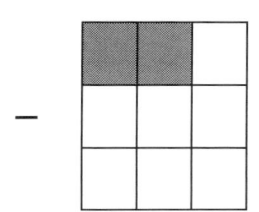

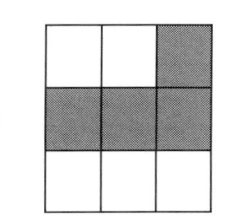

$$\frac{2}{3} - \frac{2}{9} = \frac{6}{9} - \frac{2}{9} = \frac{4}{9}$$

$$0.666˙ - 0.222˙ = 0.666˙ - 0.222˙ = 0.444˙$$

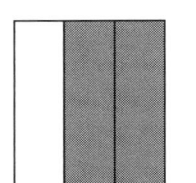

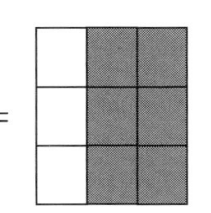

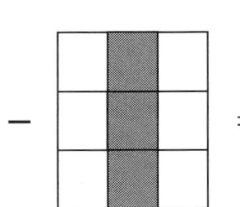

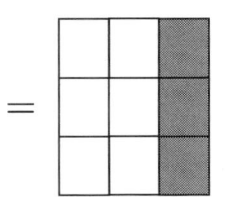

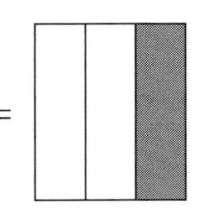

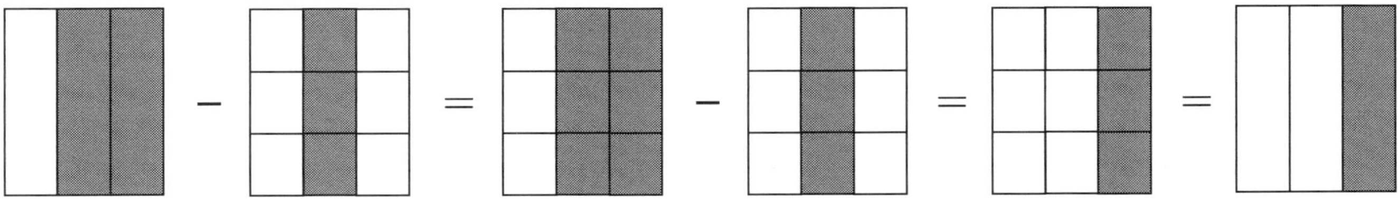

$$\frac{2}{3} - \frac{3}{9} = \frac{6}{9} - \frac{3}{9} = \frac{3}{9} = \frac{1}{3}$$

$$0.666˙ - 0.333˙ = 0.666˙ - 0.333˙ = 0.333˙ = 0.333˙$$

Thirds − Ninths

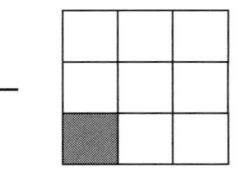

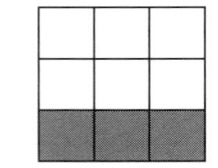

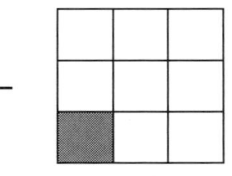

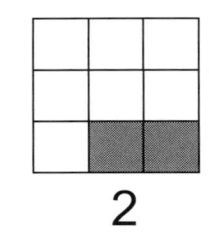

$$\frac{1}{3} - \frac{1}{9} = \frac{3}{9} - \frac{1}{9} = \frac{2}{9}$$

0.333˙ − 0.111˙ = 0.333˙ − 0.111˙ = 0.222˙

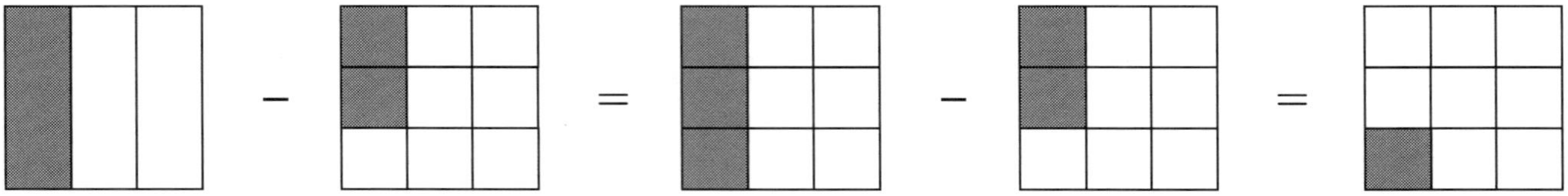

$$\frac{1}{3} - \frac{2}{9} = \frac{3}{9} - \frac{2}{9} = \frac{1}{9}$$

0.333˙ − 0.222˙ = 0.333˙ − 0.222˙ = 0.111˙

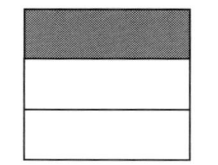

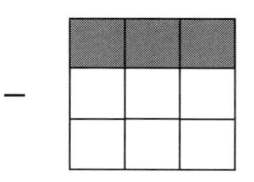

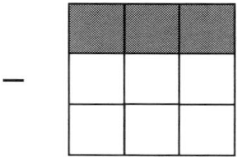

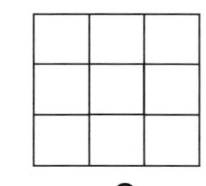

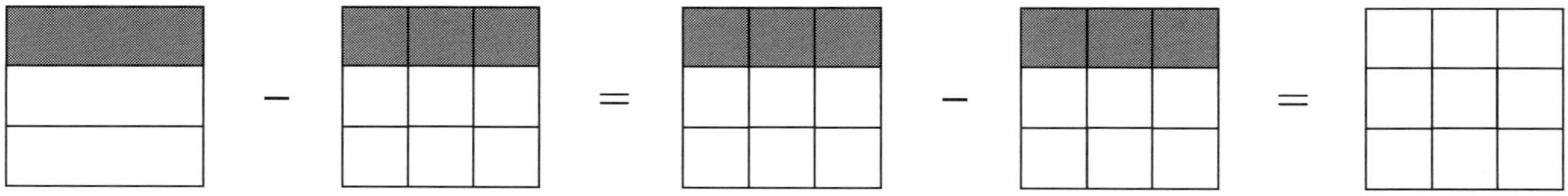

$$\frac{1}{3} - \frac{3}{9} = \frac{3}{9} - \frac{3}{9} = \frac{0}{9}$$

0.333˙ − 0.333˙ = 0.333˙ − 0.333˙ = 0.00˙

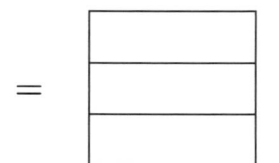

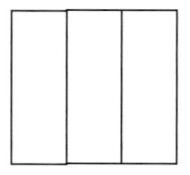

$$= \frac{0}{3} = \frac{0}{3} = 0$$

= 0.00 = 0.00 = 0

244

Sixths – Thirds

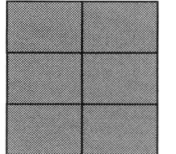

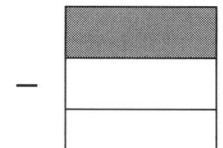

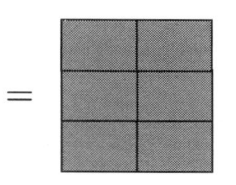

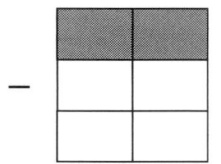

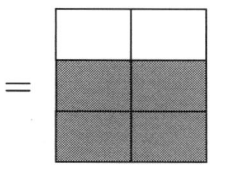

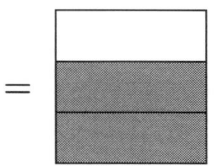

$$\frac{6}{6} - \frac{1}{3} = \frac{6}{6} - \frac{2}{6} = \frac{4}{6} = \frac{2}{3}$$

$$1.00 - 0.33˙ = 1.00 - 0.33˙ = 0.66˙ = 0.66˙$$

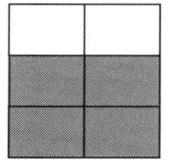

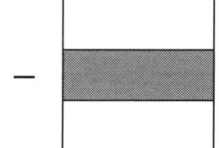

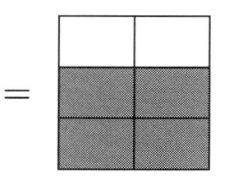

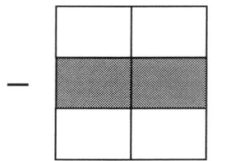

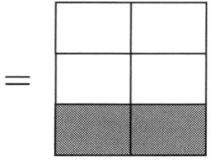

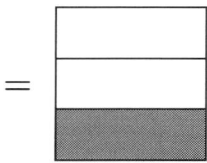

$$\frac{4}{6} - \frac{1}{3} = \frac{4}{6} - \frac{2}{6} = \frac{2}{6} = \frac{1}{3}$$

$$0.66˙ - 0.33˙ = 0.66˙ - 0.33˙ = 0.33˙ = 0.33˙$$

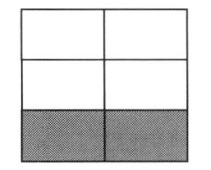

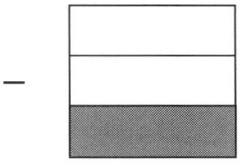

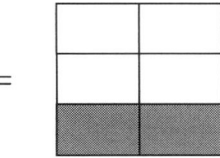

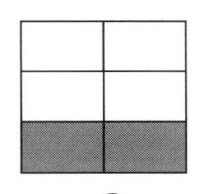

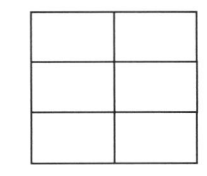

$$\frac{2}{6} - \frac{1}{3} = \frac{2}{6} - \frac{2}{6} = \frac{0}{6}$$

$$0.333˙ - 0.333˙ = 0.333˙ - 0.333˙ = 0.00$$

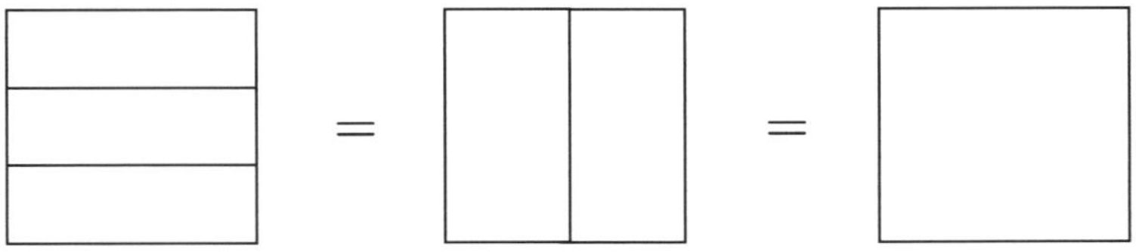

$$= \frac{0}{3} = \frac{0}{2} = 0$$

$$= 0.00 = 0.00 = 0$$

Sixths − Ninths

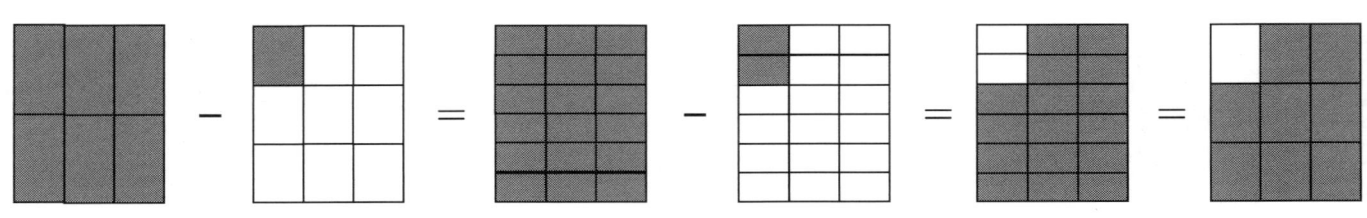

$$\frac{6}{6} - \frac{1}{9} = \frac{18}{18} - \frac{2}{18} = \frac{16}{18} = \frac{8}{9}$$

$$1.00 - 0.11\dot{} = 1.00 - 0.11\dot{} = 0.88\dot{} = 0.88\dot{}$$

$$\frac{6}{6} - \frac{2}{9} = \frac{18}{18} - \frac{4}{18} = \frac{14}{18} = \frac{7}{9}$$

$$1.00 - 0.22\dot{} = 1.00 - 0.22\dot{} = 0.77\dot{} = 0.77\dot{}$$

$$\frac{5}{6} - \frac{1}{9} = \frac{15}{18} - \frac{2}{18} = \frac{13}{18}$$

$$0.833\dot{} - 0.111\dot{} = 0.833\dot{} - 0.111\dot{} = 0.722\dot{}$$

Sixths − Ninths

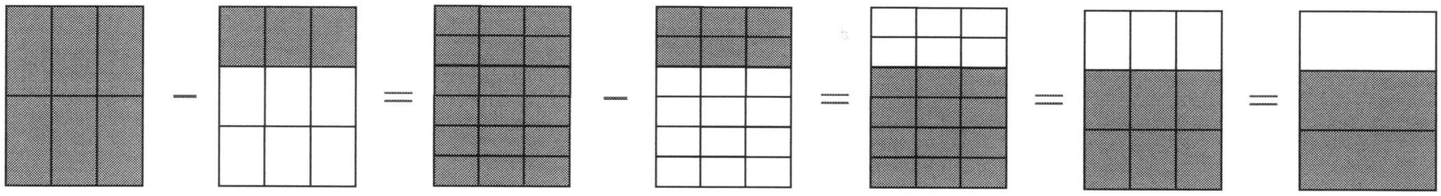

$$\frac{6}{6} - \frac{3}{9} = \frac{18}{18} - \frac{6}{18} = \frac{12}{18} = \frac{6}{9} = \frac{2}{3}$$

$$1.00 - 0.33\dot{} = 1.00 - 0.33\dot{} = 0.66\dot{} = 0.66\dot{} = 0.66\dot{}$$

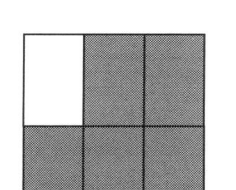

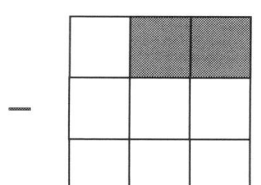

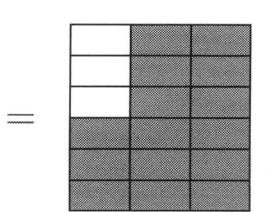

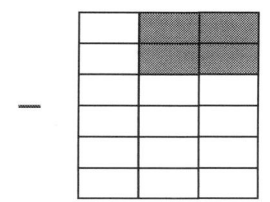

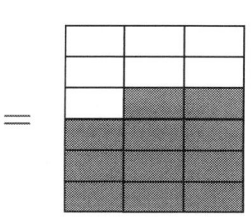

$$\frac{5}{6} - \frac{2}{9} = \frac{15}{18} - \frac{4}{18} = \frac{11}{18}$$

$$0.833\dot{} - 0.222\dot{} = 0.833\dot{} - 0.222\dot{} = 0.611\dot{}$$

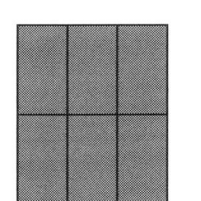

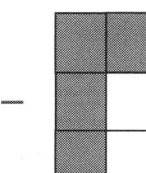

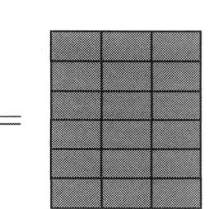

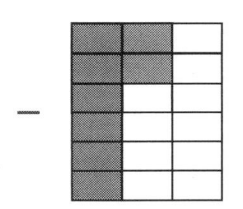

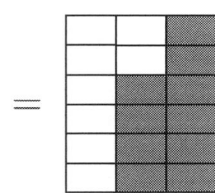

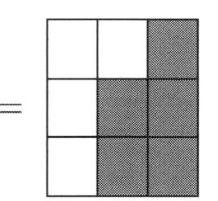

$$\frac{6}{6} - \frac{4}{9} = \frac{18}{18} - \frac{8}{18} = \frac{10}{18} = \frac{5}{9}$$

$$1.00 - 0.444\dot{} = 1.00 - 0.444\dot{} = 0.555\dot{} = 0.555\dot{}$$

Sixths − Ninths

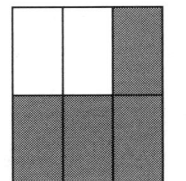

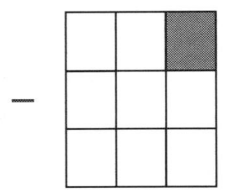

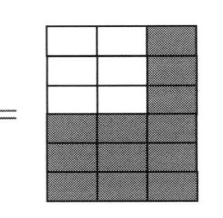

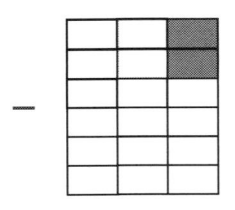

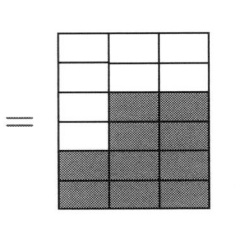

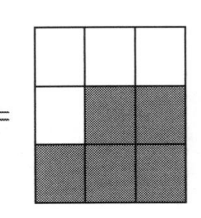

$$\frac{4}{6} - \frac{1}{9} = \frac{12}{18} - \frac{2}{18} = \frac{10}{18} = \frac{5}{9}$$

$$0.\overline{666} - 0.\overline{111} = 0.\overline{666} - 0.\overline{111} = 0.\overline{555} = 0.\overline{555}$$

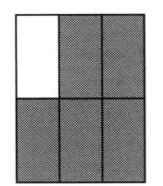

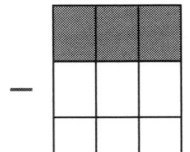

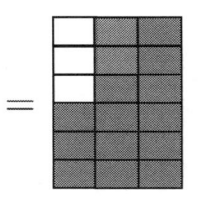

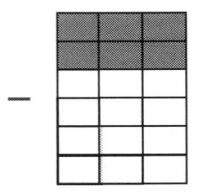

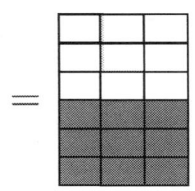

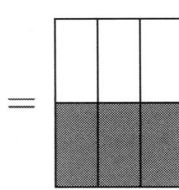

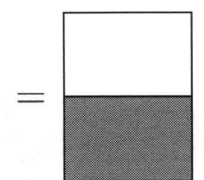

$$\frac{5}{6} - \frac{3}{9} = \frac{15}{18} - \frac{6}{18} = \frac{9}{18} = \frac{3}{6} = \frac{1}{2}$$

$$0.8\overline{3} - 0.\overline{33} = 0.8\overline{3} - 0.\overline{33} = 0.50 = 0.50 = 0.50$$

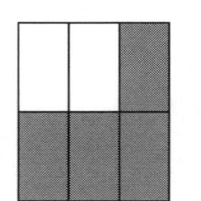

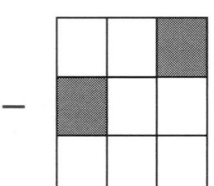

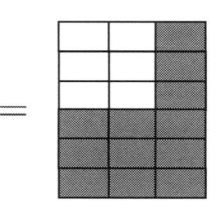

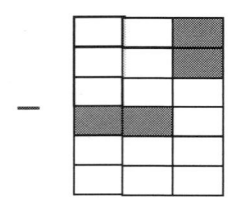

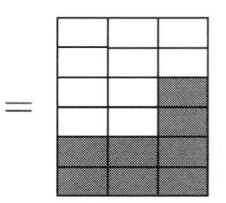

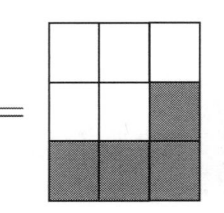

$$\frac{4}{6} - \frac{2}{9} = \frac{12}{18} - \frac{4}{18} = \frac{8}{18} = \frac{4}{9}$$

$$0.\overline{666} - 0.\overline{222} = 0.\overline{666} - 0.\overline{222} = 0.\overline{444} = 0.\overline{444}$$

Sixths – Ninths

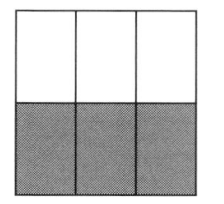

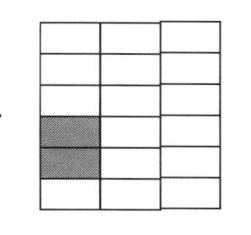

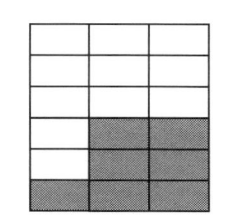

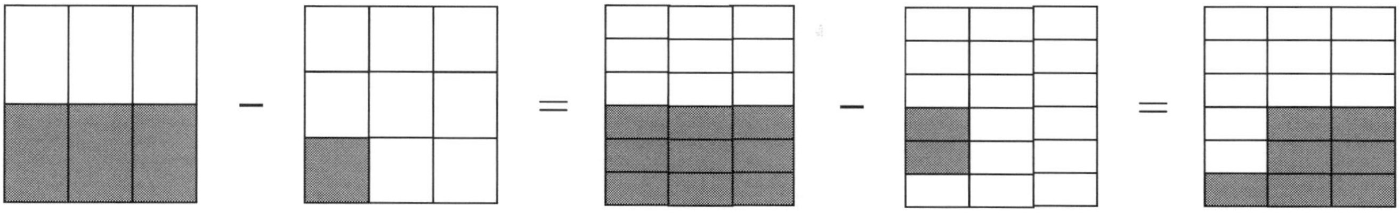

$$\frac{3}{6} - \frac{1}{9} = \frac{9}{18} - \frac{2}{18} = \frac{7}{18}$$

0.500 − 0.111˙ = 0.500 − 0.111˙ = 0.388˙

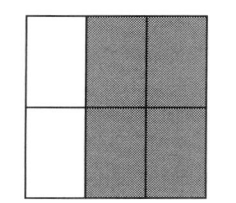

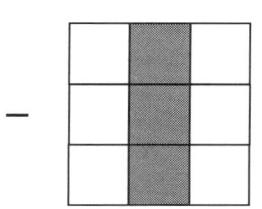

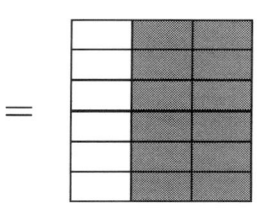

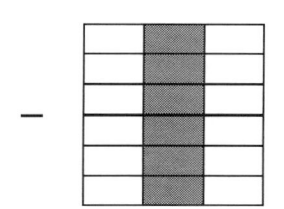

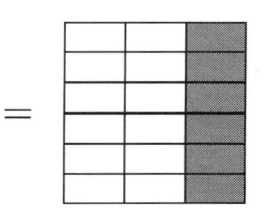

$$\frac{4}{6} - \frac{3}{9} = \frac{12}{18} - \frac{6}{18} = \frac{6}{18}$$

0.666˙ − 0.333˙ = 0.666˙ − 0.333˙ = 0.333˙

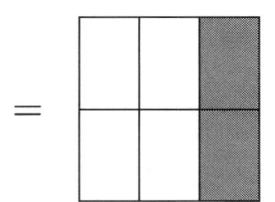

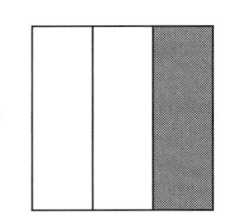

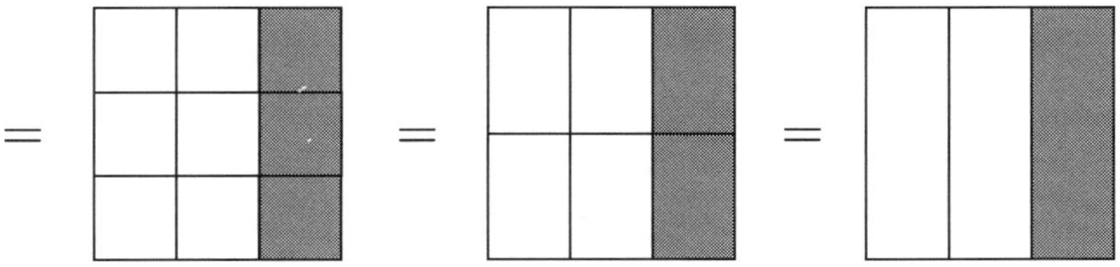

$$= \frac{3}{9} = \frac{2}{6} = \frac{1}{3}$$

= 0.333˙ = 0.333˙ = 0.333˙

Sixths – Ninths

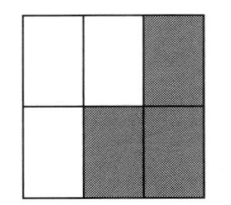

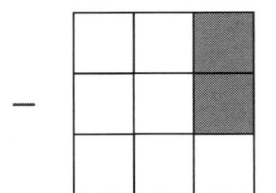

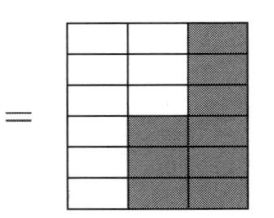

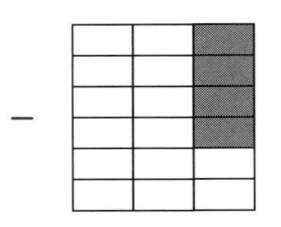

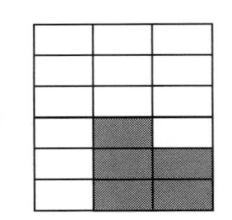

$$\frac{3}{6} - \frac{2}{9} = \frac{9}{18} - \frac{4}{18} = \frac{5}{18}$$

$$0.500 - 0.222\dot{} = 0.500 - 0.222\dot{} = 0.277\dot{}$$

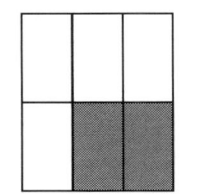

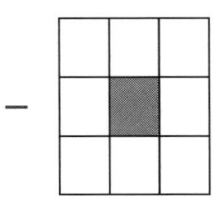

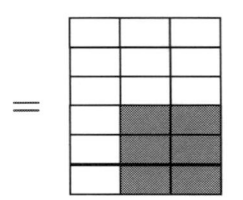

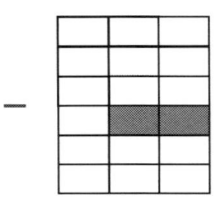

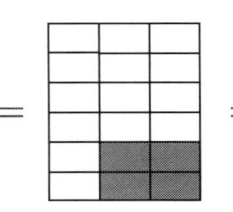

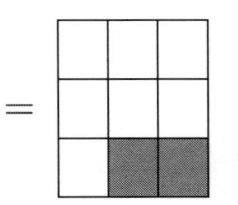

$$\frac{2}{6} - \frac{1}{9} = \frac{6}{18} - \frac{2}{18} = \frac{4}{18} = \frac{2}{9}$$

$$0.333\dot{} - 0.111\dot{} = 0.333\dot{} - 0.111\dot{} = 0.222\dot{} = 0.222\dot{}$$

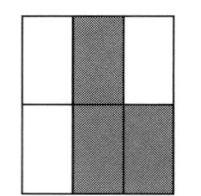

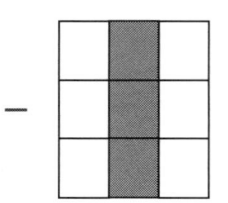

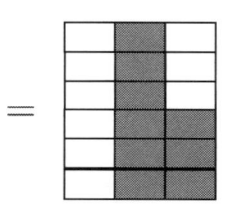

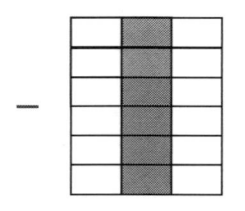

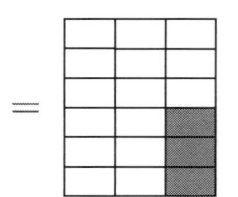

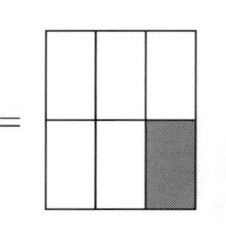

$$\frac{3}{6} - \frac{3}{9} = \frac{9}{18} - \frac{6}{18} = \frac{3}{18} = \frac{1}{6}$$

$$0.500 - 0.333\dot{} = 0.500 - 0.333\dot{} = 0.166\dot{} = 0.166\dot{}$$

Sixths − Ninths

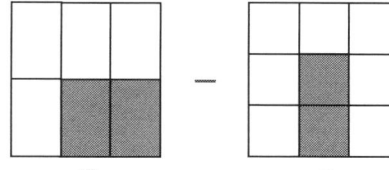

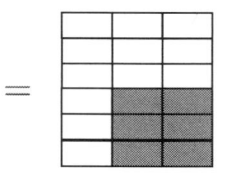

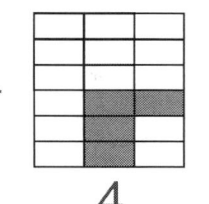

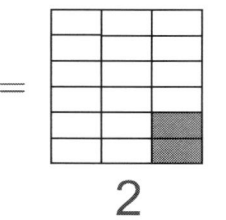

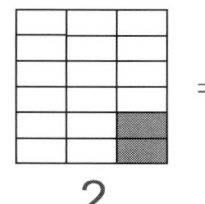

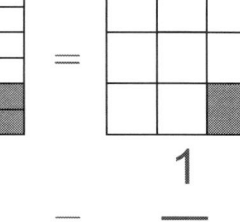

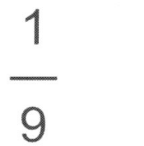

$$\frac{2}{6} - \frac{2}{9} = \frac{6}{18} - \frac{4}{18} = \frac{2}{18} = \frac{1}{9}$$

0.333˙ − 0.222˙ = 0.333˙ − 0.222˙ = 0.111˙ = 0.111˙

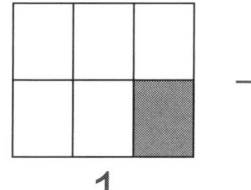

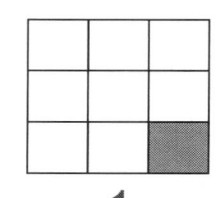

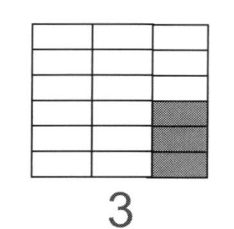

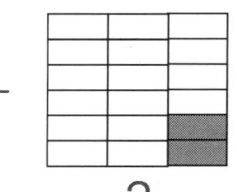

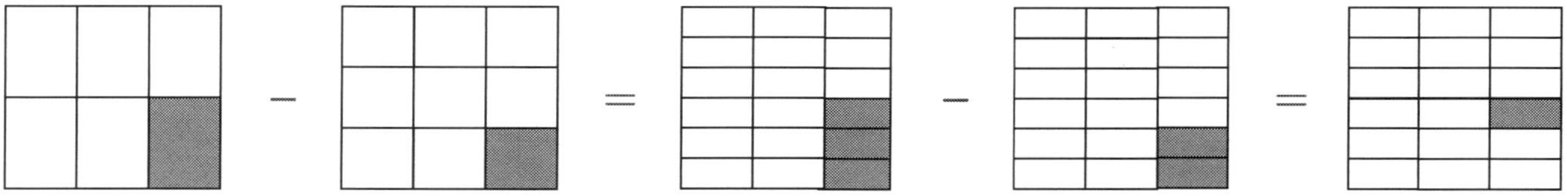

$$\frac{1}{6} - \frac{1}{9} = \frac{3}{18} - \frac{2}{18} = \frac{1}{18}$$

0.166˙ − 0.111˙ = 0.166˙ − 0.111˙ = 0.055˙

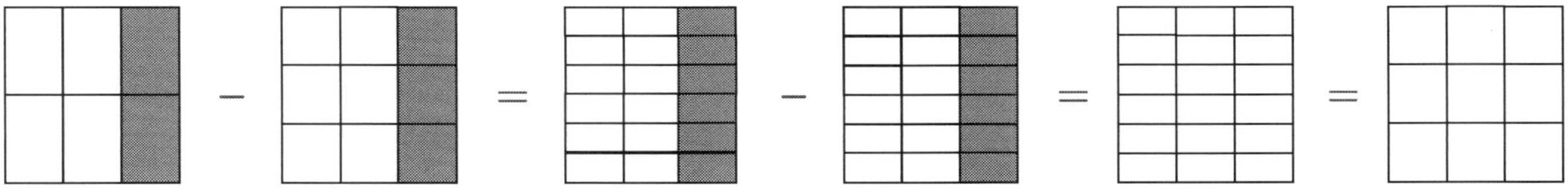

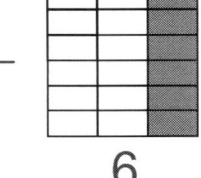

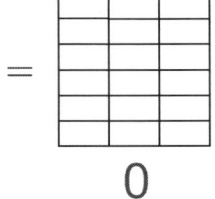

$$\frac{2}{6} - \frac{3}{9} = \frac{6}{18} - \frac{6}{18} = \frac{0}{18} = \frac{0}{9}$$

0.333˙ − 0.333˙ = 0.333˙ − 0.333˙ = 0.00 = 0.00

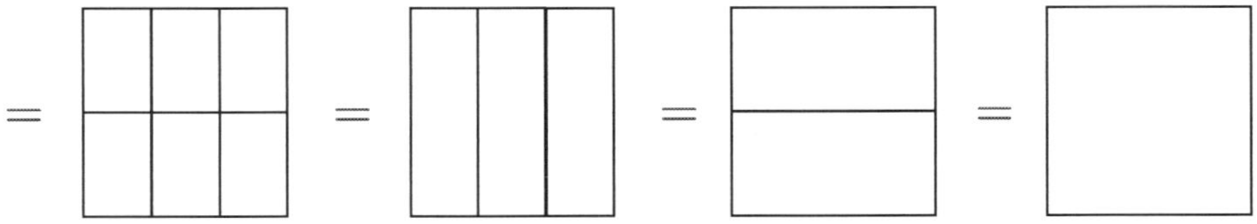

$$= \frac{0}{6} = \frac{0}{3} = \frac{0}{2} = 0$$

= 0.00 = 0.00 = 0.00 = 0

Ninths − Thirds

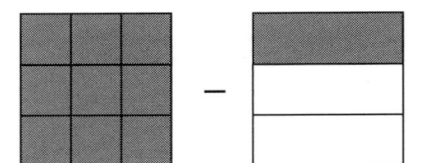

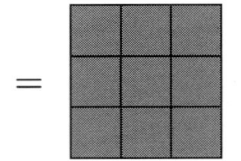

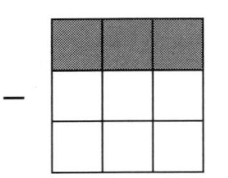

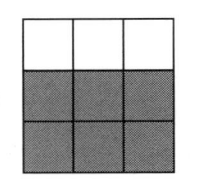

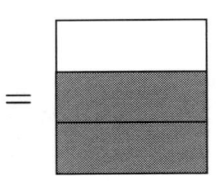

$$\frac{9}{9} - \frac{1}{3} = \frac{9}{9} - \frac{3}{9} = \frac{6}{9} = \frac{1}{3}$$

1.00 − 0.333˙ = 1.00 − 0.333˙ = 0.666˙ = 0.666˙

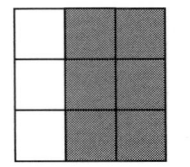

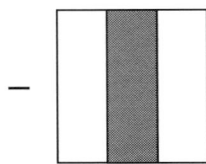

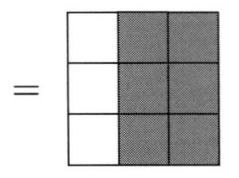

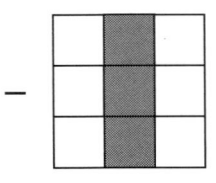

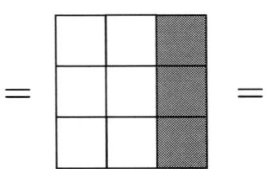

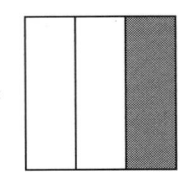

$$\frac{6}{9} - \frac{1}{3} = \frac{6}{9} - \frac{3}{9} = \frac{3}{9} = \frac{1}{3}$$

0.666˙ − 0.333˙ = 0.666˙ − 0.333˙ = 0.333˙ = 0.333˙

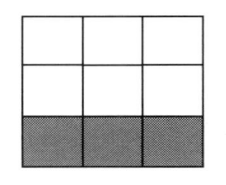

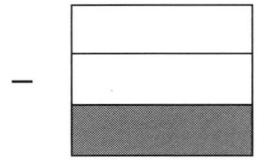

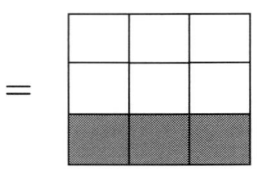

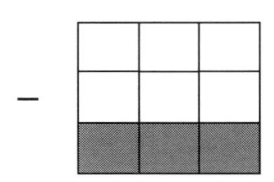

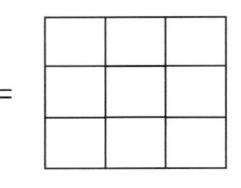

$$\frac{3}{9} - \frac{1}{3} = \frac{3}{9} - \frac{3}{9} = \frac{0}{9}$$

0.333˙ − 0.333˙ = 0.333˙ − 0.333˙ = 0.00

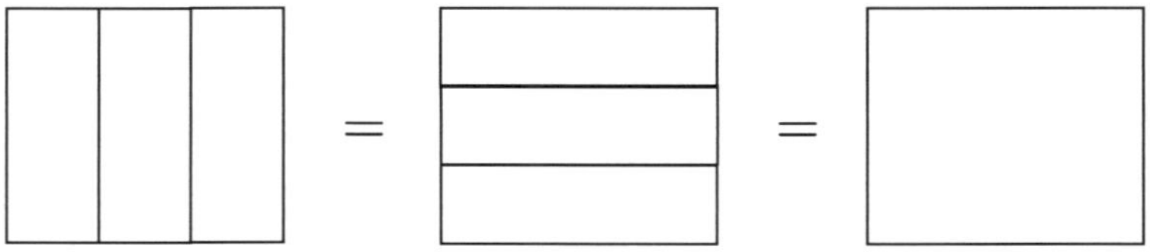

$$= \frac{0}{3} = \frac{0}{3} = 0$$

= 0.00 = 0.00 = 0

Ninths - Sixths

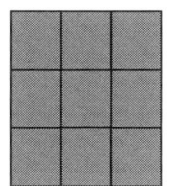

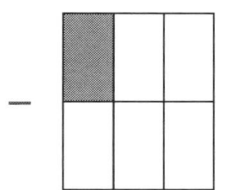

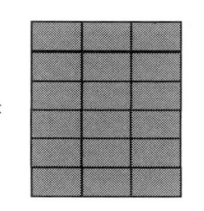

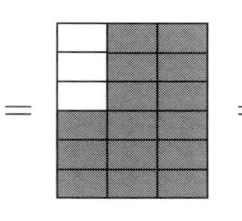

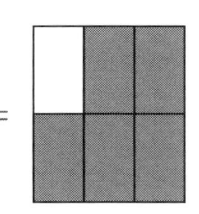

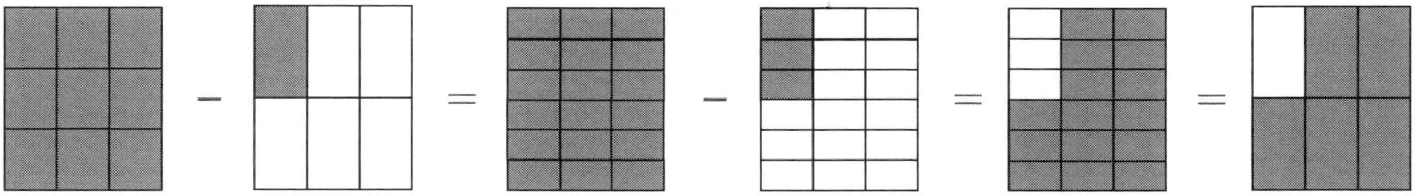

$$\frac{9}{9} - \frac{1}{6} = \frac{18}{18} - \frac{3}{18} = \frac{15}{18} = \frac{5}{6}$$

$$1.00 - 0.166˙ = 1.00 - 0.166˙ = 0.833˙ = 0.833˙$$

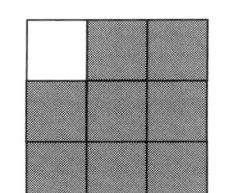

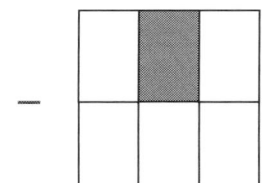

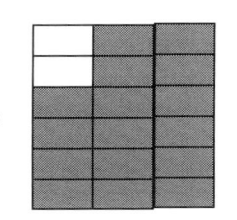

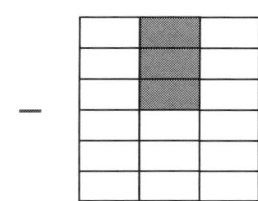

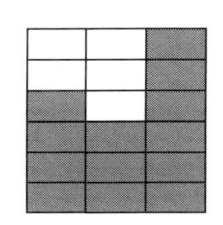

$$\frac{8}{9} - \frac{1}{6} = \frac{16}{18} - \frac{3}{18} = \frac{13}{18}$$

$$0.888˙ - 0.166˙ = 0.888˙ - 0.166˙ = 0.722˙$$

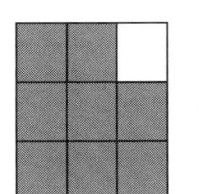

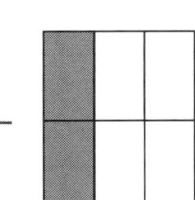

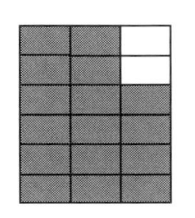

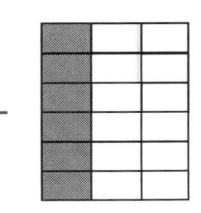

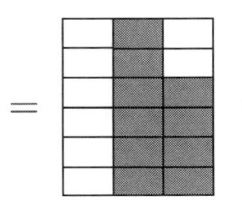

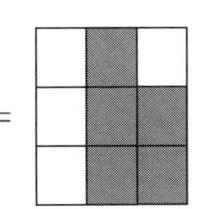

$$\frac{8}{9} - \frac{2}{6} = \frac{16}{18} - \frac{6}{18} = \frac{10}{18} = \frac{5}{9}$$

$$0.888˙ - 0.333˙ = 0.888˙ - 0.333˙ = 0.555˙ = 0.555˙$$

Ninths − Sixths

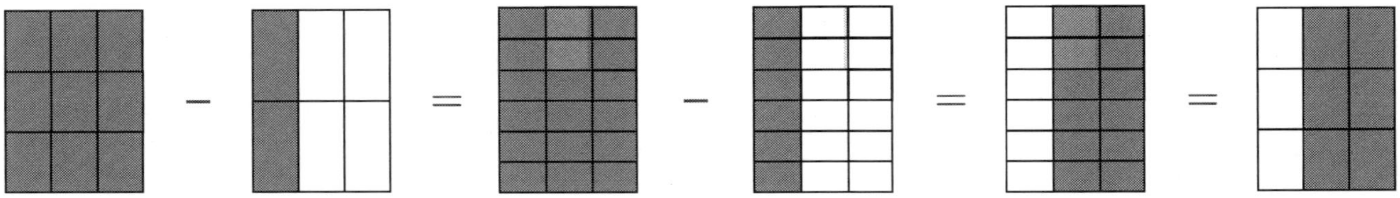

$$\frac{9}{9} - \frac{2}{6} = \frac{18}{18} - \frac{6}{18} = \frac{12}{18} = \frac{6}{9}$$

$$1.00 - 0.33˙ = 1.00 - 0.33˙ = 0.66˙ = 0.66˙$$

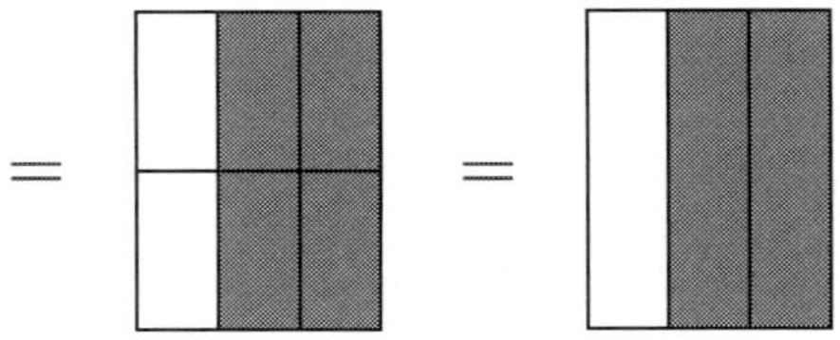

$$= \frac{4}{6} = \frac{2}{3}$$

$$= 0.66˙ = 0.66˙$$

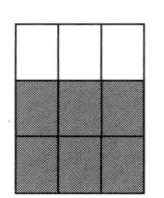

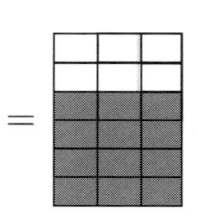

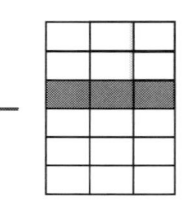

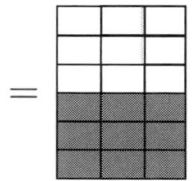

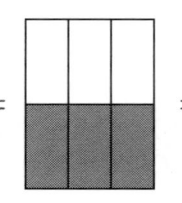

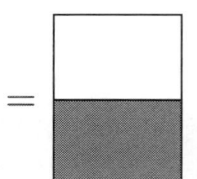

$$\frac{6}{9} - \frac{1}{6} = \frac{12}{18} - \frac{3}{18} = \frac{9}{18} = \frac{3}{6} = \frac{1}{2}$$

$$0.66˙ - 0.16˙ = 0.66˙ - 0.16˙ = 0.50 = 0.50 = 0.50$$

Ninths − Sixths

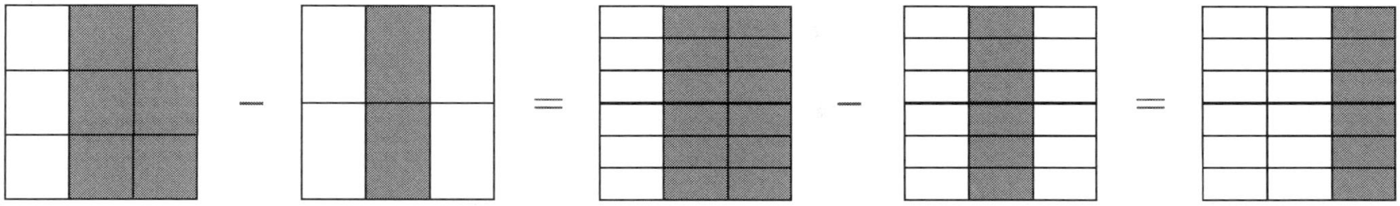

$$\frac{6}{9} - \frac{2}{6} = \frac{12}{18} - \frac{6}{18} = \frac{6}{18}$$

$$0.66\dot{} - 0.33\dot{} = 0.66\dot{} - 0.33\dot{} = 0.33\dot{}$$

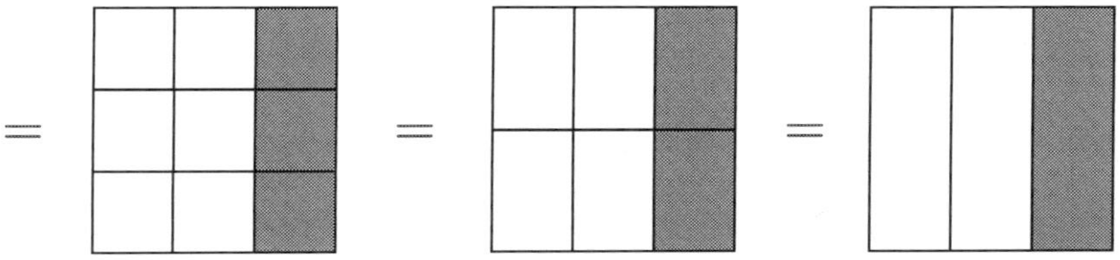

$$= \frac{3}{9} = \frac{2}{6} = \frac{1}{3}$$

$$= 0.333\dot{} = 0.333\dot{} = 0.333\dot{}$$

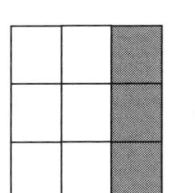

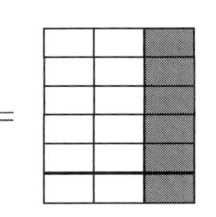

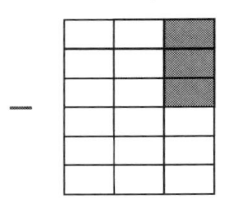

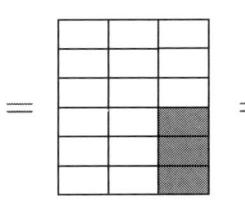

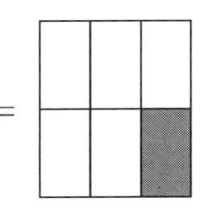

$$\frac{3}{9} - \frac{1}{6} = \frac{6}{18} - \frac{3}{18} = \frac{3}{18} = \frac{1}{6}$$

$$0.33\dot{} - 0.166\dot{} = 0.33\dot{} - 0.166\dot{} = 0.166\dot{} = 0.166\dot{}$$

Ninths − Sixths

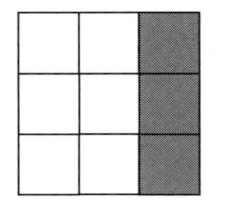

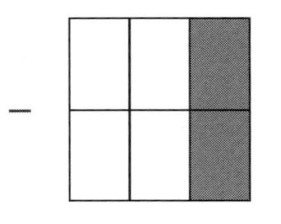

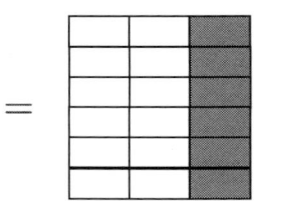

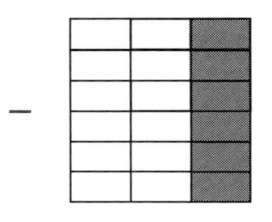

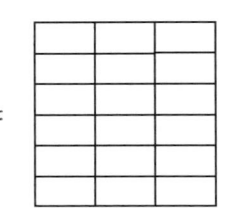

$$\frac{3}{9} - \frac{2}{6} = \frac{6}{18} - \frac{6}{18} = \frac{0}{18}$$

$$0.333^{\cdot} - 0.333^{\cdot} = 0.333^{\cdot} - 0.333^{\cdot} = 0.00$$

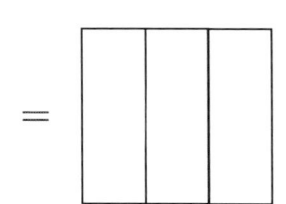

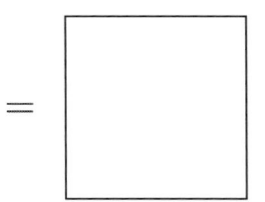

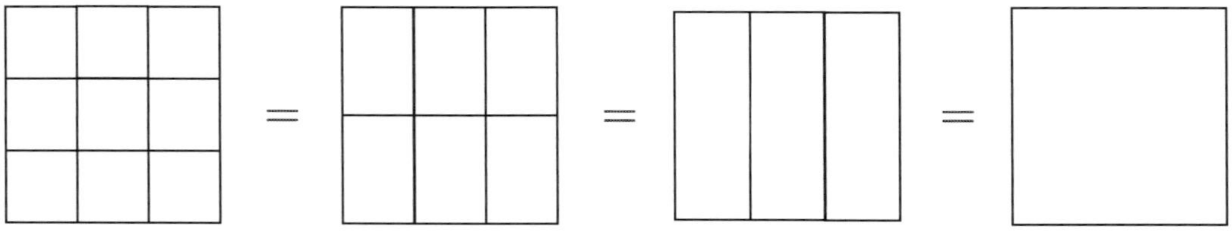

$$= \frac{0}{9} = \frac{0}{6} = \frac{0}{3} = 0$$

$$= 0.00 = 0.00 = 0.00 = 0$$

Thirds – Sixths – Ninths

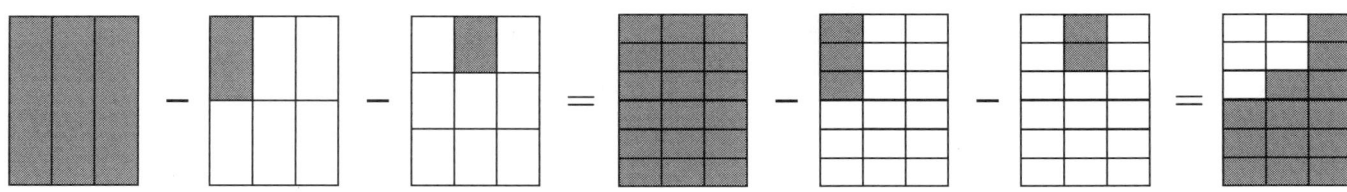

$$\frac{3}{3} - \frac{1}{6} - \frac{1}{9} = \frac{18}{18} - \frac{3}{18} - \frac{2}{18} = \frac{13}{18}$$

$$1.00 - 0.16\dot{} - 0.11\dot{} = 1.00 - 0.16\dot{} - 0.11\dot{} = 0.72\dot{}$$

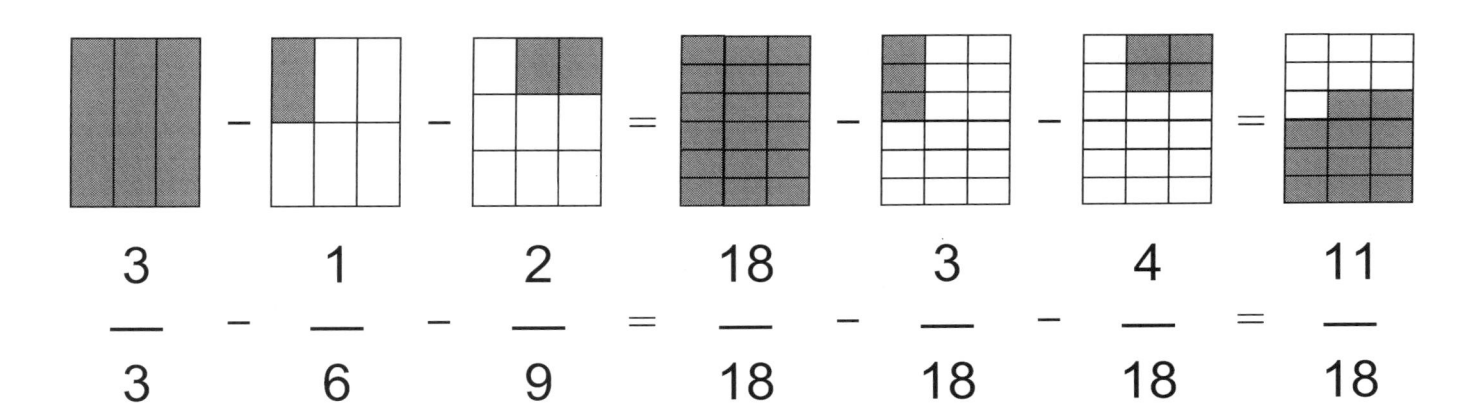

$$\frac{3}{3} - \frac{1}{6} - \frac{2}{9} = \frac{18}{18} - \frac{3}{18} - \frac{4}{18} = \frac{11}{18}$$

$$1.00 - 0.16\dot{} - 0.22\dot{} = 1.00 - 0.16\dot{} - 0.22\dot{} = 0.61\dot{}$$

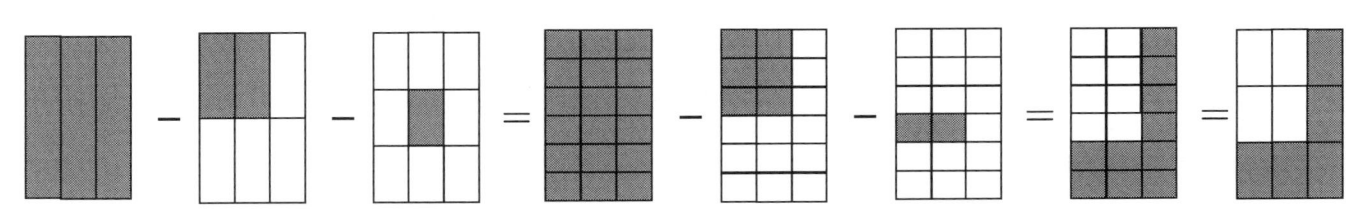

$$\frac{3}{3} - \frac{2}{6} - \frac{1}{9} = \frac{18}{18} - \frac{6}{18} - \frac{2}{18} = \frac{10}{18} = \frac{5}{9}$$

$$1.00 - 0.3\dot{} - 0.1\dot{} = 1.00 - 0.3\dot{} - 0.1\dot{} = 0.5\dot{} = 0.5\dot{}$$

Thirds – Sixths – Ninths

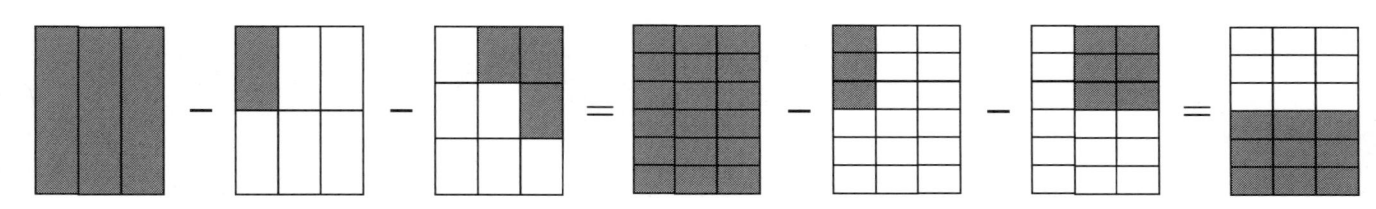

$$\frac{3}{3} - \frac{1}{6} - \frac{3}{9} = \frac{18}{18} - \frac{3}{18} - \frac{6}{18} = \frac{9}{18}$$

$$1.00 - 0.16 - 0.3\dot{} = 1.00 - 0.16 - 0.3\dot{} = 0.50$$

$$= \frac{3}{6} = \frac{1}{2}$$

$$= 0.50 = 0.50$$

$$\frac{3}{3} - \frac{1}{6} - \frac{4}{9} = \frac{18}{18} - \frac{3}{18} - \frac{8}{18} = \frac{7}{18}$$

$$1.00 - 0.16\dot{} - 0.44\dot{} = 1.00 - 0.16\dot{} - 0.44\dot{} = 0.38\dot{}$$

Thirds – Sixths – Ninths

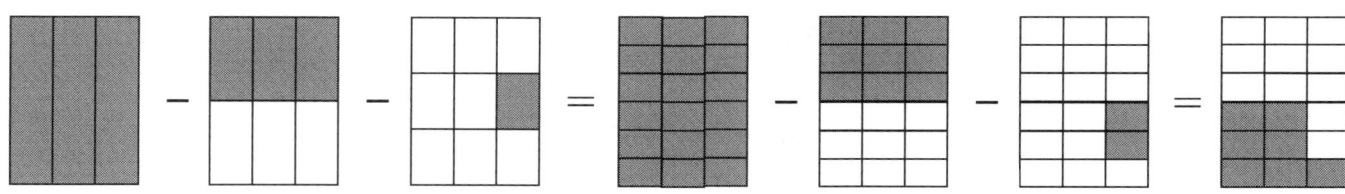

$$\frac{3}{3} - \frac{3}{6} - \frac{1}{9} = \frac{18}{18} - \frac{9}{18} - \frac{2}{18} = \frac{7}{18}$$

$$1.00 - 0.50 - 0.11˙ = 1.00 - 0.50 - 0.11˙ = 0.38˙$$

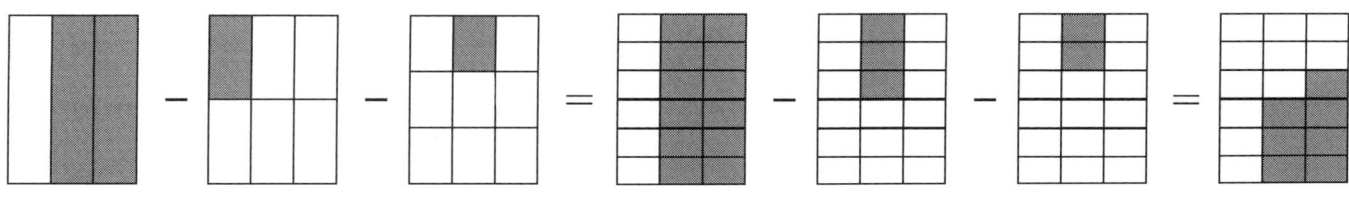

$$\frac{2}{3} - \frac{1}{6} - \frac{1}{9} = \frac{12}{18} - \frac{3}{18} - \frac{2}{18} = \frac{7}{18}$$

$$0.66˙ - 0.16˙ - 0.11˙ = 0.66˙ - 0.16˙ - 0.11˙ = 0.38˙$$

$$\frac{3}{3} - \frac{1}{6} - \frac{5}{9} = \frac{18}{18} - \frac{3}{18} - \frac{10}{18} = \frac{5}{18}$$

$$1.00 - 0.16˙ - 0.55˙ = 1.00 - 0.16˙ - 0.55˙ = 0.27˙$$

Thirds – Sixths – Ninths

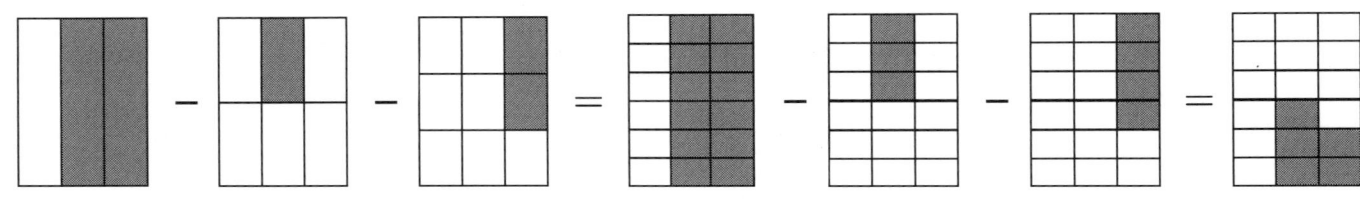

$$\frac{2}{3} - \frac{1}{6} - \frac{2}{9} = \frac{12}{18} - \frac{3}{18} - \frac{4}{18} = \frac{5}{18}$$

$$0.66\dot{} - 0.16\dot{} - 0.22\dot{} = 0.66\dot{} - 0.16\dot{} - 0.22\dot{} = 0.27\dot{}$$

$$\frac{3}{3} - \frac{4}{6} - \frac{1}{9} = \frac{18}{18} - \frac{12}{18} - \frac{2}{18} = \frac{4}{18} = \frac{2}{9}$$

$$1.00 - 0.6\dot{} - 0.1\dot{} = 1.00 - 0.6\dot{} - 0.1\dot{} = 0.2\dot{} = 0.2\dot{}$$

$$\frac{2}{3} - \frac{2}{6} - \frac{1}{9} = \frac{12}{18} - \frac{6}{18} - \frac{2}{18} = \frac{4}{18} = \frac{2}{9}$$

$$0.6\dot{} - 0.3\dot{} - 0.1\dot{} = 0.6\dot{} - 0.3\dot{} - 0.1\dot{} = 0.2\dot{} = 0.2\dot{}$$

Thirds − Sixths − Ninths

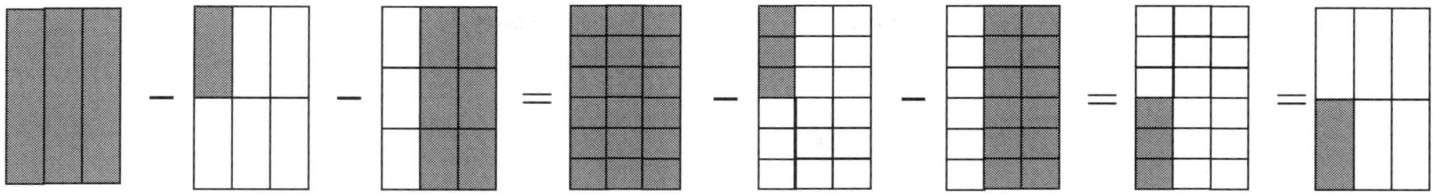

$$\frac{3}{3} - \frac{1}{6} - \frac{6}{9} = \frac{18}{18} - \frac{3}{18} - \frac{12}{18} = \frac{3}{18} = \frac{1}{6}$$

$$1.00 - 0.16 - 0.\dot{6} = 1.00 - 0.16 - 0.\dot{6} = 0.16 = 0.16$$

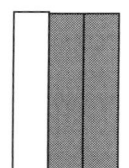

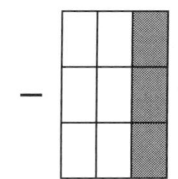

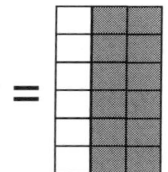

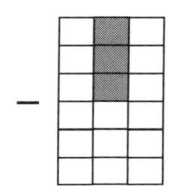

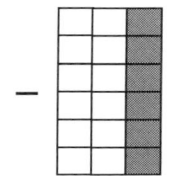

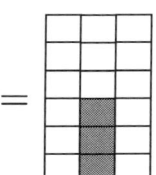

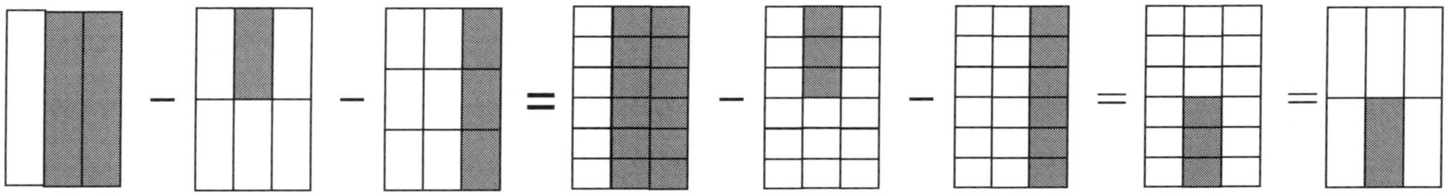

$$\frac{2}{3} - \frac{1}{6} - \frac{3}{9} = \frac{12}{18} - \frac{3}{18} - \frac{6}{18} = \frac{3}{18} = \frac{1}{6}$$

$$0.\dot{6} - 0.16 - 0.\dot{3} = 0.\dot{6} - 0.16 - 0.\dot{3} = 0.16 = 0.16$$

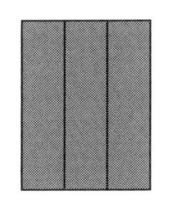

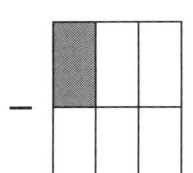

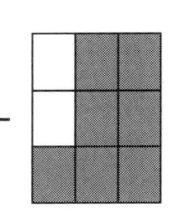

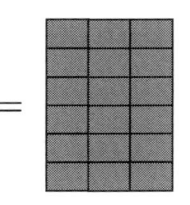

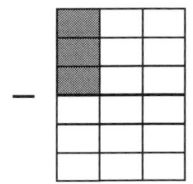

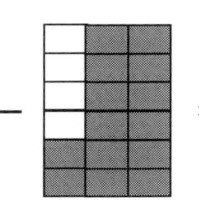

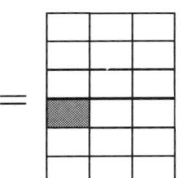

$$\frac{3}{3} - \frac{1}{6} - \frac{7}{9} = \frac{18}{18} - \frac{3}{18} - \frac{14}{18} = \frac{1}{18}$$

$$1.00 - 0.1\dot{6} - 0.7\dot{7} = 1.00 - 0.1\dot{6} - 0.7\dot{7} = 0.0\dot{5}$$

Thirds – Sixths – Ninths

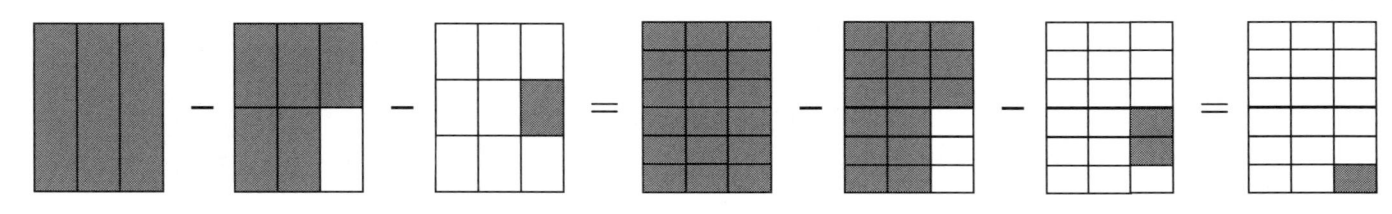

$$\frac{3}{3} - \frac{5}{6} - \frac{1}{9} = \frac{18}{18} - \frac{15}{18} - \frac{2}{18} = \frac{1}{18}$$

$$1.00 - 0.83\dot{} - 0.11\dot{} = 1.00 - 0.83\dot{} - 0.11\dot{} = 0.05\dot{}$$

$$\frac{2}{3} - \frac{1}{6} - \frac{4}{9} = \frac{12}{18} - \frac{3}{18} - \frac{8}{18} = \frac{1}{18}$$

$$0.66\dot{} - 0.16\dot{} - 0.44\dot{} = 0.66\dot{} - 0.16\dot{} - 0.44\dot{} = 0.05\dot{}$$

$$\frac{2}{3} - \frac{3}{6} - \frac{1}{9} = \frac{12}{18} - \frac{9}{18} - \frac{2}{18} = \frac{1}{18}$$

$$0.66\dot{} - 0.50 - 0.11\dot{} = 0.66\dot{} - 0.50 - 0.11\dot{} = 0.05\dot{}$$

Thirds – Sixths – Ninths

$$\frac{1}{3} - \frac{1}{6} - \frac{1}{9} = \frac{6}{18} - \frac{3}{18} - \frac{2}{18} = \frac{1}{18}$$

$$0.33^{\cdot} - 0.16^{\cdot} - 0.11^{\cdot} = 0.33^{\cdot} - 0.16^{\cdot} - 0.11^{\cdot} = 0.05^{\cdot}$$

$$\frac{2}{3} - \frac{2}{6} - \frac{3}{9} = \frac{12}{18} - \frac{6}{18} - \frac{6}{18} = \frac{0}{18} = 0$$

$$0.6^{\cdot} - 0.3^{\cdot} - 0.3^{\cdot} = 0.6^{\cdot} - 0.3^{\cdot} - 0.3^{\cdot} = 0.00 = 0$$

Sixths – Halves

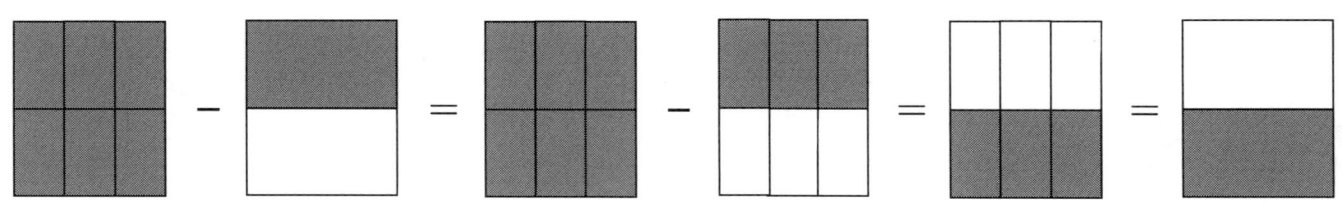

$$\frac{6}{6} - \frac{1}{2} = \frac{6}{6} - \frac{3}{6} = \frac{3}{6} = \frac{1}{2}$$

1.00 − 0.50 = 1.00 − 0.50 = 0.50 = 0.50

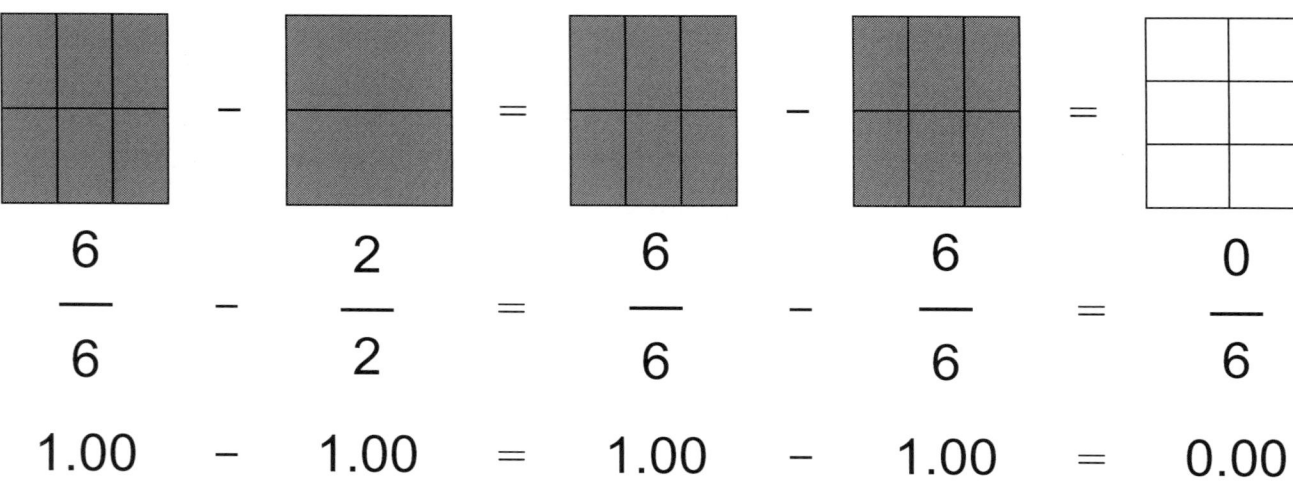

$$\frac{6}{6} - \frac{2}{2} = \frac{6}{6} - \frac{6}{6} = \frac{0}{6}$$

1.00 − 1.00 = 1.00 − 1.00 = 0.00

$$= \frac{0}{3} = \frac{0}{2} = 0$$

= 0.00 = 0.00 = 0

Halves – Thirds – Sixths

$$\frac{2}{2} - \frac{1}{3} - \frac{1}{6} = \frac{6}{6} - \frac{2}{6} - \frac{1}{6} = \frac{3}{6} = \frac{1}{2}$$

$$1.00 - 0.3\dot{} - 0.16 = 1.00 - 0.3\dot{} - 0.16 = 0.50 = 0.50$$

$$\frac{1}{2} - \frac{1}{3} - \frac{1}{6} = \frac{3}{6} - \frac{2}{6} - \frac{1}{6} = \frac{0}{6}$$

$$0.50 - 0.33\dot{} - 0.16\dot{} = 0.50 - 0.33\dot{} - 0.16\dot{} = 0.00$$

$$= \frac{0}{3} = \frac{0}{2} = 0$$

$$= 0.00 = 0.00 = 0$$

265

Quarters − Twelfths

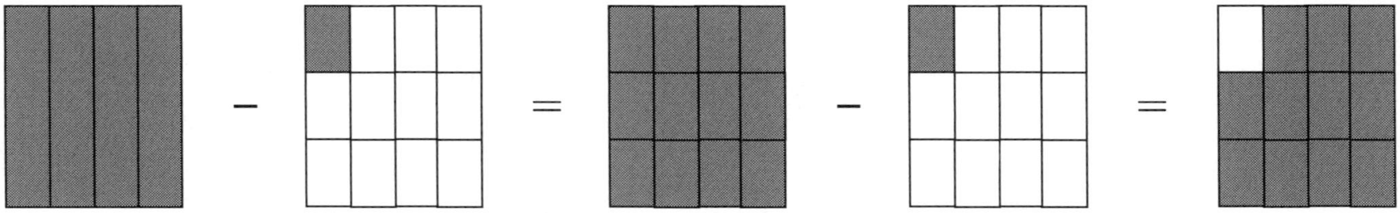

$$\frac{4}{4} - \frac{1}{12} = \frac{12}{12} - \frac{1}{12} = \frac{11}{12}$$

$$1.00 - 0.08\dot{3} = 1.00 - 0.08\dot{3} = 0.91\dot{6}$$

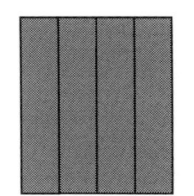

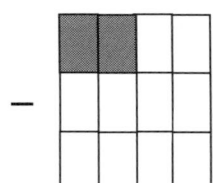

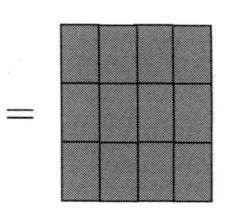

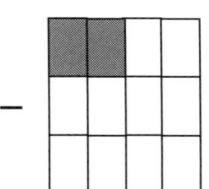

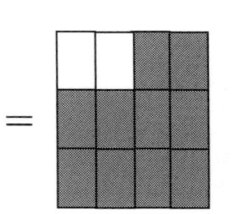

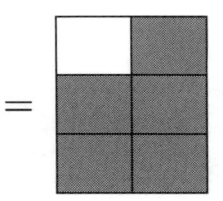

$$\frac{4}{4} - \frac{2}{12} = \frac{12}{12} - \frac{2}{12} = \frac{10}{12} = \frac{5}{6}$$

$$1.00 - 0.16\dot{6} = 1.00 - 0.16\dot{6} = 0.83\dot{3} = 0.83\dot{3}$$

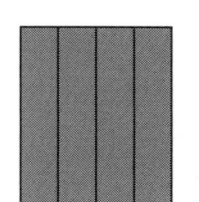

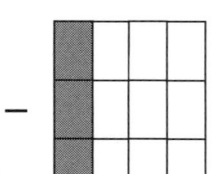

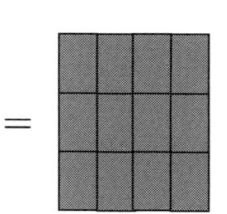

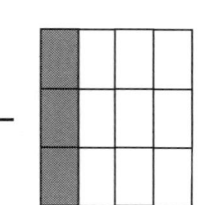

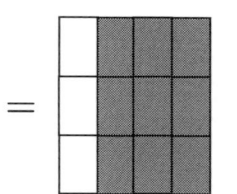

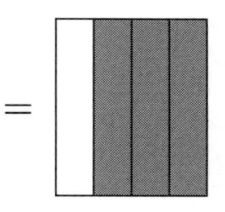

$$\frac{4}{4} - \frac{3}{12} = \frac{12}{12} - \frac{3}{12} = \frac{9}{12} = \frac{3}{4}$$

$$1.00 - 0.25 = 1.00 - 0.25 = 0.75 = 0.75$$

Quarters – Twelfths

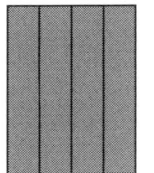

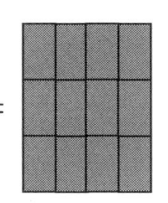

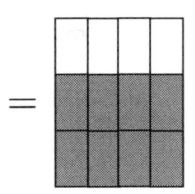

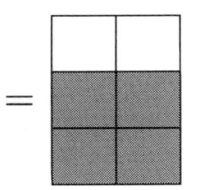

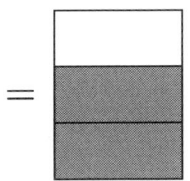

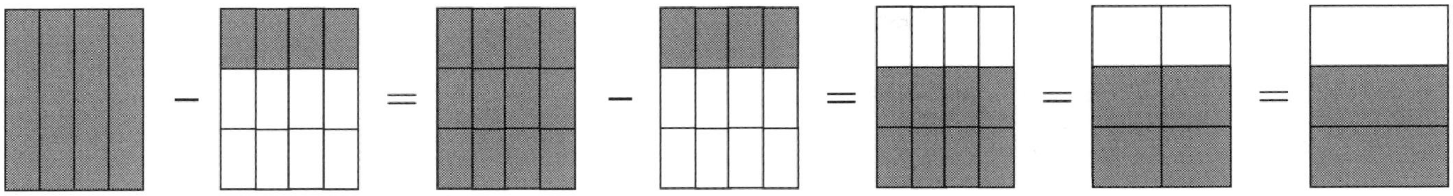

$$\frac{4}{4} - \frac{4}{12} = \frac{12}{12} - \frac{4}{12} = \frac{8}{12} = \frac{4}{6} = \frac{2}{3}$$

$$1.00 - 0.33\dot{} = 1.00 - 0.33\dot{} = 0.66\dot{} = 0.66\dot{} = 0.66\dot{}$$

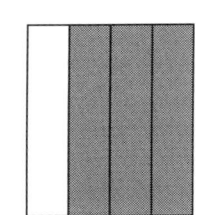

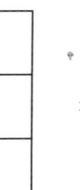

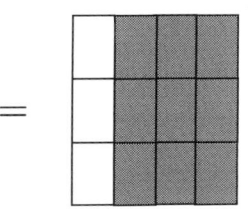

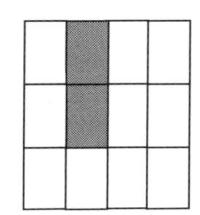

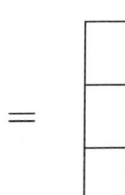

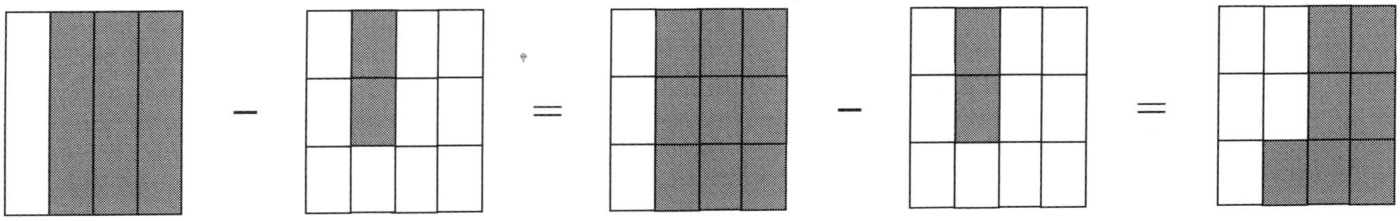

$$\frac{3}{4} - \frac{2}{12} = \frac{9}{12} - \frac{2}{12} = \frac{7}{12}$$

$$0.75 - 0.166\dot{} = 0.75 - 0.166\dot{} = 0.583\dot{}$$

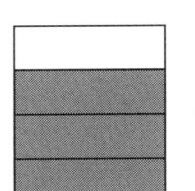

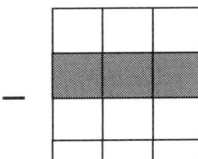

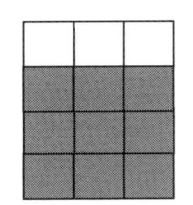

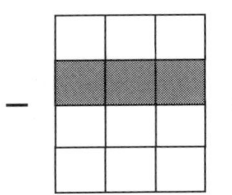

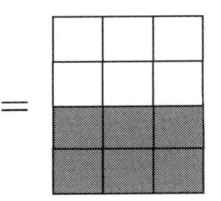

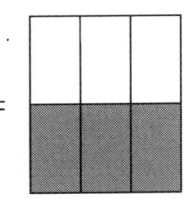

$$\frac{3}{4} - \frac{3}{12} = \frac{9}{12} - \frac{3}{12} = \frac{6}{12} = \frac{3}{6}$$

$$0.75 - 0.25 = 0.75 - 0.25 = 0.50 = 0.50$$

$$= \frac{2}{4} = \frac{1}{2}$$

$$= 0.50 = 0.50$$

$$\frac{2}{4} - \frac{1}{12} = \frac{6}{12} - \frac{1}{12} = \frac{5}{12}$$

$$0.50 - 0.083\dot{} = 0.500 - 0.083\dot{} = 0.416\dot{}$$

$$\frac{4}{4} - \frac{8}{12} = \frac{12}{12} - \frac{8}{12} = \frac{4}{12} = \frac{2}{6} = \frac{1}{3}$$

$$1.00 - 0.66\dot{} = 1.00 - 0.66\dot{} = 0.33\dot{} = 0.33\dot{} = 0.33\dot{}$$

Quarters - Twelfths

$$\frac{2}{4} - \frac{3}{12} = \frac{6}{12} - \frac{3}{12} = \frac{3}{12} = \frac{1}{4}$$

0.50 − 0.25 = 0.50 − 0.25 = 0.25 = 0.25

$$\frac{4}{4} - \frac{10}{12} = \frac{12}{12} - \frac{10}{12} = \frac{2}{12} = \frac{1}{6}$$

1.00 − 0.833˙ = 1.00 − 0.833˙ = 0.166˙ = 0.166˙

$$\frac{1}{4} - \frac{2}{12} = \frac{3}{12} - \frac{2}{12} = \frac{1}{12}$$

0.25 − 0.166˙ = 0.250 − 0.166˙ = 0.083˙

Quarters − Twelfths

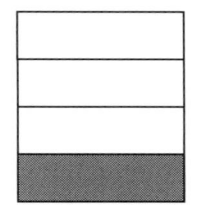

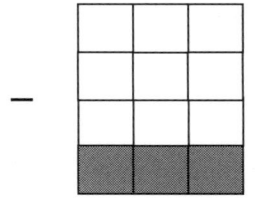

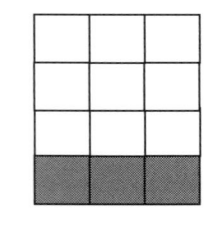

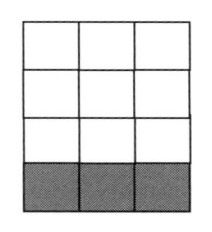

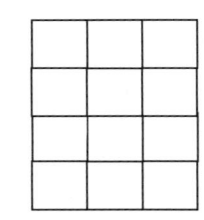

$$\frac{1}{4} - \frac{3}{12} = \frac{3}{12} - \frac{3}{12} = \frac{0}{12}$$

$$0.25 - 0.25 = 0.25 - 0.25 = 0.00$$

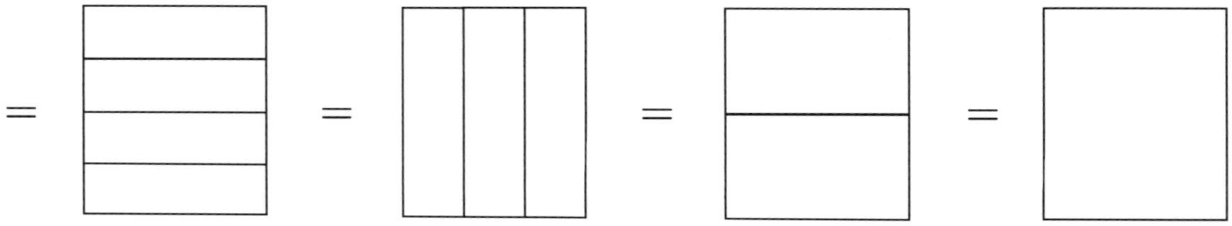

$$= \frac{0}{4} = \frac{0}{3} = \frac{0}{2} = 0$$

$$= 0.00 = 0.00 = 0.00 = 0.00$$

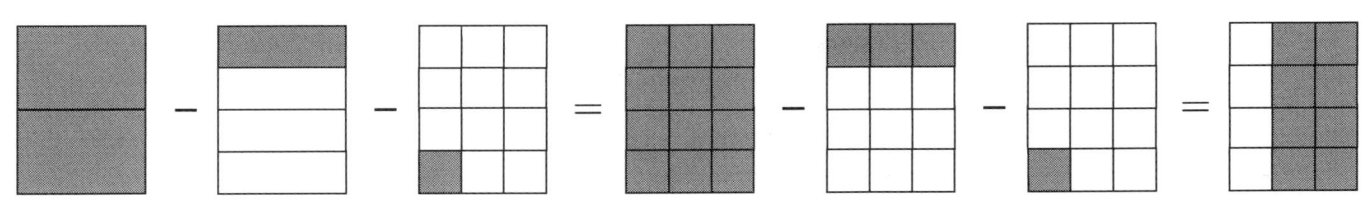

Halves – Quarters – Twelfths

$$\frac{2}{2} - \frac{1}{4} - \frac{1}{12} = \frac{12}{12} - \frac{3}{12} - \frac{1}{12} = \frac{8}{12}$$

$$1.00 - 0.25 - 0.083 = 1.00 - 0.25 - 0.083 = 0.66\dot{}$$

$$= \frac{4}{6} = \frac{2}{3}$$

$$= 0.66\dot{} = 0.66\dot{}$$

$$\frac{2}{2} - \frac{1}{4} - \frac{2}{12} = \frac{12}{12} - \frac{3}{12} - \frac{2}{12} = \frac{7}{12}$$

$$1.00 - 0.25 - 0.16\dot{} = 1.00 - 0.25 - 0.16\dot{} = 0.583$$

Halves – Quarters – Twelfths

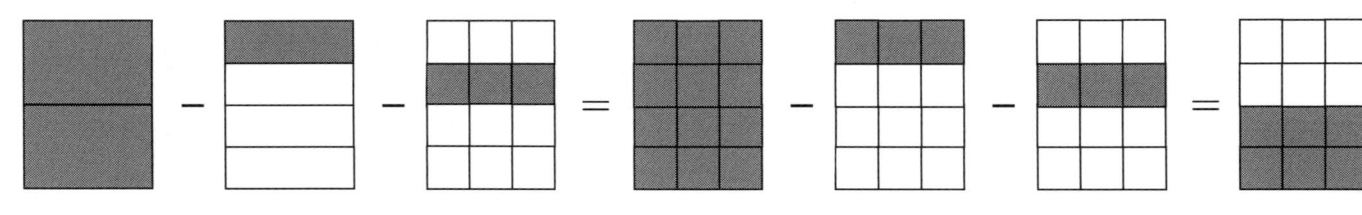

$$\frac{2}{2} - \frac{1}{4} - \frac{3}{12} = \frac{12}{12} - \frac{3}{12} - \frac{3}{12} = \frac{6}{12}$$

$$1.00 - 0.25 - 0.25 = 1.00 - 0.25 - 0.25 = 0.50$$

$$= \frac{3}{6} = \frac{2}{4} = \frac{1}{2}$$

$$= 0.50 = 0.50 = 0.50$$

$$\frac{2}{2} - \frac{1}{4} - \frac{4}{12} = \frac{12}{12} - \frac{3}{12} - \frac{4}{12} = \frac{5}{12}$$

$$1.00 - 0.25 - 0.33\dot{} = 1.00 - 0.25 - 0.33\dot{} = 0.41\dot{6}$$

Halves – Quarters – Twelfths

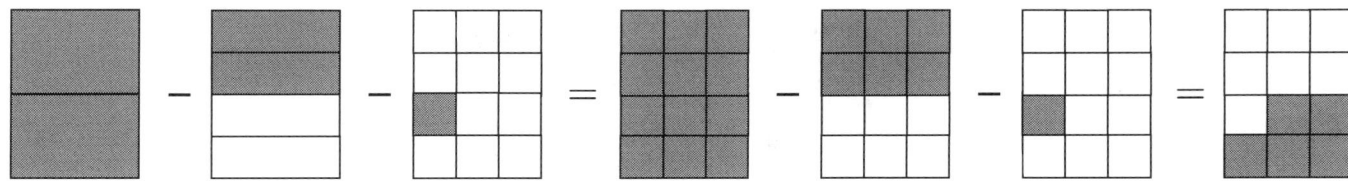

$$\frac{2}{2} - \frac{2}{4} - \frac{1}{12} = \frac{12}{12} - \frac{6}{12} - \frac{1}{12} = \frac{5}{12}$$

$$1.00 - 0.50 - 0.083 = 1.00 - 0.50 - 0.083 = 0.416$$

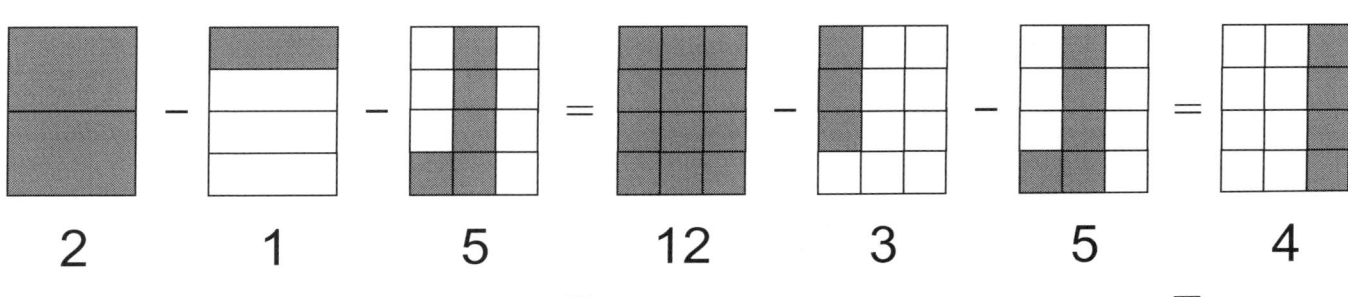

$$\frac{2}{2} - \frac{1}{4} - \frac{5}{12} = \frac{12}{12} - \frac{3}{12} - \frac{5}{12} = \frac{4}{12}$$

$$1.00 - 0.25 - 0.416 = 1.00 - 0.25 - 0.416 = 0.33\dot{}$$

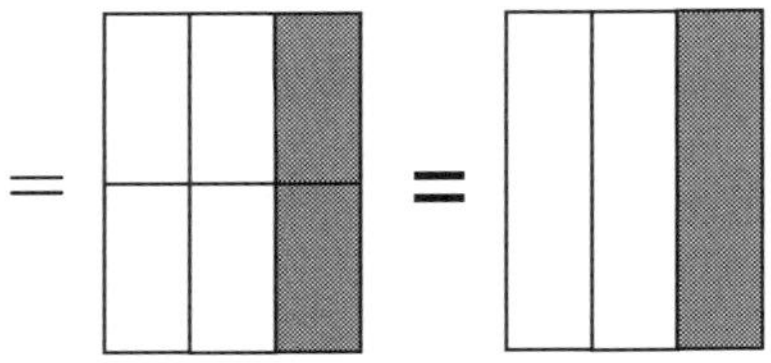

$$= \frac{2}{6} = \frac{1}{3}$$

$$= 0.33\dot{} = 0.33\dot{}$$

Halves – Quarters – Twelfths

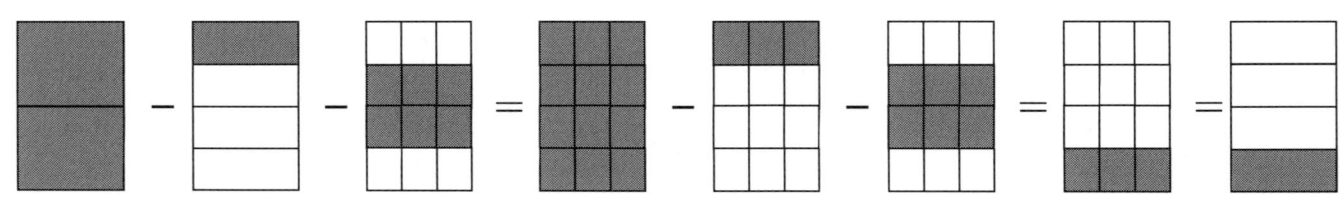

$$\frac{2}{2} - \frac{1}{4} - \frac{6}{12} = \frac{12}{12} - \frac{3}{12} - \frac{6}{12} = \frac{3}{12} = \frac{1}{4}$$

1.00 − 0.25 − 0.50 = 1.00 − 0.25 − 0.50 = 0.25 = 0.25

$$\frac{2}{2} - \frac{1}{4} - \frac{7}{12} = \frac{12}{12} - \frac{3}{12} - \frac{7}{12} = \frac{2}{12} = \frac{1}{6}$$

1.00 − 0.25 − 0.583 = 1.00 − 0.25 − 0.583 = 0.16 = 0.16

$$\frac{1}{2} - \frac{1}{4} - \frac{1}{12} = \frac{6}{12} - \frac{3}{12} - \frac{1}{12} = \frac{2}{12} = \frac{1}{6}$$

0.50 − 0.25 − 0.083 = 0.50 − 0.25 − 0.083 = 0.16 = 0.16

Halves – Quarters – Twelfths

$$\frac{2}{2} - \frac{3}{4} - \frac{1}{12} = \frac{12}{12} - \frac{9}{12} - \frac{1}{12} = \frac{2}{12} = \frac{1}{6}$$

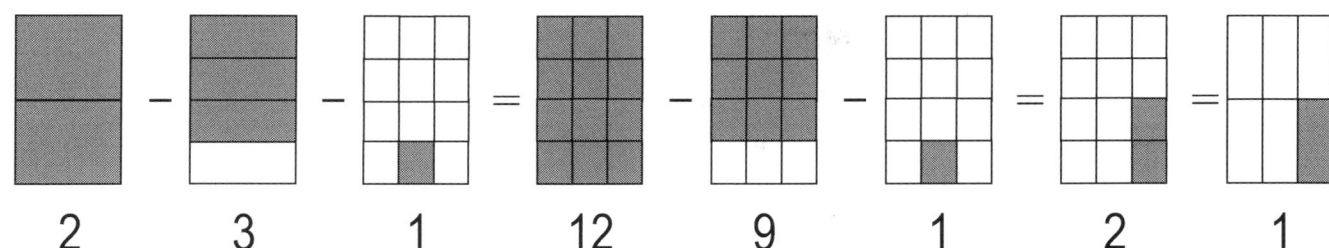

$$1.00 - 0.75 - 0.083 = 1.00 - 0.75 - 0.083 = 0.16 = 0.16$$

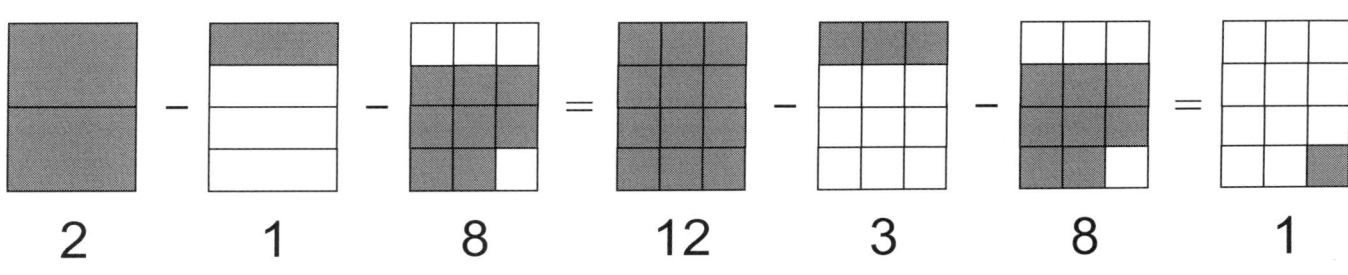

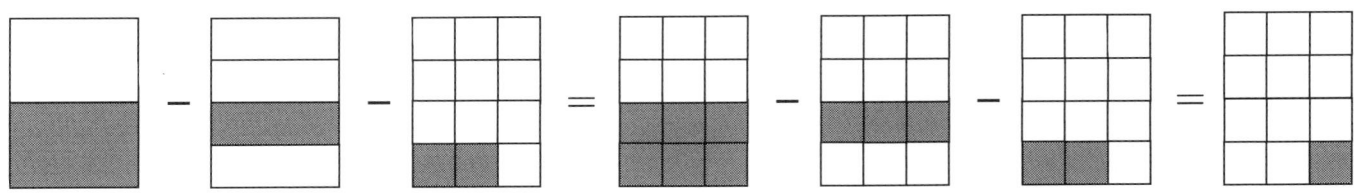

$$\frac{2}{2} - \frac{1}{4} - \frac{8}{12} = \frac{12}{12} - \frac{3}{12} - \frac{8}{12} = \frac{1}{12}$$

$$1.00 - 0.25 - 0.66^{\cdot} = 1.00 - 0.25 - 0.66^{\cdot} = 0.083$$

$$\frac{1}{2} - \frac{1}{4} - \frac{2}{12} = \frac{6}{12} - \frac{3}{12} - \frac{2}{12} = \frac{1}{12}$$

$$0.50 - 0.25 - 0.16^{\cdot} = 0.50 - 0.25 - 0.16^{\cdot} = 0.083$$

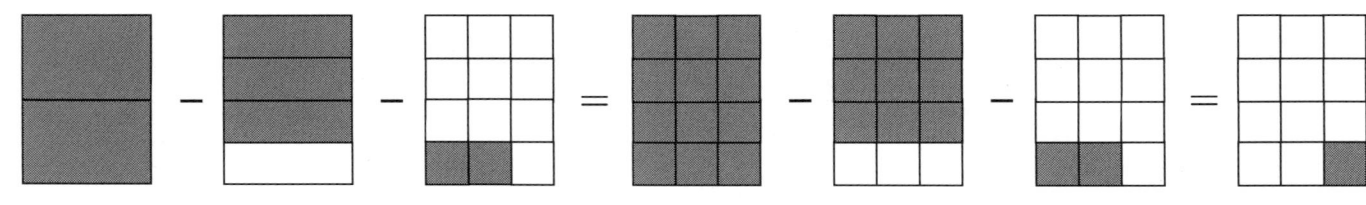

Halves – Quarters – Twelfths

$$\frac{2}{2} - \frac{3}{4} - \frac{2}{12} = \frac{12}{12} - \frac{9}{12} - \frac{2}{12} = \frac{1}{12}$$

$$1.00 - 0.75 - 0.16\dot{} = 1.00 - 0.75 - 0.16\dot{} = 0.083$$

$$\frac{1}{2} - \frac{1}{4} - \frac{3}{12} = \frac{6}{12} - \frac{3}{12} - \frac{3}{12} = \frac{0}{12}$$

$$0.50 - 0.25 - 0.25 = 0.50 - 0.25 - 0.25 = 0.00$$

$$= \frac{0}{6} = \frac{0}{4} = \frac{0}{3} = \frac{0}{2} = 0$$

$$= 0.00 = 0.00 = 0.00 = 0.00 = 0$$

Thirds – Twelfths

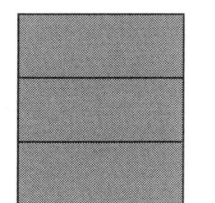

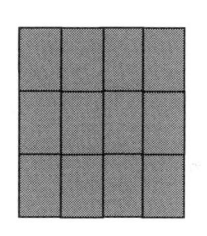

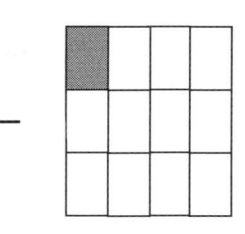

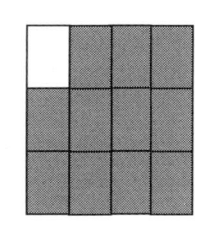

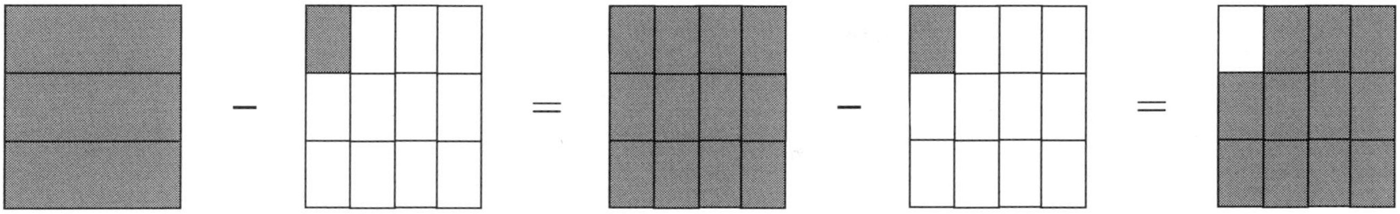

$$\frac{3}{3} - \frac{1}{12} = \frac{12}{12} - \frac{1}{12} = \frac{11}{12}$$

$$1.00 - 0.083\dot{} = 1.00 - 0.083\dot{} = 0.916\dot{}$$

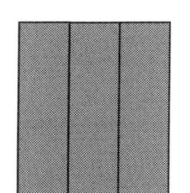

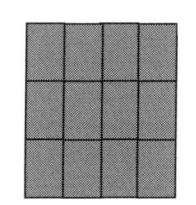

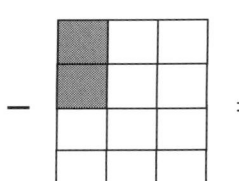

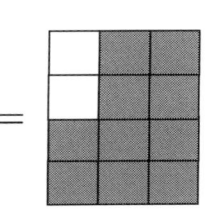

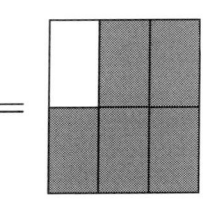

$$\frac{3}{3} - \frac{2}{12} = \frac{12}{12} - \frac{2}{12} = \frac{10}{12} = \frac{5}{6}$$

$$1.00 - 0.166\dot{} = 1.00 - 0.166\dot{} = 0.833\dot{} = 0.833\dot{}$$

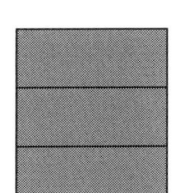

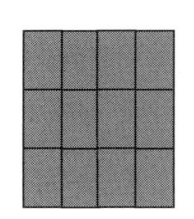

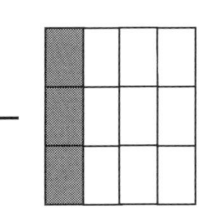

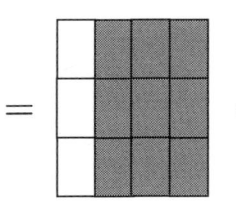

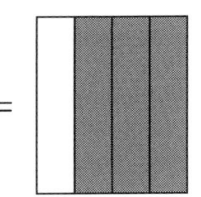

$$\frac{3}{3} - \frac{3}{12} = \frac{12}{12} - \frac{3}{12} = \frac{9}{12} = \frac{3}{4}$$

$$1.00 - 0.25 = 1.00 - 0.25 = 0.75 = 0.75$$

Thirds – Twelfths

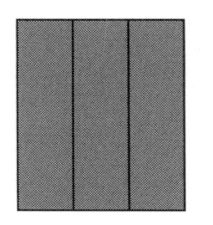

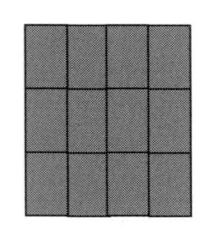

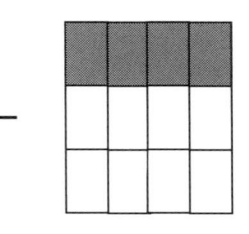

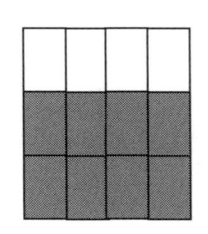

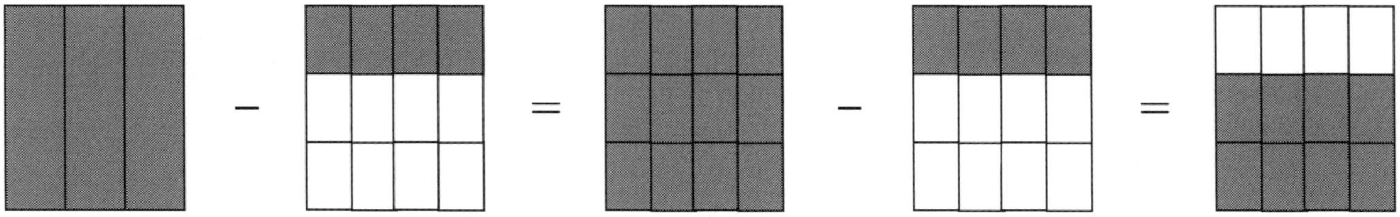

$$\frac{3}{3} - \frac{4}{12} = \frac{12}{12} - \frac{4}{12} = \frac{8}{12}$$

$$1.00 - 0.33˙ = 1.00 - 0.33˙ = 0.66˙$$

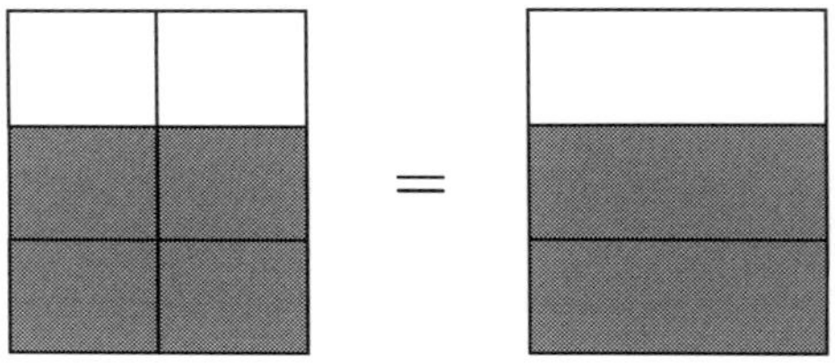

$$= \frac{4}{6} = \frac{2}{3}$$

$$= 0.666˙ = 0.666˙$$

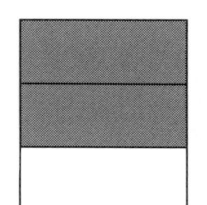

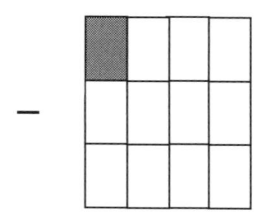

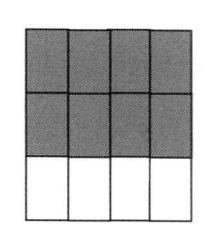

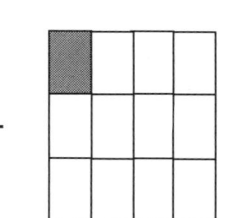

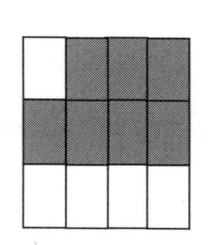

$$\frac{2}{3} - \frac{1}{12} = \frac{8}{12} - \frac{1}{12} = \frac{7}{12}$$

$$0.666˙ - 0.083˙ = 0.666˙ - 0.083˙ = 0.583˙$$

Thirds – Twelfths

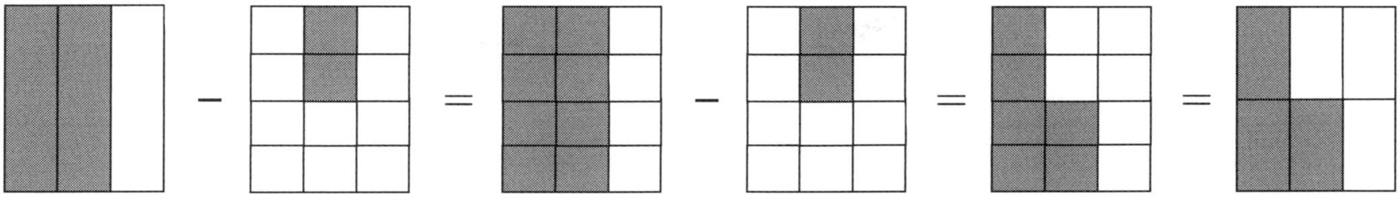

$$\frac{2}{3} - \frac{2}{12} = \frac{8}{12} - \frac{2}{12} = \frac{6}{12} = \frac{3}{6}$$

$$0.666˙ - 0.166˙ = 0.666˙ - 0.166˙ = 0.50 = 0.50$$

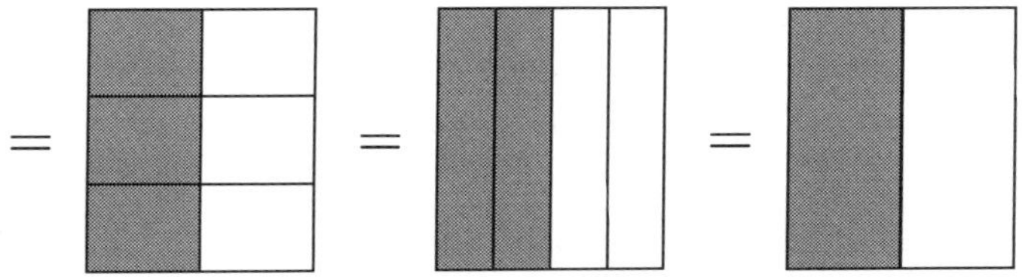

$$= \frac{3}{6} = \frac{2}{4} = \frac{1}{2}$$

$$= 0.50 = 0.50 = 0.50$$

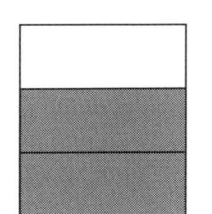

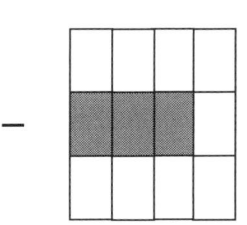

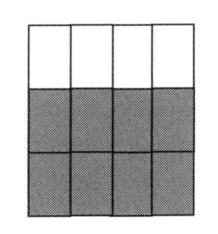

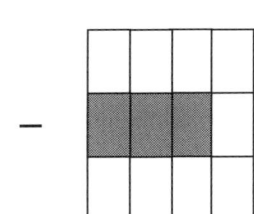

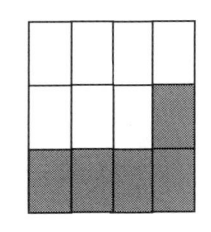

$$\frac{2}{3} - \frac{3}{12} = \frac{8}{12} - \frac{3}{12} = \frac{5}{12}$$

$$0.666˙ - 0.25 = 0.666˙ - 0.25 = 0.416˙$$

Thirds − Twelfths

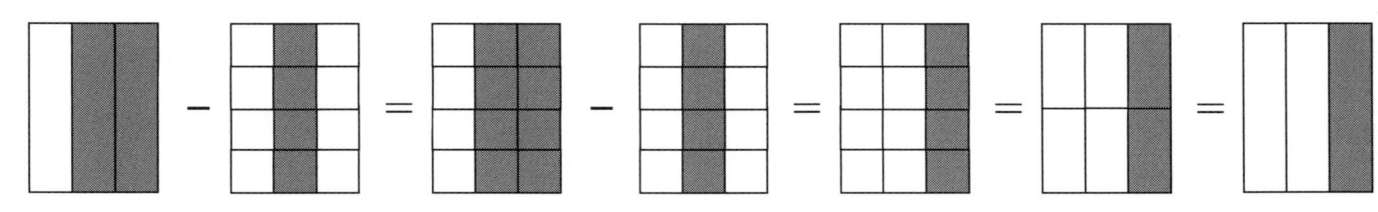

$$\frac{2}{3} - \frac{4}{12} = \frac{8}{12} - \frac{4}{12} = \frac{4}{12} = \frac{2}{6} = \frac{1}{3}$$

$$0.66\dot{} - 0.33\dot{} = 0.66\dot{} - 0.33\dot{} = 0.33\dot{} = 0.33\dot{} = 0.33\dot{}$$

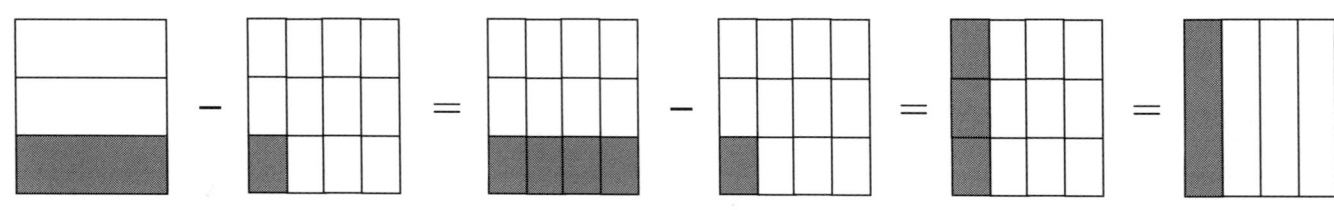

$$\frac{1}{3} - \frac{1}{12} = \frac{4}{12} - \frac{1}{12} = \frac{3}{12} = \frac{1}{4}$$

$$0.333\dot{} - 0.083\dot{} = 0.333\dot{} - 0.083\dot{} = 0.250 = 0.25$$

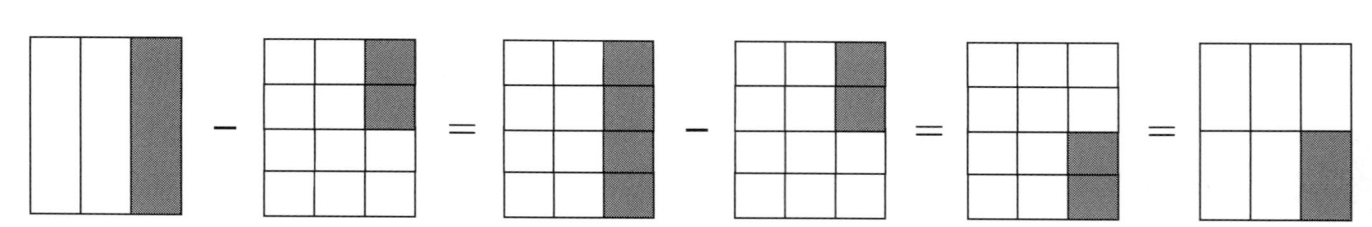

$$\frac{1}{3} - \frac{2}{12} = \frac{4}{12} - \frac{2}{12} = \frac{2}{12} = \frac{1}{6}$$

$$0.333\dot{} - 0.166\dot{} = 0.333\dot{} - 0.166\dot{} = 0.166\dot{} = 0.166\dot{}$$

Thirds − Twelfths

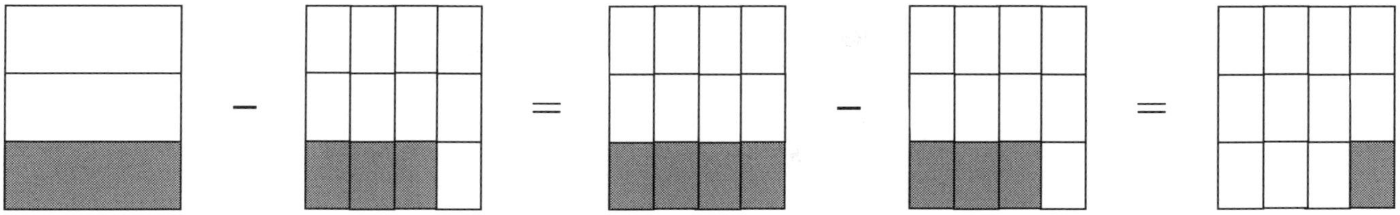

$$\frac{1}{3} - \frac{3}{12} = \frac{4}{12} - \frac{3}{12} = \frac{1}{12}$$

$$0.333^\cdot - 0.25 = 0.333^\cdot - 0.250 = 0.083^\cdot$$

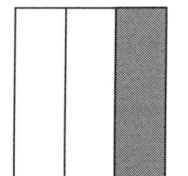

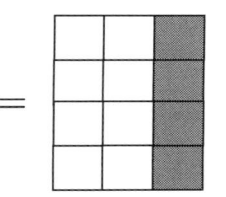

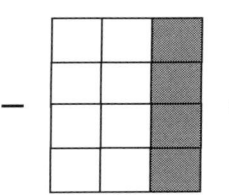

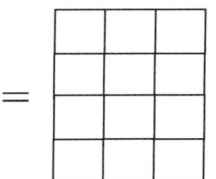

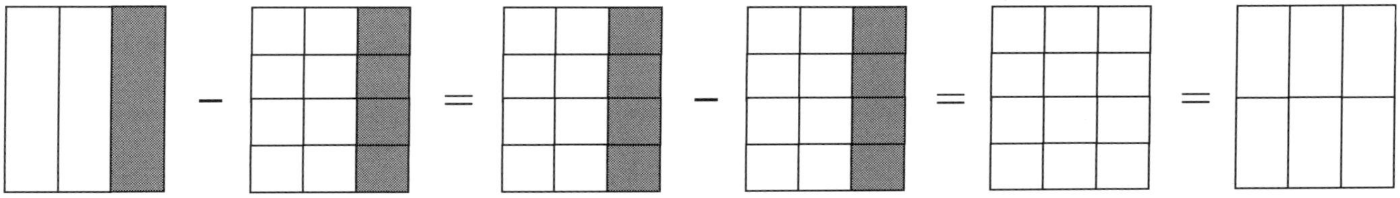

$$\frac{1}{3} - \frac{4}{12} = \frac{4}{12} - \frac{4}{12} = \frac{0}{12} = \frac{0}{6}$$

$$0.333^\cdot - 0.333^\cdot = 0.333^\cdot - 0.333^\cdot = 0.00 = 0.00$$

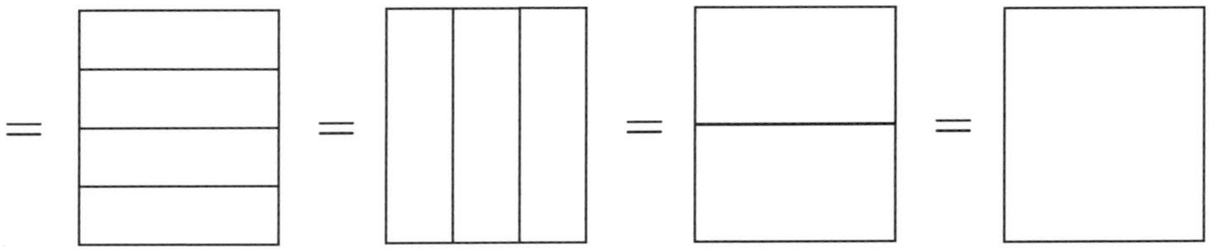

$$= \frac{0}{4} = \frac{0}{3} = \frac{0}{2} = 0$$

$$= 0.00 = 0.00 = 0.00 = 0$$

Sixths – Twelfths

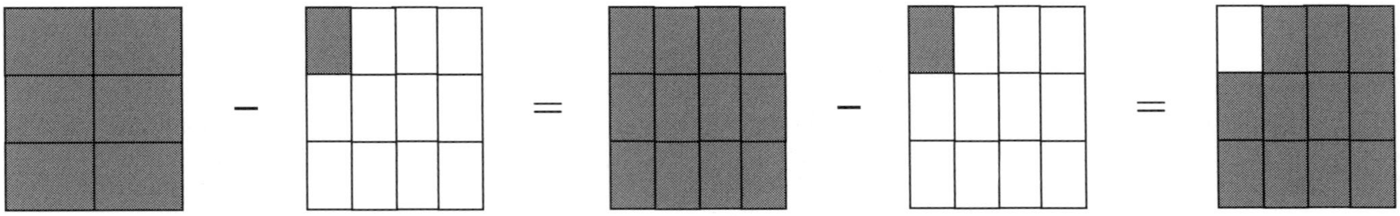

$$\frac{6}{6} - \frac{1}{12} = \frac{12}{12} - \frac{1}{12} = \frac{11}{12}$$

$$1.00 - 0.083^{\cdot} = 1.00 - 0.083^{\cdot} = 0.916^{\cdot}$$

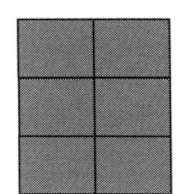

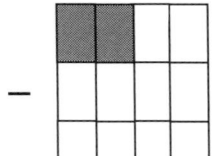

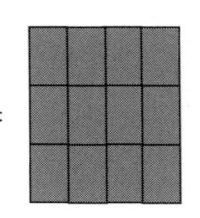

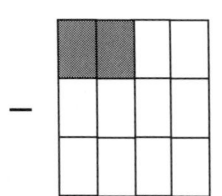

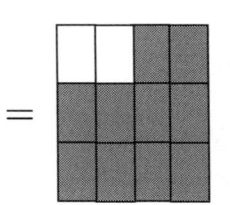

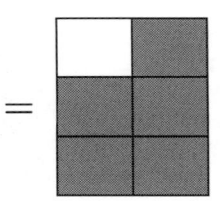

$$\frac{6}{6} - \frac{2}{12} = \frac{12}{12} - \frac{2}{12} = \frac{10}{12} = \frac{5}{6}$$

$$1.00 - 0.166^{\cdot} = 1.00 - 0.166^{\cdot} = 0.833^{\cdot} = 0.833^{\cdot}$$

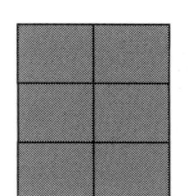

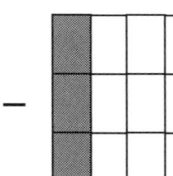

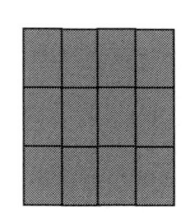

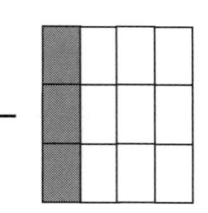

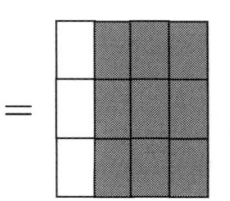

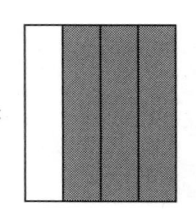

$$\frac{6}{6} - \frac{3}{12} = \frac{12}{12} - \frac{3}{12} = \frac{9}{12} = \frac{3}{4}$$

$$1.00 - 0.25 = 1.00 - 0.25 = 0.75 = 0.75$$

Sixths – Twelfths

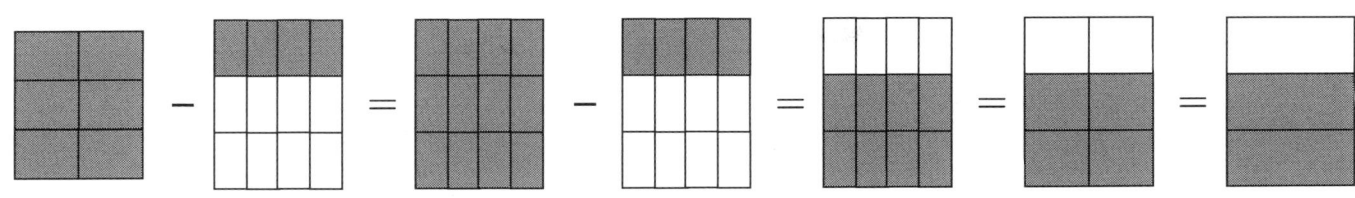

$$\frac{6}{6} - \frac{4}{12} = \frac{12}{12} - \frac{4}{12} = \frac{8}{12} = \frac{4}{6} = \frac{2}{3}$$

$$1.00 - 0.33\dot{} = 1.00 - 0.33\dot{} = 0.66\dot{} = 0.66\dot{} = 0.66\dot{}$$

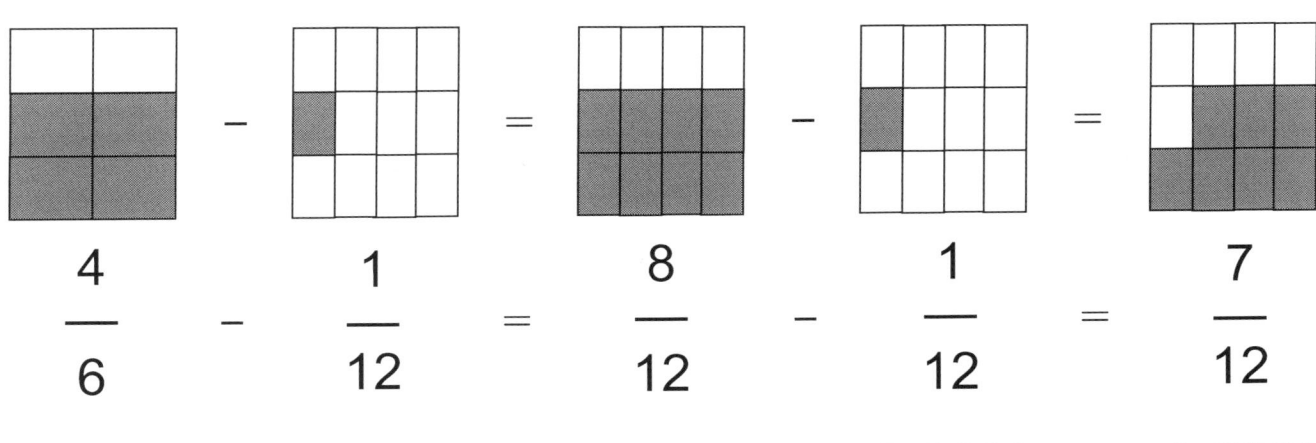

$$\frac{4}{6} - \frac{1}{12} = \frac{8}{12} - \frac{1}{12} = \frac{7}{12}$$

$$0.666\dot{} - 0.083\dot{} = 0.666\dot{} - 0.083\dot{} = 0.583\dot{}$$

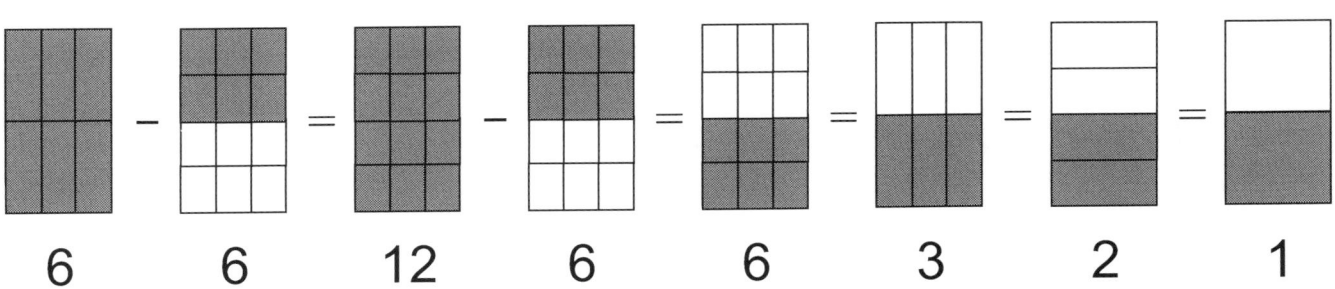

$$\frac{6}{6} - \frac{6}{12} = \frac{12}{12} - \frac{6}{12} = \frac{6}{12} = \frac{3}{6} = \frac{2}{4} = \frac{1}{2}$$

$$1.00 - 0.50 = 1.00 - 0.50 = 0.50 = 0.50 = 0.50 = 0.50$$

Sixths – Twelfths

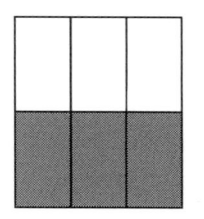

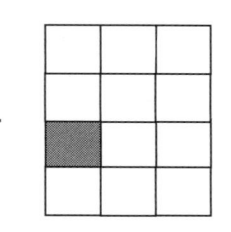

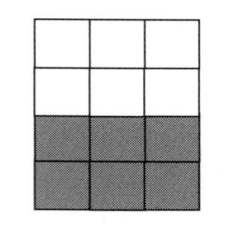

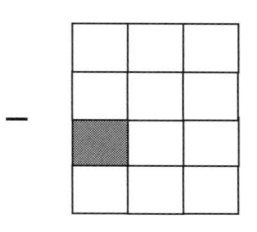

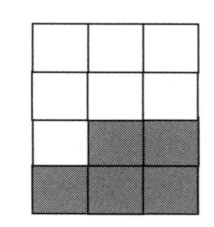

$$\frac{3}{6} - \frac{1}{12} = \frac{6}{12} - \frac{1}{12} = \frac{5}{12}$$

$$0.50 - 0.08\dot{3} = 0.500 - 0.08\dot{3} = 0.41\dot{6}$$

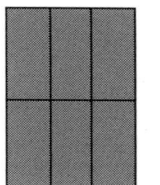

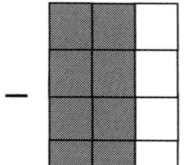

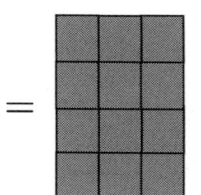

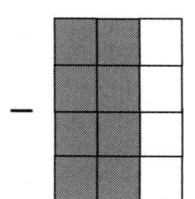

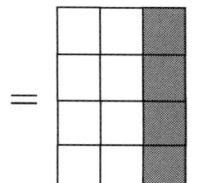

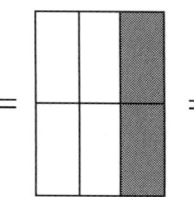

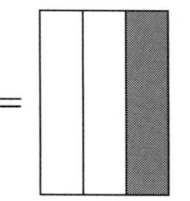

$$\frac{6}{6} - \frac{8}{12} = \frac{12}{12} - \frac{8}{12} = \frac{4}{12} = \frac{2}{6} = \frac{1}{3}$$

$$1.00 - 0.\dot{6} = 1.00 - 0.\dot{6} = 0.\dot{3} = 0.\dot{3} = 0.\dot{3}$$

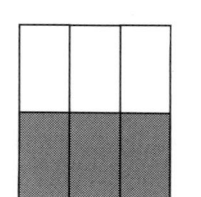

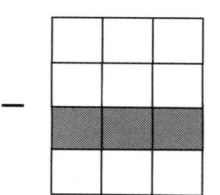

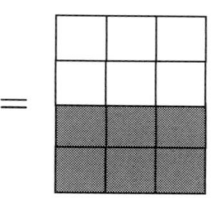

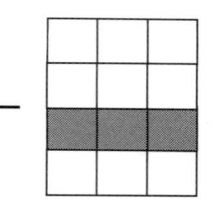

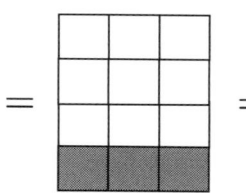

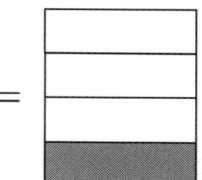

$$\frac{3}{6} - \frac{3}{12} = \frac{6}{12} - \frac{3}{12} = \frac{3}{12} = \frac{1}{4}$$

$$0.50 - 0.25 = 0.50 - 0.25 = 0.25 = 0.25$$

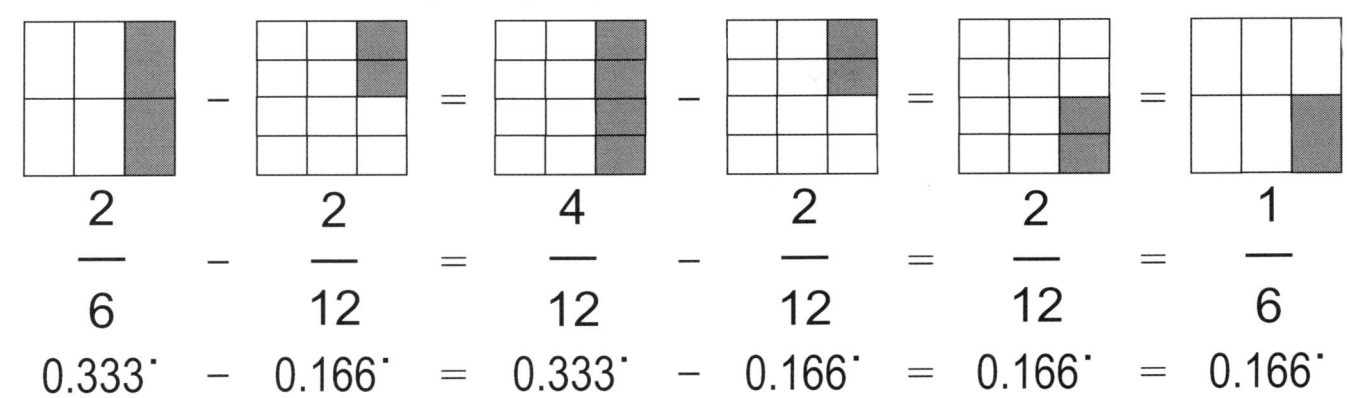

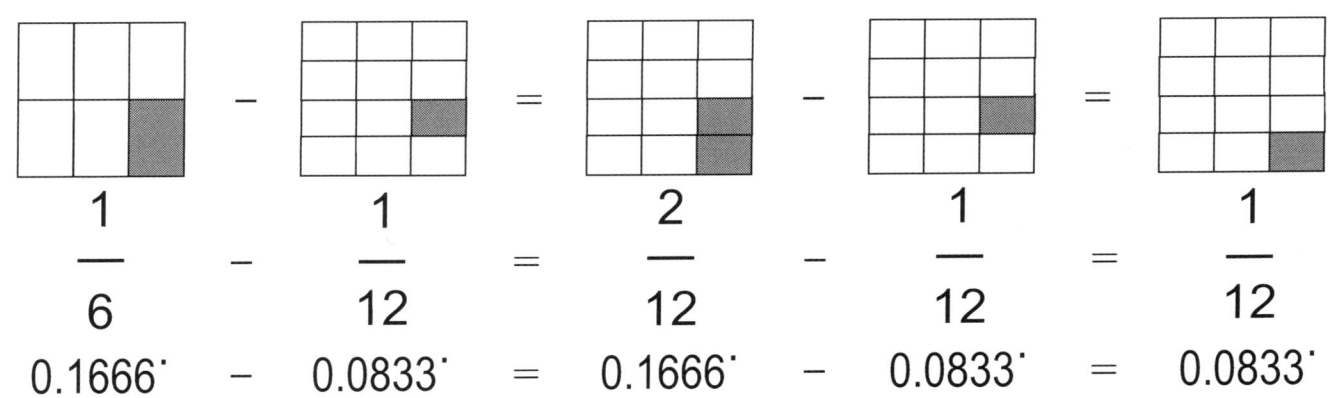

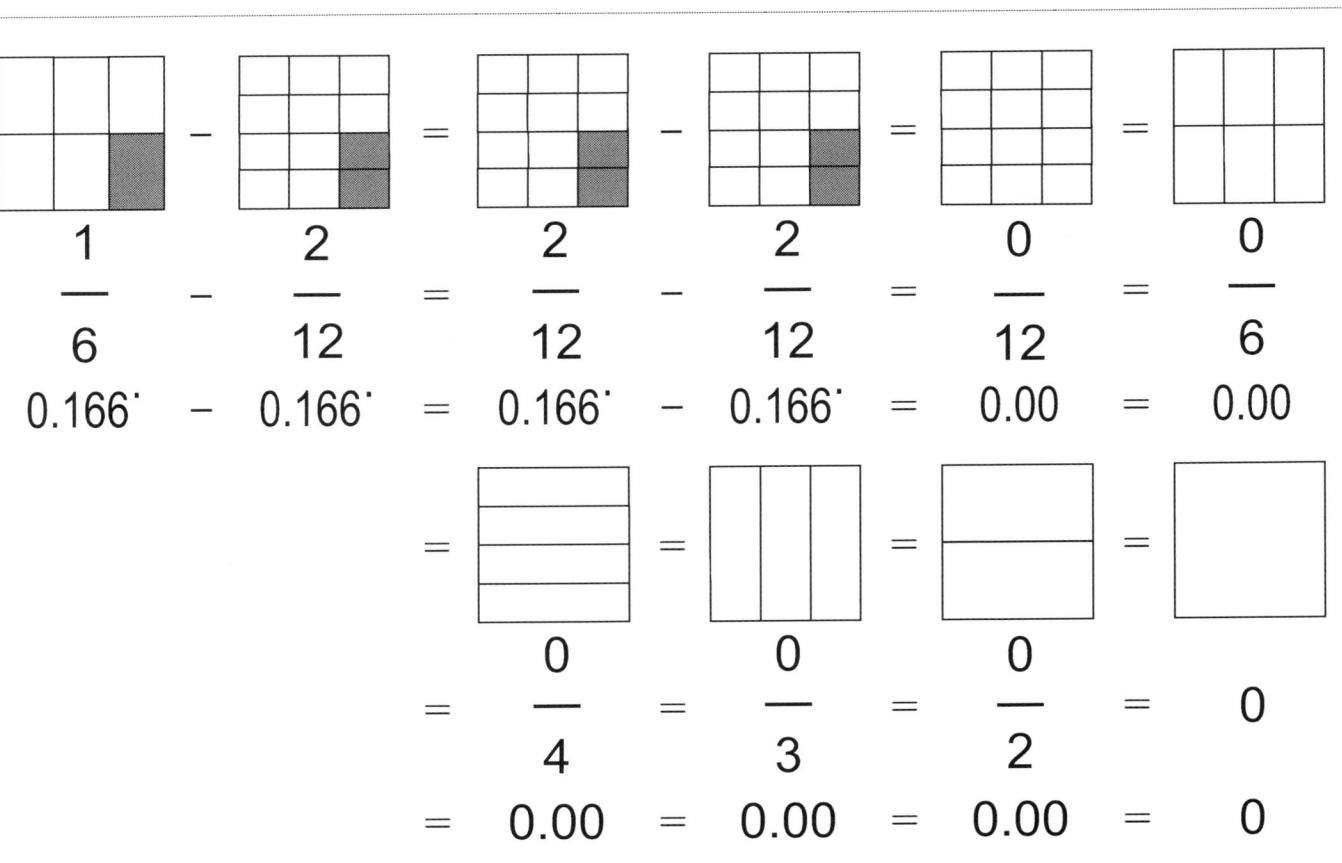

Sixths – Twelfths

$$\frac{2}{6} - \frac{2}{12} = \frac{4}{12} - \frac{2}{12} = \frac{2}{12} = \frac{1}{6}$$

$$0.333˙ - 0.166˙ = 0.333˙ - 0.166˙ = 0.166˙ = 0.166˙$$

$$\frac{1}{6} - \frac{1}{12} = \frac{2}{12} - \frac{1}{12} = \frac{1}{12}$$

$$0.1666˙ - 0.0833˙ = 0.1666˙ - 0.0833˙ = 0.0833˙$$

$$\frac{1}{6} - \frac{2}{12} = \frac{2}{12} - \frac{2}{12} = \frac{0}{12} = \frac{0}{6}$$

$$0.166˙ - 0.166˙ = 0.166˙ - 0.166˙ = 0.00 = 0.00$$

$$= \frac{0}{4} = \frac{0}{3} = \frac{0}{2} = 0$$

$$= 0.00 = 0.00 = 0.00 = 0$$

285

Thirds – Sixths – Twelfths

$$\frac{3}{3} - \frac{1}{6} - \frac{1}{12} = \frac{12}{12} - \frac{2}{12} - \frac{1}{12} = \frac{9}{12} = \frac{3}{4}$$

$$1.00 - 0.16 - 0.083 = 1.00 - 0.16 - 0.083 = 0.75 = 0.75$$

$$\frac{3}{3} - \frac{1}{6} - \frac{2}{12} = \frac{12}{12} - \frac{2}{12} - \frac{2}{12} = \frac{8}{12}$$

$$1.00 - 0.1\dot{6} - 0.1\dot{6} = 1.00 - 0.1\dot{6} - 0.1\dot{6} = 0.6\dot{6}$$

$$= \frac{4}{6} = \frac{2}{3}$$

$$= 0.6\dot{6} = 0.6\dot{6}$$

Thirds – Sixths – Twelfths

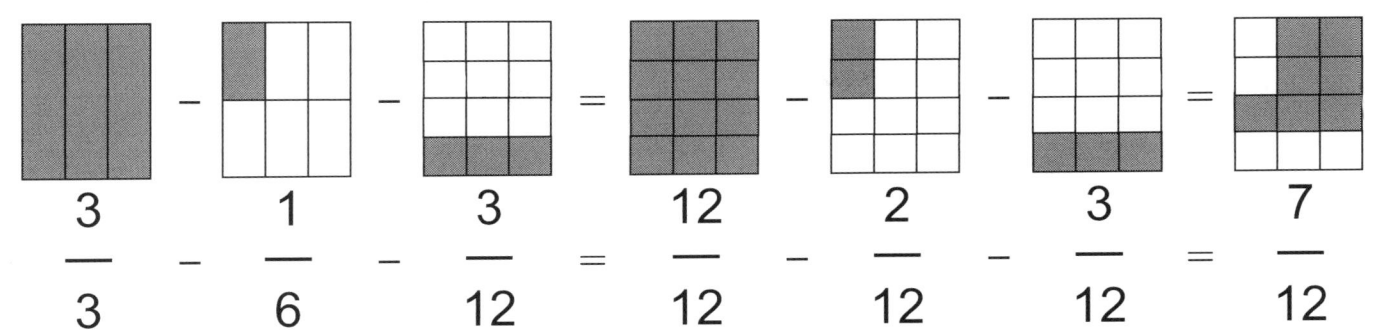

$$\frac{3}{3} - \frac{1}{6} - \frac{3}{12} = \frac{12}{12} - \frac{2}{12} - \frac{3}{12} = \frac{7}{12}$$

$$1.00 - 0.16\dot{} - 0.25 = 1.00 - 0.16\dot{} - 0.25 = 0.583$$

$$\frac{3}{3} - \frac{2}{6} - \frac{1}{12} = \frac{12}{12} - \frac{4}{12} - \frac{1}{12} = \frac{7}{12}$$

$$1.00 - 0.33\dot{} - 0.083 = 1.00 - 0.33\dot{} - 0.083 = 0.583$$

$$\frac{3}{3} - \frac{1}{6} - \frac{4}{12} = \frac{12}{12} - \frac{2}{12} - \frac{4}{12} = \frac{6}{12}$$

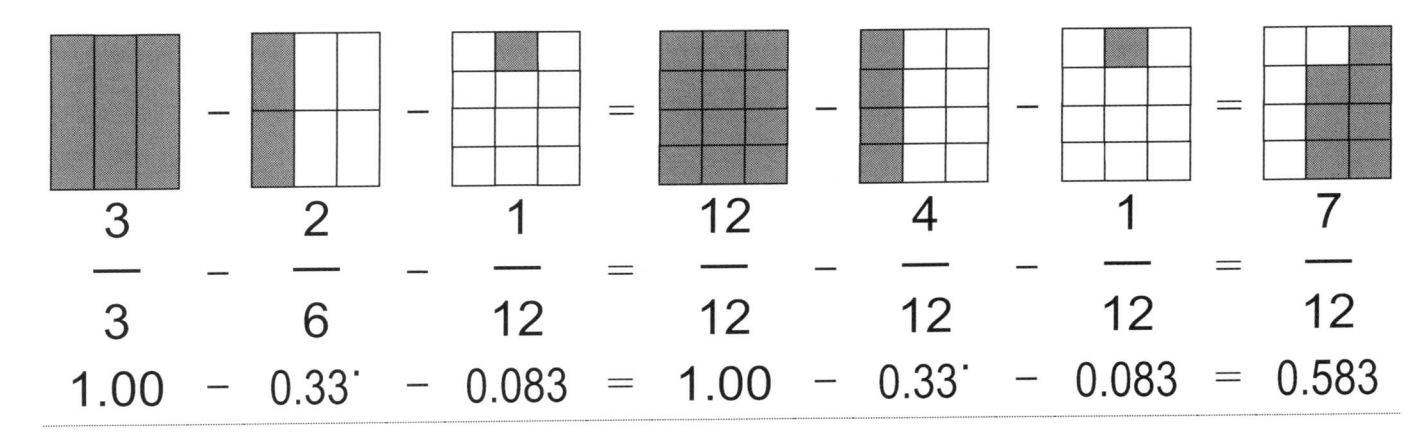

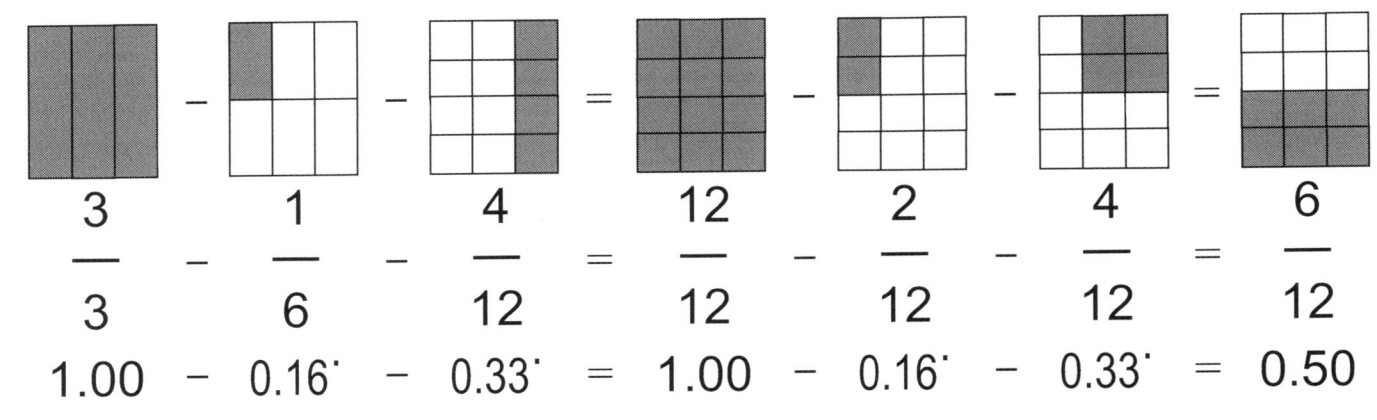

$$1.00 - 0.16\dot{} - 0.33\dot{} = 1.00 - 0.16\dot{} - 0.33\dot{} = 0.50$$

$$= \frac{3}{6} = \frac{2}{4} = \frac{1}{2}$$

$$= 0.50 = 0.50 = 0.50$$

Thirds – Sixths – Twelfths

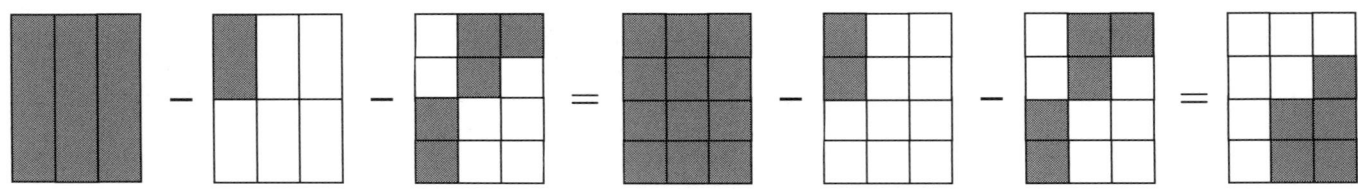

$$\frac{3}{3} - \frac{1}{6} - \frac{5}{12} = \frac{12}{12} - \frac{2}{12} - \frac{5}{12} = \frac{5}{12}$$

$1.00 - 0.1\dot{6} - 0.41\dot{6} = 1.00 - 0.1\dot{6} - 0.41\dot{6} = 0.41\dot{6}$

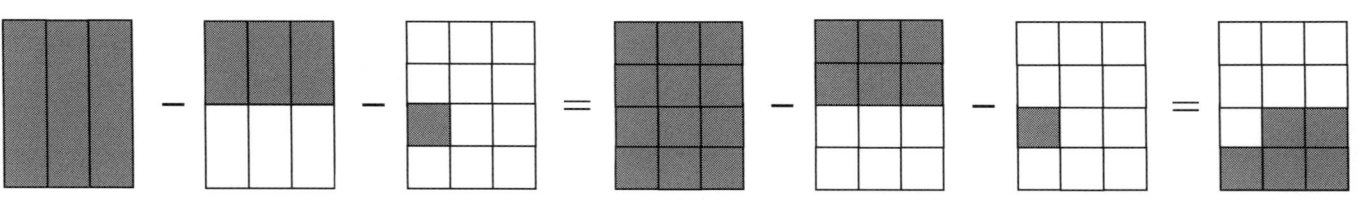

$$\frac{3}{3} - \frac{3}{6} - \frac{1}{12} = \frac{12}{12} - \frac{6}{12} - \frac{1}{12} = \frac{5}{12}$$

$1.00 - 0.50 - 0.08\dot{3} = 1.00 - 0.50 - 0.08\dot{3} = 0.41\dot{6}$

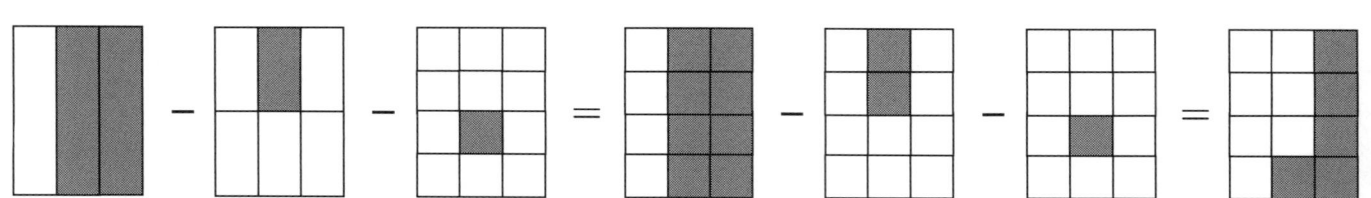

$$\frac{2}{3} - \frac{1}{6} - \frac{1}{12} = \frac{8}{12} - \frac{2}{12} - \frac{1}{12} = \frac{5}{12}$$

$0.\dot{6} - 0.1\dot{6} - 0.08\dot{3} = 0.6\dot{6} - 0.1\dot{6} - 0.08\dot{3} = 0.41\dot{6}$

Thirds – Sixths – Twelfths

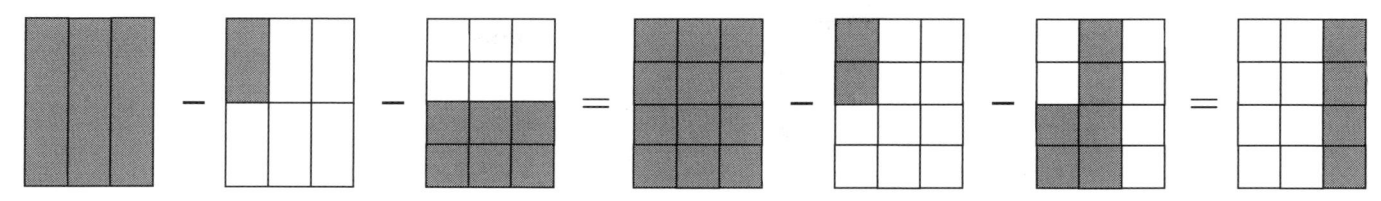

$$\frac{3}{3} - \frac{1}{6} - \frac{6}{12} = \frac{12}{12} - \frac{2}{12} - \frac{6}{12} = \frac{4}{12}$$

$$1.00 - 0.16\dot{} - 0.50 = 1.00 - 0.16\dot{} - 0.50 = 0.33\dot{}$$

$$= \frac{2}{6} = \frac{1}{3}$$

$$= 0.33\dot{} = 0.33\dot{}$$

$$\frac{3}{3} - \frac{1}{6} - \frac{7}{12} = \frac{12}{12} - \frac{2}{12} - \frac{7}{12} = \frac{3}{12} = \frac{1}{4}$$

$$1.00 - 0.16 - 0.583 = 1.00 - 0.16 - 0.583 = 0.25 = 0.25$$

289

Thirds – Sixths – Twelfths

$$\frac{3}{3} - \frac{4}{6} - \frac{1}{12} = \frac{12}{12} - \frac{8}{12} - \frac{1}{12} = \frac{3}{12} = \frac{1}{4}$$

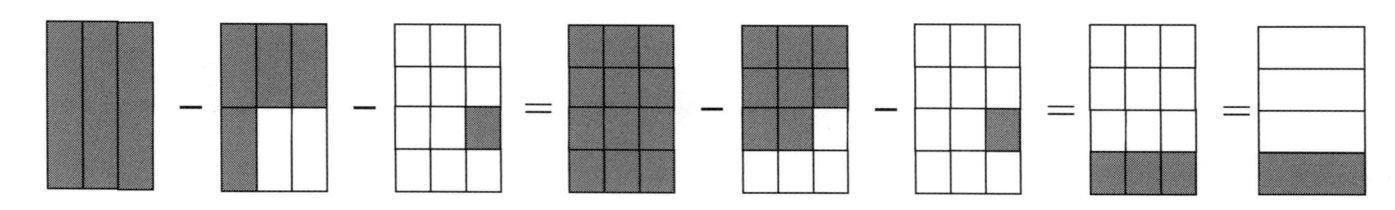

$1.00 - 0.6\dot{} - 0.083 = 1.00 - 0.6\dot{} - 0.083 = 0.25 = 0.25$

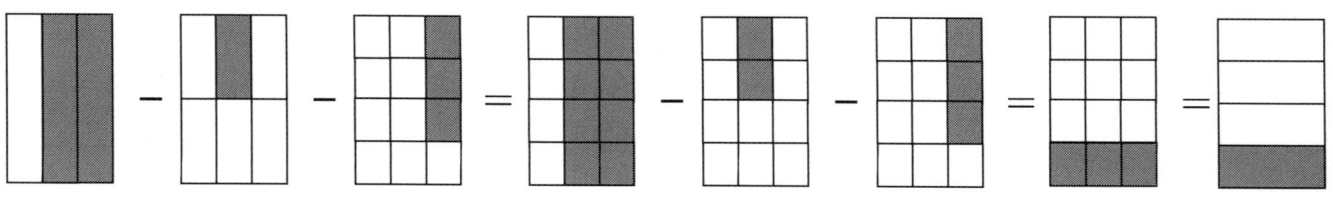

$$\frac{2}{3} - \frac{1}{6} - \frac{3}{12} = \frac{8}{12} - \frac{2}{12} - \frac{3}{12} = \frac{3}{12} = \frac{1}{4}$$

$0.6\dot{} - 0.16 - 0.25 = 0.66 - 0.16 - 0.25 = 0.25 = 0.25$

$$\frac{2}{3} - \frac{2}{6} - \frac{1}{12} = \frac{8}{12} - \frac{4}{12} - \frac{1}{12} = \frac{3}{12} = \frac{1}{4}$$

$0.6\dot{} - 0.3\dot{} - 0.083 = 0.6\dot{} - 0.3\dot{} - 0.083 = 0.25 = 0.25$

Thirds – Sixths – Twelfths

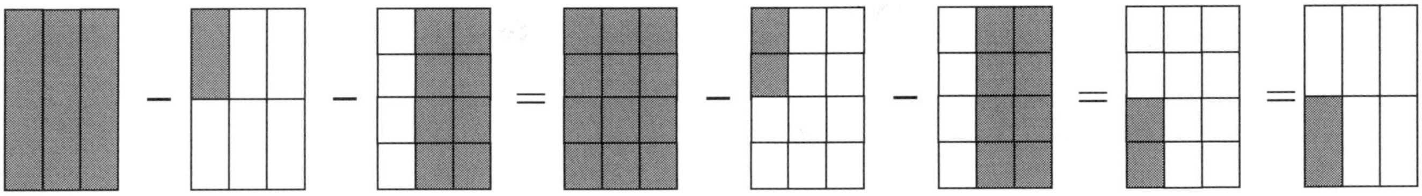

$$\frac{3}{3} - \frac{1}{6} - \frac{8}{12} = \frac{12}{12} - \frac{2}{12} - \frac{8}{12} = \frac{2}{12} = \frac{1}{6}$$

$1.00 - 0.16 - 0.6\dot{} = 1.00 - 0.16 - 0.6\dot{} = 0.16 = 0.16$

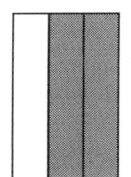

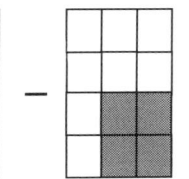

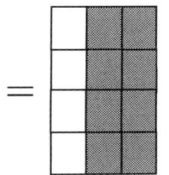

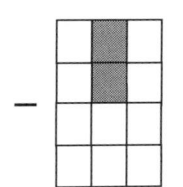

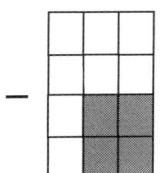

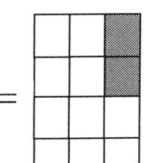

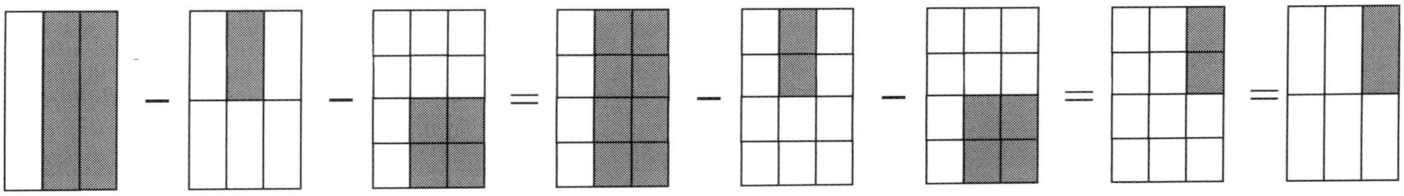

$$\frac{2}{3} - \frac{1}{6} - \frac{4}{12} = \frac{8}{12} - \frac{2}{12} - \frac{4}{12} = \frac{2}{12} = \frac{1}{6}$$

$0.6\dot{} - 0.16 - 0.3\dot{} = 0.6\dot{} - 0.16 - 0.3\dot{} = 0.16 = 0.16$

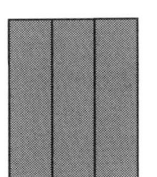

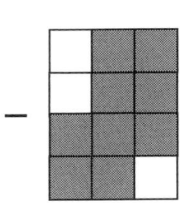

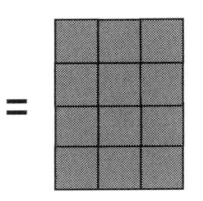

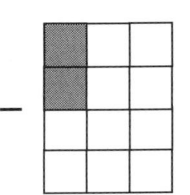

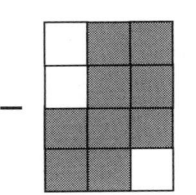

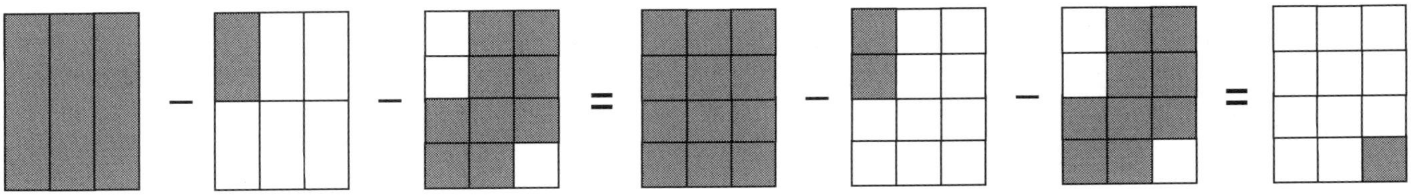

$$\frac{3}{3} - \frac{1}{6} - \frac{9}{12} = \frac{12}{12} - \frac{2}{12} - \frac{9}{12} = \frac{1}{12}$$

$1.00 - 0.16\dot{} - 0.75 = 1.00 - 0.16\dot{} - 0.75 = 0.083$

Thirds – Sixths – Twelfths

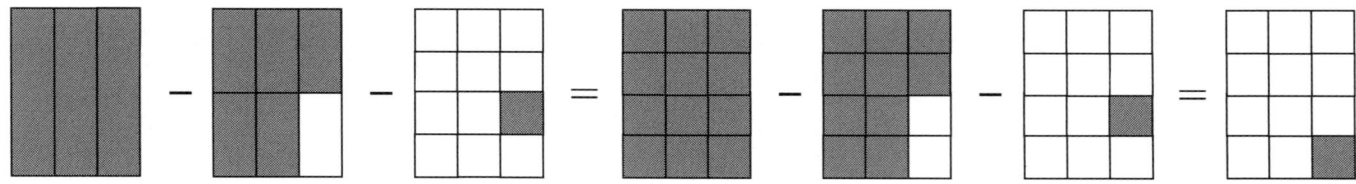

$$\frac{3}{3} - \frac{5}{6} - \frac{1}{12} = \frac{12}{12} - \frac{10}{12} - \frac{1}{12} = \frac{1}{12}$$

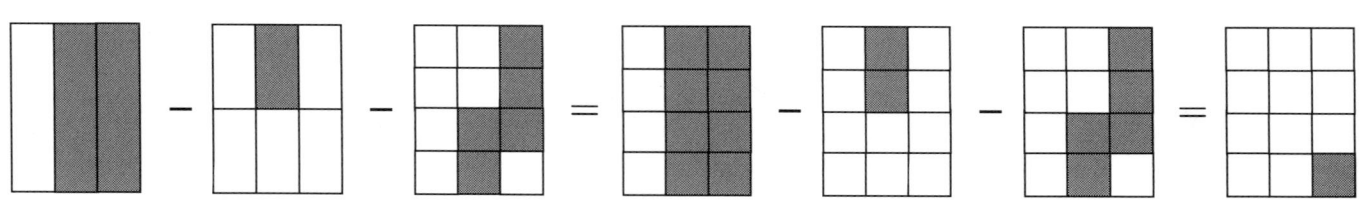

$$1.00 - 0.8\dot{3} - 0.08\dot{3} = 1.00 - 0.8\dot{3} - 0.08\dot{3} = 0.08\dot{3}$$

$$\frac{2}{3} - \frac{1}{6} - \frac{5}{12} = \frac{8}{12} - \frac{2}{12} - \frac{5}{12} = \frac{1}{12}$$

$$0.\dot{6} - 0.1\dot{6} - 0.41\dot{6} = 0.\dot{6} - 0.1\dot{6} - 0.41\dot{6} = 0.08\dot{3}$$

$$\frac{2}{3} - \frac{3}{6} - \frac{1}{12} = \frac{8}{12} - \frac{6}{12} - \frac{1}{12} = \frac{1}{12}$$

$$0.\dot{6} - 0.50 - 0.08\dot{3} = 0.\dot{6} - 0.50 - 0.08\dot{3} = 0.08\dot{3}$$

Thirds – Sixths – Twelfths

$$\frac{1}{3} - \frac{1}{6} - \frac{1}{12} = \frac{4}{12} - \frac{2}{12} - \frac{1}{12} = \frac{1}{12}$$

$$0.3\dot{} - 0.16\dot{} - 0.083 = 0.3\dot{} - 0.16\dot{} - 0.083 = 0.083$$

$$\frac{1}{3} - \frac{1}{6} - \frac{2}{12} = \frac{4}{12} - \frac{2}{12} - \frac{2}{12} = \frac{0}{12}$$

$$0.3\dot{} - 0.16\dot{} - 0.16\dot{} = 0.3\dot{} - 0.16\dot{} - 0.16\dot{} = 0.00$$

$$= \frac{0}{6} = \frac{0}{4} = \frac{0}{3} = \frac{0}{2} = 0$$

$$= 0.00 = 0.00 = 0.00 = 0.00 = 0$$

293

Quiz 2

Match each fraction subtraction with its answers

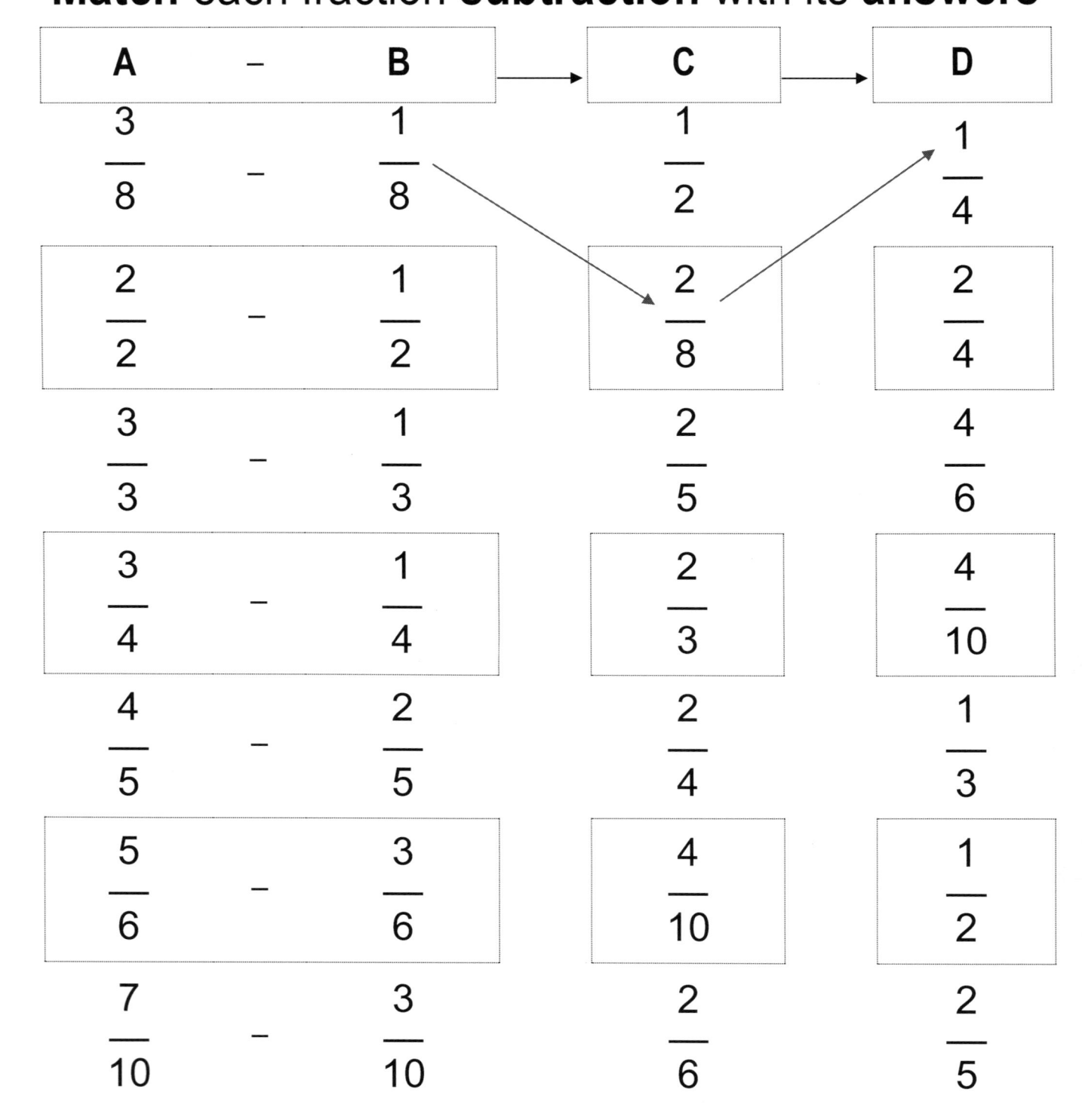

A	−	B	→	C	→	D
$\dfrac{3}{8}$	−	$\dfrac{1}{8}$		$\dfrac{1}{2}$		$\dfrac{1}{4}$
$\dfrac{2}{2}$	−	$\dfrac{1}{2}$		$\dfrac{2}{8}$		$\dfrac{2}{4}$
$\dfrac{3}{3}$	−	$\dfrac{1}{3}$		$\dfrac{2}{5}$		$\dfrac{4}{6}$
$\dfrac{3}{4}$	−	$\dfrac{1}{4}$		$\dfrac{2}{3}$		$\dfrac{4}{10}$
$\dfrac{4}{5}$	−	$\dfrac{2}{5}$		$\dfrac{2}{4}$		$\dfrac{1}{3}$
$\dfrac{5}{6}$	−	$\dfrac{3}{6}$		$\dfrac{4}{10}$		$\dfrac{1}{2}$
$\dfrac{7}{10}$	−	$\dfrac{3}{10}$		$\dfrac{2}{6}$		$\dfrac{2}{5}$

Thank you for buying my book and helping the author to keep on writing. ☺

I hope you've enjoyed reading **UNDERSTAND, ADD & SUBTRACT FRACTIONS VISUALLY**: 3-in-1 Visual Maths Fractions.

*If so, please, consider leaving a review on **Amazon.com** at* amazon.com/review/create-review?&asin=B0915VCYTG *to give this lovely book a big lending hand.* ☺

A single line, sentence or a few phrases will do. 👍

If not, please, send me your feedback, comments and corrections to: eng-s-jama@fractionsvisually.com.

Thanks.

mybook.to/B-4

amazon.co.uk/FractionsVisually

Copyright © Eng S Jama

All rights reserved.

author.to/FractionsVisually

About

Eng S Jama is an experienced electronics engineer turned an educational tutor and a self-published author.

FRACTIONS VISUALLY is for *children who think fractions are no fun* and *grown-ups who have never found the best visual resources to master basic maths fractions*.

Ages 5–11, **Year** groups 1–6 and **Key Stages** 1–2 in primary education (infants and junior schools).

ADDING FRACTIONS *STEP-BY-STEP* is for students and older learners struggling with adding fractions.
Ages 11–16 and/or year groups **7–11** in secondary schools.

```
ISBN: 979-8727324677 | http:/mybook.to/B-4
```

Titles

--- *Series #1:* **UNDERSTANDING FRACTIONS VISUALLY** ---

Colouring workbook: mybook.to/WB1-Sh-v2   **Paperback**: mybook.to/B-1
Colour paperback: mybook.to/B1-C   **Colour ebook**: mybook.to/eB1-C
Workbook: mybook.to/WB-1   **Colour workbook**: mybook.to/WB1-C

--- *Series #2:* **ADDING FRACTIONS VISUALLY** ---

Colouring workbook: mybook.to/WB2-Sh   **Paperback**: mybook.to/B-2
Colour paperback: mybook.to/B2-C   **Colour ebook**: mybook.to/Eb2-C
Workbook: mybook.to/WB2   **Colour workbook**: mybook.to/WB2-C

--- *Series #3:* **ADDING FRACTIONS *STEP-BY-STEP*** ---

Paperback: mybook.to/B-3   **Colour paperback**: mybook.to/B3-C
Workbook: mybook.to/WB3   **Colour workbook**: mybook.to/WB3-C

--- *Series #4:* **UNDERSTAND, ADD & SUBTRACT FRACTIONS VISUALLY** ---

Paperback: mybook.to/B-4   **Colour paperback**: mybook.to/B4-C

UNDERSTAND, ADD & SUBTRACT
FRACTIONS VISUALLY

Ages 5 – 11   *3-in-1 Visual Maths Fractions*   1st Edition

The only visual fractions book you need to **understand**, **add** & **subtract** fractions. It is comprehensive, convenient and completely visual.

Understanding Fractions Visually

Visual Fractions Charts, Introductions to Fractions, Halving, Quartering, Equivalent Fractions, Visual Fractions With Fractions Names, Decimal and Percentage Values. Halves, Quarters, Eighths, Fifths, Tenths, Thirds, Sixths, Ninths, Twelfths. Halves v Quarters. Quarters v Eighths. Halves v Quarters v Eighths... Quick Quizzes.

Adding Fractions Visually

How To Add Fractions with **Same** and **Different Denominators**. Finding the Lowest Common Multiples (LCM). Simplifying Fractions. Many Different Ways of Adding Halves, Quarters, Eighths, Fifths, Tenths, Thirds, Sixths, Ninths and Twelfths. Quick Quizzes. Hundreds Examples of Adding Fractions with **Same** & **Different Denominators**.

Subtracting Fractions Visually

How To Subtract Fractions with **Same** and **Different Denominators**. Simplifying Fractions. Finding the Lowest Common Multiples (LCM). Subtracting Halves, Quarters, Eighths, Fifths, Tenths, Thirds, Sixths, Ninths and Twelfths in Various Combinations. Quick Quizzes. Hundreds Examples of Subtracting Fractions with **Same** & **Different** Denominators.

Made in United States
Orlando, FL
07 January 2023

28387369R00163